RELATED TITLES FOR HIGH SCHOOL-BOUND STUDENTS

Essay Writing Step-by-Step: A Newsweek Education Program Guide for Teens

High School 411

High Stakes High School

SSAT & ISEE: For Private and Independent School Admissions

kaplansurveys.com/books

What did you think of this book? We'd love to hear your comments and suggestions. We invite you to fill out our online survey form at kaplansurveys.com/books. Your feedback is extremely helpful as we continue to develop high-quality resources to meet your needs.

Test Prep and Admissions

Catholic High School Entrance Exams (COOP/HSPT)

2005 Edition

By Helen Guler and the Staff of Kaplan Test Prep and Admissions

Simon & Schuster

NEW YORK · LONDON · SYDNEY · TORONTO

Kaplan Publishing
Published by Simon & Schuster
1230 Avenue of the Americas
New York, NY 10020

Contributing Editor: Seppy Basili
Project Editor: Sandy Gade
Production Manager: Michael Shevlin
Executive Editor: Jennifer Farthing
Interior Page Layout: Dave Chipps, Hugh Haggerty, Vincent Jeffries, Pam Beaulieu

August 2004
10 9 8 7 6 5 4 3

Manufactured in the United States of America
Published simultaneously in Canada

ISBN 0-7432-5449-X

Table of Contents

Section Four: Practice Tests

How to Use This Book

The COOP and the HSPT tests are the most common admissions exams used by Catholic schools. You should check with the specific schools you are interested in attending to see when they administer the exam and which test they use. You'll have to register to take either test, using an application form that the school can provide. After you register, you will receive a handbook of instructions and an admission ticket for the test. Be sure to bring the ticket with you on the day of the test.

You should know that the COOP and the HSPT tests cover a lot of material. To learn more specific information, read chapter one or chapter two, depending on which test you will be taking.

Next, read chapter three, "Test-Taking Strategies." Whether you are taking the COOP or the HSPT, this chapter will provide you with tips on how to answer every question, no matter its level of difficulty or the subject area that it covers.

To find out which of your skills need the most improvement, take the diagnostic quiz for the test you will be taking. Once you have reviewed the answer explanations and determined what your strengths and weaknesses are, read the skill review chapters. Use them to strengthen and hone your skills. Then, test your understanding with the practice set at the end of each skill review chapter.

Though you should complete the skill review in your problem areas first, be sure to work through all of them, since each one will give valuable strategies and practice on the various content areas of the tests.

Finally, be sure to take the practice tests at the end of the book. We've provided answer explanations for each question to help you build a systematic and effective approach that will help you do your best on whichever test you take.

Good luck!

About the Exams

Chapter One: **Facts About the COOP**

The COOP, or Cooperative Admissions exam, is given each year in October or November to eighth-graders seeking admission to specific Catholic high schools. The high schools use the exam results to make decisions about admitting applicants and to group prospective ninth-grade students into classes.

The COOP contains 7 subtests and lasts about 2 and a half hours. The subtests are: Sequences, Analogies, Quantitative Reasoning, Verbal Reasoning—Words, Verbal Reasoning—Context, Reading and Language Arts, and Mathematics. The COOP measures academic achievement as well as academic aptitude.

COOP EXAM FORMAT

The COOP contains approximately 180 multiple-choice questions. Most questions have four answer choices, A, B, C, D (odd-numbered questions) or F, G, H, J (even-numbered questions). However, some questions in the mathematics subtest have five answer choices, A, B, C, D, E (odd-numbered questions) or F, G, H, J, K (even-numbered questions). A separate answer sheet is provided to fill in your answer choices. The answer sheet is divided up into sections; each section is for a different subtest. Be careful when you fill in the answer bubbles—be sure that you're filling in the bubbles for the correct subtest!

KAPLAN TIP

The structure and contents of the COOP change slightly from year to year, but you should expect to see approximately seven subtests on the exam. Be sure that the bubbles you're filling in on your answer sheet match up with the subtest you're working on in your question booklet.

You are allowed to write in the question booklet; use this to your advantage when working through problems. Cross off answer choices as you eliminate them, circle problems you decide to skip and come back to, write out a mathematics problem as you solve it, or underline important information that helps you answer a question.

The COOP changes from year to year so that no students are more familiar than others with the test format and contents. You may see new question styles, or a different number of questions within a section. However, the content areas that the test covers remain basically the same. These are broken down into seven subtests:

Subtest	Number of Questions (approximate)	Time Allotted (approximate)
Sequences	20	15 minutes
Analogies	20	7 minutes
Quantitative Reasoning	20	15 minutes
Verbal Reasoning—Words	20	15 minutes
Verbal Reasoning—Context	20	15 minutes
Reading and Language Arts	40	40 minutes
Mathematics	40	35 minutes

Question Types

Here are explanations and examples of question types you will most likely see on the COOP exam. Directions are given for each section. Be sure to read the directions carefully before starting a subtest or section, especially since the specific question format you see may vary slightly from that presented in this book.

Test 1: Sequences

Sequence questions measure your ability to understand a rule or principle shown in a pattern or sequences of figures, letters, or numbers.

Your job is to analyze the pattern and then select the answer choice that would continue or complete the pattern.

Directions: Choose the answer that best continues the sequence.

□△○   ○□△   △○□   _____

□△○   △□○   □○△   △○□
(A)   (B)   (C)   (D)

Answer: **(A)** is the correct answer choice. Each piece of the sequence contains a square, a triangle, and a circle. Each subsequent piece of the sequence moves the last figure to the beginning of the group. In the final, missing piece, the square should be moved in front of the triangle and the circle.

Test 2: Analogies

COOP analogy questions measure your ability to detect various types of relationships among picture pairs, then extend that relationship to an incomplete picture pairs. Pictures may be made up of scenes, people, animals, objects, or symbols.

Directions: Look at the two pictures on top. Then, choose the picture that belongs in the space so that the bottom two pictures are related in the same way that the top two are related.

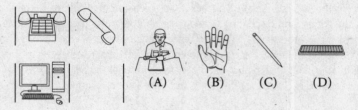

Answer: **(D)** is the correct answer choice. The receiver is a part of the entire telephone. A keyboard is part of an entire computer system.

Test 3: Quantitative Reasoning

Quantitative reasoning questions measure your aptitude for thinking with numbers. These are intentionally unlike other mathematics questions you will see on the exam since they are intended to test your reasoning ability, rather than any skills you have learned.

There are three types of quantitative reasoning questions: number relationships, visual problems, and symbol relationships. We'll cover all of them in the quantitative reasoning chapter of the book, but here is an example of one type, the visual problem.

Directions: Find the fraction of the grid that is shaded.

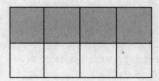

(A) $\frac{1}{8}$

(B) $\frac{4}{4}$

(C) $\frac{1}{2}$

(D) $\frac{1}{3}$

Answer: **(C)** is the correct answer choice. In this diagram, the grid is sectioned into 8 smaller squares, 4 of which are shaded. This 4 out of 8 can be expressed in fraction form as $\frac{4}{8}$ or reduced, $\frac{1}{2}$. Counting the shaded sections carefully will help you avoid errors. Create a fraction by placing the number of shaded portions as a numerator over the number of pieces in the whole in the denominator. If possible, reduce.

Test 4: Verbal Reasoning—Words

Verbal reasoning questions measure your ability to solve verbal problems by reasoning deductively, analyzing categories, and discerning relationship and patterns. This subtest contains several question types. Some require you to identify essential elements of objects or concepts, and others require you to classify words according to common characteristics. Another question type requires you to infer relationships between separate but related sets of words. We'll cover all of these in the verbal skills chapter of the book, but here is one example.

> **Directions:** Find the word that names a necessary part of the underlined word.
>
> <u>liberty</u>
>
> (A) travel
> (B) choice
> (C) vote
> (D) wilderness

Answer: **(B)** is the correct answer. *Liberty* means freedom, and a necessary part of freedom is the ability to choose. While a person who enjoys liberty may travel, *travel* is not an essential element of liberty. Likewise, we think of voting as an expression of freedom and liberty, but it does not define what the word means. *Wilderness* which is related to the wild and nature is related to freedom but does not define *liberty*.

Test 5: Verbal Reasoning—Context

This subtest measures your ability to solve verbal problems by reasoning deductively. This question type is also known as logic questions. You are required to identify essential elements of ideas presented in short passages and draw logical conclusions.

> **Directions:** Find the statement that is true according to the given information.
>
> Marisol sings in the choir. Her sister Lena takes ballet lessons. Their brother Alex plays the drums.
>
> (A) There are exactly three children in Marisol's family.
> (B) All of Marisol's family is musical.
> (C) Marisol is the oldest child in her family.
> (D) Lena is probably interested in dance.

Answer: **(D)** is the correct answer choice. The short statements do not tell us whether there are any other children in Marisol's family, nor whether all of them are musical. We are also not told the ages of Marisol and her brothers and sisters. The only thing we can say for certain, according to the statements, is that Lena is probably interested in dance.

Test 6: Reading and Language Arts

This subtest measures you ability to understand the central meaning of a passage as well as its details. It also tests your ability to understand the structure of sentences and paragraphs and how they work together to convey ideas. It tests language conventions such as punctuation and capitalization, and may cover aspects of the writing process such as topic selection, editing, and proofreading.

Directions: Read the following passage and answer the questions that follow.

"If only Moppits weren't so short!" Gadsolo exclaimed. He was standing on his tippy-toes, if you could call the little claws at the bottom of his furry legs "toes," but still he couldn't reach the rope dangling before him.

"Hurry!" Padlotto cried from the top of the cliff. "Grab on and I'll pull you up. There isn't much time."

The Moppit hopped up and down, trying to get his hands around the rope. "Ump! Harumph!" he cried as he hopped. And the hopping made him laugh.

"What in the twelve pink seas are you laughing about?" Padlotto shouted angrily.

"I can't help it," Gadsolo replied. "We Moppits are not only short, but also very silly."

"Well, you'd better wipe that smile off your face and find a way to climb up this rope," Padlotto said. "The Mucklurkers are coming."

"No!" Gadsolo gasped. He spun around and sure enough, there they were. Two slinky, slimy Mucklurkers were slithering on their green, oozy bellies toward him.

"Eek!" Gadsolo cried. With that, he jumped and grabbed on to bottom of Padlotto's rope.

Padlotto pulled, hand over hand, until the Moppit was finally safe beside him on the top of the cliff. He was grumbling and sweaty.

"What's the matter?" Gadsolo asked his human friend. "Aren't you glad to see me?"

"Moppits are short. Moppits are silly. And Moppits are also quite heavy!" Padlotto exclaimed, mopping his brow.

Where would you expect to find this passage?

(A) in a textbook about Moppits

(B) in an autobiographical book

(C) in a newspaper

(D) in a science fiction novel

Answer: **(D)** is the best answer choice. Moppits are not real creatures, so you would not expect to find them in a textbook, an autobiographical book, or a newspaper. Also, textbooks and newspapers generally don't include a lot of dialogue.

Choose the sentence that best combines the following three sentences:

Moppits are short. Moppits are silly. And Moppits are also quite heavy!

(F) Moppits are short; they are silly and they are, also, quite heavy!

(G) Moppits are: short, silly, and quite heavy!

(H) Moppits are short, silly, and quite heavy!

(J) Moppits they are short, they are silly, and they are quite heavy!

Answer: **(H)** is the best answer choice. Since the sentences all have the same subject, *Moppits*, and each contains an adjective describing the subject, the clearest and most concise way to combine the sentences is by listing the adjectives.

Test 7: Mathematics

Mathematics questions measure your understanding of math concepts. These questions include number relations, computation, estimation, operations, measurement, geometry, spatial sense, data analysis, probability, patterns, functions, and reasoning.

Directions: Read each problem and find the answer.

Mr. Wolfe drives 45 minutes to work each day. His average speed is 50 miles per hour. How far does he drive *round trip*?

(A) 37.5 miles

(B) 75 miles

(C) 225 miles

(D) 250 miles

Answer: **(B)** is the correct answer. Use the formula Rate × Time = Distance.

50 miles per hour × 45 minutes = Distance

Convert minutes to hour: 45 minutes = $\frac{3}{4}$ hour

$$50 \times \frac{3}{4} = \text{Distance} = 37.5$$

The question asks how far he drives *round trip*; 37.5 × 2 = 75 miles

HOW THE COOP IS SCORED

You will receive one point for every question that you answer correctly on the COOP. There is no penalty for incorrect answers, and each question, regardless of how difficult it is, is worth only one point. This is important since it means that it is in your best interest to guess on questions for which you are not sure of the answer. Also, since you win no additional points for answering more difficult questions, you should always answer the questions that are easier for you first in order to rack up the most points.

> **KAPLAN TIP**
>
> Be sure to fill in an answer for every question. If you don't know the answer, guess. If you can't make an educated guess, make a random guess—you may just get it right!

The points you earn, known as your **raw score**, are tallied and then converted to a **scaled score** according to a formula determined by the test developers. Converting raw scores to scaled scores allows schools to compare a student's performance on one part of the exam with his or her performance on other parts that may have included a greater or lesser number of questions. Finally, scaled scores are reported as **percentile rank**. Percentile rank shows where students stand in relationship to one another on various sections and on the test as a whole.

Chapter Two: **Facts About the HSPT**

The HSPT, or Scholastic Testing Service High School Placement Test, is given to eighth-graders seeking admission to specific Catholic high schools. Like the COOP, it is used by schools to make decisions about applicants, to place them, and to determine scholarship awards. Generally, the HSPT is administered at the school to which you want to apply. Be sure to contact the school to find out where and when the test is offered.

The standard HSPT test contains five parts and lasts about two and a half hours. The sections of the test are Verbal, Quantitative, Reading, Mathematics, and Language Skills. The Scholastic Testing Service also provides a choice of one optional test in Mechanical Aptitude, Science, or Catholic Religion. However, because many schools do not choose to administer these tests, and because the results are not included as part of your percentile ranking, this book does not cover the optional exams. If the school you are interested in does use one of these tests, be sure to ask the school for more details about its contents.

HSPT EXAM FORMAT

The HSPT contains 298 multiple-choice questions, numbered from 1 through 298. All questions have four answer choices, A, B, C, D. (NOTE: Some questions in the Verbal Skills section on the HSPT have only three answer choices, A, B, and C.) A separate answer sheet is provided to fill in answer choices.

KAPLAN TIP

Since the questions on the HSPT are numbered consecutively, it is easier to avoid filling in an answer choice on the wrong part of the bubble sheet. For example, there is only one question 5, regardless of which section of the exam you're in.

You are allowed to write in the question booklet. You can use this to your advantage when working through problems. Cross off answer choices as you eliminate them, circle problems you decide to skip and come back to, write out a mathematics problem as you solve it, or underline important information that helps you answer a question.

Question Types

Unlike the COOP, the format of the HSPT remains relatively stable from year to year. The break-down of sections, question types, and time allotted is as follows:

Test Section	Number of Questions	Time Allotted
Verbal Skills	60	16 minutes
Quantitative Skills	52	30 minutes
Reading	62	25 minutes
Mathematics	64	45 minutes
Language	60	25 minutes

Verbal Skills

This section includes synonyms, antonyms, analogies, logic, and verbal classifications. All five question-types will appear, mixed in together, on the Verbal Skills section. Knowing the directions for each of the question types is important, since it will enable you to move through the section more quickly without pausing to ponder what the question requires. We will review each question type and the directions for each in detail in chapter four of this book.

Analogy

Mechanic is to automobile as plumber is to

(A) electricity
(B) house
(C) pipe
(D) water

Answer: **(C)** is the correct answer choice. This is a functional relationship: A *mechanic* repairs an *automobile*, and a *plumber* repairs a *pipe*.

Synonym

Conclusion most nearly means

(A) finale
(B) judgment
(C) decision
(D) continuation

Answer: **(A)** is the correct answer choice. *Conclusion* means *ending*, which is closest to *finale*.

Logic

Kangaroo A jumps farther than kangaroo B. Kangaroo C
jumps farther than kangaroo A. Kangaroo C jumps farther
than kangaroo B. If the first two statements are true, the
third is

(A) true

(B) false

(C) uncertain

Answer: **(A)** is the correct answer choice. If the first two statements are true and kangaroo C
jumps farther than kangaroo A and A jumps farther than B, then C must also jump farther than B.

Verbal Classification

Which word does *not* belong with the others?

(A) poet

(B) engineer

(C) musician

(D) actor

Answer: **(B)** is the correct answer choice. An engineer is a technical profession, while the other
choices are artistic professions.

Antonym

Pretense means the *opposite* of

(A) honesty

(B) love

(C) beauty

(D) contentment

Answer: **(A)** is the correct answer choice. *Pretense* means *trickery* or *falsehood*. The opposite is
honesty.

Quantitative Skills

This section includes series, geometric comparisons, non-geometric comparisons, and number
manipulations.

Number Series

Look at this series: 15, 17, 19, 21, ... What number comes
next in the series?

(A) 22

(B) 23

(C) 24

(D) 25

Answer: **(B)** is the correct answer choice. The pattern in this series is +2; 21 + 2 = 23.

Geometric Comparisons

Examine figures A, B, and C and find the best answer.

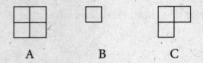

A   B   C

(A) A > B + C

(B) C < 2B

(C) A + B < C

(D) A − B = C

Answer: **(D)** is the correct answer choice. (A) contains 4 squares, (B) contains 1 square, and (C) contains 3; 4 − 3 = 1.

Non-Geometric Comparisons

Examine (a), (b), and (c) and find the best answer.

(a) $2(4 - 1)$

(b) $2 \times 4 - 1$

(c) $2 - (1 \times 4)$

(A) (b) < (a) + (c)

(B) (b) = (a)

(C) (a) + (b) > (c)

(D) (b) + (c) < (a)

Answer: **(D)** is the correct answer choice. Determine the value of (a), (b), and (c) using order of operations.

(a) $2(4 - 1) = 2(3) = 6$

(b) $2 \times 4 - 1 = 8 - 1 = 7$

(c) $2 - (1 \times 4) = 2(-4) = -8$

Then, test each answer choice to see which is true.

(A) (b) < (a) + (c)	Does 7 < 7 + (−6) = 7 < 1? **false**
(B) (b) = (a)	Does 7 = 6? **false**
(C) (a) + (b) > (c)	Does 6 + 7 > −8? **true**
(D) (b) + (c) > (a)	Does 7 + (−8) > 6 = −1 > 6? **false**

Number Manipulation

What number is 10 more than $\frac{1}{3}$ of 21?

(A) 18

(B) 15

(C) 17

(D) 24

Answer: **(C)** is the correct answer choice. First, find $\frac{1}{3}$ of 21; $\frac{1}{3} \times 21 = 7$. Then, add 10: $7 + 10 = 17$.

Reading

This section asks you to answer questions on short passages of varying styles on a range of topics.

By the late 1800s, many native peoples were being pushed off their traditional lands to make way for American expansionism. There were numerous battles of resistance, and many brave tribal leaders led the fight to keep their ancestral lands. Chief Joseph of the Nez Perce, a peaceful nation that spread from Idaho to Northern Washington, was one such leader.

Chief Joseph, known by his people as In-mut-too-yah-lat-lat (Thunder coming up over the land from the water), assumed the role of chief from his father, Old Joseph. Old Joseph was on friendly terms with the American government, and he signed a treaty that allowed his people to <u>maintain</u> most of their traditional lands. In 1863, however, following the discovery of gold in Nez Perce territory, the federal government took back almost six million acres of territory. Chief Joseph argued that his people never agreed to this second treaty and he refused to move them.

The Nez Perce were terribly outnumbered though. After months of fighting and forced marches, many of the Nez Perce were sent to a reservation in what is now Oklahoma. Many died from malaria and starvation. Chief Joseph tried every possible appeal to the federal authorities to return the Nez Perce to their land. He explained, "All men were made brothers. The earth is the mother of all people, and all people should have equal rights upon it. You might as well

KAPLAN
Test Prep and Admissions

expect the rivers to run backward as that any man who was born free should be contented when penned up and denied liberty to go where he pleases." Despite his appeals, Chief Joseph was sent to a reservation in Washington where, according to the reservation doctor, he later died of a broken heart.

According to this passage, native peoples were forced off their land by

(A) gold diggers
(B) tribal leaders
(C) the growing American nation
(D) lack of food

Answer: **(C)** is the correct answer choice. The first paragraph of the passage explains that *native peoples were being pushed off their traditional lands to make way for American expansionism.* Choice (C) is a paraphrase, or rewording, of that information.

<u>Maintain</u> as it is used in the passage, most probably means

(A) keep
(B) settle
(C) care for
(D) give back

Answer: **(A)** is the correct answer choice. The passage discusses how the Nez Perce and Chief Joseph fought for their lands. *Old Joseph...signed a treaty that allowed his people to maintain much of their traditional lands.* From the context, we can understand that *maintain* most nearly means *keep.*

Mathematics

Mathematics includes mathematical concepts and problem solving drawn from arithmetic, elementary algebra, and basic geometry.

Concepts

How many degrees does a right angle contain?

(A) 180
(B) 360
(C) 90
(D) 50

Answer: **(C)** is the correct answer choice. A right angle contains 90 degrees. A straight line contains 180 degrees, and a circle contains 360 degrees.

Problem Solving

Two years ago, Michael was four years older than half his father's age. If his father is 54 now, how old is Michael now?

(A) 30

(B) 32

(C) 26

(D) 27

Answer: **(B)** is the correct answer choice. Find the math within the story. Start with the fact

Michael's father is now 54. Two years ago ($54 - 2 = 52$), Michael was four years older than half

his father's age: $\frac{52}{2} + 4 = 30$.

Don't forget the final step. The question asks how old Michael is now: $30 + 2 = 32$.

Language Skills

Language skills questions test capitalization, punctuation, usage, spelling, and composition.

Punctuation and Capitalization

Choose the sentence that contains an error in punctuation, capitalization, or usage. If there is no error, select choice (D).

(A) Christine ordered a salad for lunch on Tuesday.

(B) What time is it? Keshia asked.

(C) We toured the Metropolitan Museum of Art on a field trip.

(D) No mistake.

Answer: **(B)** has an error in punctuation. There should be quotation marks around the question: "What time is it?" Keshia asked.

Usage

Choose the sentence that contains an error in punctuation, capitalization, or usage. If there is no error, select choice (D).

(A) Thomas is taller then his uncle.

(B) Can penguins fly?

(C) Lay the baby in the crib carefully.

(D) No mistake.

Answer: **(A)** has an error in usage. *Than* should be used for comparisons, not *then*. *Then* means *next* or *afterwards*.

Spelling

> Choose the sentence that contains an error in spelling. If
> there is no error, select choice (D).
>
> (A) Our neighborhood has many parks.
> (B) Please call me tomorrow to give me your answer.
> (C) Let's schedule our meeting for Sunday.
> (D) No mistake.

Answer: **(D)** is the correct answer choice, since there are no spelling mistakes in any of the
answer choices. Don't be tempted into selecting answers (A) through (C) even if you find no
error. There is not always an error among the answer choices.

Composition

> Choose the best word or words to complete the sentence.
>
> Dolphins seem to communicate through the use of high-
> pitched sounds, _____ no one knows what these sounds
> mean.
>
> (A) though
> (B) and
> (C) in addition
> (D) because

Answer: **(A)** is the correct answer choice. The second half of the sentence contradicts the first, so
a word of contrast such as *but* or *though* must be used.

HOW THE HSPT EXAM IS SCORED

Each question that you answer correctly on the HSPT test earns you one point. There is no penalty
or deduction for incorrect answers, so it is worthwhile to guess on questions for which you are not
sure of the answer. Also, since each question is worth one point regardless of how easy or difficult
it is, you should always answer the questions that are easier for you first. Rack up as many points
as you can, then spend any remaining minutes on questions that require more time.

> **KAPLAN TIP**
>
> Since there is no penalty for wrong answers, you should answer every question on the
> HSPT. Do your best to eliminate wrong answer choices and make an educated guess.
> However, even if you can't get rid of any choices, you should still guess. You may just
> pick the right answer.

Your **raw score**, or the total number of points you earn, is tallied and then converted to a **scaled
score** ranging from 200 to 800. The Scholastic Testing Service will also determine your
percentile rank according to your scaled score. Percentile rank shows where you stand in relationship to other students and allows the schools to more easily compare candidates. There is no
passing or failing score on the HSPT, although each school determines what is a desirable score
for its candidates.

GRIDDING—THE ANSWER GRID HAS NO HEART

Be careful when you mark your answers on the answer grid! It sounds basic, but when time is short, it's easy to get confused going back and forth between your test book and your answer grid. If you know the answer, but mark it incorrectly on the answer grid, you won't get any points, so be careful. Here are some tips to help you avoid making mistakes on the answer grid.

Always Circle the Questions You Skip

Put a big circle in your test book around any question numbers you skip. When you go back, these questions will be easy to locate. Also, if you accidentally skip a bubble on the grid, you can check your grid against your book to see where you went wrong.

Always Circle the Answers You Choose

Circling your answers in the test book makes it easier to check your grid against your book.

Grid Five or More Answers at Once

Don't transfer your answers to the grid after every question. Transfer your answers after every five questions, or wherever might be a good breaking point. That way, you won't keep breaking your concentration to mark the grid. You'll save time and you'll gain accuracy.

Be careful at the end of a section, when time may be running out. You don't want to have your answers in the test booklet and not be able to transfer them to your answer grid because you have run out of time. Make sure to transfer your answers after every five questions or so.

APPROACHING COOP AND HSPT QUESTIONS

Apart from knowing the setup of the COOP or HSPT, you need to have a system for attacking the questions. You should approach your high school admissions test with a plan. What follows is the best method for approaching test questions systematically.

Think About the Question Before You Look at the Answers

The people who write the tests love to put distracters among the answer choices. Distracters are answer choices that look like the right answer, but aren't. If you jump right into the answer choices without thinking first about what you're looking for, you are more likely to fall for one of these traps.

Work Backward If Necessary

There are usually a number of ways to get to the right answer on a question. All of the questions are multiple-choice. That means the answer is right in front of you—you just have to find it. But, if you can't figure out the answer in a straightforward way, try other techniques. We'll talk about specific Kaplan Methods in later chapters.

Pace Yourself

The COOP and HSPT give you a lot of questions in a short period of time. In order to get through an entire section, you can't spend too much time on any one question. Keep moving through the test at a good speed; if you run into a hard question, circle it, skip it, and go back later if there's time.

One caution: Don't rush through the easy problems just to save time for the harder ones. The easier problems are points in your pocket, and you don't want to work through them in such haste that you end up making careless mistakes.

Locate Quick Points If You're Running Out of Time

Some questions can be done quickly; for instance, some reading questions will ask you to identify the meaning of a particular word in a passage. These can be done at the last minute, even if you haven't read the passage. When you start to run out of time, locate and answer any of the quick points that remain.

When you take the COOP or HSPT, you have one clear objective in mind: to score as many points as you can. It's that simple. The rest of this book will help you do that.

STAY CALM

The countdown has begun. Your test date is approaching. Perhaps your anxiety is on the rise. Maybe you think you won't be ready. Maybe you already know your stuff, but you're going into panic mode anyway. Don't get carried away! It's possible to tame that anxiety and stress—before and during the test.

Remember, a little stress is good. Anxiety is a motivation to study. The adrenaline that gets pumped into your bloodstream when you're stressed helps you to stay alert and think more clearly. But if you feel that tension is preventing you from using your study time effectively, here are some things you can do to get it under control.

Take Control

Lack of control is a prime cause of stress. Research shows that if you don't have a sense of control over what is happening in your life, you can easily end up feeling helpless and hopeless. Try to identify the sources of the stress you feel. Which ones of these can you do something about? Can you find ways to reduce the stress you are feeling about any of these sources?

Focus on Your Strengths

Make a list of your qualities that will help you do well on the test. Don't be modest and under-rate your abilities. You will be able to draw on your strengths as you need them, helping you to solve difficult questions, maintain confidence, and keep test stress at a minimum. Every time you recognize a new area of strength, solve a challenging problem, or score well on a practice test, you will increase your strengths.

Imagine Yourself Succeeding

Close your eyes and imagine yourself in a relaxing situation. Breath easily and naturally. Now, think of a real-life situation in which you scored well on a test, or did well on an assignment. Focus on this success. Now, turn your thought to the exam, and keep your thoughts and feelings in line with that successful experience. Don't make comparisons between them, just imagine yourself taking the test with the same feelings of confidence and relaxed control.

Set Realistic Goals

Facing your problem areas gives you some distinct advantages. What do you want to accomplish in the study time you have remaining? Make a list of realistic goals. Perhaps it's adding 10 words a day to your vocabulary, or mastering square roots. Taking active steps to improve your in a particular area will improve your performance and boost your confidence.

Exercise Your Frustrations Away

Whether it's jogging, biking, pushups, or a pickup basketball game, physical exercise will stimulate your mind and body, and improve your ability to think and concentrate. A surprising number of students fall out of the habit of regular exercise, ironically because they are spending so much time preparing for exams. A little physical exertion will help to keep your mind and body in sync and sleep better at night.

Eat Well

Good nutrition will help you focus and think clearly. Eat plenty of fruits and vegetables, low-fat protein such as fish, skinless poultry, beans, and whole grains such as brown rice, whole wheat bread, and pastas. Don't eat a lot of sugar and high-fat snacks or salty foods. Avoid mild stimulants, such as coffee or cola. Although sometimes they can help keep you alert as you study, too much of these can also lead to agitation, restlessness, and insomnia. Better to have a large glass of water.

Keep Breathing

Conscious attention to breathing is an excellent way to manage stress while you are taking the test. Most of the people who get into trouble during tests take shallow breaths: They breathe using only their upper chest and shoulder muscles, and may even hold their breath for long periods of time. Conversely, those test takers who breathe deeply in a slow, relaxed manner are likely to be in better control during the session.

KAPLAN
Test Prep and Admissions

Stretch

If you find yourself getting spaced out or burned out as you study or take the test, stop for a brief moment and stretch. Flex your feet and arms. Even though you will be pausing on the test for a moment, it's a moment well spent. Stretching will help to refresh you and refocus your thoughts.

Now, apply these strategies as you work through the review chapters and practice tests in this book.

"Managing Stress" adapted from "The Kaplan Advantage Stress Management System" by Dr. Ed Newman and Bob Verini, © 1996 by Kaplan, Inc.

CFOR Diagnostic Quiz
Answer Sheet

| SECTION TWO |

Diagnostic Quizzes

COOP Diagnostic Quiz
Answer Sheet

Remove (or photocopy) this answer sheet and use it to complete the practice test.

Sequences

1. Ⓐ Ⓑ Ⓒ Ⓓ   3. Ⓐ Ⓑ Ⓒ Ⓓ   5. Ⓐ Ⓑ Ⓒ Ⓓ

2. Ⓐ Ⓑ Ⓒ Ⓓ   4. Ⓐ Ⓑ Ⓒ Ⓓ

Analogies

1. Ⓐ Ⓑ Ⓒ Ⓓ   3. Ⓐ Ⓑ Ⓒ Ⓓ   5. Ⓐ Ⓑ Ⓒ Ⓓ

2. Ⓐ Ⓑ Ⓒ Ⓓ   4. Ⓐ Ⓑ Ⓒ Ⓓ

Quantitative Reasoning

1. Ⓐ Ⓑ Ⓒ Ⓓ   3. Ⓐ Ⓑ Ⓒ Ⓓ   5. Ⓐ Ⓑ Ⓒ Ⓓ

2. Ⓐ Ⓑ Ⓒ Ⓓ   4. Ⓐ Ⓑ Ⓒ Ⓓ

Verbal Reasoning—Words

1. Ⓐ Ⓑ Ⓒ Ⓓ   3. Ⓐ Ⓑ Ⓒ Ⓓ   5. Ⓐ Ⓑ Ⓒ Ⓓ

2. Ⓐ Ⓑ Ⓒ Ⓓ   4. Ⓐ Ⓑ Ⓒ Ⓓ

Verbal Reasoning—Context

1. Ⓐ Ⓑ Ⓒ Ⓓ   3. Ⓐ Ⓑ Ⓒ Ⓓ   5. Ⓐ Ⓑ Ⓒ Ⓓ

2. Ⓐ Ⓑ Ⓒ Ⓓ   4. Ⓐ Ⓑ Ⓒ Ⓓ

Reading and Language Arts

1. Ⓐ Ⓑ Ⓒ Ⓓ Ⓔ   4. Ⓐ Ⓑ Ⓒ Ⓓ   7. Ⓐ Ⓑ Ⓒ Ⓓ   10. Ⓐ Ⓑ Ⓒ Ⓓ

2. Ⓐ Ⓑ Ⓒ Ⓓ Ⓔ   5. Ⓐ Ⓑ Ⓒ Ⓓ   8. Ⓐ Ⓑ Ⓒ Ⓓ

3. Ⓐ Ⓑ Ⓒ Ⓓ Ⓔ   6. Ⓐ Ⓑ Ⓒ Ⓓ   9. Ⓐ Ⓑ Ⓒ Ⓓ

Mathematics

1. Ⓐ Ⓑ Ⓒ Ⓓ Ⓔ   4. Ⓐ Ⓑ Ⓒ Ⓓ   7. Ⓐ Ⓑ Ⓒ Ⓓ   10. Ⓐ Ⓑ Ⓒ Ⓓ

2. Ⓐ Ⓑ Ⓒ Ⓓ Ⓔ   5. Ⓐ Ⓑ Ⓒ Ⓓ   8. Ⓐ Ⓑ Ⓒ Ⓓ

3. Ⓐ Ⓑ Ⓒ Ⓓ Ⓔ   6. Ⓐ Ⓑ Ⓒ Ⓓ   9. Ⓐ Ⓑ Ⓒ Ⓓ

COOP Diagnostic Quiz

SEQUENCES

Directions: For questions 1–5, choose the answer that best continues the sequence.

1.

2.

3. 18   16   ___   12   10   8
    (A) 15
    (B) 13
    (C) 14
    (D) 11

4. 1   3   9   ___   81   243
    (A) 54
    (B) 27
    (C) 21
    (D) 45

5. Z1   Y2   X3   W4   ___

    (A) V5

    (B) V4

    (C) S4

    (D) X5

ANALOGIES

Directions: For questions 1–5, look at the two pictures on top. Then, choose the picture that belongs in the space so that the bottom two pictures are related the same way that the top two are related.

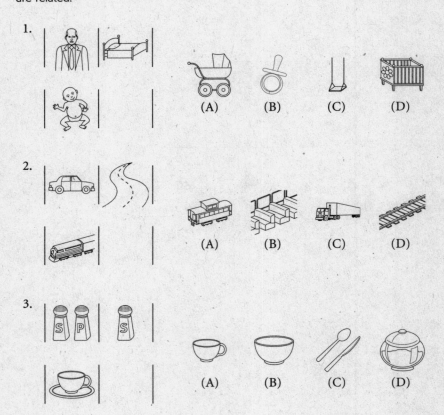

4.

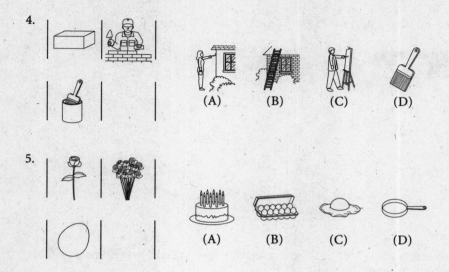

5.

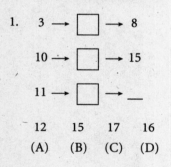

QUANTITATIVE REASONING

Directions: For questions 1–2, find the relationship of the numbers in the left column to the numbers in the right column. Choose the number that should replace the blank.

1. 3 → ☐ → 8

    10 → ☐ → 15

    11 → ☐ → __

12	15	17	16
(A)	(B)	(C)	(D)

2. 7 → ☐ → 14

    4 → ☐ → 8

    9 → ☐ → __

18	3	20	19
(A)	(B)	(C)	(D)

Directions: For question 3, find the fraction of the grid that is shaded.

3.

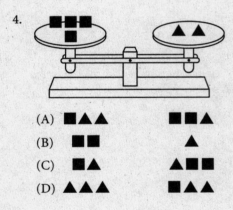

(A) $\dfrac{4}{16}$

(B) $\dfrac{5}{5}$

(C) $\dfrac{5}{8}$

(D) $\dfrac{1}{2}$

Directions: For questions 4–5, the scale shows sets of shapes of equal weight. Find a set that would also balance the scale.

4.

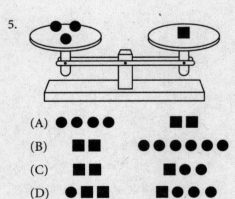

(A) ■▲▲   ■■▲

(B) ■■   ▲

(C) ■▲   ▲■■

(D) ▲▲▲   ■▲▲

5.

(A) ●●●●   ■■

(B) ■■■   ●●●●●●

(C) ■■■   ■●●

(D) ●■■   ■●●●

VERBAL REASONING—WORDS

Directions: For questions 1–3, find the word that names a necessary part of the underlined word.

1. <u>restriction</u>

   (A) forbid
   (B) strict
   (C) contract
   (D) sign

2. <u>celebration</u>

   (A) balloon
   (B) cake
   (C) party
   (D) birthday

3. <u>wisdom</u>

   (A) age
   (B) knowledge
   (C) books
   (D) teacher

Directions: For questions 4–5, the words in the top row are related in some way. The words in the bottom row are related in the same way. Find the word that competes the bottom row of words.

4. bread   slice   crumb

   water   puddle

   (A) pebble
   (B) lake
   (C) river
   (D) drop

5. pen   pencil   paint

   drawing   photograph

   (A) paper
   (B) painting
   (C) camera
   (D) clay

VERBAL REASONING—CONTEXT

Directions: For questions 1–5, find the statement that is true according to the given information.

1. Jane attends high school at Lincoln High. She bicycles to school everyday.

   (A) Jane knows how to ride a bicycle.
   (B) Jane is a fast bicyclist.
   (C) There is no bus service from Jane's house to school.
   (D) Jane locks up her bicycle outside school.

2. The weather forecast says it will probably rain on Saturday. The Browns are planning a picnic on Saturday.

   (A) The Browns will change their picnic to Sunday.
   (B) The Browns will not go on their picnic.
   (C) The Browns should bring umbrellas if they go on their picnic on Saturday.
   (D) The Browns will get wet on their picnic.

3. The Blue Ridge Mountains are in Tennessee. Coby has hiked in the Blue Ridge Mountains.

   (A) Coby is from Tennessee.
   (B) Coby is a good athlete.
   (C) The Blue Ridge Mountains are high.
   (D) Coby has been to Tennessee.

4. Miss Battle is a kindergarten teacher. In order to attend kindergarten, a child must be at least five years old.

   (A) Miss Battle is five years old.
   (B) None of the children in Miss Battle's class are six years old.
   (C) The children in Miss Battle's class are at least five years old.
   (D) Miss Battle loves children.

5. Daffodils bloom only in spring. Daffodils are blooming.

   (A) Crocuses are also blooming.
   (B) Daffodils wilt easily.
   (C) Daffodils are yellow.
   (D) It is spring.

READING AND LANGUAGE ARTS

Directions: Follow the directions for questions 1–10.

Read the following passage and answer questions 1–4.

If you have never heard of the tulip craze, you won't believe it's true. The story begins in the 1550s when Dutch botanist Carolus Clusius brought the first tulip bulbs from Turkey to Holland. Clusius planted the flower bulbs in his own small garden and refused to give any to the locals. The rarity of the flower, of course, only made it more desirable to Clusius' neighbors. It wasn't long before some of them broke into Clusius' garden and stole his tulip bulbs. This is how the Dutch tulip trade started.

People fell in love with these colorful flowers. Because they were beautiful and hard to get, tulips soon became a status symbol for the well-to-do. For the next seventy years, the price of tulips increased dramatically. Everyone wanted them.

Though the early tulip buyers were people who loved flowers, later buyers were interested in trading tulip bulbs for money. By 1636, tulips were established as a trading commodity on the Amsterdam Stock Exchange. People were willing to spend vast amounts of money to obtain one rare tulip bulb in the hopes that they could trade it for profit. Though tulips had no practical use, no perfume, and no medicinal benefit, some people sold everything they owned just to buy one tulip bulb. At the height of tulip mania, the price of a single bulb could range from $17,000 to $76,000 in today's value. Tulip clerks were appointed to record tulip transactions, and laws were passed to control the tulip craze.

It wasn't long before the bubble burst. When some people began to sell their tulip holdings, tulip prices slowly began to weaken. The public's confidence in the value of tulips suddenly declined. People panicked and everyone tried to sell their tulips at once. In a period of just six weeks, tulip prices crashed dramatically. Although the Dutch government tried to pass regulations to help the market, tulip prices continued to fall. Tulip prices plummeted so that a bulb that had been worth the equivalent of $76,000 was suddenly worth less than one dollar. Trade in Holland took years to recover from this great shock.

1. In the last paragraph, the word *plummeted* means

   (A) rose slowly

   (B) fell rapidly

   (C) stayed steady

   (D) grew quickly

2. The selection suggests that after the early buyers, people bought tulips

   (A) as an indication of their wealth

   (B) because they loved the flowers

   (C) to annoy Clusius

   (D) to protect people from stealing them

3. The title that best expresses the main idea of this selection is

    (A) The First Stock Market
    (B) Why People do Crazy Things
    (C) The History of the Tulip
    (D) The Tulip Craze

4. The writer of this selection most likely feels that

    (A) people are always reasonable and predictable
    (B) flowers are a good investment
    (C) the tulip craze can teach us about human behavior
    (D) the tulip craze was a strange event that would never happen today

5. Here are two sentences related to the passage:
    People used to keep tulip bulbs in their homes.
    Tulips were considered too valuable to plant in gardens.

    Select the answer choice that best combines these sentences into one.

    (A) People used to keep tulip bulbs in their homes; tulips were considered too valuable to plant in gardens.
    (B) People used to keep tulip bulbs in their homes and that is why the tulips were considered too valuable to plant in gardens.
    (C) People used to keep tulip bulbs in their homes however tulips were considered too valuable to plant in gardens.
    (D) People used to keep tulip bulbs in their homes because tulips were considered too valuable to plant in gardens.

6. Choose the sentence that is written correctly.

    (A) During tulip mania, outsiders found it difficult to understand the great popularity of the flower.
    (B) During tulip mania; outsiders found it difficult to understand the great popularity of the flower.
    (C) During tulip mania. Outsiders found it difficult to understand the great popularity of the flower.
    (D) During tulip mania—outsiders found it difficult to understand the great popularity of the flower.

7. Choose the sentence that best completes this paragraph.

    Tulips are still popular today in Holland. They are also an important export product for the Dutch.

    (A) Tulip mania will never be forgotten.
    (B) There are many varieties of tulips.
    (C) Today, Holland exports 1.2 billion tulip bulbs a year.
    (D) Almost every Dutch garden boasts at least one type of tulip.

Here is a story a student wrote about visiting Holland. Read the story then answer questions 8–10.

(1) Last summer my family visited Holland. (2) We flew to Amsterdam. (3) Amsterdam is the capital city. (4) We spent a week there, touring many interesting sites. (5) Amsterdam is very different from New York City. (6) There are bicycles everywhere they ride bikes.

8. Which is the best way to write sentence 4?

   (A) We spent a week there, and toured many interesting sites.

   (B) We spent a week there, where we have toured many interesting sites.

   (C) We spent a week there, touring many interesting sites.

   (D) Best as is.

9. Which is the best way to write sentence 6?

   (A) People ride bicycles everywhere.

   (B) Everywhere people are there riding bicycles.

   (C) There are bicycles everywhere riding.

   (D) Best as is.

10. What is the best way to combine sentences 2 and 3?

    (A) We flew to Amsterdam, capital city.

    (B) We flew to Amsterdam, the capital city.

    (C) We flew to the city which is the capital and that city is Amsterdam.

    (D) Best as is.

MATHEMATICS

Directions: Read each problem and find the correct answer.

1. $\dfrac{2}{3} + \dfrac{1}{8} =$

   (A) $\dfrac{19}{24}$

   (B) $\dfrac{1}{8}$

   (C) $\dfrac{3}{4}$

   (D) 11

   (E) none of these

2. 12.2 – 3.5 =

   (A) 7.5

   (B) 10.7

   (C) 9.7

   (D) 8.7

   (E) none of these

3. 8 × –2 =

   (A) 12

   (B) 16

   (C) –16

   (D) 6

   (E) none of these

Read the chart, then answer questions 4–6.

The 9th grade at Youngstown High put on a play. The table shows the total amounts in ticket sales for each of the three performances.

	Student Ticket Sales	Adult Ticket Sales
Friday night	$220	$280
Saturday night	$260	$375
Sunday night	$140	$225

4. Which number below best shows the part of the total ticket sales brought in on Friday night?

   (A) $\frac{3}{10}$

   (B) $\frac{1}{3}$

   (C) 30%

   (D) .03

5. If each student ticket costs $2.50, how many students attended the play in all?

   (A) 1,040

   (B) 520

   (C) 248

   (D) 210

6. If half of the 196 adults who attended also bought a bag of popcorn for .50 cents, how would you find the amount of money raised in popcorn sales?

    (A) Divide 196 by 2 and add .5.

    (B) Divide 196 by 2 and multiply by .5.

    (C) Multiply 196 by 2 and multiply by .5.

    (D) Divide 196 by .5 and multiply by .5.

7. What is the area of the rectangle?

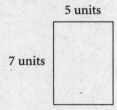

5 units

7 units

    (A) 27 square units

    (B) 24 square units

    (C) 30 square units

    (D) 35 square units

8. Farrah jogs 2 miles every morning. It takes her 40 minutes to finish her morning jog. About how fast is she jogging?

    (A) 8 miles per hour

    (B) 6 miles per hour

    (C) 3 miles per hour

    (D) 80 miles per hour

9. If $-1 < x < 3$, and x is an integer, which of the following represents the set of possible values of x?

    (A) $\{1, 2\}$

    (B) $\{1, 2, 3\}$

    (C) $\{0, 1, 2\}$

    (D) $\{-1, 0, 1, 2\}$

10. Rene has 3 dollars less than twice as much as her sister. If x represents the amount of money her sister has, which expression could represent the amount of money Rene has?

    (A) $\dfrac{1}{3(2x)}$

    (B) $2x - 3$

    (C) $(x - 3)/2$

    (D) $2x + 3$

ANSWER KEY

Sequences

1. D
2. A
3. C
4. B
5. A

Analogies

1. D
2. D
3. A
4. A
5. B

Quantitative Reasoning

1. D
2. A
3. D
4. B
5. B

Verbal Reasoning—Words

1. A
2. C
3. B
4. D
5. B

Verbal Reasoning—Context

1. A
2. C
3. D
4. C
5. D

Reading and Language Arts

1. B
2. A
3. D
4. C
5. D
6. A
7. C
8. C
9. A
10. B

Mathematics

1. A
2. D
3. C
4. B
5. C
6. B
7. D
8. C
9. C
10. B

ANSWERS AND EXPLANATIONS

Sequences

1. D

Each square has one more line than the previous one. The next in the sequence should have another diagonal line, choice (D).

2. A

The pattern consists of triangles and circles. Only (A) contains triangles and circles. There is no reason to believe the next in the pattern should be shaded or contain squares.

3. C

The pattern is −2; 16 − 2 = 14.

4. B

The pattern is ×3; 9 × 3 = 27.

5. A

Letters are decreasing toward A and the numbers are increasing. The next letter should be V and the next number, 5.

Analogies

1. D

An adult sleeps in a bed, a baby sleeps in a crib.

2. D

A car rides on a road, a train rides on a track.

3. A

A salt shaker is one item of the pair pictured to the left. A cup is one item of the pair pictured to the left.

4. A

The brick is used by the man to lay bricks, the paint can and brush are used by the woman to paint. It is not the same kind of paint and brush that an artist would use.

5. B

Roses are usually sold by the dozen, and eggs are also usually sold by the dozen.

Quantitative Reasoning

1. D

Each number in the right column is 5 more than the number in the left column. The relationship is +5. The missing number is 11 + 5 = 16.

2. A

The number in the right column is two times the number in the left column. The relationship is ×2. The missing number is 9 × 2 = 18.

3. D

Count the total pieces of the rectangle and count the number of pieces shaded. There are 8 large pieces and 3 of them are shaded. Also, two halves of 2 more pieces are shaded. So, 4 pieces of 8 are shaded, or $\frac{4}{8}$, which reduces to $\frac{1}{2}$.

4. B

The diagram shows that 4 squares equal 2 triangles. Therefore, 2 squares = 1 triangle, or answer choice (B).

5. B

Three circles equal 1 square, so 2 squares equal 6 circles.

Verbal Reasoning—Words

1. A

A restriction forbids some action. That is the necessary part of the word since it defines what the word does. While a sign may post a restriction, such as "no swimming" this is not a necessary part of the word. Likewise, a contract is not necessary to have a restriction. Choice (B), strict, is a distracter choice. Restrictions may be strict, but again, this is not what defines the word.

2. C

A celebration marks a festive event. A party is a celebration. All the other elements, balloon, cake, birthday, are not necessary parts of a celebration.

3.   B

Wisdom is the state of being wise or knowledgeable. Therefore, knowledge is a necessary part of wisdom. One doesn't have to be old to be wise, and wisdom can be found without books. Likewise, a teacher is not necessary to acquire wisdom.

4.   D

The words above the line are related because they are decreasing parts of a whole; a slice is a smaller piece of bread; a crumb is the smallest bit. The words below the line are related in the same way; a puddle is made up of water and a drop is the smallest component of a puddle.

5.   B

Above the line are all types of things to create art. Below the line are all pieces of art. Only choice (B) is another type of art.

Verbal Reasoning—Context

1.   A

Since Jane bicycles to school, she must know how to ride a bicycle. This is the only conclusion we can draw with certainty from the information given.

2.   C

It is said that it will *probably* rain. There is no certainty. The information does not state told whether or not this forecast will cause the Browns to cancel or postpone their picnic. However, they should bring umbrellas in case they decide to go.

3.   D

If Coby has hiked in the Blue Ridge Mountains, and the Blue Ride Mountains are in Tennessee, Coby has been to Tennessee.

4.   C

The information states that *in order to attend kindergarten a child must be at least five years old.* Some of the students may be older than that. Choice (C) is the correct answer.

5.   D

Daffodils bloom only in spring and they are blooming. Therefore, it must be spring.

Reading and Language Arts

1.   B

The paragraph explains that in just six weeks, tulip prices *plummeted* to less than one dollar. They fell rapidly.

2.   A

The passage explains that at first, people bought tulips because they loved them. As prices grew, they later bought the flowers as a way to show off and prove that they were wealthy.

3.   D

This selection is mainly about the tulip craze in Holland. The title should reflect the selection's main idea.

4.   C

This is the best answer choice because the theme of the passage is that the tulip craze was an interesting example of how people behaved.

5.   D

These two sentences have a effect-cause relationship. The word *because* best connects them.

6.   A

The phrase *during tulip mania* should be set of with a comma.

7.   C

The second sentence brings up the idea of tulips as an export product. The last sentence should expand on this idea.

8.   C

The word *spended* is incorrect. The correct past tense verb is *spent*.

9.   A

This sentence is the clearest because it has a simple subject and verb.

10. B

This is the most clear and correct way to combine the two sentences.

Mathematics

1. A

Change the fractions to a common denominator. The lowest common denominator is 24.

$$\frac{2}{3} + \frac{1}{8} = \frac{16}{24} + \frac{3}{24} = \frac{19}{24}.$$

2. D

Line up the decimal points and subtract. You will have to borrow.

$$\begin{array}{r} 12.2 \\ -\ 3.5 \\ \hline 8.7 \end{array}$$

3. C

A positive number multiplied by a negative one will give a negative product. $8 \times -2 = -16$.

4. B

Total ticket sales = all student tickets + all adult tickets, so $620 + 880 = 1,500$. Friday night sales = $280 + 220 = 500$; $\frac{500}{1,500} = \frac{1}{3}$.

5. C

Add all student tickets , $220, $260, $140 and divide by 2.50

$$\frac{620}{2.5} = 248.$$

6. B

Translate the word problem into math. "half of the 196 adults $= \frac{196}{2}$" "bought a bag of popcorn for .50 cents" $\left(\frac{196}{2}\right) \times 0.5$.

Divide 196 by 2 and multiply by .5

7. D

Area of rectangle = length × width = $5 \times 7 = 35$ square units.

8. C

Distance = Rate × Time

$$40 \text{ minutes} = \frac{40}{60} = \frac{2}{3} \text{ hour}$$

$$2 \text{ miles} = \text{rate} \times \frac{2}{3} \text{ hour}$$

$$\text{rate} = 2 \div \frac{2}{3}$$

$$\text{rate} = \frac{2}{1} \times \frac{3}{2} = \frac{6}{2} = 3 \text{ miles per hour}$$

9. C

The statement says that x is greater than -1 and less than 3, therefore x could be 0, 1, or 2.

10. B

Translate the word problem into math. Three dollars less than twice as much as x is equivalent to: $2x - 3$.

HSPT Diagnostic Quiz
Answer Sheet

Remove (or photocopy) this answer sheet and use it to complete the practice test.

Verbal Skills

1. Ⓐ Ⓑ Ⓒ Ⓓ   4. Ⓐ Ⓑ Ⓒ Ⓓ   7. Ⓐ Ⓑ Ⓒ Ⓓ   10. Ⓐ Ⓑ Ⓒ Ⓓ

2. Ⓐ Ⓑ Ⓒ Ⓓ   5. Ⓐ Ⓑ Ⓒ Ⓓ   8. Ⓐ Ⓑ Ⓒ Ⓓ   11. Ⓐ Ⓑ Ⓒ Ⓓ

3. Ⓐ Ⓑ Ⓒ Ⓓ   6. Ⓐ Ⓑ Ⓒ Ⓓ   9. Ⓐ Ⓑ Ⓒ Ⓓ   12. Ⓐ Ⓑ Ⓒ Ⓓ

Quantitative Skills

13. Ⓐ Ⓑ Ⓒ Ⓓ   16. Ⓐ Ⓑ Ⓒ Ⓓ   19. Ⓐ Ⓑ Ⓒ Ⓓ   22. Ⓐ Ⓑ Ⓒ Ⓓ

14. Ⓐ Ⓑ Ⓒ Ⓓ   17. Ⓐ Ⓑ Ⓒ Ⓓ   20. Ⓐ Ⓑ Ⓒ Ⓓ

15. Ⓐ Ⓑ Ⓒ Ⓓ   18. Ⓐ Ⓑ Ⓒ Ⓓ   21. Ⓐ Ⓑ Ⓒ Ⓓ

Reading

23. Ⓐ Ⓑ Ⓒ Ⓓ   26. Ⓐ Ⓑ Ⓒ Ⓓ   29. Ⓐ Ⓑ Ⓒ Ⓓ   32. Ⓐ Ⓑ Ⓒ Ⓓ

24. Ⓐ Ⓑ Ⓒ Ⓓ   27. Ⓐ Ⓑ Ⓒ Ⓓ   30. Ⓐ Ⓑ Ⓒ Ⓓ   33. Ⓐ Ⓑ Ⓒ Ⓓ

25. Ⓐ Ⓑ Ⓒ Ⓓ   28. Ⓐ Ⓑ Ⓒ Ⓓ   31. Ⓐ Ⓑ Ⓒ Ⓓ   34. Ⓐ Ⓑ Ⓒ Ⓓ

Mathematics

35. Ⓐ Ⓑ Ⓒ Ⓓ   38. Ⓐ Ⓑ Ⓒ Ⓓ   41. Ⓐ Ⓑ Ⓒ Ⓓ   44. Ⓐ Ⓑ Ⓒ Ⓓ   47. Ⓐ Ⓑ Ⓒ Ⓓ

36. Ⓐ Ⓑ Ⓒ Ⓓ   39. Ⓐ Ⓑ Ⓒ Ⓓ   42. Ⓐ Ⓑ Ⓒ Ⓓ   45. Ⓐ Ⓑ Ⓒ Ⓓ   48. Ⓐ Ⓑ Ⓒ Ⓓ

37. Ⓐ Ⓑ Ⓒ Ⓓ   40. Ⓐ Ⓑ Ⓒ Ⓓ   43. Ⓐ Ⓑ Ⓒ Ⓓ   46. Ⓐ Ⓑ Ⓒ Ⓓ

Language

49. Ⓐ Ⓑ Ⓒ Ⓓ   52. Ⓐ Ⓑ Ⓒ Ⓓ   55. Ⓐ Ⓑ Ⓒ Ⓓ   58. Ⓐ Ⓑ Ⓒ Ⓓ

50. Ⓐ Ⓑ Ⓒ Ⓓ   53. Ⓐ Ⓑ Ⓒ Ⓓ   56. Ⓐ Ⓑ Ⓒ Ⓓ   59. Ⓐ Ⓑ Ⓒ Ⓓ

51. Ⓐ Ⓑ Ⓒ Ⓓ   54. Ⓐ Ⓑ Ⓒ Ⓓ   57. Ⓐ Ⓑ Ⓒ Ⓓ   60. Ⓐ Ⓑ Ⓒ Ⓓ

HSPT Diagnostic Quiz

VERBAL SKILLS

Directions: Choose the answer that most nearly means the given word.

1. Humble most nearly means

    (A) weak

    (B) modest

    (C) poor

    (D) proud

2. Emulate most nearly means

    (A) copy

    (B) brag

    (C) tease

    (D) omit

Directions: Choose the answer that does *not* belong with the others.

3. Which word does *not* belong with the others?

    (A) ample

    (B) considerable

    (C) miniscule

    (D) substantial

4. Which word does *not* belong with the others?

    (A) transmit

    (B) inhibit

    (C) broadcast

    (D) communicate

Directions: Choose the answer that matches the relationship given.

5. Calendar is to date as map is to

   (A) location
   (B) time
   (C) appointment
   (D) identity

6. Counselor is to advice as teacher is to

   (A) instruction
   (B) blackboard
   (C) student
   (D) law

Directions: Choose the answer that means the same as the underlined word.

7. a <u>nomadic</u> tribe

   (A) agricultural
   (B) savage
   (C) settled
   (D) wandering

8. an <u>intricate</u> pattern

   (A) colorful
   (B) complex
   (C) vivid
   (D) traditional

Directions: Choose the answer that most nearly means the opposite of the given word.

9. Aggravate means the *opposite* of

   (A) improve
   (B) annoy
   (C) decline
   (D) anger

10. Reveal means the *opposite* of

    (A) uncover
    (B) conceal
    (C) display
    (D) convey

Directions: Choose the best answer to each question.

11. Mrs. Rangal cooks dinner for the Rangal family on weeknights. Mr. Rangal cooks dinner for the Rangal family on the weekend. Mr. Rangal cooks dinner more often than Mrs. Rangal. If the first two statements are true, the third is

    (A) true
    (B) false
    (C) uncertain

12. Carl runs faster than Joseph. Monty runs faster than Carl. Monty runs faster than Joseph. If the first two statements are true, the third is

    (A) true
    (B) false
    (C) uncertain

QUANTITATIVE SKILLS

Directions: Choose the best answer to each question.

13. What number is 3 more than 30% of 90?

    (A) 33
    (B) 30
    (C) 3
    (D) 16

14. Look at this series: 1, 8, 15, _____, 29… What number belongs in the blank in the series?

    (A) 20
    (B) 22
    (C) 21
    (D) 23

15. What number is $\frac{1}{3}$ the average of 10, 14, 11, and 13?

    (A) 5
    (B) 6
    (C) 4
    (D) 12

16. Examine (a), (b), and (c) and find the best answer

    (a) 100% of 20

    (b) 20% of 100

    (c) 20% of 100%

    (A) (b) is greater than (a)

    (B) (a) is greater than (b) and (c)

    (C) (c) is greater than (a) but less than (b)

    (D) (a) and (b) are equal

17. A small flower store earns $450 dollars per day. If the store is open 6 days a week, how many dollars does the store earn in 4 weeks?

    (A) $10,800

    (B) $8,800

    (C) $10,000

    (D) $10,050

18. On a field trip to the zoo, 60 eighth graders visit the reptile exhibit. This is $\frac{3}{4}$ of the students in the entire eighth grade. How many students are in the eighth grade?

    (A) 90

    (B) 45

    (C) 20

    (D) 80

19. Which of the following sets of integers may replace the * to make the sentence below true?

    6 < * < 10

    (A) {5, 6}

    (B) {7, 8, 9}

    (C) {8, 9, 10}

    (D) {6, 7, 8, 9, 10}

20. If a box of chocolates costs y dollars, then 3 boxes of chocolates, in dollars, cost

    (A) $3 - y$

    (B) $3y$

    (C) $\frac{y}{3}$

    (D) $y + 3$

21. In which case are the numbers arranged in order of value with the smallest one first?

    (A) .53, $\frac{1}{3}$, 50%

    (B) .90, $\frac{1}{9}$, 33%

    (C) .25, $\frac{2}{3}$, 85%

    (D) 47%, $\frac{2}{5}$, .70

22. What is the next number in the series 72, 36, 18, 9, …

    (A) 8
    (B) 4
    (C) 3
    (D) 4.5

READING

Directions: Read each passage and answer the questions that follow.

The name Fort Knox brings to mind images of solid gold bricks, stretching as far as the eye can see. However, very few people have ever laid eyes on the gold bullion reserves stored in Fort Knox, Kentucky. The bullion depository is a classified facility. No visitors are permitted inside and no gold is removed.

The gold bricks in Fort Knox are an <u>asset</u> of the United States government. Gold was originally put there to insure the U.S. dollar to other nations. During the Gold Acts of 1933 and 1934, the federal banks began collecting gold coins. By late 1934 the Treasury Department realized it needed a safe place to house this gold. Fort Knox was chosen because it is far from the country's borders. It is a safe distance from any possible invaders, and it has rough <u>terrain</u> that makes it easy to protect. Also, the First Cavalry, one of the fastest moving military units, is located in Fort Knox.

The first gold shipment arrived at Fort Knox in 1937. Forty trains, each with 200 cars, brought the gold to Fort Knox. The largest amount of gold held at Fort Knox was 649.6 million ounces. This record amount was reached in December of 1941. Worried that the war raging in Europe might spill over the into United Sates, officials decided to temporarily move the gold, as well as the Declaration of Independence from Washington D.C. to Fort Knox. In 1944, when danger of enemy attack had passed, the Declaration was returned to Washington, D.C.

Presently, there are 147.3 million ounces of gold housed in Fort Knox. Each ounce is valued at $42.22. One standard gold bar weighs 27.5 pounds, or about 400 ounces. A standard bar is 7 inches by $3\frac{5}{8}$ inches and 1 and $\frac{3}{4}$ inches. Each bar is worth over $16,000.

This gold is well protected. Fort Knox is built from granite that has been lined with concrete and reinforced with steel. The gold bars are kept within a concrete vault. The vault door weighs more than 20 tons. That's over 40,000 pounds! No one person knows the combination to the vault. Several members of the depository staff must dial separate combinations known only to them. The depository contains its own emergency power plant, water system, and other facilities in case of attack.

23. As used in the passage, the word <u>terrain</u> most nearly means

    (A) landscape

    (B) features

    (C) rocks

    (D) inhabitants

24. A good title for this passage might be

    (A) A Safe Place

    (B) The Combination to the Vault

    (C) The Gold Standard

    (D) All the Gold in Fort Knox

25. How much does one gold bar weigh?

    (A) 400 ounces

    (B) 25 pounds

    (C) 7 pounds

    (D) 42 pounds

26. Which of the following is correct?

    (A) The Declaration of Independence was moved to Fort Knox in 1937.

    (B) The Declaration of Independence was moved to Fort Knox during World War II.

    (C) The Declaration of Independence is still in the vault at Fort Knox.

    (D) George Washington put the Declaration of Independence in the vault at Fort Knox.

27. You would expect to find the kind of information in this passage in

    (A) a science book

    (B) a thesaurus

    (C) an encyclopedia

    (D) none of these

28. As used in the passage, the word <u>asset</u> most nearly means

(A) insurance

(B) protection

(C) possession

(D) tax

29. According to the passage, if you were comparing the gold kept in Fort Knox 1941 to the gold kept in Fort Knox today you would find

(A) each gold brick is heavier today

(B) there is more gold now

(C) the gold today is less valuable

(D) there is less gold now

30. Why did the author write this passage?

(A) to tell a funny story

(B) to teach about Fort Knox

(C) to persuade readers to buy gold

(D) to explain why gold is valuable

Directions: Choose the answer that means the same as the underlined word.

31. a celebrity <u>endorsement</u>

(A) advertisement

(B) declaration

(C) scandal

(D) portrait

32. a casual <u>acquaintance</u>

(A) friend

(B) statement

(C) contact

(D) outfit

33. a <u>mutinous</u> crew

(A) strong

(B) rebellious

(C) magnificent

(D) competitive

KAPLAN
Test Prep and Admissions

34. a <u>grave</u> mistake

    (A) serious

    (B) unimportant

    (C) careless

    (D) accidental

MATHEMATICS

Directions: Choose the best answer to each question.

35. Which of the following represents the total number of degrees in the measure of a circle?

    (A) $36\pi°$

    (B) $90°$

    (C) $180°$

    (D) $360°$

36. The measure of angle A in the figure below is

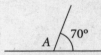

    (A) $110°$

    (B) $90°$

    (C) $80°$

    (D) $100°$

37. When multiplying a number by 10^3, the decimal point will move

    (A) one place to the right

    (B) three places to the right

    (C) three places to the left

    (D) four places to the left

38. Which of the following pairs contain a number and its reciprocal?

    (A) $\left(\dfrac{1}{3}, \dfrac{2}{3}\right)$

    (B) $\left(\dfrac{2}{3}, \dfrac{3}{2}\right)$

    (C) $(23, 32)$

    (D) $(-2, 2)$

39. Which fraction shows the greatest value?

(A) $\frac{6}{7}$

(B) $\frac{7}{8}$

(C) $\frac{4}{5}$

(D) $\frac{5}{6}$

40. The least common multiple of 3 and 8 is

(A) 12

(B) 4

(C) 24

(D) 16

41. A theater sold 120 tickets for the afternoon show at $20 per ticket and 155 tickets for the evening show at $24 per ticket. How much did the theater earn in ticket sales that one day?

(A) $3,960

(B) $5,120

(C) $6,120

(D) $2,720

42. Solve: $11 - 2 = 2\frac{1}{12}$

(A) $7\frac{11}{12}$

(B) $8\frac{11}{12}$

(C) $9\frac{11}{12}$

(D) $10\frac{1}{12}$

43. Solve: $8 + (-4) + 6 + (-7) =$

(A) 3

(B) 11

(C) 25

(D) −2

44. Mrs. Jones paid $326.52 for her cable bill last year. Approximately how much, on average, did she pay per month?

    (A) $30.10
    (B) $28.00
    (C) $27.00
    (D) $30.50

45. If $5(2x - 3) = 42$, then $x =$

    (A) 57
    (B) 42
    (C) 4.7
    (D) 5.7

46. Three years ago, Marisa's mother was 3 times as old as Marisa. How is Marisa's mother now if Marisa is 15?

    (A) 39
    (B) 36
    (C) 24
    (D) 30

47. If the 8% sales tax on a sweater is $4.16, what is the price of the sweater, not including the tax?

    (A) $56.16
    (B) $62
    (C) $60.02
    (D) $52

48. The ratio of $\frac{2}{7}$ to $\frac{5}{4}$ is

    (A) 36:8
    (B) 8:35
    (C) 5:14
    (D) 10:28

LANGUAGE

Directions: For questions 49–52 choose the sentence that contains an error in punctuation, capitalization, or usage. If there is no error, select choice (D).

49. (A) Neither the blue nor the red pen is on the table.
    (B) I always prefer to arrive on time.
    (C) She is certainly more talkative than her sister.
    (D) No mistake.

50. (A) A letter is in the mailbox now.
    (B) Their's nothing I can do at the moment.
    (C) How many cans are in the cupboard?
    (D) No mistake.

51. (A) Aunt elisa is visiting us tomorrow.
    (B) We won't be late if we leave now.
    (C) Does he play on the team?
    (D) No mistake.

52. (A) We requested a room with a view.
    (B) I never agreed to that.
    (C) Which sweater do you like better?
    (D) No mistake.

Directions: For questions 53–56, choose the sentence that contains a spelling error. If there is no error, select choice (D).

53. (A) I received the bill yesterday.
    (B) Jack always reads the sports colum.
    (C) Compared to Louise, I am punctual.
    (D) No mistake.

54. (A) The job will take approximately 2 hours.
    (B) Please include specific examples.
    (C) All of the merchundise is on sale.
    (D) No mistake.

55. (A) We highly recommend the movie.
    (B) I made a note on my calender.
    (C) Maxine canceled the appointment.
    (D) No mistake.

56. (A) Please stop tapping your toes; you are irratating me.

    (B) The delivery is scheduled for noon.

    (C) Have you noticed how hazy it is today?

    (D) No mistake.

Directions: For questions 57–60, choose the best answer to each question.

57. Choose the words that best complete the following sentence.

    The club needs to decide _____.

    (A) where to go on its spring trip this year.

    (B) this year where to go on its spring trip

    (C) about its spring trip this year and where to go.

    (D) to go where on its spring trip.

58. Choose the word that is a clear connective to complete the sentence below.

    Jonathan believed that he had done his best; _____, he was content when he received his score.

    (A) however

    (B) therefore

    (C) moreover

    (D) none of these

59. Which sentence does not belong in the paragraph below?

    (1) Located north of Afghanistan, in central Asia, Uzbekistan is a dry, landlocked country. (2) Only 10% of the country consists of irrigated river valleys. (3) The capital, Tashkent, lies in the valley of the River Chirchik. (4) During the period of Soviet occupation, it was one of the poorest areas of the region. (5) It is now the third largest cotton exporter in the world, as well as a major producer of gold and natural gas.

    (A) sentence 1

    (B) sentence 2

    (C) sentence 3

    (D) sentence 5

60. Where should the following sentence be placed in the paragraph below?

However, if Shakespeare did not invent the stories, he did pen the marvelous words that make his writings poetic and unique.

(1) Though William Shakespeare is renowned as a brilliant playwright, many of his readers are not aware that the Bard did not completely invent his works. (2) Many of his plots and themes were borrowed from Renaissance literature. (3) In fact, most can be directly attributed to popular dramas of the day.

(A) before sentence 1

(B) before sentence 2

(C) after sentence 1

(D) after sentence 3

ANSWER KEY

Verbal Skills

1. B
2. A
3. C
4. B
5. A
6. A
7. D
8. B
9. A
10. B
11. B
12. A

Quantitative Skills

13. B
14. B
15. C
16. D
17. A
18. D
19. B
20. B
21. C
22. D

Reading

23. A
24. D
25. A
26. B
27. C
28. C
29. D
30. B

31. B
32. C
33. B
34. A

Mathematics

35. D
36. A
37. B
38. B
39. B
40. C
41. C
42. B
43. A
44. C
45. D
46. A
47. D
48. B

Language

49. D
50. B
51. A
52. D
53. B
54. C
55. B
56. A
57. A
58. B
59. C
60. D

ANSWERS AND EXPLANATIONS

Verbal Skills

1. B

Humble means polite, reserved, or modest.

2. A

To emulate is to imitate or copy.

3. C

Miniscule means small, while all the other choices mean large amounts.

4. B

These words have to do with sharing information. However, inhibit most nearly means to prohibit.

5. A

A calendar shows dates, a map shows locations.

6. A

A counselor's job is to give advice, a teacher's job is to give instruction.

7. D

A nomadic tribe wanders from place to place.

8. B

An intricate pattern is complex.

9. A

To aggravate means to make worse. Choice (A), *improve*, is the opposite

10. B

To reveal is to show something hidden. The opposite is (B), *conceal*.

11. B

Because the first two statements are true and Mrs. Rangal cooks 5 nights a week as compared with Mr. Rangal's two nights a week, she must cook dinner more often than Mr. Rangal.

12. A

Because the first two statements are true and Carl runs faster than Joseph, Monty must run faster than Joseph too.

Quantitative Skills

13. B

30% of $90 = .30 \times 90 = 27$; $27 + 3 = 30$.

14. B

Each number is 7 more than the preceding one. The number in the blank should be
$15 + 7 = 22$.

15. C

First, calculate the average of the four numbers:

$$10 + 14 + 11 + 13 = \frac{48}{4} = 12.$$

Then, multiply by $\frac{1}{3}$:

$$12 \times \frac{1}{3} = 4.$$

16. D

Calculate the value of (a), (b), and (c)

(a) $100\% \times 20 = 20$

(b) 20% of $100 = .2 \times 100 = 20$

(c) 20% of $100\% = .2 \times 1 = .2$

Evaluate each answer choice; (a) and (b) are equal. Therefore, choice (D) is correct.

17. A

6 days a week $\times$ 4 weeks = 24 days.

$24 \times 450 = 10,800$

18. D

$\frac{3}{4}$ of the students in the eighth grade = 60 students

$\frac{1}{4}$ of the students in the eighth grade = $60 \div 3 = 20$

$\frac{4}{4}$, or all the students on the trip = $20 \times 4 = 80$ students

19. B

The sentence states that the numbers that may be placed in * are greater than 6 and less than 10. The numbers 7, 8, and 9 are greater than 6 and less than 10. Therefore, the members 7, 8, and 9 may replace *.

20. B

In order to obtain the cost of three boxes we must multiply the number of boxes bought by the cost per box, $3y$.

21. C

By writing all the numbers as decimals, we can compare them easily.

(A) .53, .33, .50—the smallest one is not first.

(B) .90, .11, .33—the smallest one is not first.

(C) .25, .66, .85—the smallest one is first here.

(D) .47, .40, .70—the smallest one is not first.

22. D

The pattern is that each number is divided by 2. The next number is 9 divided by 2, or 4.5.

Reading

23. A

As it is used in the passage, the word *terrain* means a piece of land, or a landscape.

24. D

A good title should contain the main idea of the passage. This passage is about the gold in Fort Knox. Therefore, choice (D) is the best answer.

25. A

This is a detail question. The answer, 400 ounces, is found in paragraph 4.

26. B

This is a detail question. Information about the Declaration of Independence is found in paragraph 3. The Declaration was moved to Fort Knox for safe keeping in 1941 during World War II and was returned to Washington D.C. after the war.

27. C

This passage is factual. It could be found in an encyclopedia article.

28. C

Reread the sentence containing the word asset and a few sentences after it to figure out the meaning of the word. The gold is kept in Fort Knox by the government. It belongs to, or is a possession of, the government.

29. D

Paragraph 3 states: *The largest amount of gold held at Fort Knox was 649.6 million ounces. This record amount was reached in December of 1941.* Paragraph 4 states: *Presently, there are 147.3 million ounces of gold housed in Fort Knox.* Thus, there is less gold in Fort Knox now.

30. B

The information in the passage is not funny, nor does it persuade the reader to do something. Although it tells about the value of the gold, it does not explain why the Declaration of Independence is valuable. This passage was written to inform readers about Fort Knox.

31. B

A celebrity endorsement is a declaration given by a celebrity.

32. C

A causal acquaintance is a contact.

33. B

A mutinous crew is rebellious.

34. A

A grave mistake is serious.

Mathematics

35. D

A circle measures 360 degrees.

36. A

A straight line measures 180 degrees. Since the measure of the given angle is 70 degrees, $180 - 70 = 110$.

37. B

$10^3 = 1,000$. To multiply by 1,000, move the decimal point 3 places to the right. The number is getting larger.

38. B

Reciprocals are fractions turned upside down so that one fraction is the inverse of the other.

39. B

To compare more readily, convert all answer choices to decimals.

Thus, $\frac{6}{7} \approx .85$

$\frac{7}{8} \approx .87$

$\frac{4}{5} \approx .8$

$\frac{5}{6} \approx .83$

$\frac{7}{8}$ is the largest.

40. C

The least common multiple of 3 and 8 is 24; in other words, 24 is the smallest number in which both 3 and 8 divide evenly without a remainder.

41. C

$(20 \times 120) + (155 \times 24) = 2,400 + 3,720 = 6,120$

42. B

Convert 11 into $10\frac{12}{12}$ then subtract $2\frac{1}{12} = 8\frac{11}{12}$.

43. A

When adding two numbers with different signs, subtract the absolute values and keep the sign of the number with the larger absolute value. $8 + (-4) = 4$; $4 + 6 = 10$; $10 + (-7) = 3$.

44. C

Round 326.52 to 327 and divide by 12 because there are 12 months in a year.

$\frac{327}{12} = 27.25$, which is approximately equal to 27.

45. D

Isolate x to solve. First, multiply using the distributive property; $10x - 15 = 42$. Add 15 to each side of the equal sign; $10x = 42 + 15$; $10x = 57$. Divide each side by 10; $x = \frac{57}{10} = 5.7$

46. A

Let x equal Marisa's mother's age.

Marisa is now 15. Three years ago her mother was three times as old as Marisa. Thus, three years ago:

$3(15 - 3) = x$

$3(12) = x$

$36 = x$

Marisa's mother's age now $= 36 + 3 = 39$

47. D

$.08x = 4.16$

$x = \frac{4.16}{.08} = 52$

48. B

Ratios can be expressed as fractions:

$\frac{2}{7}$

$\frac{5}{4}$

To divide a fraction by a fraction, multiply by the reciprocal of the number being divided by. The problem becomes $\frac{2}{7} \times \frac{4}{5} = \frac{8}{35}$, which can also be expressed as 8:35.

Language

49. D

There are no mistakes.

50. B

Their's is incorrect. The correct word is *there's*, the contraction for *there is*.

51. A

Elisa, a proper name, should be capitalized.

52. D

There are no mistakes.

53. B

The correct spelling is *column*.

54. C

The correct spelling is *merchandise*.

55. B

The correct spelling is *calendar*.

56. A

The correct spelling is *irritating*.

57. A

The meaning of the sentence is clearest when the adverbial phrase follows the verb.

58. B

The first phrase is the reason for the second. *Therefore* is the correct connective.

59. C

Information about the capital is not related to the general flow of the paragraph that introduces the topic of Uzbekistan and then discusses its economic status.

60. D

The word *however* indicates a change in direction of the ideas of the paragraph. It should come at the end of the paragraph, after sentence 3.

| SECTION THREE |

Skill Review

Chapter Four: **Verbal Skills**

Verbal skills questions account for a sizeable portion of your raw score on the HSPT and COOP. There are 60 verbal skills questions on the HSPT and approximately 30 on the COOP. These questions can appear in several formats: synonyms, antonyms, words-in-context, analogies, and verbal classification. (On the HSPT, short logic questions will also appear on the Verbal Skills section; we'll cover these in the reasoning chapter of this book.)

In this chapter, we'll review each of the vocabulary-based question types. On both the COOP and HSPT, several formats of verbal skills questions will appear mixed in together. Therefore, it is really important that you feel comfortable with each type of question and are able to switch gears quickly between question types in order to answer as accurately as possible.

No matter what the question type, a strong vocabulary is a large part of doing well on these sections and we'll discuss how to build your vocabulary at the end of the chapter. Obviously, the more words you know, the better. But our goal is to rack up points on the test, not to memorize every word in the dictionary. The strategies covered here will help you get closer to the correct answer choice, even if you don't always know the exact meaning of the words in question.

QUESTION TYPE 1—SYNONYMS

A synonym is a word that is similar in meaning to another word. *Fast* is a synonym for *quick*. *Garrulous* (whether you know it or not) is a synonym for *talkative*. On the COOP or HSPT, a synonym question will read: "Fast most nearly means…." It will be followed by four answer choices.

> Genuine most nearly means
>
> (A) authentic
> (B) valuable
> (C) ancient
> (D) damaged

KAPLAN TIP

Questions with the phrase *most nearly means* are synonym questions. Look for a word in the answer choices that means the same as the word in the question.

Sometimes you will know the word in the question. Sometimes you won't. Sometimes you'll know all the words in the answer choices, and sometimes you won't. We'll give you the Kaplan Three-Step Method for Synonyms when you know the word. Then, we'll give you some great tactics to use when you don't know all the words in the question.

THE KAPLAN THREE-STEP METHOD FOR SYNONYMS

Step 1: Define the stem word.

Step 2: Find the answer choice that best fits your definition.

Step 3: If no choice fits, think of other definitions for the stem word and go through the choices again.

Let's take another look at the example above, using the Kaplan Three-Step Method.

Step 1—Define the Stem Word

What does *genuine* mean? Something genuine is something real, such as a real Picasso painting, rather than a forgery. Your definition might be something like this: *Something genuine can be proven to be what it claims to be.*

Step 2—Find the Answer Choice That Best Fits Your Definition

Go through the answer choices one by one to see which one fits best. Your options are: *authentic; valuable, ancient, damaged,* and *historical.* Something genuine could be worth a lot or not much at all, old or new, in good shape or bad, or even recent or historical. The only word that really means the same thing as *genuine* is (A) *authentic.*

Step 3—If No Choice Fits, Think of Other Definitions for the Stem Word and Go Through the Choices Again

In this instance, one choice fits. Now, take a look at the following example:

Grave most nearly means

(A) regrettable

(B) unpleasant

(C) serious

(D) careful

Maybe you defined *grave* as a burial location. You looked at the choices, and didn't see any words like *tomb* or *coffin.* What to do? Move to Step 3, and go back to the stem word, thinking about other definitions. Have you ever heard of a "grave situation"? *Grave* can also mean *serious* or *solemn,* so you can see that (C) *serious,* now fits perfectly. If none of the answer choices seems to work with your definition, there may be a secondary definition you haven't considered yet.

AVOIDING PITFALLS

The Kaplan Three-Step Method for Synonyms should always be the basis for tackling every question, but there are a few other things you need to know to perform your best on synonym questions. Fortunately, there are only two pitfalls to watch out for.

Pitfall 1—Running Out of Time

Pace yourself. You have a limited amount of time, so make sure you use it wisely. Never waste time on a question you don't know; just circle it and come back to it later. Be careful, since question types may be mixed together. Be sure to read the question again before answering it. You don't want to make the mistake of answering a synonym question as an antonym or vice versa!

Pitfall 2—Choosing Tempting Wrong Answers

The test makers choose their wrong answer choices very carefully. Sometimes that means throwing in answer traps that will tempt you, but that aren't right. Be a savvy test taker; don't fall for these distracters!

What kinds of wrong answers are we talking about here? In synonym questions, there are two types of answer traps to watch out for: answers that are almost right, and answers that sound like the stem word. Let's illustrate both types to make it concrete.

Delegate most nearly means

(A) delight

(B) assign

(C) decide

(D) manage

Favor most nearly means

(A) award

(B) prefer

(C) respect

(D) improve

In the first example, choices (A), and (C) might be tempting, because they all start with the prefix *de-*, just like the stem word, *delegate*. It's important that you examine all the answer choices, because otherwise you might choose (A) and never get to the correct answer, (B).

In the second example, you might look at the word *favor* and think, oh, that's something positive. It's something you do for someone else. It sounds a lot like choice (A), *award*. Maybe you pick (A) and move on. If you do that, you would be falling for a trap! The correct answer is (B) *prefer*, since *favor* is being used as a verb, and *to favor* someone or something is to like it better than something else—in other words, to prefer it. If you don't read through all of the choices, you might be tricked into choosing a wrong answer.

At this point, you have a great set of tools for answering most synonym questions. You know how to approach them and you know some traps to avoid. But what happens if you don't know the word in the question? Should you just give up and move on? No way! Here are some techniques to help you figure out the meaning of a tough vocabulary word and answer a hard synonym question.

WHAT TO DO IF YOU DON'T KNOW THE WORD

Technique 1: Look for familiar roots and prefixes.

Technique 2: Use your knowledge of foreign languages.

Technique 3: Remember the word in context.

Technique 4: Use word charge.

Let's examine each technique more closely.

Technique 1—Look for Familiar Roots and Prefixes

Having a good grasp of how words are put together will help you tremendously on synonym questions, particularly when you don't know a vocabulary word. If you can break a word into pieces that you do understand, you'll be able to answer questions that you might have thought too difficult to tackle.

Look at the words below. Circle any prefixes or roots that you know.

benevolence

insomnia

inscribe

conpsire

verify

Bene means good; *somn* has to do with sleep; *scrib* has to do with writing; *con* means doing something together; and *ver* has to do with truth. So, if you were looking for a synonym for *benevolence*, you'd definitely want to choose a positive, or "good" word.

Technique 2—Use Your Knowledge of Foreign Languages

Do you study a foreign language? If so, it can help you decode lots of vocabulary words on the COOP or HSPT, particularly if it's one of the Romance languages (French, Spanish, Italian, Portuguese). Look at the example words below. Do you recognize any foreign language words in them?

facilitate

dormant

explicate

Facile means easy in Italian; *dormir* means to sleep in Spanish; and *expliquer* means to explain in French. A synonym for each of these words would have something to do with these general meanings.

Technique 3—Remember the Word in Context

Sometimes a word might look strange sitting on the page by itself, but if you think about it, you realize you've heard it before in other phrases. If you can put the word into context, even if that context is cliché, you're on your way to deciphering its meaning.

Illegible most nearly means

(A) illegal

(B) twisted

(C) unreadable

(D) eligible

Have you heard this word in context? Maybe someone you know has had his or her handwriting described as illegible. What is illegible handwriting?

Remember to try to think of a definition first, before you look at the answer choices.

Some of the answer choices here are tricks. Which ones are tempting wrong answers, meant to remind you of the question word? The correct answer is (C).

Here's another example:

Laurels most nearly means

(A) vine

(B) honor

(C) lavender

(D) cushion

Have you heard the phrase "don't rest on your laurels"? What do you think it might mean?

The phrase "don't rest on your laurels" originated in ancient Greece, where heroes were given wreaths of laurel branches to signify their accomplishments. Telling someone to not rest on his laurels is the same thing as telling him to not get too smug, living off the success of one accomplishment, rather than striving for improvement.

Technique 4—Use Word Charge

Even if you know nothing about the word, have never seen it before, don't recognize any prefixes or roots, and can't think of any word in any language that it sounds like, you can still take an educated guess by using word charge.

What do we mean by word charge? Word charge refers to the sense that a word gives you as to whether it's a positive word or a negative word.

vilify: This sounds like *villain*, a word most people would say is bad.

glorify: This sounds like *glorious*, a word most people would say is good.

Let's say that vilify has a negative charge (–) and glorify has a positive charge (+). On all synonym questions, the correct answer will have the same charge as the stem word, so use your instincts about word charge to help you when you're stuck on a tough word.

Often words that sound harsh have a negative meaning, while smooth-sounding words tend to have positive meanings. If *cantankerous* sounds negative to you, you would be right: It means difficult to handle.

You can also use prefixes and roots to help determine a word's charge. *Anti*, *mal*, *de*, *dis*, *un*, *in*, *im*, *a*, and *mis* often indicate a negative, while *pro*, *ben*, and *magn* are often positives.

Not all words sound positive or negative; some sound neutral. But, if you can define the charge, you can probably eliminate some answer choices on that basis alone. Word charge is a great technique to use when answering antonym questions, too.

QUESTION TYPE 2—ANTONYMS

Antonyms are words that have the opposite meaning of one another. *Slow* is the antonym of *fast*; *taciturn* is the antonym of *garrulous*. (Remember *garrulous* from our synonym section? Just throwing in a little review here….)

Antonym questions are clearly identifiable on the HSPT since they include the word *opposite*. An antonym question will read: "Generous means the *opposite* of…."

Use the Kaplan Three-Step Method for Synonyms when dealing with antonym questions. But just remember, now you're looking for a word that means the OPPOSITE of the one given. It's a good idea to circle the word *opposite* in the question, to make sure you don't accidentally look for a synonym.

THE KAPLAN THREE-STEP METHOD FOR ANTONYMS

Step 1: Define the word. Then, think of a word that means the opposite.

Step 2: Find the answer choice that best fits your definition.

Step 3: If no choice fits, think of other definitions for the stem word and go through the choices again.

Use roots, context, or word charge to help you if you don't know the definition of the question word.

Let's practice with an example:

Dear means the opposite of

(A) beloved

(B) close

(C) cheap

(D) family

Step 1—Define the Word. Then, Think of a Word That Means the Opposite.

Dear is a pretty familiar word. You know it from the beginning of a letter as in "Dear Aunt Sue." So, you might define *dear* as *a term for someone you love*. The opposite might be *a term for someone you hate or dislike*.

Step 2—Find the Answer Choice That Best Fits Your Definition

When we look at the answer choices—*beloved, close, cheap, family*—none of them fits our definition of the opposite of *dear* as *someone disliked or hated*. Since *dear* is an "easy" word, we have to figure that perhaps our definition is a little off. We have to refocus it.

Step 3—If No Choice Fits, Think of Other Definitions for the Stem Word and Go Through the Choices Again

When we use the term "Dear Aunt Sue," or "Dear Sir," what are we saying about that person? We say that we care about them and think that they are valuable. Okay, so let's use *valuable* as our new definition of *dear*. Our antonym would then be the opposite of *valuable—worthless*, perhaps.

Which of the answer choices comes closest to *worthless*? Choice (C), *cheap* is closest to worthless. That's the correct answer.

When you don't find an obvious answer choice for a word you know, you can suspect that there is an alternate meaning for that word. Use your knowledge of the word's primary meaning and see if you can expand on it to arrive at the correct answer.

You can also use your knowledge of word roots, familiarity with the word in context, and word charge to help you select the answer to antonym questions.

When using word charge on antonym questions, don't forget you're looking for words with the **opposite** charge. If the question word has a positive charge, your answer choice should have a negative one, and vice versa.

QUESTION TYPE 3—WORDS-IN-CONTEXT

We already discussed how trying to recall the context, or situation, in which you've heard a word can help you answer synonym or antonym questions. On the HSPT, there are also question types that already put the vocabulary word in context for you. These words-in-context questions appear on the Reading section of the HSPT, and they look like this:

grant a <u>reprieve</u>

strict <u>regulations</u>

<u>annual</u> earnings

<u>valid</u> argument

Of course, each question is followed by four answer choices. It is essential to realize that you are looking for a word that means the same (or most nearly the same) as the underlined word. In essence, these are fancy synonym questions, in which the context is already provided for you.

Approach words-in-context questions as you would any other synonym question, but use the context to your advantage. It may help jog your memory of an otherwise unknown word, or help you clarify your definition.

THE KAPLAN THREE-STEP METHOD FOR WORDS-IN-CONTEXT

Step 1: Define the word.

Step 2: Find an answer choice that best fits your definition.

Step 3: Refocus the definition. Use the context provided to help you clarify the word.

Use all the techniques at your disposal if you don't know the question word.

Hey, wait a minute! What if you don't know the word *disposal* used in the sentence above? Let's treat that as a words-in-context question and use the Kaplan Three-Step Method for Words-in-Context to find the answer.

Step 1—Define the Word

techniques at your <u>disposal</u>

Use the context, the surrounding words, to help you determine your definition. (Notice the context is not "garbage disposal"—if it were, *disposal* would have a different meaning.) The context given is *techniques at your disposal.* These must be techniques you can use. So our definition of *disposal* is therefore *something that you can use, useable,* or *at hand.*

Step 2—Find the Answer Choice That Best Fits Your Definition

techniques at your <u>disposal</u>

(A) worthless

(B) dislikeable

(C) available

(D) memorable

Which of the answer choices is most like our definition *at hand* or *useable*? Choice (C), *available*, fits best.

What if our definition doesn't fit?

Step 3—Refocus the Definition. Use the Context Provided to Help You Clarify the Word.

Here's another example.

<u>field</u> of study

(A) garden

(B) area

(C) space

(D) object

A field is an open space. However, using the context *of study* can help us avoid going down a wrong path to begin with. Since *field* is used in the phrase *field of study*, we are not talking about a real open space with grass, but rather a general area or region. Given that definition, move on to Step 2. Which answer choice fits best? Choice (B).

Think about the context in which you've seen the underlined words below. Then jot down a possible definition of each one and choose answer that best fits your definition.

WORKING BACKWARD

What if you just can't think of a definition for the underlined word? Try working backward.

Working backward means plugging in your answer choices and asking yourself if they could possibly mean the same as the underlined word. This technique is especially useful for words-in-context questions. Let's examine how this works.

<u>dry</u> wit

(A) sarcastic

(B) moldy

(C) unusual

(D) pathetic

Given the context, we know that *dry* here can't mean the opposite of *wet*. The context already clues us in to the fact that *dry* has something to do with wit, or being clever.

Let's say you just don't know what *dry wit* could be. Go to the answer choices and ask yourself if each one could apply to the context, and therefore mean the same as the word *dry*.

Choice (A): Could you have *sarcastic wit*? Yes, someone could be sarcastically witty.

Choice (B): Could you have *moldy wit*? Moldy wit? That doesn't make sense. Eliminate this answer choice.

Choice (C): Could you have *unusual wit*? Perhaps, but it doesn't sound as good as choice (A).

Choice (D): Could you have *pathetic wit*? No, that doesn't make sense. *Pathetic* means *pitiable*. *Pitiable cleverness* doesn't make sense. Eliminate this answer choice.

Choice (A) is the best answer. You've got it!

QUESTION TYPE 4—VERBAL CLASSIFICATION

Verbal classification questions on the HSPT ask you to find the word that is different from the rest of the choices, and doesn't belong with them. Synonym, antonym, and words-in-context questions all require you to define one word. Verbal classification questions require you not only to define a word, but also to figure out whether it belongs in a category with a group of other words. Verbal classification on the HSPT looks like this:

Which word does *not* belong with the others?

(A) approve
(B) scorn
(C) criticize
(D) deride

Three of the answer choices fit into the same category, and one of them does not. Your job is to find the one that does not belong.

The best approach to use? The Kaplan Three-Step Method for Verbal Classification!

THE KAPLAN THREE-STEP METHOD FOR VERBAL CLASSIFICATION

Step 1:   Define the words in the answer choices.

Step 2:   Think of the category, and find the answer choice that does not belong to that category.

Step 3:   If necessary, refocus and go through the choices again.

Although the Three-Step Method is slightly different for verbal classification questions, the foundation remains the same. Define first and find and answer second. By doing this, you will avoid becoming confused by wrong or trick answers.

Let's revisit some of our examples and see how the method works on verbal classification questions.

Step 1—Define the Words in the Answer Choices

Yes, you need to define each answer choice. It doesn't have to be an extensive or complicated definition, just a brief "label" to help you focus on what the word means.

Your labels might look something like this:

> Which word does *not* belong with the others?
>
> (A) approve—*says okay*
> (B) scorn—*says bad things about*
> (C) criticize—*says bad things about*
> (D) deride—*?*

Step 2—Think of the Category, and Find the Answer Choice that Does Not Belong to that Category

Assuming that you don't know the word *deride*, you at least know that (B) and (C), have to do with disapproval. So let's define your category as *disapproval*.

Which word doesn't belong? Choice (A), *approval*. Notice how you were able to arrive at the right answer choice even though you didn't know all the words in the answer choices.

Let's try another one.

> Which word does *not* belong with the others?
>
> (A) gloomy
> (B) depressed
> (C) hazy
> (D) fair

Step 1—Define the Words in the Answer Choices

Read all four answer choices, and jot down a brief definition next to each one.

(A) gloomy—*sad, dark*
(B) depressed—*sad*
(C) hazy—*foggy*
(D) fair—*bright? pretty?*

Step 2—Think of the Category, and Find the Answer Choice that Does Not Belong to that Category

On a quick first reading, *gloomy* and *depressed* both have to do with dark moods. You might define the category as *dark moods*.

But remember, we're looking for the choice that doesn't belong. If you initially defined the category as *dark moods*, you would find that two answer choices—*hazy* and *fair*—don't belong. Since there can be only one correct answer choice (only one word that does not belong), we know that our initial definition of the category as *dark moods* is not on target. Therefore, we need to move on to Step 3.

Step 3— If Necessary, Refocus and Go Through the Choices Again

Look at the answer choices. Choices (C) and (D) have to do with weather. So does (A). Three out of four answer choices fall into the same category. Let's refocus our definition then and call the category *types of weather*.

Therefore, choice (B) doesn't belong. This is the correct answer choice.

The example above illustrates an important point. Although it might seem helpful to move quickly, cutting out steps, or selecting an answer without reading all the answer choices carefully, can actually cost you more time in the end.

On the other hand, recognizing types of categories, such as members of a group, or parts of a whole, will help you arrive more quickly at a correct answer choice on verbal classification questions.

> **KAPLAN TIP**
>
> Trying to select an answer in a verbal classification question without carefully reading all the answer choices can lead you down the wrong path and cost you more time in the end.

QUESTION TYPE 5—ANALOGIES

Analogy questions ask you to compare two words and then extend the relationship to another sets of words.

Simply put, an analogy is a comparison. When you say, "She's as slow as molasses," or "He eats like a horse," you're making an analogy. In the first example, you're comparing the person in question with molasses, and in the second example, you're comparing the person with a horse.

Analogy questions on the HSPT are mixed in with the rest of the verbal skills questions we just covered. HSPT analogies look like this:

> Bird is to nest as bear is to
>
> (A) cub
>
> (B) paw
>
> (C) tree
>
> (D) cave

One set of words—*bird* and *nest*—is given. The second set—*bear* and *?*—is incomplete. Your job is to find an answer choice that will create the same relationship between the second set of words as exists in the first set.

Analogies may seem pretty weird at first glance. However, once you become familiar with the format, you'll find that they are pretty straightforward and very predictable. With practice, you can learn to get analogy questions right even when you don't know all of the vocabulary words involved.

KAPLAN TIP

On the COOP, analogy questions actually use pictures instead of words. Don't panic! The Kaplan Three-Step Method for Analogies works just as well for pictures as it does for words. Go to chapter thirteen in this book to learn more about COOP analogies.

THE KAPLAN THREE-STEP METHOD FOR ANALOGIES

Step 1:   Build a bridge.

Step 2:   Predict your answer choice, and select an answer.

Step 3:   Adjust your bridge if necessary.

What does it mean to "build a bridge"? A bridge is a sentence you create to express the relationship between the words in the stem pair. Building a bridge helps you zone in on the correct answer and helps you avoid falling for wrong answer traps. Let's take a closer look to see how it works.

Step 1—Build a Bridge

In every analogy question, there's a strong, definite connection between the two stem words. Your first task is to figure out this relationship.

A bridge is a short sentence that relates the two words in the question, and every pair of words will have a strong bridge that links them. In our original example, a good bridge would be, "A bird lives in a nest."

Step 2—Predict your Answer Choice and Select an Answer

You figured out how the words *bird* and *nest* are related. Now, you need to determine which answer choice relates to *bear* in the same way. Use your bridge to do that.

Our bridge was: A bird lives in a nest.

Apply the same bridge to the incomplete pair: A bear lives in a _____.

So when we predict the answer choice, we come up with a place where a bear lives: a cave.

Bird is to nest as bear is to

(A) cub
(B) paw
(C) tree
(D) cave

Cave, our predicted answer is indeed among the answer choices, choice (D).

Take a moment to look at the incorrect answer choices: *cub*, *paw*, and *tree*. They are all related in some way to the words in the question, but not in the way our bridge defined. Building a strong bridge is essential to predicting an answer, selecting a correct answer choice, and avoiding traps.

What if your bridge doesn't work? Sometimes you may find that even though you came up with a bridge, none of the answer choices fits. In this case, your bridge is either too broad or too narrow. You'll need to refocus it. That's where Step 3 comes in.

Step 3—Adjust your Bridge if Necessary

Let's see how you can adjust a weak bridge using the example below.

Fish is to gill as mammal is to

(A) arm
(B) wing
(C) foot
(D) lung

Let's say you create this bridge: "A fish has a gill." Then you went to the answer choices and plugged in the bridge:

(A) A mammal has an arm.
(B) A mammal has a wing.
(C) A mammal has a foot.
(D) A mammal has a lung.

Every choice fits! In this case, the bridge was too general, so you'll need to adjust your bridge.

What would a good adjustment be? Try to create the most specific relationship between the words, because the more specific your bridge is, the fewer choices will match it. A good bridge for this pair might be: "A fish uses a gill to breathe." Now try plugging that bridge into the answer choices.

    (A) A mammal uses an arm to breathe? No.

    (B) A mammal uses a wing to breathe? No.

    (C) A mammal uses a foot to breathe? No.

    (D) A mammal uses a lung to breathe? Yes!

It should now be easier to see the correct answer: Fish is to gill as mammal is to lung, choice (D).

> **KAPLAN TIP**
>
> When making a bridge, a good rule is to relate the words in such a way that you'd be able to insert the phrase "by definition" and the relationship would hold true. For example: "A poodle, by definition, is a type of dog." If you can't use "by definition" in the sentence that relates the words, your bridge isn't strong, and it needs to be reworked.

BUILDING CLASSIC BRIDGES

Building strong bridges takes practice. However, because relationships between items in analogy questions need to be strong and definite, there are some bridges that appear again and again. We call these **classic bridges**. Get to know these bridges; you'll be able to identify them quickly and save yourself a lot of time getting to the correct answer choice on analogy questions. As you read through each one, use the space provided to come up with an example of your own.

Bridge 1: Character

One word characterizes the other.

    Quarrelsome is to argue… Someone quarrelsome is characterized by a tendency to argue.

    Vivacious is to energy… Someone vivacious is characterized by a lot of energy.

    Your example: _____

Bridge 2: Lack

One word describes what someone or something lacks (or does not have).

    Coward is to bravery… A coward lacks bravery.

    Braggart is to modesty… A braggart lacks modesty.

    Your example: _____

Bridge 3: Function

One word names an object; the other word defines its function or what it is used for.

Scissors is to cut… Scissors are used to cut.

Pen is to write… A pen is used to write

Your example: _____

Bridge 4: Degree

One word is a greater or lesser degree of the other word.

Deafening is to loud… Something deafening is extremely loud.

Hovel is to mansion… A hovel is a mansion of a poor degree. (Including the specific "poor degree" might help you hone in on the right answer choice.)

Your example: _____

Bridge 5: Example

One word is an example of, or type of, the other word.

Measles is to disease… Measles is a type of disease.

Apartment is to home… An apartment is a type of home.

Your example: _____

Bridge 6: Group

One word is made up of several of the other word.

Forest is to trees… A forest is made up of many trees.

Bouquet is to flowers… A bouquet is made up of many flowers.

Your example: _____

WHAT TO DO IF YOU'RE STUCK

1. Backsolve.

2. Make an educated guess.

3. Remember the context.

4. Use word charge.

Even with your arsenal of tools, you may run into analogy questions where you don't know what to do. Perhaps you won't know what a word in the question means, or how the words relate to one another. What should you do?

There are a few strategies that will really up your chances of getting the question right, even if you're stuck.

Backsolve

What is backsolving? It may sound like an obscure form of chiropractic medicine, but it's actually just a nifty way of approaching analogies when you can't answer them directly.

Basically, you skip right past the question and head straight for the answer choices. You may be wondering, "How you can figure out the answer without knowing what the question is asking?" Well, you can't necessarily figure out the answer right away, but you can start to eliminate clearly wrong answer choices, leaving fewer options to choose from. When you rule out choices that you know can't be right, the odds are better that you'll pick the right choice from what's left.

> Awl is to tool as rose is to
>
> (A) vase
> (B) flower
> (C) bird
> (D) daisy

Even if you didn't know that an awl is a type of tool, what could you rule out? Well, in (A), there's no definite connection between *rose* and *vase*. A rose could be put in a vase, but it also could be left in the wild. Additionally, any other flower could also be put in a vase. Rule out (A) as having a weak bridge. There is also no relationship by definition between *rose* and *bird*, choice (C), except that they're both living things. Choice (D) is also not a strong relationship by definition: Although *rose* and *daisy* are both flowers, one is not defined in terms of the other. ("Both are" is NOT a good bridge—it's an answer trap! Avoid answer choices in which this is the only bridge that you can create to link the two words.)

In the example above, only (B) has a strong, definite relationship to *rose*. The words *rose* and *flower* are joined by a classic "type of" bridge: A rose is a type of flower.

> **KAPLAN TIP**
>
> Watch out for the "both are" trap on analogy questions. For instance, bread and bananas are both types of food, but what exactly is their relationship? Bananas aren't a type of bread, a lack of bread, or a function of bread. If both words are part of a larger group, but there's no connection, by definition, between the words themselves, it's an answer trap.

By eliminating even one illogical answer choice, you'll narrow down your choices and have a better chance of getting the question right. Always keep your eye out for "both are" traps and weak bridges as you work through analogy questions, and you'll rack up lots of points on even the toughest questions.

Make an Educated Guess

What if you reach the point where you can't figure out the bridge, and you can't rule out wrong answer choices?

You know the six classic bridges. You know they show up a lot on analogy questions. So, even if you don't know the exact definition of one (or both!) words, you could make an educated guess about the bridge. For example, say you saw this question:

Word is to philologist as bug is to

What might the bridge be? Well, a *philologist* sounds like a type of person (since it ends in -*ologist*), and a *word* is a thing, so maybe a philologist does something with words. *Philologist* is a tricky word, but you could make a great guess by saying that a philologist studies words, which is exactly right!

Remember the Context

Sometimes a word sounds familiar, but you can't remember why. If that happens, use the context to help you determine their meaning. For example,

Crescendo is to music as climax is to

What does *crescendo* mean? Maybe you don't know. But the fact that it is already linked to music in the question clues you in to the fact that *crescendo* has something to do with music. Climax therefore has something to do with…. Predict your answer choice, then look at the answers to see which one fits best.

Use Word Charge

Some words give you the feeling that they're either positive or negative. Use this sense to help you figure out the bridge between words in the question when you don't actually know what one of them means—or both!

So how does word charge help you find the right answer? Once you determine the charge of the words in the question, you can look for a word in the answer choices that completes the second phrase with the same charge relationship. If the words in the question have the same charge (+, +) or (−, −) the two next words should have the same charge. That charge can be either both positive, or both negative, but it must be the same. If the words in the question have opposite charges (+, −) or (−, +), the two following words should have opposite charges.

Work through this example to see how word charge works.

Imprison is to confine as undermine is to

(A) unleash

(B) broaden

(C) weaken

(D) protect

Imprison is negative. *Confine* is negative. So the word charges for the two words in the question are (−, −).

Undermine is negative. The word that completes this phrase therefore needs to be negative, so that we have a (−, −) relationship, like that in the words in the question.

(A) *Unleash* is to let off a leash. This may be either positive or negative, depending on the situation. Rule it out.

(B) *Broaden* is positive. We're looking for a word with a negative charge. Rule it out.

(C) *Weaken* is negative. That fits.

(D) *Protect* is positive. We're looking for a word with a negative charge. Rule it out.

Choice (C) is the best answer choice.

VOCABULARY-BUILDING STRATEGIES

You have a lot of strategies and skills at your disposal for the verbal skills questions on the COOP or HSPT. You should be ready to handle any verbal skills question that comes your way if you put your knowledge into practice.

One of the best ways to prepare for the COOP, the HSPT, and many other standardized tests is to expand your vocabulary. You don't need to sit down and memorize the dictionary. Just spend about 30 minutes a day using any of the techniques below. We recommend dividing your vocabulary study into two daily sessions. Spend some time learning new words during the first session, and review them again later before the end of the day. Scientific research shows that this is the best way to optimize retention. (Don't know the meaning of *retention*? Look it up!)

> **KAPLAN TIP**
>
> Expanding your vocabulary is a great way to prepare for the COOP or HSPT. Divide your vocabulary study time into two daily sessions: Spend around 15 minutes learning new words during the first session, and review them again later before the end of the day.

Look It Up

Challenge yourself to find at least five words a day that are unfamiliar to you. You could find these words listening to a news broadcast, or reading a magazine or novel. In fact, books that you choose to read for enjoyment normally contain three to five words per page that are unfamiliar to you.

Write down these words, look them up in the dictionary, and record their definitions in a notebook.

But don't only write the word's definition. Below your definition, use the word in a sentence. This will help you to remember the word, and to anticipate possible context questions. Ask a teacher, parent, or someone else with a strong vocabulary to check your sentences to make sure you've used the word correctly.

Use Flash Cards

Periodically, transfer the words from your notebook to flash cards. On one side of the card write the word, on the other side, record its definition. You might find it helpful to put your context phrase on either side of the card as well. Keep your flash cards with you (in your bag or back-pack), and practice with them during the day.

Make Lists of Synonyms and Antonyms

Another great way to expand your vocabulary is to make groupings of words with the same meaning. Use a thesaurus to find synonyms (and antonyms) of common words.

For example, you might look up the word *talkative*. Then fold a piece of paper in half lengthwise; in one column make a list of all the synonyms you find for *talkative*, and in the other column record all the antonyms. (Make sure that you make some mark on the paper to remind you that the two columns are opposites!)

Study Word Roots, Prefixes, and Suffixes

Knowing some word roots, prefixes, and suffixes will expand your vocabulary, and will help you guess the meaning of a word if you are not sure.

You can pick up a book with word roots from the library, or ask your librarian to help you find a list on the computer and print it out. As you memorize roots, be sure to record words that use them in a notebook, write them in sentences, and put them on your flash cards.

Use Your New Words in Conversation

As much as possible, use your new words in everyday conversation. This is a great sign that you've mastered the new vocabulary words, and it will also ensure that you don't forget the new words.

While it's impossible to know exactly which of the many words you'll study may appear on the COOP or HSPT, expanding your vocabulary isn't important only on test day. A rich vocabulary will stand you in good stead for future study, work, and simply expressing yourself—not to mention that a million-dollar vocabulary is just plain impressive!

VERBAL SKILLS PRACTICE SET

1. Usurp most nearly means

(A) seize

(B) grease

(C) admit

(D) attack

2. Unscrupulous most nearly means

(A) moral

(B) clever

(C) tidy

(D) dishonest

3. Fatigued means the *opposite* of

(A) argumentative

(B) fragile

(C) energetic

(D) exhausted

4. Which word does *not* belong?

(A) river

(B) lake

(C) waterfall

(D) brook

5. Furtive is to secret as blatant is to

(A) controlled

(B) hurried

(C) obvious

(D) complex

6. Destitute means the *opposite* of

(A) wealthy

(B) hungry

(C) hopeless

(D) plentiful

7. business acumen

(A) sharpness

(B) zeal

(C) cruelty

(D) competition

8. ample supplies

(A) stored

(B) plentiful

(C) moldy

(D) delayed

9. Iota is to amount as miniature is to

(A) dollhouse

(B) size

(C) drop

(D) number

10. Which word does *not* belong?

(A) kick

(B) grasp

(C) grab

(D) pitch

ANSWERS AND EXPLANATIONS

1.   A

This is a synonym question. Come up with your own definition first, if you know the word. Your definition might be something like this: *Usurp* means *to grab*. If you can define the word, move on to the answer choices. If you haven't try to use other means to come up with a definition. Maybe you've heard the word used in this context: "usurp a throne." This context could help you define *usurp* as *take without permission*. Even if you are unable to come up with a definition, you could eliminate (B) which sounds suspiciously like a trick, the -*surp* somehow making you think of grease. The answer choice closest in meaning to *usurp* is (A), *seize*.

2.   D

This is a synonym question. *Unscrupulous* means *without scruples or morals*. The answer choice that best fits this definition is *dishonest*. Perhaps you've heard the word used in the context, "He has no scruples." Having no scruples is negatively charged. If you don't know the meaning of the word *unscrupulous*, look for an answer choice that is also negatively charged. Only choice (D) fits. It is the correct answer.

3.   C

This is an antonym question. Define the word, and think of an opposite. *Fatigued* means tired or worn out; the opposite is *energetic*, choice (C).

4.   B

This is a verbal classification question. Read all the answer choices and think about what three out of four of them have in common. *River*, *waterfall*, and *brook* are bodies of water that flow. A lake is contained. *Lake* does not belong.

5.   C

This is an analogy question. Build a bridge between the first two words, and use it to determine what the missing word should be. Your bridge here might be: *Furtive* is in a *secret* manner. *Blatant* is in a *clear* manner. Which answer choice means the closest to *clear*? Choice (C), *obvious*.

6.   A

This is an antonym question. *Destitute* means *poor*; the opposite is *wealthy*. If you did not know the meaning of the question word, use word charge to help you hone in on the right answer. *Destitute* has a negative charge. The opposite, or antonym, should have a positive charge. Choices (A) and (D) have a positive charge. Take your best guess from these remaining answer choices.

7.   A

This is a words-in-context question. Think of a definition first. *Acumen* is *intelligence* or *cunning*. Choice (A) best fits the definition. If you are unable to think of a definition, work backward plugging in the answer choices. *Business sharpness*? Makes sense. *Business zeal*? Possibly, but it doesn't sound as good. *Business cruelty*? Doesn't really make sense. *Business competition*? That sounds good. Now that you've ruled out choice (C), take your best guess.

8.   B

This is a words-in-context question. If you are able to, think of a definition first. *Ample* means *enough*. Choice (B), *plentiful* best fits this definition. If you are unable to think of a definition, try using word charge to eliminate poor answer choices. *Ample* is positively charged. The strongest positively charged answer choice is (B). Choices (C) and (D) are both negatively charged, while (A) does not really carry any charge.

9.   B

This is an analogy question. Build a bridge first, then think of a word that fits into the relationship you defined. An *iota* is *a small amount*, a *miniature* is *a small size*. *Size*, our definition, is actually one of the answer choices, choice (B).

10.   A

This is a verbal classification question. *Grasp*, *grab*, and *pitch* are all done with the arms, but *kick* is an action performed with the legs. Be sure to read through each item and think about what they have in common before rushing to select a choice. If you worked too quickly, you might have chosen *pitch*, since it sounds more sporty than the other choices.

Chapter Five: **Reading Comprehension**

Reading comprehension skills are important to have when you take the COOP or HSPT tests. You'll be presented with anywhere from five to eight passages ranging in length from one to six paragraphs. Each passage has approximately five questions. These questions test your ability to understand what you've read.

In previous years, the COOP Reading Comprehension subtest included only passages. Currently, some language mechanics and organization skills are tested in this section as well. We'll address those topics in chapter six. For now, we'll focus on the passages and the questions that accompany them.

Because time is of the essence on the COOP and HSPT exams, it's important to approach the passages in a systematic way. Reading habits that serve you well in school can prove too time-consuming for this type of exam. Avoid these common reading traps:

- Reading too slowly
- Continually rereading things you do not understand
- Spending more time on the passages than on the questions

All of these traps involve pacing yourself. Normally, it's a good idea to read slowly and deliberately and to stick with something you are reading until it makes sense. However, what normally works will not help you on test day.

READING ON TESTS IS DIFFERENT FROM EVERYDAY READING

You don't usually read to gather points, do you? An essential thing to remember as you approach the COOP or HSPT reading passages is that the points come from the questions, not the passages.

Read the passage to answer questions and rack up points. If you spend your time focusing on all the subtle nuances or details of a given passage, you may not have time to answer the questions (and earn points) when you are finished. Yes, you may know all the details of 12th century manuscript illumination, but this won't help you get into the school of your choice.

Therefore, as you work through this chapter, there are two things you need to do:

- Be aware of your reading habits. Notice how you approach each passage and whether you are getting bogged down in the details.
- Remember that the point is to earn points on the test. Make the questions your priority.

How do you do that? Use our systematic approach to focus on the questions and the points.

THE KAPLAN FOUR-STEP METHOD FOR READING COMPREHENSION QUESTIONS

Step 1. Read the passage.

Step 2. Decode the question.

Step 3. Research the detail.

Step 4. Predict the answer, and check the answer choices.

Like the Kaplan Method for the other question types, the Kaplan Four-Step Method for Reading Comprehension Questions requires you to do most of your work *before* you actually look at the answer choices. It's very tempting to read the questions and immediately dive into the answer choices. Don't do this. The work you do up front will save you more time in the long run and increase your ability to avoid tempting wrong answer choices.

Step 1—Read the Passage

The first thing you're going to do is read through the passage. However, it's important to realize that while you are reading the passage, you do not need to memorize it or take it apart. Instead, look for the main idea and paragraph topics (note the general idea of the passage and where it seems to be going).

For example, if you saw the following passage on the COOP or HSPT, these are some things you might want to note.

Franklin was remembered for many things; he was also a diplomat.

Benjamin Franklin is well-known as a founding father, an inventor, and a philosopher. He is remembered for the clever yet humorous writings of *Poor Richard's Almanac*, which offered advice such as "Early to bed, early to rise, makes a man healthy, wealthy and wise." The scientist Franklin discovered electricity through his experiments with lightning. He was also the first American diplomat. From 1776 to 1778, Benjamin Franklin led a three-man envoy to France in an effort to win French support for American independence.

In Paris, Franklin charmed French aristocrats and intellectuals. They welcomed him as the embodiment of the New World Enlightenment thinking. His likeness was etched on medallions, rings, watches, and snuffboxes. Fashionable upper class ladies wore their hair in a style imitating Franklin's fur cap. Franklin used his popularity and diplomatic talent to convince France to recognize American independence and sign the Treaty of Alliance with the thirteen states. The treaty was brilliantly negotiated, and Franklin managed to include an article stating that no payment would need to be made to secure the alliance.

Franklin was popular and successful in France.

After the American Revolution, Franklin became the first American Minister to be received by a foreign government. He was aged 73 at the time. In 1785, Thomas Jefferson followed Franklin as ambassador to France. When the French Foreign Minister asked Jefferson, "It is you who replace Dr. Franklin?" Jefferson replied, "No one can replace him, Sir; I am only his successor."

Jefferson followed Franklin, but respected the man who came before him.

Notice that we've kept our comments very broad on this initial reading of the passage. The goal is to recognize the major themes and perhaps a few details. There's no reason to focus too closely on any particular thing because we don't know yet whether the questions will ask about it or not.

Step 2—Decode the Questions

About four or five questions will follow each passage. The first thing you'll need to do with each question is decode it. In other words, you need to figure out exactly what the question is asking before you can answer it. Be sure the question makes sense to you.

Here's an example of a question that might follow the Benjamin Franklin passage.

According to the passage, what was the goal of Franklin's first mission to France?

In other words, why did Franklin go to France?

(A) to charm the French people

(B) to win support for the American Revolution

(C) to get help drafting the Constitution

(D) to be received by a foreign government

This is a detail question. However, we did not originally note details when we first read the passage. We were waiting to see which ones were asked about in the questions. Now that we know, we can move on to Step 3.

KAPLAN TIP

Figure out what the question is asking from you before you read the answer choices.

Step 3—Research the Details

Remember, we didn't want to waste time memorizing too many details before we knew which ones were in the questions. Now that we know the detail that is being questioned—why Franklin went to France—we can go back and find it.

You should have noted when you read the passage that the first paragraph is about Franklin's role as a diplomat. Scan this paragraph for details about where he went and why.

Even if you have some memory of the detail, avoid answering based solely on your recollection. Check the passage to make sure your memory is right. This technique will also keep you from trying to memorize details. Memorizing details is a waste of time on the test.

Step 4—Predict the Answer and Check the Answer Choices

When you find the detail in the passage, think about the purpose that it serves. Why does the author mention Franklin's *effort to win French support for American independence*? What does that mean? It could mean he wanted financial support or to form an alliance against the British. Now that you have an idea of the correct answer, look for an answer choice that matches your idea.

(A) to charm the French people

(B) to win support for the American Revolution

(C) to get help drafting the Constitution

(D) to be received by a foreign government

Answer choice (B) is the only one that fits the idea you've already come up with. That's it! You've got it. Now that you've seen the Kaplan Method at work, let's practice some more strategies for dealing with the passages.

THE QUESTIONS

When you begin the reading comprehension section on your exam, knowing what type of questions to expect will help you constructively read the passage. There are four question types that you could be asked after each passage.

Main Idea Questions

A main idea question asks you to summarize the topic of the entire passage. You may see a main idea question in a variety of forms. Some examples of these forms are as follows:

- What is this passage mostly about?
- Which of the following is a good title for this passage?
- The information in this passage could help you answer which of these questions?

Decode the question, and you realize that they are asking the same thing. All of these questions are asking about the main idea of the passage as a whole.

KAPLAN TIP

A key strategy for main idea questions is to look for an answer choice that summarizes the entire passage, not just a detail or a paragraph.

Detail Questions

A detail question asks you to research information that is directly stated in the passage. For example:

- Which of the following is a result of photosynthesis?
- What is the first stage of child development?
- Which Roman Emperor conquered the Celts?

All of the detail questions above are asking for specific information, and they are all straightforward. All you have to do is locate the information in the passage. A key strategy is to research the details by relating the facts from the question to a specific paragraph and then rereading that paragraph to find the detail you're looking for.

Inference Questions

The answers to inference questions will not be stated outright in the passage, but will be hinted at strongly. It is your job to figure out what those hints mean when put together. Here are some examples of inference questions:

- This passage is most likely found in a
- The author of this passage is probably
- The next thing that will most likely happen is

Inference questions usually ask you to predict what might happen next, or what would be a logical next paragraph. Likewise, questions that ask you about the author's purpose, the author's identity, or the author's attitude toward the topic are inference questions.

For instance, if a passage goes on about the wonders of exploring archeological excavations, the author is, most likely, an archeologist. If, on the other hand, the passage discusses the negative impact of archeological digs, you can most likely infer that the author is not an archeologist.

We will discuss what skills are involved in answering inference questions more in this chapter. You will need to use those inference skills to figure out things that are not stated directly.

Vocabulary-in-Context Questions

Vocabulary-in-context questions ask you to figure out the meaning of a word used in the passage. Although it may be a word that you recognize, treat vocabulary-in-context questions as a type of research question. Often, the obvious meaning is not the correct answer.

- What does the author mean by choosing the word *misguided* to describe the plan?
- In this passage, the word *futile* most nearly means
- Based on the passage, a good definition for *exorbitant* is

Even if you think you know the meaning of the word, always go back and locate the word within the passage. Read a sentence or two before the word, the sentence in which it is used, and a sentence or two after it. The context of the word will provide enough clues to its meaning.

THE PASSAGE

As you learned earlier, reading for the COOP or HSPT test is not exactly like the reading you do in school or at home. In general, you usually read to learn, or you read for pleasure. It's a petty safe bet that you're not reading the COOP or HSPT passages for the fun of it. If you do happen to enjoy them, great! However, it should still be clear that you are not reading these passages for enjoyment. You are reading them to answer questions and earn points. Anything that doesn't help you get a point is a waste of time for the purpose of the test. Therefore, you want to read in such a way that will help maximize your chance of getting points on the questions. The questions will ask you about the main idea, a few details, and a few inferences. Keep in mind that you need to get enough out of the passage to help you deal with the questions. Here are some strategies to do just that.

COOP and HSPT Reading Strategies

Mark it Up

You can write in the test booklet, so use this to your advantage. You do not need to take a lot of notes, but do not leave the passage and surrounding space blank. Use it to keep track of the main idea of the whole passage and of the various paragraphs. Your notes will help to you find the information you need to answer the questions later.

Focus on the First Third of the Passage

Sure, you may find the passages boring. That's an unfortunate fact of the test. Although you cannot count on being entertained, you can count on being presented with a well-organized passage. This means that the author is overwhelmingly likely to present the important information at the beginning of the passage. Odds are that you'll be able to answer the inevitable main idea question based on the first third of the passage.

Look for the Main Idea

All you really need to understand is the main idea and the paragraph topics. Remember that you can research the details as you need them, as long as you have an idea of where to look.

Use the Paragraph Topics

The first two sentences of each paragraph should tell you what it's about. The rest of the paragraph is likely to be more detail heavy. Just as you should pay more attention to the beginning of the passage, you should also pay more attention to the beginning of each paragraph.

Don't Worry About the Details

Don't waste time reading and rereading parts that you don't understand. As long as you have a general idea of where the details are, you don't have to know what they are. Remember, you can look them up later. This is another example of why marking up the passage is so useful. You can circle or underline the details that seem important. Furthermore, as long as you've made a note of the paragraph topic, you should be able to go back and find the detail within it. Details will always be located within the paragraph that deals with the general topic.

Break it Down

Sometimes you'll come across difficult language or technical jargon in the passages, especially in the science passages. As much as possible, try not to get bogged down by language that you find confusing. The underlying topic is usually pretty straightforward. It can be very helpful to put confusing language into your own words. Remember, you don't have to understand every word to summarize or paraphrase. All you need is a general understanding.

Keep Moving

Aim to spend no more than 2–3 minutes reading a passage. Remember, reading the passage doesn't earn you points.

CRITICAL READING SKILLS

So far, you've learned a great method by which to approach all reading comprehension passages and question types. You've also been introduced to strategies that should help you work through the passages efficiently. Now, it's time to look a little more closely at the skills you'll need to use while reading a passage. These skills are summarizing, researching, and making an inference. Practicing these skills will make you a more effective COOP or HSPT reader.

Summarizing

For the purposes of the COOP or HSPT test, summarizing means capturing in a single phrase what the entire passage is about. We've already shown you the types of main idea questions you could see; these questions ask about the passage as a whole. Wrong answers will include choices that deal only with one paragraph or some other smaller component of the passage. You will need to look for the answer that deals with the entire passage. If you've thought about the main idea ahead of time, you're more likely to go directly to the correct answer choice.

> The Homestead Act was one of the most important bills passed in the history of the United States. Signed into law in 1862 by Abraham Lincoln, this act made vast amounts of public land available to private citizens. Under the Homestead Act, 270 million acres, or 10% of the area of the United States, was claimed and settled. For a small filing fee of $18, five years of residency, and a lot of back-breaking labor, anyone dedicated to land ownership could win an impressive 160-acre parcel of land.

The qualifying requirements were seemingly scant. A homesteader simply had to be the head of a household and at least 21 years old. Each homesteader had to build a home, make improvements to the land, and farm it for five years. After this time, the settler would be eligible to "prove up," or prove all the conditions had been met. If successful, he or she would be able to keep the land. Hopeful people from all walks of life came to the West lured by the promise of "free" land.

This passage is mainly about

(A) how to apply to be a homesteader

(B) proving requirements for homesteaders

(C) the Homestead Act's effect on land ownership

(D) all the acts that Abraham Lincoln signed

The question is basically asking which choice best summarizes what the entire passage is about. Only one answer choice sums up the contents of both paragraphs. (A) and (B) are both details. (D) is too broad; all the acts that Lincoln signed are not discussed in the passage. Choice (C) summarizes the whole passage. The passage discusses the importance of the Homestead Act making public land available for people to own. Although there are a few details explaining how the land was given out, the main idea of the passage is that this act made it possible for people to own land.

Researching

Whereas summarizing is important in helping you answer main idea questions, researching is important in helping you answer detail questions. Researching means knowing where to look for the details. Generally, if you jot down paragraph topics in the blank space around the text, you should have a good map to help you locate the details. Once you know where to look, just scan the passage for key phrases found in the question.

extratropical storms, layers of cold and warm air

From fall through winter, extratropical storms dominate the weather across much of the United States and other parts of the globe. These extratropical storms originate outside the tropics and generally move west to east across the oceans and continents. In areas of the storm that are ahead of a warm front, warm air flows over colder air that is closer to the ground. Thus, one layer of air that is above 32 degrees Fahrenheit is caught between a layer of colder air near the ground and a layer of colder air higher up.

rain, sleet, or snow determined by temperature of layers

Whether we experience snow, sleet, or freezing rain is determined by the temperatures of the layers of air when precipitation begins. Precipitation that begins as snow in the higher level of colder air will become rain if it meets a layer of air that's above 32 degrees Fahrenheit. However, if the layer of cold air near the ground is relatively thick, the falling rain will freeze into ice pellets, which are generally called sleet. On the other hand, if the layer of cold air near the ground is relatively thin, the falling rain will not become ice unless it hits something. This is freezing rain. In places where there is no layer of warm air, precipitation falls all the way to the ground as snow. Often, rain, freezing rain, and snow will fall together as a storm moves by, leaving an icy coating on exposed surfaces.

Take a look at the passage and paragraph topics above. Note that the topics are very general. They just note the general topics of the paragraphs. If you saw the following questions, would you know where to locate the answers?

Which of the following is true of extratropical storms?

(A) they dominate winter weather

(B) they originate in the tropics

(C) they move from east to west

(D) they cause tornados

The first paragraph deals with extratropical storms.

According to the passage, what causes precipitation to fall as snow?

(A) it meets a layer of ice as it hits the ground

(B) it begins high in the atmosphere

(C) it does not meet any layer of warm air as it hits the ground

(D) it moves from west to east as it travels the globe

The second paragraph deals with the details of why precipitation becomes either rain, freezing rain, sleet, or snow.

Making an Inference

Making an inference means coming to a conclusion based on information that is hinted at, but not directly stated. In other words, making an inference means reading between the lines. What did the author almost say, but not state outright?

Inferences will not stray too far from the language of the text. Wrong answer choices on inference questions will often fall beyond the subject matter of the passage.

As the saying goes, Rome wasn't built in a day. Writing a top-notch essay takes time, planning, and careful revision. But in order to revise, you must first have something down on paper. Many students feel that this is the most difficult part of the composition process.

Brainstorming is often a helpful way to overcome writer's block. Sit quietly somewhere with a piece of blank paper and your chosen topic. Note all the things that occur to you on that topic. For example, if you were writing an essay about horses, you might jot down *fast*, *beautiful*, *Arabian Stallion*, *work horses*, or anything else that jars your imagination. Once you have some ideas down on paper, you can begin to organize them.

According to the passage, the first step in the writing process is

(A) carefully revising

(B) purchasing necessary supplies

(C) daydreaming about the topic

(D) jotting down ideas

This short passage discusses the writing process. The question asks what is the first step in the process. Yet, there is no sentence in the passage that states directly: *The first step of the writing passage is…* However, in the first paragraph, the author mentions that *in order to revise, you must first have something down on paper*. Getting something down must be the first step. Now that we've predicted what the answer should be, it's time to check the answer choices for a match.

Revising (A) can't occur until writing has been done. *Purchasing supplies* (B) is not getting something down on paper; neither is daydreaming (C). Choice (D) is the only choice that is close to our predicted answer.

Notice how information in the passage allowed us to come to a reasonable conclusion. We were not directly told that jotting down ideas was the first step to writing an essay. We were able *infer* it based on the way the passage presented the information.

A WORD ABOUT TYPES OF PASSAGES

There are several passage types you may see on the COOP or HSPT test. The topics of interest can be from any field and of any variation. Here are a few areas of interest that the passages may be about.

Science

These passages are about a scientific topic such as life science, physical science, or earth science. They may be packed with details. Remember not to worry about the details or try to memorize them. Use paragraph topic sentences to help you relocate the details you need later.

Social Science

These passages are about areas such as history, linguistics, culture, or any other social science. The author may have a point of view he or she is arguing. There may also be a comparison between old and new ideas about the topic. Try to notice the author's tone, but treat these passages as you would any other. Keep your first reading broad and avoid focusing on any one detail until after you have encountered it in a detail question.

Fiction

These may be short stories, or first or third person narratives. A selection may discuss the actions or internal thoughts of a character. The exact identity of the characters or the precise location of the story may only be hinted at rather than stated. Don't let this bother you. As always, keep your initial reading general. Notice the tone or the type of story. *Mystery story about a girl*, for example, could be a helpful main idea notation for this type of passage.

Whereas different passages may lend themselves better to different question types, i.e., science passages are full of details for detail questions and short stories are great for inference questions about a character or what might happen next, it is important to read every type of passage in the same strategic way we've discussed. Regardless of whether the passage is a fiction passage, a scientific passage, or a social science passage, always note the main idea. Jot down the topic of each paragraph, and circle or underline details you believe may be asked about later.

A REMINDER ABOUT TIMING

Plan to spend approximately 2–3 minutes reading the passage and no more than 30 seconds on each question. When you start practicing, you'll probably find yourself spending more time on the passages. That's okay. However, you need to pay attention to your timing, and cut the time down as you improve. Remember, you don't need to memorize every detail or understand every subtle thought. Get through the passage and get on to the questions, where the points lie.

Now it's time to practice some reading comprehension passages and questions. Make sure you mark up the passage, noting the main idea and paragraph topics. Research the details and predict your answers. Most importantly, remember that it's all about the questions.

READING COMPREHENSION PRACTICE SET

Directions: Read the passages and answer the questions that follow.

A nuclear reaction is a change in the structure of the nuclei, or center, of an atom. The energy created during a nuclear reaction results in nuclear energy, or atomic energy. Some nuclear energy is produced naturally. The Sun and stars, for example, continually generate heat and light by nuclear reactions. The nuclear reactions that occur on the Sun, as on all other stars, are nuclear fusion reactions. In these reactions, the nuclei of atoms are joined together or fused. This occurs only at extremely high temperatures.

The nuclear energy that is produced by humans in nuclear reactor power plants is based on a different type of nuclear reaction. These plants depend on the energy released during nuclear fission to generate power. In nuclear fission, energy is released by the splitting of atomic nuclei.

Because of its many favorable properties, the element uranium is the primary fuel used in nuclear power plants. Uranium nuclei can be easily split. One split uranium nuclei can release many fragments, which then split other nuclei. This is known as a chain reaction. In addition, uranium is also a cost-efficient energy producer. One ton of uranium can be used to produce more energy than is produced by several million tons of coal or barrels of oil.

1. A good title for this passage would be

   (A) The Power of the Sun
   (B) What is Nuclear Energy?
   (C) Favorable Properties
   (D) Explaining Nuclear Fission

2. According to the passage, nuclear reactions on the Sun differ from those of nuclear power plants because

   (A) they release more energy
   (B) they use more uranium than power plants
   (C) they join rather than separate atomic nuclei
   (D) they occur at higher temperatures

3. This text could probably be found in

   (A) a magazine article on the history of nuclear power plants
   (B) a brochure put out by a group opposed to nuclear energy
   (C) a scientific textbook explaining various types of energy
   (D) a debate about the pros and cons of nuclear energy

Although history has referred to Genghis Khan and the Mongolian army as Mongolian <u>hordes</u>, Mongolian superiority was most likely not a result of their over-whelming numbers. The quality, not the quantity, of the Mongolian warrior was the key to Mongolian military victories. Each Mongolian warrior was extremely well trained, disciplined, and prepared.

The Mongolian army was tightly organized according to the decimal system. The largest unit of fighters was a *tjumen*, which consisted of 10,000 soldiers. A large army would be made up of three *tjumens*: one of infantry troops who would perform close combat and two others whose job was to encircle the opponent. Each *tjumen* consisted of ten regiments; one thousand troops made up a regiment. Each of these 1,000-strong regiments, or *mingghans*, was further broken down into squadrons of 100 men. The 100-men *jaghun* was then broken down further into groups of ten. Each group of ten, known as an *arban*, elected its commander by a majority vote. This process worked from level to level, although the Khan was personally appointed by the leaders of the *tjumen*. This appointment was based on ability, rather than age or social status.

On the battlefield, each unit was expected to participate in a major coordinated effort and at the same time be able to act independently. Thus, warriors carried an extensive collection of equipment, which allowed them to engage in larger joint efforts and also perform on their own. This equipment included a battle-axe, a curved sword, a lance, and two Mongolian bows. One bow was designed for rapid use on horseback. The other was heavier and more useful from a long-range ground position. Each rider also carried a sharpening stone for his metal arms, a knife, an awl, and a needle and thread in case he needed to repair his equipment in the field.

The warrior's dress was also extremely important military equipment. Because the winter temperatures in Siberia and Mongolia fell well below zero, warm clothing was essential. Mongols wore felt socks and heavy leather boots. They would typically don a coat of fur or sheepskin, under which they wore several layers of wool. Even a Mongolian warrior's underclothes were designed for military use. They preferred Chinese silk for this purpose. Not only was it warm, but heavy silk could also prevent an arrow from piercing human skin. If an arrow did penetrate into a warrior's arm or chest, it could be drawn out by pulling the silk thread around it. If the arrow were poisoned, this technique might also keep the poison from entering the bloodstream.

4. The author's attitude toward the Mongolian army is one of

   (A) fear

   (B) respect

   (C) disbelief

   (D) awe

5. The smallest unit of the Mongolian army was

   (A) a *jaghun*

   (B) a *tjumen*

   (C) a *mingghan*

   (D) an *arban*

6. This passage is mostly about

   (A) Mongolian battle equipment
   (B) Genghis Khan's victories in China
   (C) the organization of the Mongolian army
   (D) reasons for Mongolian military success

7. According to the passage, Mongolian warriors were expected to be

   (A) excellent farmers and horsemen
   (B) well-dressed and fashionable
   (C) independent yet cooperative
   (D) competitive and mistrustful

8. As used in the passage, the word <u>hordes</u> most nearly means

   (A) leaders
   (B) barbarians
   (C) masses
   (D) warriors

   Originally, the plaid, coarse wool of the Scottish tartan was only intended to be a decorative fabric. However, because they were made of coarse local wool and relied on a limited range of color dyes, the tartan soon became associated with particular districts and communities. In areas such as the Scottish Highlands, where there was a strong clan presence, the clan of a visitor from another area could be deduced by the color of his tartans. Thus, the tartan came to symbolize clan membership.

   After the rebellion of Charles Edward Stuart, wearing the tartan of the Scottish Highlands was prohibited by law. The Highland Regiments, independent companies of soldiers who policed the area, were the only ones allowed to wear it. They used a dark tartan, which came to be called the Black Watch. The Black Watch was the basis of many patterns involving white, red, and yellow. It is still the official government tartan, and is considered a universal one that everyone may wear.

9. This passage could help you answer which of the following questions?

   (A) Why are tartans associated with clan membership?
   (B) Who is Charles Edward Stuart?
   (C) How many tartan patterns are there?
   (D) How many people wear tartans today?

10. What is the Black Watch?

   (A) a Highland Regiment
   (B) the tartan pattern of Charles Edward Stuart
   (C) a pattern of tartan
   (D) a group of pirates

ANSWERS AND EXPLANATIONS

1. B

This is a main idea question. The notes you made while reading this passage should help you hone in on the correct answer. Notice that the wrong answer choices are details from the passage. Whereas the passage does discuss the power of the Sun, uranium's favorable properties, and nuclear fission, these are not the main idea of the entire passage.

2. C

This is a detail question. Use your paragraph topics to locate information about nuclear reactions on the Sun. Then, do the same to locate information about reactions in power plants. In reactions on the Sun, the nuclei of atoms are joined together, whereas reactions in power plants use nuclear fission in which energy is released by the splitting of atomic nuclei. Notice how the wrong answer choices take details out of context from the passage. The passage mentions releasing energy, uranium, and high temperatures of the Sun, but this information does not serve as a comparison between the reactions on the Sun and those that occur in power plants.

3. C

This is an inference question. Use your knowledge of the main idea of the passage together with clues based on the style of the text. This is about nuclear energy; the information is presented in a factual way. Choice (A) is not information included in the passage, and choices (B) and (D) both would contain strong opinions not expressed in the passage.

4. B

This is an inference question. Although the author does not state his or her attitude about the Mongolian army directly, there are many clues in the passage that allow us to reach a logical conclusion. The first paragraph alone uses the adjectives *superior*, *well trained*, *disciplined*, and *prepared*. The author obviously respects the Mongolian army.

5. D

This is a detail question. You should not have memorized the definitions of each of these foreign words or spent too much time on them as you read. Instead, you should have circled or underlined them so that you could find them more easily. Remember to research detail questions by locating the information you need using your topic sentences, and then rereading it before you answer the question.

6. D

This is a main idea question. Choices (A), (B), and (C) take details from the passage (although victories in China are not discussed). Only choice (D) is the main idea of the entire passage.

7. C

This is a detail question. Use your topic sentences to help you locate the answer to this question in paragraph 3. The correct answer is a rephrasing of sentence 1 from paragraph 3, which states: *On the battlefield, each unit was expected to participate in a major coordinated effort and at the same time be able to act independently.* Notice that the wrong answer choices are either not mentioned at all in the passage (*farmers* or *mistrustful*), or are taken out of context (well-dressed). Only (C) works for this question.

8. C

This is a detail question. Locate the information in the passage. Sentence 1 of paragraph 1 states: *Although history has referred to Genghis Khan and the Mongolian army as Mongolian hordes, Mongolian superiority was most likely not a result of their overwhelming numbers.* If superiority is not a result of overwhelming numbers, a horde must be an overwhelming number or a mass. The wrong answer choices are taken out of context and are not directly supported by research within the passage.

9. A

This is a main idea question. Noting the main idea and the paragraph topics could help you answer this question quickly. The first paragraph of the passage explains why tartans are associated with membership in different clans. The passage does not explain who Charles Edward Stuart is. It also does not discuss how many tartan patterns there are today or how many people currently wear tartans.

10. C

This is a detail question. Remember to research the detail using your paragraph topics. Sentences 2 and 3 of paragraph 2 provide the information necessary to answer this question.

Chapter Six: **Language Arts**

Language Arts is a broad category that includes spelling, punctuation, grammar, usage, and composition.

On the HSPT there are 60 language arts questions. The questions ask you to identify an incorrect sentence from among the answer choices. If all of the sentences are correct, select choice (D).

(A) Fridays and Saturdays we play field hockey.

(B) Franklin Elementary School is located on birch street.

(C) Miss Hampton discussed the situation with Peter's coach.

(D) No mistake.

The composition questions require you to choose the answer choice that best expresses a particular idea.

Choose the group of words that best completes the sentence.

The children had been playing in the park; _____ .

(A) they were covered in mud

(B) and because of that they were covered in mud

(C) they were covered in mud

(D) covered in mud

On the COOP, language arts questions follow reading passages. They test the same skills of punctuation, spelling, grammar, usage, and composition, but they tend to follow the theme of the passage rather than introduce new ideas.

For example, if the reading passage is about camels, you might see a question like this:

Read the paragraph below.

There are two kinds of camels, the Arabian and the Bactrian camel. The Arabian camel has only one hump, whereas the Bactrian camel has two humps. The humps store fat, which the camel can absorb as nutrition when food becomes scarce.

absorb as nutrition when food becomes scarce.

Which of the answer choices would be the best introductory sentence to the paragraph?

(A) The camel is native to the desert regions of Asia and northern Africa.

(B) A camel can survive without water for several days.

(C) The Arabian camel usually stands taller than the Bactrian camel.

(D) Both types of camels have been domesticated for hundreds of years.

HOW TO APPROACH LANGUAGE ARTS ERROR QUESTIONS

On the HSPT, this question type can be challenging because you are given three sentences as answer choices and are required to decide whether there is an error in any of the sentences. Because, by nature, we suspect that there *is* an error, many test-takers spend too much time searching and searching for an elusive error. What may, in fact, be a correct sentence starts to become suspect as we continue to search for the error. How do you approach these questions without driving yourself crazy or wasting too much time? (Remember, there are 60 questions to get through in this section.) Use the Kaplan Three-Step Method.

THE KAPLAN THREE-STEP METHOD FOR LANGUAGE ARTS ERROR QUESTIONS

Step 1. Read each sentence **one time** carefully, looking for identifiable mistakes. (We'll point out some common mistakes as we go through the punctuation, grammar, and usage review that follows.)

Step 2. Circle the mistake within the incorrect answer choice if there is one. If there is no error, circle choice D. Blacken the appropriate box on your answer sheet and move on.

Step 3. If the question is really confusing you, put a check mark next to it and come back to it later, only if you have more time after finishing the entire section.

To do your best on language arts questions, you'll have to work at a good pace, zero in on the error, and have confidence in your chosen answer so that you avoid wasting time reading and rereading all the choices. You've got to have a firm grasp of correct punctuation, grammar, spelling, and usage. You also need to be able to recognize common errors.

This chapter will give you the skill review you need to succeed in these areas. We'll review punctuation, grammar, and usage, and then discuss proper composition. Even if you think you've seen the material in English class, don't give in to the temptation to rush through it.

PUNCTUATION REVIEW

Capitals

Capitalize proper names.

George lives on Front Street. (Notice that "Street" is capitalized because it is part of the proper name.)

First Avenue is the largest thoroughfare in town.

The Tigers won five of their last ten games.

Capitalize holidays.

Independence Day is July 4th.

Vincent cooked an enormous turkey for Thanksgiving.

Capitalize the first letter of a person's title when it precedes their proper name.

Mr. Smith

Principal Young

Dr. McCullough

Aunt Rose

However, when the title is used without the proper name, it remains lowercase. See the following example:

Tim's dad is the coach of the baseball team.

Because the coach is not mentioned by name, *coach* is not capitalized.

Capitalize days of the week and months of the year.

We walk to school Mondays, Tuesdays, and Wednesdays.

In July, we often go to the shore.

Capitalize the first word of a direct quotation.

Henry told us, "Sit on the bench outside the office."

"Sit on the bench," Henry told us, "outside the office."

Commas

Use commas to separate the last two items in a long series.

If more than two items are listed in a series, they should be separated by commas. The final comma—the one that precedes the word *and*—may be omitted. An omitted final comma would not be considered an error on the COOP or HSPT.

EXAMPLE: My recipe for cornbread includes cornmeal, butter, eggs, and milk.

ALSO CORRECT: My recipe for cornbread includes cornmeal, butter, eggs and milk.

Look out for commas placed before the first element of a series, or after the last element.

INCORRECT: Jason watches television, morning, noon, and night.

INCORRECT: Action programs, cartoons, and soap operas, are his favorite shows.

Use commas to separate two or more adjectives before a noun.

EXAMPLE: It was a long, dull novel.

It is incorrect to place a comma after the last adjective in a series.

INCORRECT: The novel was a long, dull, travesty.

Use commas to set off parenthetical clauses and phrases.

If a phrase or clause is not necessary to the main idea expressed by a sentence, it is parenthetical and should be separated by commas.

EXAMPLE: Heather, who always attends practice, is the best athlete on the team.

In this example, the phrase *who always attends practice* is not necessary information. The main idea here is that Heather is the best player on the team. The clause in the middle merely serves to further describe her; it is therefore set off by commas.

Use commas after introductory phrases.

EXAMPLE: After the storm, there was a rainbow.

EXAMPLE: Having driven two hundred miles in one day, we were exhausted.

When combining independent clauses with *and*, *but*, *for*, *nor*, *or*, *so*, and *yet*, use a comma before the conjunction.

EXAMPLE: The dinner was burning, and the smoke alarm was going off.

EXAMPLE: Lena tried to make a pot roast, but she burned it.

Semicolons

Like commas, semicolons can be used to separate independent clauses. As we saw in the previous examples, two related independent clauses that are connected by a conjunction such as *and, but, nor,* or *yet* should be punctuated with a comma. If the words *and, but, nor,* or *yet* are not used, the clauses should be separated by a semicolon.

EXAMPLE: The question of who built the pyramids of Egypt has been an ongoing debate; scholars and Egyptologists continue to argue about the number and identity of the workers.

EXAMPLE: The question of who built the pyramids of Egypt has been an ongoing debate, yet one historian believes she has the answer.

Colons

In standard written English, the colon is used only as a means of signaling that what follows is a list, definition, explanation, or restatement of what has gone before. A word or phrase such as *like the following, as follows, namely,* or *this* is often used along with the colon to make it clear that a list, summary, or explanation is coming up.

EXAMPLE: The rules are as follows: No running, horseplay, or splashing is permitted in the pool area.

EXAMPLE: This is our schedule for the field trip: cookie factory, park, and zoo.

The Apostrophe

The apostrophe has two distinct functions. It is informally used with contracted verb forms to indicate that one or more letters have been eliminated, i.e. *he's* (*he is*), *they're* (*they are*), *there's* (*there is*), *let's* (*let us*), etc.

EXAMPLE: The girl's a member of the varsity basketball team. (The girl is a member of the varsity basketball team.)

EXAMPLE: There's a chocolate donut on the floor. (There is a chocolate donut on the floor.)

The apostrophe is also used to indicate the possessive form of a noun.

EXAMPLE: The boy's uniform was covered in mud.

With plural nouns that end in *s* the apostrophe is placed on the end of the word to indicate possession.

EXAMPLE: The girls' team sang victory songs all the way home.

Careful: *It's* is the contraction *it is*.

EXAMPLE: It's getting late. (It is getting late.)

The possessive *its* does not have an apostrophe.

EXAMPLE: The dog drank all the water in its bowl.

Punctuation with Quotation Marks

Direct quotes should be placed within quotation marks. If there is an introductory clause, a comma precedes the first quotation mark and the first word of the quotation is capitalized. The ending punctuation goes within the quotation mark.

EXAMPLE: John asked, "How do you do?"

If the quotation is followed by a clause, set it aside with a comma.

EXAMPLE: "I'm fine," Sue replied.

If the quotation is broken, punctuate the sentence as follows:

EXAMPLE: "How often," Carlos asked, "do you walk your dog?"

On the HSPT, grammar is tested along with punctuation and usage in the same question type. Of the statements given in a multiple-choice question, you might find that the punctuation in all statements is correct, but there could still be a mistake in grammar in one of the sentences. Hone your ability to identify mistakes (or decide if there is no mistake) by studying the following basic grammar review.

GRAMMAR REVIEW

Subject-Verb Agreement

The form of a verb must match, or agree with, its subject in two ways: person and number.

Agreement of Person

When we talk about *person*, we're talking about whether the subject and verb of a sentence show that the author is making a statement about him or herself (first person), the person he or she is speaking to (second person), or some other person, place, or thing (third person).

The first person subjects are *I* and *we*.

> EXAMPLE: We are bicycling from New York to Vermont. I am training every other day for the event.

The second person subject is *you*.

> EXAMPLE: Are you sure you wouldn't like to join us?

The third person subjects are *he*, *she*, *they*, *it*, and names of people, places, and things.

> EXAMPLE: The dog yaps day and night.

Agreement of Number

When we talk about *number*, we're talking about whether the subject and verb show that one thing is being discussed (singular) or that more than one thing is being discussed (plural).

> INCORRECT: The children catches the bus to school every morning.

> CORRECT: The children catch the bus to school every morning.

Be especially careful of subject-verb agreement when the subject and verb are separated by a long string of words.

> INCORRECT: Truth, the ultimate goal of all research, are elusive.

> CORRECT: Truth, the ultimate goal of all research, is elusive.

> **KAPLAN TIP**
>
> Underline the subject and verb in each answer choice. Then, make sure they agree.

Pronouns

A pronoun is a word that is used in place of a noun. The antecedent of a pronoun is the word to which the pronoun refers.

> EXAMPLE: Research has shown that green tea may help prevent cavities because it reduces plaque and bacteria.

Occasionally, the antecedent will appear in a sentence *after* the pronoun.

EXAMPLE: Because it helps prevent cavities, tea is a healthy beverage.

KAPLAN TIP

Make sure you're clear on what antecedent a pronoun refers to. Ask yourself what is *it* or who is *she* or *he* or *they* referring to. Does the sentence make this clear? If not, there may be a problem with usage or grammar.

Pronouns and Agreement

In grammatically correct writing, a pronoun must clearly refer to and agree with its antecedent.

Number and person agreement of pronouns is frequently tested on the COOP and HSPT.

	Singular	**Plural**
First Person Pronouns	I, me, my, mine	we, us, our, ours
Second Person Pronouns	you, your, yours	you, your, yours
Third Person Pronouns	he, him, she, her, it, one, his, her, hers, its, one's	their, theirs

Number Agreement

Pronouns must agree in number with their antecedents. A singular pronoun should stand for a singular antecedent. A plural pronoun should stand for a plural antecedent. Here's a typical pronoun error.

INCORRECT: The school refused to let Ann Marie attend the class field trip because their rules required her to have a permission letter.

What does the plural possessive *their* rules refer to? The singular noun *school*. The singular possessive is what we need here.

CORRECT: The school refused to let Ann Marie attend the class field trip because its rules required her to have a permission letter.

Careful: *Everyone*, *each*, and *every* are singular pronouns

INCORRECT: Everyone brought their favorite picture to share with the class

CORRECT: Everyone brought his favorite picture to share with the class.

Careful: It is acceptable to use *his*, *her*, or *his or her* if gender is mixed or unknown. Do not use the third person pronoun *they* or *their* to avoid dealing with the masculine or feminine issue.

INCORRECT: Everyone has to complete their work on time if this project is to succeed.

CORRECT: Everyone has to complete his or her work on time if this project is to succeed.

Helpful Hints

Each, *every*, *either*, *anybody*, or *much* requires a singular verb.

> EXAMPLE: **Everyone admires** her extensive vocabulary.

Both, *few*, *several*, *many*, or *others* require a plural verb.

> EXAMPLE: **Many comment** on her writing ability as well.

All, *any*, *more*, *most*, *some*, or *a part of* requires a singular or plural verb depending on the number being referenced.

> EXAMPLE: **All** of the guests **had** checked out of the hotel by noon. (singular verb)
>
> EXAMPLE: **Most** citizens **vote** on election day. (singular verb)
>
> EXAMPLE: When times are difficult, **most rise** to the challenge. (plural verb)

Person Agreement

Pronouns must not only agree in number with their antecedent but in *person* too. That is, a first-person pronoun should stand for a first-person antecedent and so on.

> EXAMPLE: Caroline and Joe completed their laboratory report yesterday.

One more thing to remember about which pronoun to use with which antecedent: Never use the relative pronoun *which* to refer to a person. Use *who*, *whom*, or *that*.

> INCORRECT: The woman which is waving is my sister.
>
> CORRECT: The woman who is waving is my sister.

Pronouns and Case

A more subtle type of pronoun error is one in which the pronoun is in the wrong case. Look at the following chart.

	Subjective Case	Objective Case
First Person Pronouns	I, me, my, mine	me, us
Second Person Pronouns	you	you
Third Person Pronouns	he, she, it, they, one	him, her, it, them, one
Relative Pronouns	who, that, which	whom, that which

When to Use Subjective Case Pronouns

As the name implies, use the subjective case for the **subject** of a sentence.

> EXAMPLE: She is a daring mountain climber.
>
> INCORRECT: Danny, Cary, and me are going to the town fair.
>
> CORRECT: Danny, Cary, and I are going to the ballet.

Use the subjective case after a linking verb, such as *to be*.

EXAMPLE: It is I.

Use the subjective case when making comparisons between the subject of verbs that are not stated but understood.

EXAMPLE: Wilson is faster than they (are).

When to Use Objective Case Pronouns

Use the objective case when the pronoun is the **object** of a verb. An object receives an action.

EXAMPLE: I told him.

Use the objective case for the object of a preposition.

EXAMPLE: I smiled at her.

EXAMPLE: I sat between Mark and her.

Use the objective case after infinitives and gerunds (the *-ing* form).

EXAMPLE: To give him a nice gift, we all contributed five dollars.

EXAMPLE: Writing her was a good idea.

Who and Whom

Use *who* if the unknown person is the subject of a verb.

EXAMPLE: Sylvester, who is afraid of the dark, sleeps with a nightlight on.

Look at the pronoun within the clause *who is afraid of the dark*. Notice that *who* is the subject.

Use *whom* if the unknown person is the object of a verb.

EXAMPLE: Sylvester, whom I gave a nightlight, thanked me.

Look at the pronoun within the clause *whom I gave a nightlight*. Notice that *whom* is the object. That is, *Sylvester* received something, while *I* performed the action of giving.

Myself/Me and Yourself/You

Use the reflexive pronoun if the subject is acting on his/her/itself or the action was performed *by oneself* (alone).

INCORRECT: He met with Barbara and myself.

CORRECT: He met with Barbara and me.

CORRECT: I discovered the answer myself.

Sentence Structure

A **sentence** is a group of words that expresses a complete thought. To express a complete thought, a sentence must contain a subject, about which something is stated, and a verb, which in turn states something about that subject.

EXAMPLE: Lions roar.

EXAMPLE: Searching through the cupboards, John found an old can of soup.

Every sentence contains at least one **clause**—a group of words that contains a subject and verb. *Lions roar*, and *John found* are both clauses.

A **phrase** is a group of words that does not have both a subject and a verb. *Searching through the cupboards* is a phrase. Important! A phrase is not a complete sentence; it is a sentence fragment.

Sentence Fragments

On the COOP or HSPT, some of those innocent-looking groups of words beginning with capital letters and ending with periods are only masquerading as sentences. In reality, they are sentence fragments.

A sentence fragment is *grammatically incomplete* because it lacks a subject or verb or because other elements necessary to complete a logical thought are missing.

INCORRECT: Arches and vaulted ceilings typical of Romanesque architecture.

This is not a complete sentence because there is no verb to say something about the subject *arches and vaulted ceilings*.

Careful: Don't let strings of long difficult words distract you. Read carefully to be sure whether or not a sentence contains a verb.

INCORRECT: Because we arrived late.

Even though this fragment contains a subject (*we*) and a verb (*arrived*), it's not a complete sentence because it doesn't express a complete thought. We don't know what happened *because we arrived late.*

Run-on Sentences

Whereas a sentence fragment is unacceptable because it is incomplete, a run-on sentence is unacceptable because it is too complete.

A run-on sentence is actually two complete sentences (or more) stuck together with either just a comma or with no punctuation at all.

INCORRECT: The team practiced diligently, it received a gold ribbon.

INCORRECT: The team practiced diligently it received a gold ribbon.

Section Three: Skill Review

There are a number of ways to fix this kind of problem. They all involve inserting a punctuation mark or a connecting word to properly connect the two clauses.

Join the clauses with a semicolon.

> CORRECT: The team practiced diligently; it received a gold ribbon.

Join the clauses with a coordinating conjunction (*and, but, for, nor, or, so,* or *yet*) and a comma.

> CORRECT: The team practiced diligently, and it received a gold ribbon.

Join the clauses with a subordinating conjunction (*after, although, if, since,* or *while*).

> CORRECT: Since the team practiced diligently, it received a gold ribbon.
>
> OR
>
> CORRECT: The team received a gold ribbon because it practiced diligently.

Finally, the two halves of a run-on sentence can be written as two separate complete sentences.

> CORRECT: The team practiced diligently. It received a gold ribbon.

Verbs

On the COOP and HSPT, you'll find items that are wrong because a verb is in the wrong tense. To spot this kind of error, you need to be familiar both with the way each tense is used and with the ways the tenses are used together. English has six tenses, and each of these has a simple form and a progressive form.

	Simple Form	Progressive Form
Present	I walk	I am walking
Past	I walked	I was walking
Future	I will walk	I will be walking
Present Perfect	I have walked	I have been walking
Past Perfect	I had walked	I had been walking
Future Perfect	I will have walked	I will have been walking

Using the Present Tense

Use the present tense to describe a state or action occurring in the present time.

> EXAMPLE: I am happy.
>
> EXAMPLE: They are studying the Holy Roman Empire.

Use the present tense to describe things that are true.

> EXAMPLE: The sky is blue.
>
> EXAMPLE: The earth is round.

Using the Past Tense

Use the simple past tense to describe an event or state that took place at a specific time in the past and is now finished.

> EXAMPLE: The class dissected a frog in biology class.

Using the Future Tense

Use the future tense to describe actions expected to take place in the future. The future tense is also used to express promises.

> EXAMPLE: It will rain tomorrow.

> EXAMPLE: I will call you tonight.

Often, future actions begin with a form of the verb *to be*, as in *be going to*. This is considered acceptable and correct.

> EXAMPLE: I am going to call you tonight.

Using the Present Perfect Tense

Use the present perfect tense for actions and states of being that start in the past and continue up and into the present time.

> EXAMPLE: I have been attending Jefferson Junior High for the last two years.

Use the present perfect for actions and states of being that happened a number of times in the past and may happen again in the future.

> EXAMPLE: We have visited the planetarium several times.

Use the present perfect to describe an event that happened at an unspecified time in the past.

> EXAMPLE: Anna has given me her opinion already.

Using the Past Perfect Tense

The past perfect tense is used to represent past actions or states that were completed before other past actions or states. The more recent past event is expressed in the simple past, and the earlier past event is expressed in the past perfect.

> EXAMPLE: When the alarm clock rang this morning, I noticed that I had set it for eight o'clock rather than seven. (the earlier event—setting the clock—is expressed in past perfect.)

Using the Future Perfect Tense

Use the future perfect tense for a future state or event that will take place before another future event.

> EXAMPLE: By Saturday, I will have finished the entire novel.

Using the Proper Past Participle Form

Perfect tenses use a participle form of a base verb.

> EXAMPLE: I have planted tomatoes in the garden.

The past participle is formed by adding -*ed* to the base form, unless it is an irregular verb. Irregular verbs have two different forms for simple past and past participle tenses. If you use the present, past, or future perfect tense, make sure that you use the past participle and not the simple past tense.

INCORRECT: I have swam in that lake before.

CORRECT: I have swum in that lake before.

The following are some of the most common irregular verbs.

IRREGULAR VERBS		
Infinitive	**Simple Past**	**Past Participle**
arise	arose	arisen
become	became	become
begin	began	begun
blow	blew	blown
break	broke	broken
come	came	come
do	did	done
draw	drew	drawn
drink	drank	drunk
drive	drove	driven
eat	ate	eaten
fall	fell	fallen
fly	flew	flown
freeze	froze	frozen
give	gave	given
grow	grew	grown
hang	hung	hung
know	knew	known
ride	rode	ridden
rise	rose	risen
run	ran	run
see	saw	seen
shake	shook	shaken
shrink	shrank	shrunk
sing	sang	sung
speak	spoke	spoken
take	took	taken
throw	threw	thrown

Could Have, Should Have, Would Have, Might Have

The words *could*, *should*, *would*, and *might* which express possibility, impossibility, or necessity must be followed by *have*.

Careful: People often incorrectly say *could of*. This is incorrect.

INCORRECT: I could of gone if I had enough money.

CORRECT: I could have gone if I had enough money.

Adjectives and Adverbs

On the COOP and HSPT, you may find an occasional item that's wrong because it uses an adjective where an adverb is called for, or vice versa.

An **adjective** modifies, or describes, a noun or pronoun.

EXAMPLE: A man with a gray beard sat on an old tree stump.

EXAMPLE: The moldy, rotting apple had been sitting in my refrigerator for months.

An **adverb** modifies a verb, an adjective, or another adverb. Most, but not all, adverbs end in *-ly* (Don't forget that some adjectives—*friendly, lovely*—also end in *–ly*)

EXAMPLE: The detective worked ceaselessly to solve the mystery. (The adverb *ceaselessy* describes how the detective worked.)

EXAMPLE: The builders finished surprisingly quickly. (*Surprisingly* describes the adverb *quickly*.)

Adverbs of place show where an action is done.

EXAMPLE: They travel internationally.

Adverbs of time show when an action is done or the duration or frequency of that action.

EXAMPLE: We purchased a jet recently.

EXAMPLE: The office is temporarily closed.

Adverbs Modifying Noun Phrases

Some adverbs of degree can modify noun phrases.

EXAMPLE: That dinner was quite delicious.

Adverbs Modifying Determiners, Numerals and Pronouns

Adverbs such as *almost*, *nearly*, *hardly*, and *about* can be used.

EXAMPLE: Hardly anyone has purchased their ticket yet.

Careful: The word *hardly* means *barely*. The adverbial form of the adjective *hard* is *hard*.

EXAMPLE: We worked hard planting the hedges.

Parallel Structure

On the COOP and HSPT, and in good writing, constructions must be expressed in matching or parallel form. Make sure that when a sentence contains a list or makes a comparison, the items being listed or compared exhibit parallel structure.

Items in a List

INCORRECT: I love skipping, jumping, and to play tiddlywinks.

INCORRECT: I love to skip, jump, and to play tiddlywinks.

CORRECT: I love to skip, jump, and play tiddlywinks

ALSO CORRECT: I love to skip, to jump, and to play tiddlywinks.

ALSO CORRECT: I love skipping, jumping, and playing tiddlywinks.

Items in a Comparison

Comparisons must do more than just exhibit parallel structure; they must make sense. Most faulty comparisons are wrong based on the notion that you can't compare apples and oranges. A good comparison is not only grammatically similar, but also logically similar.

INCORRECT: To paint an apple is not the same as tasting it.

CORRECT: To paint an apple is not the same as to taste it.

ALSO CORRECT: Painting an apple is not the same as tasting it.

INCORRECT: The rules of chess are more complex than checkers.

CORRECT: The rules of chess are more complex than those of checkers.

ALSO CORRECT: Chess is more complex than checkers.

Comparatives and Superlatives

Use the **comparative form** when comparing two items.

EXAMPLE: Martina is a strong tennis player. She is a stronger player than Bobby is. (The *is* may be omitted since it is understood.)

EXAMPLE: They finished more quickly than we. (*Than we did* is understood.)

Careful: Remember to use the correct form of the pronoun.

INCORRECT: She is a stronger player than him. (This is incorrect since the subjective case of the pronoun must be used.)

CORRECT: She is a stronger player than he. (The *is* is understood.)

CORRECT: She is the stronger player of the two.

Careful: Avoid repetitiveness in comparisons.

INCORRECT: The oil painting is more prettier than the watercolor is.

CORRECT: The oil painting is prettier than the watercolor is.

The **superlative** form of the adjective is used when the person, place, or thing defined, is the best—it has no comparison, nothing is in its class. The superlative form can be recognized by the word *the* before the adjective.

EXAMPLE: August is the hottest month.

EXAMPLE: In my opinion, French cuisine is the best.

Careful: *Good, better, best* is the correct progression of this adjective. *Bad, worse, worst* is the correct progression of this adjective.

INCORRECT: It is more better to make an effort and fail than not to try at all.

CORRECT: It is better to make an effort and fail than not to try at all.

STYLE REVIEW

Good writing is not only grammatically correct, but also stylistically clear. We'll review some problems with style in the following pages and show you how to correct these problems.

Pronouns and Reference

We noted earlier that pronouns *refer to* their antecedents and must agree in person and number with their antecedent. Mistakes in grammar and problems with clarity occur when they do not. Another kind of pronoun reference problem exists when a pronoun either doesn't refer to any antecedent at all or doesn't refer clearly to one, and only one, antecedent.

UNCLEAR: Francesco likes the music they play on this radio station.

The sentence is poorly written because it is unclear. Who are *they*? We can't tell because the pronoun has no antecedent.

CORRECT: Francesco likes the music that the disc jockeys play on this radio station.

Careful: Sometimes a pronoun seems to have an antecedent until you read more closely and realize that the word that appears next to the antecedent is not a noun, but an adjective, a possessive form, or a verb. Remember, the antecedent of a pronoun should be a noun.

INCORRECT: When you are cooking, be careful to watch it.

CORRECT: When you are cooking dinner, be careful to watch it.

Here are other examples of pronoun reference problems:

INCORRECT: Veronica has always been interested in medicine and has decided to become one.

CORRECT: Veronica has always been interested in medicine and has decided to become a doctor.

Don't use pronouns with remote references. A pronoun that is too far away from what it refers to is said to have a remote antecedent; this type of sentence structure is considered incorrect.

INCORRECT: Joe started jogging, and as a result lost a lot of weight. It was very good for his heart. (What does the pronoun *it* refer to? Losing weight or jogging?)

CORRECT: Joe started jogging because it was very good for his heart, and as a result he lost a lot of weight. (The antecedent of it is clearly *jogging*.)

Make sure pronouns have a clear, precise reference rather than a broad (and faulty) one.

INCORRECT: Bullfrogs live in areas where the water rarely recedes, such as rivers, lakes, and farm ponds. They sing during summer months to mark their territory. (*They* is too far away from its antecedent *bullfrogs* and thus seems as if it might refer to *rivers, lakes, and ponds.*)

CORRECT: Bullfrogs live in areas where the water rarely recedes, such as rivers, lakes, and farm ponds. Bullfrogs sing during summer months to mark their territory.

Misreference

Remote antecedents can also cause confusion in the following way:

POOR: The president sent a memo to Charlie, and he will address the problem right away.

(In this sentence it is unclear what *he* refers to, Charlie or the president.)

BETTER: The president sent a memo to Charlie, and Charlie will address the problem right away.

Dangling Modifiers

In order to avoid confusion, clauses and phrases should clearly relate to the elements they modify.

INCORRECT: <u>To write a clear sentence</u>, <u>subject and verb should agree</u>.
               phrase   clause

Who is writing the sentence? Certainly not the subject and verb; they can't write.

CORRECT: To write a clear sentence, you should make sure the subject and verb agree.

Here are some more examples:

INCORRECT: When driving across the bridge, the sun blinded him.

CORRECT: When driving across the bridge, he was blinded by the sun.

INCORRECT: Knowing little about astronomy, the charts and maps confused me.

CORRECT: Knowing little about astronomy, I was confused by the charts and maps.

Redundancy

Redundancy means repetitiveness. Words or phrases are redundant when they have basically the same meaning as something already stated in the sentence. Don't use two phrases when only one is sufficient.

INCORRECT: Blackmore University was established and founded in 1906.

CORRECT: Blackmore University was established in 1906.

Double Negatives

In standard written English, double negatives are redundant and wrong.

INCORRECT: "I didn't say nothing!" he protested.

CORRECT: "I didn't say anything!" he protested.

INCORRECT: I do not want to hear no complaints.

CORRECT: I do not want to hear any complaints.

Careful: *Cannot help but* is a double negative, so is *can't hardly*. Both are incorrect.

Relevance

A good sentence contains only related or relevant ideas. Unrelated information, even when set off in parenthesis, should be avoided. If an idea is unrelated to the main point of the sentence, it should be cut and moved to another sentence that is, in turn, related to the general point.

IRRELEVANT: Constructing the new baseball field will cost the community over forty thousand dollars (though the entire town loves to watch the Tigers play).

RELEVANT: Constructing the new baseball field will cost the community over forty thousand dollars. Decision makers feel this investment is worthwhile however, since the entire town loves to watch the Tigers play.

Wordiness

Wordiness, also creates a style and clarity problem.

WORDY: Our fascination with celebrities that we love to read about supports the multibillion dollar industry of gossip magazines.

CONCISE: Our fascination with celebrities supports the multibillion dollar industry of gossip magazines.

WORDY: We were in agreement with each other that Max was charitable to a fault.

CONCISE: We agreed that Max was charitable to a fault.

Commonly Misused Words

accept/except

To *accept* means to receive or agree to something, whereas *except* is usually a preposition meaning excluding, although it can also mean to leave out.

INCORRECT: Can you except my apology?

CORRECT: Can you accept my apology

CORRECT: Everyone except Sam will attend the meeting.

affect/effect

These are easy to confuse. To *affect* means to have an *effect* on something. When the word is being used as a verb, the proper word to use is almost always *affect;* when it's being used as a noun, the proper word to use is almost always *effect.* (It should be noted that *effect* can also be a verb, meaning to bring about or cause to happen.)

INCORRECT: The news effected me deeply.

CORRECT: The news affected me deeply. (Affect is a verb, meaning it had an *effect* on me.)

CORRECT: What are the effects of the new medicine on rats? (*Effect* is a noun, in this case a plural noun.)

already/all ready

Already means earlier or previously. *All ready* means all of us are ready.

INCORRECT: Are you ready all ready?

CORRECT: I've already finished the assignment.

altogether/all together

Altogether means completely. *All together* means as one group.

CORRECT: Carlene was altogether happy with the experiment's results.

CORRECT: Let's go all together.

among/between

In most cases, use *between* for two items and *among* for more than two.

EXAMPLE: The rivalry between the Tigers and the Bears has gone on for years.

EXAMPLE: Among the various choices, I prefer the first.

However, use common sense. Sometimes *among* is not appropriate.

EXAMPLE: Plant the trees in the area between the road, the wall, and the fence.

amount/number

Amount should be used to refer to an uncountable quantity. *Number* should be used to refer to a countable quantity.

>   EXAMPLE: The amount of food he threw away would feed a substantial number of people.

anyway

Anyway means in any way possible, or regardless. *Anyways* is incorrect. Don't use it.

>   INCORRECT: Anyways, I hope we can still go.

>   CORRECT: Anyway, I hope we can still go.

>   CORRECT: Frank insisted on winning anyway possible.

as/like

Like is a preposition; it takes a noun object. *As*, when functioning as a conjunction, introduces a subordinate clause. Remember, a clause is part of a sentence containing a subject and a verb.

>   EXAMPLE: He sings like an angel.

>   EXAMPLE: He sings as an angel sings.

as…as…

The idiom is *as…as…*.

>   INCORRECT: That dress is as nice than this one.

>   CORRECT: That dress is as expensive as this one.

beside/besides

Beside means by the side of or next to. *Besides* means moreover.

>   INCORRECT: Set the book besides the photo album.

>   CORRECT: Set the book beside the photo album.

>   CORRECT: Besides being an excellent athlete, I am also a brilliant mathematician.

fewer/less

Use *fewer* before a plural noun; use *less* before a singular one.

>   EXAMPLE: There are fewer people in the audience tonight than there were last night.

>   EXAMPLE: We paid less money for our ticket than you did.

neither…nor…

The correlative conjunction is *neither…nor…*.

>   EXAMPLE: We are neither tired nor hungry.

Avoid the redundancy caused by using *nor* after a negative.

>   INCORRECT: Alice's departure was not noticed by Sue nor Debby.

>   CORRECT: Alice's departure was not noticed by Sue or Debby.

its/it's

Many people confuse *its* and *it's*. *Its* is possessive; *it's* is a contraction of *it is*.

>   EXAMPLE: The cat licked its paws.

>   EXAMPLE: It's raining cats and dogs.

lay/lie/laid

Lay means to put or to place. The past tense of *lay* is *laid*, the past participle *has laid*, and the continuous form *is/was laying*.

Lie means to recline, to stay, or to rest. The past is *lay*, the past participle *has lain*, the continuous form, *is/was lying*.

Careful: *Lay* is both the present tense of *lay* (as *in put or place*) and the past tense of *lie* (as in *lie down*).

>   EXAMPLE: Please lay the tablecloth over the picnic table.

>   EXAMPLE: We laid the tarp over the sofa so it wouldn't get dirty when we painted the room.

>   EXAMPLE: The cat is lying on the table, and he doesn't want to be bothered.

>   EXAMPLE: Duncan lay down because he was feeling tired.

Lying is also to the continuous of the verb *to lie*, meaning not to tell the truth.

than/then

Use *than* in making comparisons. Use *then* for time.

>   INCORRECT: Dolores is more graceful then I.

>   CORRECT: Dolores is more graceful than I.

>   CORRECT: First wash the one, then the other.

their/they're/there

Many people confuse *their, there,* and *they're. Their* is possessive; *they're* is a contraction of *they are*.

>   EXAMPLE: The girls rode their bikes home.

>   EXAMPLE: They're training for the marathon.

There has two uses: It can indicate place and it can be used as an expletive—a word that doesn't do anything in a sentence except delay the subject.

>   EXAMPLE: Put the book over there.

>   EXAMPLE: There will be fifteen runners competing for the prize.

Passive Voice

The passive voice uses the verb *to be* with a past participle. The subject is usually affected rather than acting. Although passive voice is grammatically correct, excessive or unfounded use of the passive voice is considered poor style. It is often clearer to state the information with an active subject and verb.

PASSIVE: My finger was bitten by the gerbil.

ACTIVE: The gerbil bit my finger.

A Word About Spelling

Approximately 10 questions on the Language Arts section of the HSPT will ask you to identify mistakes in spelling. Unfortunately, it is impossible to predict which of the thousands of words in the English dictionary will appear on these questions.

Spend some time studying lists of commonly misspelled words. Ask your English teacher or local librarian to help you find these lists. The words on them are the ones you're most likely to see on the HSPT.

Improving your spelling requires a time commitment, and there are few spelling rules in English. Sounding things out may help, or it may not, especially if you are not certain of the word's pronunciation. However, remember:

i before e, except after c, except when it sounds like *a* as in *neighbor* and *weigh*

EXAMPLE: society, transient, receive

A word of more than one syllable ending in a single vowel and a single consonant, which has the accent on the final syllable, doubles that consonant before a suffix beginning with a vowel.

EXAMPLE: occur—occurring

EXAMPLE: prefer—preferred

If the final syllable has no accent, do not double the consonant.

EXAMPLE: benefit + *ing* = benefiting

If a word ends with a silent e, drop the e before adding a suffix that begins with a vowel.

EXAMPLE: hope—hoping, like—liking

When a word ends in e, drop the final e before a suffix beginning with a vowel.

EXAMPLE: small + *er* = smaller

EXAMPLE: move + *able* = movable

Do not drop the e when the suffix begins with a consonant.

EXAMPLE: manage—management, like—likeness, use—useless

When *y* is the last letter in a word and the *y* is preceded by a consonant, change the *y* to *i* before adding any suffix except those beginning with *i*.

> EXAMPLE: pretty—prettier, hurry—hurried, deny—denied

Spelling is one area where knowing your own strengths and weaknesses is important. If you tend to have trouble spelling, you may decide to go against your instinct when selecting an answer choice. In other words, if a word looks right to you, but you know you are a terrible speller, you may guess that the word is actually spelled incorrectly. Vice versa, if a word sounds wrong to you, but you admit you're not sure of its pronunciation, you may decide that word is actually correct.

Finally, if you are not certain whether or not a word is spelled correctly, take your best guess and move on. Remember, there is no penalty for guessing, and you have a one in four chance of picking the correct answer choice.

COMPOSITION

Some questions on the COOP or HSPT will ask you how to best organize a paragraph, sentence, or theme. Keep these four principles in mind.

Four Steps to Clear Composition

1. Each paragraph should be limited to a single topic or major idea.
2. The topic sentence should reflect the content.
3. The writing should be concise.
4. Transitions should be used when shifting ideas.

Each Paragraph Should Be Limited to a Single Topic or Main Idea

For clarity's sake, it is preferable that each paragraph of an essay or theme address one major idea rather than jump around between various thoughts or points. Extraneous ideas, or those irrelevant to that particular major point should be removed.

> POOR: The Browns are looking forward to their holiday in Australia next week. Mrs. Brown is excited about snorkeling in the coral reefs and Mr. Brown is happy to have a week away from work to relax. **Mr. Brown used to sing opera when he was younger.** They hope to visit the opera house in Sydney. (Notice how the third sentence is unrelated to the theme of the Brown's holiday in Australia.)

> BETTER: The Browns are looking forward to their holiday in Australia next week. Mrs. Brown is excited about snorkeling in the coral reefs, and Mr. Brown is happy to have a week away from work to relax. **They'd also like to see that famous Australian animal, the kangaroo.** They also hope to visit the opera house in Sydney. (This sentence better fits the general theme of the paragraph.)

KAPLAN
Test Prep and Admissions

The Topic Sentence Should Reflect the Content

Just as each paragraph must address one major idea, the topic sentence of that paragraph should appropriately reflect the content of the paragraph.

POOR: **Many Americans know about the pyramids of Egypt, although they may not realize that there are pyramids much closer to home in Central America.** Deep within the jungles of Mexico and Guatemala lie the mysterious pyramids of the Maya. The Mayan were noted for their skill with astronomy and farming, as well for their elaborate and highly decorated ceremonial architecture. **The pyramids of Egypt were built as monuments to the pharaohs.** (This sentence does not relate to the topic sentence of the paragraph—that there are pyramids in Central America.)

BETTER: **Many Americans know about the pyramids of Egypt, although they may not realize that there are pyramids much closer to home in Central America.** Deep within the jungles of Mexico and Guatemala lie the mysterious pyramids of the Maya. The Mayan were noted for their skill with astronomy and farming, as well for their elaborate and highly decorated ceremonial architecture. **The Maya built temple-pyramids, palaces, and observatories all without metal tools.** (This paragraph is better organized; all sentences relate to the topic sentence, which introduces the idea of pyramids in Central America.)

The Writing Should Be Concise

Watch out for run-on sentences, redundancy, and overly lengthy sentences or paragraphs. A sentence should be no more than two lines in length. A paragraph should be between 3–5 sentences long.

POOR: Senator Robbins is running for re-election on a platform of economic reform, she intends to reduce city spending and increase taxes so that more citizens can benefit from additional services such as better transportation, clean streets, and having safer neighborhoods. (Not only is this a run-on sentence, but the items in the final list—better transportation, clean street, and having safer neighborhoods—are not parallel.)

BETTER: Senator Robbins is running for re-election on a platform of economic reform. She intends to reduce city spending and increase taxes so that more citizens can benefit from additional services. She plans to improve transportation, street cleaning, and safety. (Notice how the last sentence has been rewritten but keeps parallel construction. All the items in the list are nouns.)

Transitions Should Be Used When Shifting Ideas

Transitional words and phrases show how sentences or paragraphs are logically linked. A poorly chosen or incorrect transitional word can completely alter the meaning of a sentence or paragraph.

POOR: John is tired, so he will not rest until he finishes the job at hand. (This is not a logical transition. *John is tired, so he will not rest.* That doesn't make sense.)

BETTER : Although John is tired, he will not rest until he finishes the job at hand. (The transitional word *although* makes the idea clear. Despite the fact that John is tired, he will not rest. We understand from this sentence that John is hard-working and determined.)

Transitional Words

Words that show an idea is moving in the **same direction**: *and, also, besides, moreover, in addition*

Words that show **contrast**: *but, meanwhile, on the other hand, yet, however, on the contrary*

Words that show **emphasis**: *in fact, most of all, in any, even*

Words that **illustrate** a point: *for example, for instance*

Words of **conclusion**: *accordingly, so, therefore, consequently*

Words of **concession**: *of course, naturally, in fact*

Words of **time**: *formerly, meanwhile, after, later, at the same time, in the first place, first, second, finally*

Words that express a **condition**: *nevertheless, even though, although*

Words to point out **cause/effect**: *it follows that, accordingly, for this reason*

Words of **comparison**: *similarly, in comparison, still*

Questions that Ask for Transitional Words

On the COOP or HSPT, some questions will ask you to find a logical, transitional word to complete an idea or sentence. Look for clues within a sentence or paragraph that tell you how the first clause or phrase of a sentence is related to the second.

EXAMPLE: It is raining, _____ we will still go to the beach.

The first clause *it is raining* contains one idea. The second clause *we will still go to the beach* contradicts the general notion that rain would cause us to cancel a trip to the beach. A word of contrast is required here. Look for an answer choice that contains a word of contrast such as *but, however,* or *yet.*

Practice, Practice, Practice

Way to go! You've worked through the basic rules of grammar, punctuation, and usage. The more you practice, the more these principles will become like second-nature to you. Be sure to complete the practice set. Try to work at a good pace, spending no more than a minute on each question. Read each sentence carefully, circling mistakes as you spot them. Put a check mark next to the questions that cause you difficulty, but don't leave any question unanswered. Finally, check your answers, read the answer explanations, and see whether your instincts on the questions that caused you difficulty were correct.

LANGUAGE ARTS PRACTICE SET

Directions: In questions 1-3, look for errors in punctuation, capitalization, or usage. If there is no error, select choice D.

1. (A) "Is there room for me in the car?" Janet asked.
   (B) The shore is three miles from the center of town.
   (C) The Hawks beat the bluejays two to one.
   (D) No mistake.

2. (A) There's no business like show business.
   (B) Sue's mother warned her to be careful.
   (C) What are the chances of winning?
   (D) No mistake.

3. (A) Who has my briefcase?
   (B) If there ready, let's go.
   (C) Uncle Tito plays the bongo drums.
   (D) No mistake.

Directions: For questions 4–6, look for mistakes in spelling only.

4. (A) I'd like to address your concerns immediately.
   (B) Please register your complaint with customer service.
   (C) Ocassionaly, we update our records.
   (D) No mistake.

5. (A) We separated the blue papers from the red ones.
   (B) Heather communicated the message to Dawn.
   (C) Knowledge is the key to power.
   (D) No mistake.

6. (A) I am including a photo of our trip.
   (B) The coach encouraged us to do our best.
   (C) It is unecessary to call before you come.
   (D) No mistake.

Directions: For questions 7–10, follow the directions for each question.

7. Choose the words that best complete the following sentence.
   The school's tennis team is _____
   (A) known for its competitive players.
   (B) known for the competitiveness of its players when they compete.
   (C) known because its players are said to be competitive.
   (D) known to be competitive and have competitive players.

8. Choose the best word to complete the sentence.
   We left our house on time, _____ we still arrived late.
   (A) consequently
   (B) therefore
   (C) so
   (D) none of these

9. Choose the sentence that is correctly written.

   (A) The pizza, as we know it, was developed in the late 18th century.

   (B) Pizza as we know it now, was developed before in the late 18th century.

   (C) Pizza, as we now know it, was developed by its developers in the late 18th century.

   (D) As we know it, the current pizza, was developed in the late 18th century.

10. Read the two sentences.

    In about 1889, Queen Margherita toured her kingdom and saw many people eating this large, flat bread.

    The people were mostly peasants.

    Which of the following sentences best combines the two sentences above?

    (A) In about 1889, Queen Margherita toured her kingdom and saw many people eating this large, flat bread; the people were mostly peasants.

    (B) In about 1889, Queen Margherita toured her kingdom and saw many people, the people were mostly peasants, eating this large, flat bread.

    (C) In about 1889, Queen Margherita toured her kingdom and saw many peasants eating this large, flat bread.

    (D) In about 1889, Queen Margherita toured her kingdom and saw many people eating this large, flat bread and the people were mostly peasants.

ANSWERS AND EXPLANATIONS

1. C

The word *Bluejays* should be capitalized since it is the name of a team.

2. D

There are no mistakes.

3. B

Look at the use of *there* in choice (B). It should be *they are,* or *they're.* Although you've spotted the error, read the final answer choice just to be sure.

4. C

The correct spelling is *occasionally.*

5. D

There are no mistakes.

6. D

The correct spelling is *unnecessary.*

7. A

The most concise and clearest answer choice is (A). Choices (B), (C) and (D) are unnecessarily wordy.

8. D

The first clause states that *we left on time*, the second clause contradicts this since *we arrived late*. The linking word must show a contrast. There are no contrasting transition words, so (D) is the best answer.

9. A

Good writing must be grammatically correct and clear and to the point. Choice (B) is redundant. Choice (C) is also redundant. Choice (D) implies that we already know pizza was developed in the late 18th century.

10. C

When combining these sentences, avoid creating a run-on sentence. Choice (C) best combines the two ideas by making the direct object *peasants*. Choice (A) is a run-on sentence. It is better to keep these two sentences separate than combine them with a semicolon. Choice (B) is too wordy. Choice (D) is a run-on sentence.

Chapter Seven: **Math Skills**

Math counts for a large portion of your score on the test. On the HSPT there are approximately

110 mathematics questions, which is about $\frac{1}{3}$ of the test. On the COOP, there are approximately

40 mathematics questions, which is about $\frac{1}{4}$ of the test.

The good news is

- A limited amount of concepts are tested.
- This is most likely math you've already been exposed to in school.

We will review mathematics later in this chapter, but first, it is important to develop a game plan for how to approach mathematics questions on the test.

HOW TO APPROACH MATH QUESTIONS

Before we dive in to the actual math, let's take a step back and build some strategies for how to approach math problems in general. You've done math before. You've most likely seen most of the math concepts you'll encounter on the COOP or HSPT. However, you need to approach math a little differently on the test than you would in another situation.

Remember, you'll have a limited amount of time, so you need to use it wisely. Also, remember that each question is worth the same amount of points. Since time is of the essence, and since each question is worth only one point, you need to decide whether spending more than 30 seconds on any one question is the best use of your time.

Since there is no penalty for guessing, you should answer all the questions, however, you may choose to set a problem aside and come back to it later.

Read through the Question and Make Your Decision

Of course you're going to read through the question. Our point here is that while you need to read the question carefully and deliberately before you start solving the problem. If you don't, it's easy to make careless mistakes.

Consider the following problem:

> Jane is a salesperson for PDQ Carpet Company. In the last
> three years she earned $36,000, $38,000, and $40,000 dollars
> annually. What is her average monthly income?

(A) 36,000

(B) 3,000

(C) 30,000

(D) 12,000

It's crucial that you pay close attention to precisely what the question is asking. This question contains a classic trap that's very easy to fall into if you don't read it carefully. Did you notice that the question is asking you to solve for Jane's *monthly* income, rather than her yearly income? Solving for her yearly income would be careless, but it's easy to be careless when you're working quickly.

The other reason to read the entire question carefully before you start solving is that you may save yourself some work. If you start answering too quickly, you may assume a problem is more difficult than it actually is. Similarly, you might assume that the problem is less difficult that it actually is and skip a necessary step or two.

Another reason to read carefully before answering is that you probably shouldn't solve every problem on your first pass.

Decide Whether to Do the Problem or Skip it for Now

Each time you approach a new math problem you have the option of doing it, or putting it aside.

1. If you can solve the problem relatively quickly and efficiently, do it! This is the best option.
2. If you think you can solve it, but it will take you a long time, circle the number in your test booklet and go back to it later. Remember that when you go back to problems you have skipped the first time, you'll want to fill in an answer, even if it's a random guess. Don't underestimate your ability to eliminate wrong answer choices even when you don't know how to solve a problem. Each answer choice you eliminate increases your chances of guessing correctly.
3. If you have no idea what to do, circle the problem and move on. Save your time for the problems you can solve.

Here's another example

> Which value of x would make the following equation true?
>
> $$\frac{1}{2} = \frac{x^3}{12}$$
>
> (A) $\sqrt[3]{6}$
>
> (B) $\sqrt{2}$
>
> (C) 9
>
> (D) 28

Different test takers will have different reactions to this question. Some students may quickly see the process they need to take in order to solve this. Others may see the exponent (the little 3 above the *x*) and run screaming from the room. We don't recommend this approach. However, if you know that you habitually have difficulty with exponents, you may choose to save this problem for later or make an educated guess.

Here's the solution to the question. Don't worry if any of this is unfamiliar to you, we'll review working with fractions and other math concepts later in this chapter.

First, multiply each numerator by the denominator on the other side of the equation:

$$12 = 2x^3$$

Next, isolate the unknown *x* by dividing each side of the equation by 2.

$$\frac{12}{2} = \frac{2x^3}{2}$$

This leaves you with $6 = x^3$

To find the value of *x* divide each side by its cube root.

$$x = \sqrt[3]{6}$$

If you choose to tackle any given problem, look for the fastest method. What is the fastest method? The method that is fastest for you.

> Patricia is *a* years old and her brother Mark is 5 years older than she. In terms of *a*, how old will Mark be in 3 years?
>
> (A) $3(a + 5)$
>
> (B) $a + 5 - 3$
>
> (C) $a + 3$
>
> (D) $a + 5 + 3$

You could solve the problem using algebra. If Patricia is *a* years old, then Mark is *a* + 5 years old. In three years, he will be *a* + 5 + 3 yeas old. Thus, (D) is the correct answer choice.

You could also solve the problem by picking numbers. Let's say Patricia is 12 years old, that makes Mark who is 5 years older, 17. In 3 years, he'll be 20. Now, substitute Patricia's age, 12, for the unknown *a* in all the answer choices and see which equation gives us the result we're looking for—20. Once you try all the answer choices, only (D) works.

As you see, there is often more than one way to do a particular problem. The best method is the one that will help you arrive at the correct answer accurately and quickly.

Some people *get* algebra. Others have a harder time with it. The same is true for geometry, word problems, ratios, etc. Know your strengths and make decisions about how to approach math problems accordingly.

Make an Educated Guess

Don't leave any answers blank on the COOP or HSPT test. Since there's no penalty for wrong answers, there is no harm in guessing when you don't know the answer.

Random guessing doesn't hurt, but you should guess strategically whenever possible. Remember, each answer choice you eliminate increases your odds of choosing the correct answer.

> **What is the greatest prime factor of 26 and 265?**
>
> (A) 13
>
> (B) 4
>
> (C) 2
>
> (D) 5

If you read this problem and either could not remember how to find a factor, let alone a prime factor, or if you were running out of time and wanted to save your time for other questions, you should be able to eliminate at least one answer choice pretty easily. Do you see which one?

Since all multiples of 5 end in either 5 or 0, the number 5 cannot be a factor of 26. So, choice (D) must be incorrect.

ARITHMETIC REVIEW

On the COOP or HSPT, math skills include basic computation, using whole numbers, fractions, decimals, and percentages. You need to have a firm grasp of arithmetic concepts such as number properties, factors, divisibility, units of measure, ratio and proportion, percentages, and averages. These skills may be tested in basic operations or in word problems. This section will review these important concepts and give you a chance to practice problems dealing with these subjects. Even if you feel that you know them, spend time on this section. The more you practice, the more comfortable you will feel working with numbers on these tests.

First, take a look at a few definitions.

Number Type:	Definition:	Examples:
Real Numbers	Any number that can name a position on a number line, regardless of whether that position is negative or positive.	-75% .5 $\frac{3}{4}$ $\begin{array}{c}\text{-5 -4 -3 -2 -1 0 1 2 3 4 5}\end{array}$
Rational Numbers	Any number that can be written as a ratio of two integers, including whole numbers, integers, terminating decimals, and repeating decimals.	$5 = \frac{5}{1}, 2 = \frac{2}{1}, 0 = \frac{0}{1}, -6 = \frac{-6}{1}$ $2\frac{50}{100}$, or $\frac{250}{100}$ $\frac{1}{3}$ (.33333)
Whole Numbers	Zero and the positive integers are the whole numbers.	0, 1, 2, 3...
Integers	Whole numbers, including 0 and negative whole numbers.	-500, -2, 0, 1, 53
Fractions	A **fraction** is a number that is written in the form $\frac{A}{B}$ where A is the numerator and B is the denominator. An **improper fraction** is a number that is greater than 1 (or less than -1) that is written in the form of a fraction. Improper fractions can be converted to a **mixed number**.	$\frac{-5}{6}, \frac{3}{17}, \frac{1}{2}, \frac{899}{901}$ $\frac{-65}{64}, \frac{9}{8}, \frac{57}{10}$ $-1\frac{1}{64}, 1\frac{1}{8}, 5\frac{7}{10}$
Positive/Negative	Numbers greater than 0 are positive numbers; numbers less than 0 are negative;. 0 is neither positive nor negative.	Positive: 1, 5, 900 Negative: -64, -40, -11, $\frac{-6}{13}$
Even/Odd	An even number is an integer that is a multiple of 2. NOTE: 0 is an even number. An odd number is an integer that is not a multiple of 2.	Even numbers: -6, -2, 0, 4, 12, 190 Odd numbers: -15, -1, 3, 9, 453
Prime Numbers	An integer greater than 1 that has no factors other than 1 and itself; 2 is the only even prime number.	2, 3, 5, 7, 11, 13, 59, 83
Consecutive Numbers	Numbers that follow one after another, in order, without skipping any.	Consecutive integers: 3, 4, 5, 6 Consecutive even integers: 2, 4, 6, 8, 10 Consecutive multiples of 9: 9, 18, 27, 36
Factors	A positive integer that divides evenly into a given number with no remainder.	The complete list of factors of 12: 1, 2, 3, 4, 6, 12
Multiples	A number that a given number will divide into with no remainder.	Some multiples of 12: 0, 12, 24, 60

Odds and Evens

Even ± Even = Even	$2 + 2 = 4$
Even ± Odd = Odd	$3 + 3 = 5$
Odd ± Odd = Even	$3 + 3 = 6$
Even × Even = Even	$2 \times 2 = 4$
Even × Odd = Even	$2 \times 3 = 6$
Odd × Odd = Odd	$3 \times 3 = 9$

Positives and Negatives

There are few things to remember about positives and negatives.

Adding a negative number is basically subtraction.

$6 + (-4)$ is really $6 - 4$ or 2.

$4 + (-6)$ is really $4 - 6$ or -2.

Subtracting a negative number is basically addition.

$6 - (-4)$ is really $6 + 4$ or 10.

$-6 - (-4)$ is really $-6 + 4$ or -2.

Multiplying and dividing positives and negatives is like all other multiplication and division, with one catch. To figure out whether your product is positive or negative, simply count the number of negatives you had to start. If you had an odd number of negatives, the product is negative. If you had an even number of negatives, the product is positive.

$$6 \times (-4) = -24 \text{ (1 negative} \rightarrow \text{negative product)}$$

$$(-6) \times (-4) = 24 \text{ (2 negatives} \rightarrow \text{positive product)}$$

$$(-1) \times (-6) \times (-4) = -24 \text{ (3 negatives} \rightarrow \text{negative product)}$$

Similarly,

$$-24 \div 3 = -8 \text{ (1 negative} \rightarrow \text{negative quotient)}$$

$$-24 \div (-3) = 8 \text{ (2 negatives} \rightarrow \text{positive quotient)}$$

Absolute Value

Absolute value describes how far a number on the number line is from zero. It doesn't matter in which direction the number lies—to the right on the positive side, or to the left on the negative side.

For example, the absolute value of both 3 and −3 is 3.

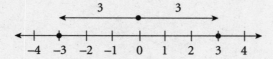

To find the absolute value of a number, simply strip the number within the vertical lines of its sign.

$$|4| = 4$$
$$|-4| = 4$$

When absolute value expressions contain different arithmetic operations, perform the operation first, and then strip the sign from the result.

$$|-6 + 4| = |-2| = 2$$
$$|(-6) \times 4| = |-24| = 24$$

Sets

A set is a group of numbers that share particular qualities. For example, even numbers are a set—a set of integers that are divisible by two. Likewise, odd numbers are a set—a set of integers that are not divisible by two. The symbols {} represent set notation. Thus, a set of numbers including the integers 3, 7, and 11, would be indicated like this: {3, 7, 11}

The symbol ∩ represents intersection. The intersection of two sets consists of the elements that are common to both sets.

Factors and Multiples

To find the prime factorization of a number, keep breaking it down until you are left with only prime numbers.

To find the prime factorization of 168:

$$168 = 4 \times 42$$
$$= 4 \times 6 \times 7$$
$$= 2 \times 2 \times 2 \times 3 \times 7$$

To find the greatest common factor (GCF) of two integers, break down both integers into their prime factorizations and multiply all prime factors they have in common. The greatest common factor is the largest factor that goes into a one or more numbers.

For example, if you're looking for the greatest common factor of 40 and 130, first identify the prime factors of each integer.

$$40 = 4 \times 10$$
$$= 2 \times 2 \times 2 \times 5$$

$$140 = 10 \times 14$$
$$= 2 \times 5 \times 2 \times 7$$
$$= 2 \times 2 \times 5 \times 7$$

Next, see what prime factors the two numbers have in common and then multiply these common factors.

Both integers share two 2's and one 5, so the GCF is $2 \times 2 \times 5$ or 20.

If you need to find a common multiple of two integers, you can always multiply them. However, you can use prime factors to find the least common multiple (LCM). To do this, multiply all of the prime factors of each integer as many times as they appear. Don't worry if this sounds confusing, it becomes pretty clear once it's demonstrated. Take a look at the example to see how it works.

To find a common multiple of 20 and 16:

$$20 \times 16 = 320$$

320 is a common multiple of 20 and 16, but it is not the *least* common multiple.

To find the least common multiple of 20 and 16 first find the prime factors of each integer:

$$20 = 2 \times 2 \times 5$$
$$16 = 2 \times 2 \times 2 \times 2$$

Now, multiply each prime integer as many times as it appears: $2 \times 2 \times 2 \times 2 \times 5 = 80$

The Order of Operations

You need to remember the order in which arithmetic operations must be performed. PEMDAS (or Please Excuse My Dear Aunt Sally) may help you remember the order.

Please = Parentheses

Excuse = Exponents

My Dear = Multiplication and Division (from left to right)

Aunt Sally = Addition and Subtraction (from left to right)

$$3^3 - 8(3 - 1) + 12 \div 4$$
$$= 3^3 - 8(2) + 12 \div 4$$
$$= 27 - 8(2) + 12 \div 4$$
$$= 27 - 16 + 3$$
$$= 11 + 3$$
$$= 14$$

Divisibility Rules

If you've forgotten—or never learned—divisibility rules, spend a little time with this chart. Even if you remember the rules, take a moment to refresh your memory. There are no easy divisibility rules for 7 and 8.

Divisible by	The Rule	Example: 558
2	The last digit is even.	a multiple of 2 because 8 is even
3	The sum of the digits is a multiple of 3.	a multiple of 3 because 5 + 5 + 8 = 18, which is a multiple of 3
4	The last 2 digits comprise a 2-digit multiple of 4.	NOT a multiple of 4 because 58 is not a multiple of 4
5	The last digit is 5 or 0.	NOT a multiple of 5 because it doesn't end in 5 or 0
6	The last digit is even AND the sum of the digits is a multiple of 3.	a multiple of 6 because it's a multiple of both 2 and 3
9	The sum of the digits is a multiple of 9.	a multiple of 9 because 5 + 5 + 8 = 18, which is a multiple of 9
10	The last digit is 0.	not a multiple of 10 because it doesn't end in 0

Properties of Numbers

Here are some essential laws or properties of numbers.

Commutative Property for Addition

When adding two or more terms, the sum is the same regardless of which number is added to which.

$$3 + 2 = 2 + 3$$

$$a + b = b + a$$

Associative Property for Addition

When adding two or more terms, the sum is the same, regardless of the order in which the terms are added.

$$2 + (5 + 3) = (2 + 5) + 3$$

$$a + (b + c) = (a + b) + c$$

Commutative Property for Multiplication

When multiplying two or more terms, the result is the same regardless of which number is multiplied by which.

$$2 \times 4 = 4 \times 2$$

$$ab = ba$$

Associative Property for Multiplication

When multiplying groups, the product is the same regardless of the order in which the groups are multiplied.

$$2 \times (4 \times 3) = (2 \times 4) \times 3$$

$$a(b \times c) = (a \times b) \times c$$

Distributive Property of Multiplication

When multiplying groups, the product is the same as multiplying each group separately and summing the result.

$$2 \times 3 = 2 \times (1 + 1 + 1)$$

$$x \times 3y = x \times (y + y + y)$$

Fractions and Decimals

Generally, it's a good idea to reduce fractions when solving math questions. To do this, simply cancel all factors that the numerator and denominator have in common.

$$\frac{28}{36} = \frac{4 \times 7}{4 \times 9} = \frac{7}{9}$$

To add fractions, get a common denominator and then add the numerators.

$$\frac{1}{4} + \frac{1}{3} = \frac{3}{12} + \frac{4}{12} = \frac{3 + 4}{12} = \frac{7}{12}$$

To subtract fractions, get a common denominator and then subtract the numerators.

$$\frac{1}{4} - \frac{1}{3} = \frac{3}{12} - \frac{4}{12} = \frac{3 - 4}{12} = \frac{-1}{12}$$

To multiply fractions, multiply the numerators and multiply the denominators.

$$\frac{1}{4} \times \frac{1}{3} = \frac{1 \times 1}{4 \times 3} = \frac{1}{12}$$

To divide fractions, invert the second fraction and multiply. In other words, multiply the first fraction by the reciprocal of the second fraction.

$$\frac{1}{4} \div \frac{1}{3} = \frac{1}{4} \times \frac{3}{1} = \frac{1 \times 3}{4 \times 1} = \frac{3}{4}$$

Comparing Fractions

To compare fractions, multiply the numerator of the first fraction by the denominator of the second fraction to get a product. Then, multiply the numerator of the second fraction by the denominator of the first fraction to get a second product. If the first product is greater, the first fraction is greater. If the second product is greater, the second fraction is greater.

Here's an example:

$$\text{Compare } \frac{2}{5} \text{ and } \frac{5}{8}.$$

1. Multiply the numerator of the first fraction by the denominator of the second.

   $2 \times 8 = 16$

2. Multiply the numerator of the second fraction by the denominator of the first.

   $5 \times 5 = 25$

3. The second product is greater, therefore, the second fraction, $\frac{5}{8}$ is greater than $\frac{2}{5}$.

To convert a fraction to a decimal, divide the denominator into the numerator.

To convert $\frac{8}{25}$ to a decimal, divide 25 into 8.

$$\frac{8}{25} = 0.32$$

To convert a decimal to a fraction, first set the decimal over 1. Then, move the decimal over as many places as it takes until it is immediately to the right of the digit farthest to the right. Count the number of places that you moved the decimal. Then, add that many 0's to the 1 in the denominator.

$$0.3 = \frac{0.3}{1} = \frac{3.0}{10} \text{ or } \frac{3}{10}$$

$$0.32 = \frac{0.32}{1} = \frac{32.0}{100} \text{ or } \frac{8}{25}$$

Common Percent Equivalencies

Being familiar with the relationships among percents, decimals, and fractions can save you time on test day. Don't worry about memorizing the following chart. Simply use it to review relationships you already know (e.g., $50\% = 0.50 = \frac{1}{2}$) and to familiarize yourself with some that you might not already know. To convert a fraction or decimal to a percent, multiply by 100%. To convert a percent to a fraction or decimal, divide by 100%.

Fraction	Decimal	Percent
$\frac{1}{20}$	0.05	5%
$\frac{1}{10}$	0.10	10%
$\frac{1}{8}$	.125	12.5%
$\frac{1}{6}$	$.16\overline{6}$	$16\frac{2}{3}\%$
$\frac{1}{5}$	.20	20%
$\frac{1}{4}$	.25	25%
$\frac{1}{3}$	$.33\overline{3}$	$33\frac{1}{3}\%$
$\frac{3}{8}$	.375	37.5%
$\frac{2}{5}$	.40	40%
$\frac{1}{2}$	.50	50%
$\frac{3}{5}$	.60	60%
$\frac{2}{3}$	$.66\overline{6}$	$66\frac{2}{3}\%$
$\frac{3}{4}$	.75	75%
$\frac{4}{5}$	.80	80%
$\frac{5}{6}$	$.83\overline{3}$	$83\frac{1}{3}\%$
$\frac{7}{8}$	.875	87.5%

Rounding

You might be asked to estimate or round a number on the COOP or HSPT test. Rounding might also help you determine an answer choice. There are a few simple rules to rounding. Look at the digit to the right of the number in question. If it is a 4 or less, leave the number in question as it is and replace all the numbers to the right with 0's.

For example, round of 765,432 to the nearest 100. The 4 is the hundred's digit, but you have to look at the digit to the right of the hundred's digit, which is the ten's digit, or 3. Since the ten's digit is 3, the hundred's digit remains the same and the ten's and one's digits both become 0. Therefore, 765,432 rounded to the nearest 100 is 765,400.

If the number to the right of the number in question is 5 or greater, increase the number in question by 1 and replace all the numbers to the right with 0's.

593 rounded to the nearest 100 would round to 600.

Place Units

Rounding requires that you know the place unit value of the digits in a number. You will probably also encounter questions on the COOP or HSPT that ask you the place value of a digit in a number. Though these seem obvious, be sure to answer these questions carefully because glancing at a large number and answering too quickly may lead you to select a wrong answer choice.

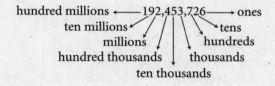

Symbols of Inequality

An inequality is a mathematical sentence in which two expressions are joined by symbols such as ≠ (not equal to), > (greater than), < (less than), ≥ (greater than or equal to), ≤ (less than or equal to). Examples of inequalities are:

$5 + 3 \neq 7$ 5 plus 3 is not equal to 7

$6 > 2$ 6 is greater than 2

$8 < 8.5$ 8 is less than 8 and a half

$x \leq 9 + 6$ x is less than or equal to 9 plus 6

$c \geq 10$ c is greater than or equal to 10 (c is an algebraic variable. That means, it varies, and could be any number greater than or equal to 10.)

Exponents and Roots

Exponents are the small raised numbers written to the right of a number or variable. A variable is the letter term used in algebra. We'll get to that in the next chapter. For now, remember that an exponent indicates the number of times that a number (or variable) is to be used as a factor. On the COOP or HSPT, you'll usually deal with numbers or variables that are squares (multiplied by itself twice) and cubes (multiplied by itself 3 times).

You should remember the squares of 1 through 10.

square = a number to the second power   **cube = a number to the third power**

2^2	$2 \times 2 = 4$		2^3	$2 \times 2 \times 2 = 8$
3^2	$3 \times 3 = 9$		3^3	$3 \times 3 \times 3 = 27$
4^2	$4 \times 4 = 16$		4^3	$4 \times 4 \times 4 = 64$
5^2	$5 \times 5 = 25$		5^3	$5 \times 5 \times 5 = 125$
6^2	$6 \times 6 = 36$			
7^2	$7 \times 7 = 49$			
8^2	$8 \times 8 = 64$			
9^2	$9 \times 9 = 81$			
10^2	$10 \times 10 = 100$			

To add or subtract terms consisting of a coefficient (the number in front of the variable) multiplied by a power (a power is a base raised to an exponent), both the base and the exponent must be the same. As long as the bases and the exponents are the same, you can add the coefficients.

$x^2 + x^2 = 2x^2$ —the base (x) and the exponent (2) are the same, you can add these.

$3x^4 - 2x^4 = x^4$ —again, the base (x) and the exponent (4) are the same, you can subtract these.

$x^2 + x^3$ cannot be combined. The exponents are different (2) and (3).

$x^2 + y^2$ cannot be combined. The bases are different (x) and (y).

To multiply terms consisting of coefficients multiplied by powers having the same base, multiply the coefficients and add the exponents.

$2x^5 \times (8x^7) = (2 \times 8)(x^{5+7}) = 16x^{12}$

To divide terms consisting of coefficients multiplied by powers having the same base, divide the coefficients and subtract the exponents.

$$6x^7 \div 2x^5 = (6 \div 2)(x^{7-5}) = 3(x^2)$$

To raise a power to an exponent, multiply the exponents.

$$(x^2)^4 = x^{2 \times 4} = x^8$$

A square root of a non-negative number is a number that, when multiplied by itself, produces the given quantity. The radical sign $\sqrt{}$ is used to represent the positive square root of a number, so $\sqrt{25} = 5$, since $5 \times 5 = 25$.

To add or subtract radicals, make sure the numbers under the radical sign are the same. If they are, you can add or subtract the coefficients outside the radical signs.

$$2\sqrt{2} + 3\sqrt{2} = 5\sqrt{2}$$

$\sqrt{2} + \sqrt{3}$ cannot be combined.

To simplify radicals, factor out the perfect squares under the radical, unsquare them, and put the result in front of the radical sign.

$$\sqrt{32} = \sqrt{16 \times 2} = 4\sqrt{2}$$

To multiply or divide radicals, multiply (or divide) the coefficients outside the radical. Multiply (or divide) the numbers inside the radicals.

$$\sqrt{x} \times \sqrt{y} = \sqrt{xy}$$

$$3\sqrt{2} \times 4\sqrt{5} = 12\sqrt{10}$$

$$\frac{\sqrt{x}}{\sqrt{y}} = \sqrt{\frac{x}{y}}$$

$$12\sqrt{10} \div 3\sqrt{2} = 4\sqrt{5}$$

To take the square root of a fraction, break the fraction into two separate roots and take the square root of the numerator and the denominator.

$$\sqrt{\frac{16}{25}} = \frac{\sqrt{16}}{\sqrt{25}} = \frac{4}{5}$$

The Power of 10

The exponent of a power of 10 tells you how may zeros to add. For example, 10 to the 10th power has 10 zeros.

The exponent of a power of 10 indicates how many zeros the number would contain if it were written out. For example, $10^4 = 10,000$ (4 zeros) since the product of 4 factors of 10 is equal to 10,000.

When multiplying a number by a power of 10, move the decimal point to the right the same number of places as the number of zeros in that power of 10.

$$0.0123 \times 10^4 = 123$$

When dividing by a power of 10, move the decimal point, to the left.

$$43.21 \div 10^3 = 0.04321$$

Multiplying by a power with a negative exponent is the same as dividing by a power with a positive exponent. Therefore, when you multiply by a number with a positive exponent, move the decimal to the right. When you multiply by a number with a negative exponent, move the decimal to the left.

For example:

$$10^3 = 1,000 = 1,000$$

Percents

Remember these formulas: Part = Percent × Whole or $\text{Percent} = \dfrac{\text{Part}}{\text{Whole}}$

From Fraction to Percent

To find part, percent, or whole, plug the values you have into the equation and solve.

$$44\% \text{ of } 25 = 0.44 \times 25 = 11$$

42 is what percent of 70?

$$42 \div 70 = 0.6$$

$$0.6 \times 100\% = 60\%$$

To increase or decrease a number by a given percent, take that percent of the original number and add it to or subtract it from the original number.

To increase 25 by 60%, first find 60% of 25.

$$25 \times 0.6 = 15$$

Then, add the result to the original number.

$$25 + 15 = 40$$

To decrease 25 by the same percent, subtract the 15.

$$25 - 15 = 10$$

Average, Median, and Mode

$$\text{Average} = \frac{\text{sum of the terms}}{\text{number of the terms}}$$

The average of 15, 18, 15, 32, and 20 $= \dfrac{15 + 18 + 15 + 32 + 20}{5} = \dfrac{100}{5} = 20$

When there are an odd number of terms, the median of a group of terms is the value of the middle term, with the terms arranged in increasing order.

Suppose that you want to find the median of the terms 15, 18, 15, 32, and 20. First, put the terms in order from small to large: 15, 15, 18, 20, 32. Then, identify the middle term. The middle term is 18.

When there is an even number of terms, the median is the average of the two middle terms with the terms arranged in increasing order.

Suppose that you want to find the mode of the terms 15, 18, 15, 32, and 20. The mode is the value of the term that occurs most; 15 occurs twice, so it is the mode.

Ratios, Proportions, and Rates

Ratios can be expressed in two forms.

The first form is $\dfrac{a}{b}$.

If you have 15 dogs and 5 cats, the ratio of dogs to cats is $\dfrac{15}{5}$. (The ratio of cats to dogs is $\dfrac{5}{15}$) Like any other fraction, this ratio can be reduced; $\dfrac{15}{5}$ can be reduced to $\dfrac{1}{3}$. In other words, for every three dogs, there's one cat.

The second form is $a:b$.

The ratio of dogs to cats is 15:5 or 3:1. The ratio of cats to dogs is 5:15 or 1:3.

Pay attention to what ratio is specified in the problem. Remember that the ratio of dogs to cats is different from the ratio of cats to dogs.

To solve a proportion, cross-multiply and solve for the variable.

$$\frac{x}{6} = \frac{2}{3}$$

$$3x = 12$$

$$x = 4$$

A rate is a ratio that compares quantities measured in different units. The most common example is miles per hour. Use the following formula for such problems:

$$\text{Distance} = \text{Rate} \times \text{Time or } D = R \times T$$

Remember, although not all rates are speeds, this formula can be adapted to any rate.

Units of Measurement

You will most likely see at least a few questions that include units of measurement on the COOP or HSPT. You are expected to remember these basic units of measurement. Spend some time reviewing the list below.

Distance

1 foot = 12 inches

1 yard = 3 feet = 36 inches

1 kilometer = 1,000 meters

metric: 1 meter = 10 decimeters = 100 centimeters = 1,000 millimeters

(Remember the root *deci* is 10; the root *centi* is 100, the root *milli* is 1,000)

Weight

1 pound = 16 ounces

metric: A gram is a unit of mass. A kilogram is 1,000 grams.

Volume

8 ounces = 1 cup

2 cups = 1 pint

1 quart = 2 pints

4 cups = 1 quart

1 gallon = 4 quarts

metric: A liter is a unit of volume. A kiloliter is 1,000 liters.

Don't worry, you won't be expected to remember the formulas for converting metric and U.S. equivalents or vice versa. On questions such as these, the formula is provided.

However, you must be careful when approaching a problem that includes units of measurement. Be sure that the units are given in the same format. You may have to convert pounds to ounces or feet to yards (or vice versa) to arrive at the correct answer choice.

A Word About Word Problems

You can expect to see a lot of word problems on the COOP or HSPT test. Some of these will be algebra problems, asking you to solve for an unknown. We'll get into those in the next chapter. Some of them however, will just be asking you to perform arithmetic equations. Your job is to find the math within the story.

Here's an example:

> A grocery store charges $.99 for a liter of milk, $1.49 for a half pound of tomatoes, and $.49 for a jar of tomato sauce and $1.25 for a box of pasta. If Reggie buys 2 liters of milk, 1 pound of tomatoes, a jar of tomato sauce and 2 boxes of pasta, what is his bill?
>
> (A) $7.90
> (B) $7.95
> (C) $6.36
> (D) $8.36

If you sort through the story, you realize that the question is asking you to add the amounts of each item that Reggie bought. Read the question carefully to make sure you have the correct number of each item he bought, then add the amounts.

$.99 \times 2 = 1.98$ (The price of two liters of milk.)

$1.49 \times 2 = 2.98$ (The price given was per half pound; Reggie bought 1 full pound.)

$.49$ (The price of one jar of sauce.)

$1.25 \times 2 = 2.50$ (The price of two boxes of pasta.)

Now, add these numbers together to get the total.

$$
\begin{array}{r}
1.98 \\
2.98 \\
.49 \\
\underline{2.50} \\
\$7.95 \ (B)
\end{array}
$$

Often, word problems can seem tricky because it may be hard to figure out precisely what you are being asked to do. It can be difficult to translate English into math. The following table lists some common words and phrases that turn up in word problems, along with their mathematical translation.

When you see:	Think:
sum, plus, more than, added to, combined total	+
minus, less than, difference between, decreased by	−
is, was, equals, is equivalent to, is the same as, adds up to	=
times, product, multiplied by, of, twice, double, triple	x
divided by, over, quotient, per, out of, into	÷

MATH SKILLS PRACTICE SET

1. Which of the following demonstrates the commutative property of addition?

    (A) $1 + 3 = 4$

    (B) $1 + 3 = 3 + 1$

    (C) $1 + 3 = \dfrac{1}{3} \times \dfrac{3}{1}$

    (D) $1 + 3 = 1 - (-3)$

2. What is the least common multiple of 12 and 8?

    (A) 12

    (B) 24

    (C) 18

    (D) 96

3. Which of the following is an even multiple of both 2 and 6?

    (A) 435

    (B) 247

    (C) 322

    (D) 426

4. All of the following can be a product of a negative integer and a positive integer EXCEPT

    (A) -6

    (B) 1

    (C) -1

    (D) -2

5. What is the sum of five consecutive integers if the middle one is 9?

    (A) 50

    (B) 55

    (C) 45

    (D) 30

6. $2^3(3 - 1)^2 + (-4)^2 =$

    (A) 48

    (B) 32

    (C) 136

    (D) -48

7. If x is an even integer and $8 < x < 17$, what is the mean of all possible values of x?

    (A) 10

    (B) 11

    (C) 13

    (D) 12

8. Which of the following numbers is closest to the product of 52.3×10.4?

    (A) 5,000

    (B) 500

    (C) 6,000

    (D) 60

9. Which of the following is 53,298 rounded off to the nearest 100?

    (A) 53,290

    (B) 52,000

    (C) 53,300

    (D) 53,000

10. If 40% of x is 8, what is $x\%$ of 40?

    (A) 80

    (B) 30

    (C) 10

    (D) 8

ANSWERS AND EXPLANATIONS

1. B

The commutative property of addition states that when adding two or more terms, the sum is the same, no matter the order in which the terms are added.

2. B

The least common multiple of two integers is the product of their prime factors, each raised to the highest power with which it appears. The prime factorization of 12 is $2 \times 2 \times 3$, the prime of factorization of 8 is $2 \times 2 \times 2$. So their LCM is $2 \times 2 \times 2 \times 3 = 24$. You could also find their LCM by checking out the multiples of the larger integer (12) until you find one that's also a multiple of the smaller.

3. D

If a number is a multiple of both 2 and 6, it must satisfy the divisibility rules of both: its last digit must be even, its digits must add up to a multiple of 3. Only choice (D) fits both requirements $4 + 2 + 6 = 12$. You could have quickly eliminated choice (A) and (B) which are not even numbers.

4. B

Remember to count the number of negatives to determine whether the product of negative and positive integers is either negative or positive. An odd number of negatives will yield a negative number, while an even number of negatives will yield a positive number. Since choice (B) is a positive integer, it is not the product of a negative and a positive integer.

5. C

This is a simple addition problem. If the middle integer is 9, place them in order. You would have: $7 + 8 + 9 + 10 + 11 = 45$.

6. A

Remember PEMDAS. Perform the operation in parenthesis first.

$2^3(3 - 1)^2 + (-4)^2 = 2^3(2)^2 + (-4)^2$. Exponents next, $8(4) + 16$. Multiplication next, and addition or subtraction last: $32 + 16 = 48$.

7. C

x is an even integer greater than 8 but less than 17. Thus, x could be 10, 12, 14, or 16. The mean of all its possible values $= \dfrac{(10 + 12 + 14 + 16)}{4} = \dfrac{52}{4} = 13$. Be sure to read each question carefully. This question required two steps. If you read to quickly, you might have missed the second step that was finding the mean of all the possible values of x.

8. B

This is a rounding off question. You can round off 52.3 to 50 and 10.4 to 10; $50 \times 10 = 500$.

9. C

To round off to the nearest 100 look at the tens digit. If it is 5 or greater, round the hundreds digit up. If the tens digit is 4 or smaller, keep the same hundreds digit. Here, the tens digit is 9, so you must round the hundreds digit up to 3 and replace the digits to the right with zeros.

10. D

This problem is not difficult if you remember that $a\%$ of $b = b\%$ of a. In this case, $x\%$ of b (the number 40) $= b$ (the number 40)% of $x = 8$. If you didn't remember this, you could have solved for x with the formula percent $\times$ whole $=$ part. Thus, $\dfrac{40}{100} = \dfrac{8}{x}$. When we cross multiply and solve for x we get $40x = 800$, $x = \dfrac{800}{40}$, so $x = 20$. We now need to determine $x\%$ of 40. $x = 20$; 20% of 40 $= 20 \times 40 = 8$.

Chapter Eight: **Algebra Basics**

Algebra problems will appear in two forms on the COOP or HSPT: as regular math problems and as word problems. This chapter will give you a chance to review the basic algebra concepts that you'll see on the test. (Word problems are covered in the next chapter and will build on the concepts from this chapter.)

WHAT IS ALGEBRA?

Algebra has been called *math with letters*. Just like arithmetic, the basic operations of algebra are addition, subtraction, multiplication, division, roots. Instead of numbers though, algebra uses letters to represent unknown or variable numbers. Why would you work with a variable? Let's look at an example.

> You buy 2 bananas from the supermarket for 50 cents total.
> How much does one banana cost?

That's a simple equation, but how would you write it down on paper if you were trying to explain it to a friend?

Perhaps you would write: $2 \times \underline{\ ?\ } = 50$ cents.

Algebra gives you a systematic way to record the question mark.

$2 \times b = 50$ cents or $2b = 50$ cents, where $b =$ the cost of 1 banana.

Algebra is a type of mathematical shorthand. The most commonly used letters in algebra are a, b, c and x, y, z.

The number 2 in the term $2b$ is called a **coefficient**. It is a constant that does not change.

To find out how much you paid for each banana, you could use your equation to solve for the unknown cost.

$$2b = 50 \text{ cents}$$

$$\frac{2b}{2} = \frac{50}{2}$$

$$b = 25 \text{ cents}$$

ALGEBRAIC EXPRESSIONS

An expression is a collection of quantities made up of constants and variables linked by operations signs such as + and −.

Let's go back to our fruit example. Let's say you have 2 bananas and you give one to your friend. You could express this in algebraic terms as:

$2b - b$

$2b - b$ is an example of an algebraic expression, where b = one banana.

In fact, it is a binomial expression. A monomial expression has only 1 constant and variable, a polynomial expression has two or more. Since there are two, it is called a binomial.

$2b$ = monomial
$2b - b$ = binomial
$2(b + x)$ = binomial
$2 + b^2 + y$ = trinomial or **polynomial**

On the COOP or HSPT an algebraic expression is likely to look something like this:

$(11 + 3x) - (5 - 2x) =$

In addition to algebra, this problem tests your knowledge of positives and negatives, and the order of operations (PEMDAS).

The main thing you need to remember about **expressions** on the COOP or HSPT is that you can only combine like terms.

Let's talk about fruit once more. Let's say in addition to the 2 bananas you purchased you also bought 3 apples and 1 orange. You spent 4 dollars total. We can express our purchases as $2b + 3a + 1o = 4.00$. Now, b = the cost of 1 banana, a = the cost of 1 apple, and o = the cost of one orange.

However, let's say that once again you forgot how much each banana cost. You could NOT add the six items, divide them into 4.00 to get the cost of each one. They're different items.

> **KAPLAN TIP**
>
> Remember you can only combine like terms. Combine a's with a's , x's with x's, or coefficients that have the exact same variable.

While you cannot solve expressions with unlike terms, you *can* simplify them. For example, to combine monomials or polynomials, simply add or subtract the coefficients of terms that have the exact same variable. When completing the addition or subtraction, do not change the variables.

$$6a + 5a = 11a$$
$$8b - 2b = 6b$$
$$3a + 2b - 8a = 3a - 8a + 2b = -5a + 2b \text{ or } 2b - 5a$$

Coefficient = The number that comes before the variable. In $6x$, 6 is the coefficient.

Variable = The variable is the letter that stands for an unknown. In $6x$, x is the variable.

Monomial = One variable: $6x$ is a monomial.

Polynomial = More than one variable: $6xy$ is a polynomial.

To review, you cannot combine:

$6a + 5a^2$ —Why not? The variables are not exactly alike. (One is a the other is a^2)

or

$3a + 2b$ —Why not? The variables are not exactly alike. (One is a the other is b)

For algebraic expressions, make sure you only combine like terms.

Multiplying and dividing monomials is a little different. Unlike addition and subtraction, you can multiply and divide terms that are different. When you multiply monomials, multiply the coefficients of each term. (In other words, multiply the numbers that come before the variables.) Add the exponents of like variables. Multiply different variables together.

$$(6a)(4b) =$$
$$= (6 \times 4)(a \times b)$$
$$= 24ab$$

$$(6a)(4ab) =$$
$$= (6 \times 4)(a \times a \times b)$$
$$= (6 \times 4)(a^{1+1} \times b)$$
$$= 24a^2b$$

Use the FOIL method to multiply and divide binomials. FOIL stands for **F**irst **O**uter **I**nner **L**ast.

$$(y + 1)(y + 2) =$$
$$= (y \times y) + (y \times 2) + (1 \times y) + (1 \times 2)$$
$$= y^2 + 2y + y + 2$$
$$= y^2 + 3y + 2$$

EQUATIONS

The key to solving equations is to do the same thing to both sides of the equation until you have your variable isolated on one side of the equation and all of the numbers on the other side.

$$8a + 4 = 24 - 2a$$

First, subtract 4 from each side so that the left side of the equation has only variables.

$$8a + 4 - 4 = 24 - 2a - 4$$
$$8a = 20 - 2a$$

Then, add $2a$ to each side so that the right side of the equation has only numbers.

$$8a + 2a = 20 - 2a + 2a$$
$$10a = 20$$

Finally, divide both sides by 10 to isolate the variable.

$$\frac{10a}{10} = \frac{20}{10}$$
$$a = 2$$

Treat Both Sides Equally

Always perform the same operation to both sides to solve for a variable in an equation.

Sometimes you're given an equation with two variables and asked to solve for one variable in terms of the other. This means that you must isolate the variable for which you are solving on one side of the equation and put everything else on the other side. In other words, when you're done, you'll have x (or whatever the variable you're looking for is) on one side of the equation and an expression on the other side.

Solve $7x + 2y = 3x + 10y - 16$ for x in terms of y.

Since you want to isolate x on one side of the equation, begin by subtracting $2y$ from both sides.

$$7x + 2y - 2y = 3x + 10y - 16 - 2y$$
$$7x = 3x + 8y - 16$$

Then, subtract $3x$ from both sides to get all the x's on one side of the equation.

$$7x - 3x = 3x + 8y - 16 - 3x$$
$$4x = 8y - 16$$

Finally, divide both sides by 4 to isolate x.

$$\frac{4x}{4} = \frac{8y - 16}{4}$$
$$x = 2y - 4$$

SUBSTITUTION

If a problem gives you the value for a variable, just plug the value into the equation and solve. Make sure that you follow the rules of PEMDAS and are careful with your calculations.

If $x = 15$ and $y = 10$, what is the value of $4x(x - y)$?

Plug 15 in for x and 10 in for y.

$4(15)(15 - 10) =$

Then, solve.

$(60)(5) = 300$

PICKING NUMBERS

Picking numbers is a very useful strategy for avoiding lots of tedious calculations. Basically, instead of solving the expression and figuring out which answer choice matches your answer, you plug choices back into the expression until one fits.

Some typical questions that can be solved by picking numbers are:
- age stated in terms of variables
- remainder problems
- percentages or fractions of variables
- positive and negative variable calculations
- questions with algebraic expressions as answers

KAPLAN TIP

Don't be afraid to pick numbers out of thin air if the answer choices contain variables. Also, remember to pick easy workable numbers. Avoid 1 and 0 as these values may cause you problems.

INEQUALITIES

Solve **inequalities** like you would any other equation. Isolate the variable for which you are solving on one side of the equation and everything else on the other side of the equation.

$$4a + 6 > 2a + 10$$
$$4a - 2a > 10 - 6$$
$$2a > 4$$
$$a > 2$$

The only difference here is that instead of finding a specific value for *a*, you get a range of values for *a*. That is, *a* can be any number greater than 2. The rest of the math is the same.

There is, however, one *crucial* difference between solving equations and inequalities. **When you multiply or divide an inequality by a negative number, you must change the direction of the sign.**

$$-5a > 10$$

$$\frac{a}{-5} > \frac{10}{-5}$$

$$a < -2$$

If this seems confusing, think about the logic. You're told that −5 times something is greater than 10. This is where your knowledge of positives and negatives comes into play. You know that negative × positive = negative and negative × negative = positive. Since −5 is negative and 10 is positive, −5 has to be multiplied by something negative to get a positive product. Therefore, *a* has to be *less* than −2, not *greater* than it. If *a* > −2, then any value for *a* that is greater than −2 should make −5*a* greater than 10. Say *a* is 20; −5*a* would be −100 which is certainly NOT greater than 10.

ALGEBRA BASICS PRACTICE SET

1. What is the value of $a(b - 2) + \dfrac{bc}{a}$ if $a = 2, b = 6$ and $c = 4$?

    (A) 20

    (B) 12

    (C) 24

    (D) 32

2. If $= 5$ and $d = 2$, then $2c + d =$

    (A) 32

    (B) 20

    (C) 22

    (D) 35

3. What is the value of x in the equation $6x - 7 = y$, if $y = 11$?

    (A) 12

    (B) 8

    (C) 4

    (D) 3

4. If $x = \sqrt{3}, y = 2$, and $z = \dfrac{1}{2}$, then $x^2 - 5yz + y^2 =$

    (A) 1

    (B) 2

    (C) 4

    (D) 7

5. $(3d - 7) - (5 - 2d) =$

    (A) $d - 12$

    (B) $5d - 2$

    (C) $5d + 12$

    (D) $5d - 12$

6. If x is an odd integer and y is an even integer, which of the following expressions MUST be odd?

    (A) $2x + y$

    (B) $2(x + y)$

    (C) $x^2 + y^2$

    (D) $xy + y$

7. If $90 \div x = 9n$, then what is the value of nx?

   (A) 10

   (B) $9x$

   (C) 900

   (D) $90xn$

8. For what value of y is $4(y - 5) = 2(y + 3)$?

   (A) -13

   (B) 13

   (C) 7

   (D) -8

9. What is the value of x in the following equation?
   $$\frac{1}{2} + x = 6.5$$

   (A) 3.5

   (B) 3.25

   (C) 5.5

   (D) 6

10. If $2(a + m) = 5m - 3 + a$, what is the value of a, in terms of m?

    (A) $\dfrac{3m}{2}$

    (B) 3

    (C) $4m + 33$

    (D) $3m - 3$

ANSWERS AND EXPLANATIONS

1. A

Plug in $a = 2$, $b = 6$, and $c = 4$

$$2(6 - 2) + \frac{6(4)}{2}$$

$$2(4) + \frac{24}{2}$$

$$8 + 12 = 20$$

2. C

Since we're told the value of d, we can plug it into the

equation $= 5$ to find the value of c. We are told that $d = 2$,

so $= 5$ can be rewritten as $\frac{c}{2} = 5$. Since $\frac{c}{2} = 5$, multiply

both sides of the equation by 2 to isolate c and determine

it's value. $\frac{c}{2} \times 2 = 5 \times 2$. $c = 10$. Now, we can plug the

values of c and d into the expression: $2(10) + 2 =$

$20 + 2 = 22$.

3. D

We are told that $y = 11$, so first we'll replace the y in the
equation with 11, and then we can solve for x.

$$6x - 7 = y$$
$$6x - 7 = 11$$

Now, we can add 7 to both sides:

$$6x - 7 + 7 = 11 + 7$$
$$6x = 18$$

Next, we divide both sides by 6:

$$\frac{6x}{6} = \frac{18}{6}$$
$$x = 3$$

4. B

Remember, $5yz$ means $5 \cdot y \cdot z$. First, we will replace x, y,
and z with the values given. Then, we will carry out the
indicated operations using the PEMDAS order of operations—Parentheses, Exponents, Multiplication and Division,
Addition and Subtraction.

$$x^2 - 5yz + y^2 = (\sqrt{3})^2 - 5 \cdot 2 \cdot \frac{1}{2} + 2^2$$

$$= 3 - 5 \cdot 2 \cdot \frac{1}{2} + 4$$

$$= 3 - 5 + 4$$

$$= -2 + 4$$

$$= 2$$

5. D

Subtract:

$$3d - 7 - 5 - (-2d)$$

Combine like terms:

$$3d - (-2d) - 7 - 5$$
$$5d - 12$$

Note that $3d$ minus $-2d$ equals $+5d$, because subtracting
a negative is the same as adding a positive.

6. C

We know that x is odd and y is even. Let's say that $x = 3$
and $y = 4$.

(A) $2x + y$; $2(3) + 4 = 6 + 4 = 10$; 10 is even, so this
isn't correct.

(B) $2(x + y)$; $2(3 + 4) = 2(7) = 14$; 14 is even.

(C) $x^2 + y^2$; $3^2 + 4^2 = 9 + 16 = 25$; 25 is odd, so (C) is
correct.

7. A

This problem looks harder than it really is. If $90 \div x = 9n$,
then $9n \cdot x = 90$, or $9nx = 90$ and
$nx = 10$.

8. **B**

Multiply through and solve for y by isolating it on one side of the equation:

$$4(y - 5) = 2(y + 3)$$
$$4y - 20 = 2y + 6$$
$$4y - 20 - 6 = 2y$$
$$4y - 26 - 4y = 2y - 4y$$
$$\frac{-26}{-2} = \frac{-2y}{-2}$$
$$13 = y$$

9. **D**

Isolate x on one side of the equation:

$$\frac{1}{2} + x = 6.5$$
$$\frac{1}{2} - \frac{1}{2} + x = 6.5 - \frac{1}{2}$$
$$x = 6$$

This problem is easy when you remember the decimal equivalent of $\frac{1}{2}$ is .5.

10. **D**

Multiply through and then find a in terms of m by isolating a on one side of the equation:

$$2(a + m) = 5m - 3 + a$$
$$2a + 2m = 5m - 3 + a$$
$$2a + 2m - a - 2m = 5m - 3 + a - 2m - a$$
$$a = 3m - 3$$

Chapter Nine: **Algebra Word Problems**

Understanding algebra word problems is probably one of the most useful math skills you can have. The great thing about word problems is that, unlike some other areas tested on the COOP or HSPT, they're not only important on test day, they're useful in everyday life. Whether you're figuring out how much a piece of clothing will cost you with sales tax, or calculating your earnings, algebraic word problems help you figure out unknown amounts.

Regardless of their usefulness in everyday life, we still need to approach word problems as we have every other question on the test—as an opportunity to win points. Like other topics we've covered so far, Kaplan has a systematic approach to help you do your best.

THE KAPLAN THREE-STEP METHOD FOR WORD PROBLEMS

Step 1: Decode the question.

Step 2: Set up an equation.

Step 3: Solve for the unknown.

Step 1—Decode the Question

In order to solve a question, any question, you first need to know what it is asking you to do. You need to translate the English into math.

When you see:	Think:
sum, plus, more than, added to, combined total	+
minus, less than, difference between, decreased by	−
is, was, equals, is equivalent to, is the same as, adds up to	=
times, product, multiplied by, of, twice, double, triple	×
divided by, over, quotient, per, out of, into	÷
what, how much, how many, a number	x, n, a, b, etc.

In the previous table you see how algebraic variables come into play solving word problems. The letter, or variable, stands for the unknown amount we need to find.

Let's translate one:

> In a class of 30 students, 12 have birthdays in the summer, 8 have birthdays in the fall, and 6 have birthdays in the winter. How many students have their birthday in the spring?

The *how many* in the phrase, clues us in to the fact that we can use an algebraic equation to help us solve this problem.

Here's another example:

> Amy is 18 months older than her brother Sean and three years older than her sister Katie. If the sum of their ages is 20 years, approximately how old is Amy?

What is the question looking for? Amy's age.

Step 2—Set Up an Equation

Now that we know what's being asked of us, we have to set up an equation to find Amy's age.

Let x = Amy's age. That means that Sean's age is $x - 18$ (If x = Sean's age, then Amy's age would be $x + 18$) and Katie's age is $x - 3(12)$.

The sum of all their ages is 20, so:

$$x + x - 18 + x - (3 \times 12) = 20 \times 12$$

Hopefully you noticed that this is a trick question. Ages are given in months and in years. We have to convert everything to the same measurement in order to solve correctly. That's why we multiplied the 3 and the 20 by 12, because there are 12 months in a year.

Step 3—Solve for the Unknown

We know what's being asked of us, we set up an equation, the only thing left to do is the math. Make sure you do your calculations in the right order and properly.

$$x + x - 18 + x - (3 \times 12) = 20 \times 12$$
$$3x - 54 = 240$$
$$3x - 54 + 54 = 240 + 54$$
$$3x = 294$$
$$x = 98$$

Amy is 98 years old? How could that be?

Remember, we were working with months. Don't forget to translate the number of months back into years when you are finished.

$\frac{98}{12} \approx 8$ years old.

WORD PROBLEMS WITH FORMULAS

Some of the more challenging word problems may involve translations with mathematic formulas. For example, you might see questions dealing with averages, rates, or areas of geometric figures. (More about geometry later.) Since the COOP and HSPT do not provide formulas for you, you have to know them going in. For example:

> If a truck driver travels at an average of speed of 50 miles per hour for 6.5 hours, how far will the driver travel?

To answer this question, you need to remember the distance formula.

$$(\text{Distance} = \text{Rate} \times \text{Time}) \text{ or } D = r \times t$$

Once you know the formula, you can plug in the numbers:

$D = 50 \times 6.5$

$D = 325$ miles

Here's another example:

> Thomas took an exam with 60 questions on it. If he finished all the questions in two hours, how many minutes on average did he spend answering each question?

$$\text{Average} = \frac{\text{sum of terms}}{\text{number of terms}}$$

$$x = \frac{(2 \text{ hours x 60 minutes})}{60 \text{ questions}} = \frac{180}{60} = 3 \text{ minutes per question}$$

You may have noticed there's a trick in this question as well. Do you see it? The time it took for Thomas to finish the exam is given in *hours*, but the question is asking how many *minutes* each question took. Be sure to read each the question carefully so you don't fall for tricks like this.

WORD PROBLEM STRATEGIES

Picking Numbers

Words problems are a great place to pick numbers. Here's the Kaplan Three-Step Method for Picking Numbers.

THE KAPLAN THREE-STEP METHOD FOR PICKING NUMBERS

Step 1:   Pick simple, easy to use numbers for each variable.

Step 2:   Solve the problem using the numbers you pick.

Step 3:   Plug your numbers into each answer choice. The choice that gives you the same numerical solution you arrived at in Step 2 is correct.

A few things to remember:

- You can pick numbers only when the answer choices contain variables.
- Pick easy numbers rather than realistic ones. Keep the numbers small and manageable, but avoid 0 and 1.
- Remember that you have to try all the answer choices. If more than one works, pick another set of numbers.
- Don't pick the same number for more than one variable.
- Always pick 100 for percent questions.

Backsolving

Here are some things you should know about backsolving:

- You can backsolve when the answer choices contain only numbers.
- Always start with answer choice with a middle value. For example, if your choices are 1, 7, 35, and 12, you should start with 12.
- If the middle value is not correct, you can usually eliminate 2 or more choices simply by determining whether the value must be higher or lower.

ALGEBRA WORD PROBLEMS PRACTICE SET

1. Andrew bought a camera on sale at a 20% discount. It was marked down from its regular price of $120. If there is an 8% sales tax on the sale price, how much did Andrew pay for the camera?

    (A) $24.00
    (B) $103.68
    (C) $127.68
    (D) $105.68

2. Edward has $400 more than Robert. After Edward spends $60 on groceries, he has 3 times more money than Robert. How much money does Robert have?

    (A) 140
    (B) 120
    (C) 90
    (D) 170

3. A dry cleaning store charges $3.50 to clean men's shirts, $4.00 to clean men's pants, and $5.00 to clean men's jackets. If Jose brings 10 items for cleaning and pays a total of $48, what is the average price he has paid per item?

    (A) $3.50
    (B) $2.22
    (C) $5.00
    (D) $4.80

4. Rene's dress shop is suffering from slow business. Rene decides to mark down all her merchandise. The next day, she sells 33 winter coats. Now, only 30% of the winter coats she had in stock remains. How many winter coats were in stock before the sale?

    (A) 990
    (B) 99
    (C) 110
    (D) 1,110

5. The price of a stock decreased by 20%. By what percent must the price increase to return to its original value?

    (A) 25%
    (B) 50%
    (C) 20%
    (D) 120%

6. Mrs. Bailer divides the amount of money she has between her 4 children. Mr. Bailer then adds $2 to the amount each one receives so that each child now has a total of $5.25. Which of the following equations shows this relationship?

    (A) $4x + 2 = 5.25$

    (B) $\dfrac{x}{4} + 2 = 5.25$

    (C) $4x = 5.25 + 2$

    (D) $4(x + 2) = 5.25$

7. A worker earns $16 for the first 40 hours she works each week, and one and a half times this much for every hour over 40 hours. If she earned $700 for one week's work, how many hours did she work?

    (A) 3.3
    (B) 3
    (C) 2.5
    (D) 4

8. Liza has 40 less than three times the number of books that Janice has. If B is equal to the number of books that Janice has, which of the following expressions shows the total number of books that Liza and Janice have together?

    (A) $4B - 40$
    (B) $3B - 40$
    (C) $4B$
    (D) $4B + 40$

9. The Tigers had 5 times as many losses as they had ties in a season. If the Tigers did not win any of their games, which could be the total number of games they played in the season?

   (A) 16
   (B) 5
   (C) 10
   (D) 12

10. Ruth has finished 3 chapters of an 8-chapter novel in just one evening of reading. If she reads an additional $\frac{1}{10}$ of the novel tomorrow night, what part of the novel will she have finished?

   (A) $\frac{4}{10}$
   (B) $\frac{1}{2}$
   (C) $\frac{19}{40}$
   (D) $\frac{36}{80}$

ANSWERS AND EXPLANATIONS

1. B

This problem has several steps. First, find out what the sale price of the camera was.

It was discounted 20% from $120.

$$x = .20 \times \$120 = \$24$$

Next, subtract the discount from the total amount to find out the sale price.

$$\$120 - \$24 = \$96$$

(You could also arrive at the sale price by using the formula part = percent × whole.)

Since the camera was discounted 20%, Andrew really paid 80% of the whole.

$$x = .80 \times \$120 = \$96$$

Now, multiply the sale price by the tax of .08 to find out how much tax Andrew paid.

$$\$96 \times .08 = \$7.68$$

Finally, add the tax to the sale price to find the total Andrew paid for his purchase.

$$\$96 + \$7.68 = \$103.68$$

2. D

Translate the words into math and solve for the unknown. Let x = the unknown amount of money Robert has.

"Edward has 400 more than Robert": $x + 400$
After he spends $60 on groceries": $x + 400 - 60$
"he has 3 times more than Robert": $x + 400 - 60 = 3x$

Now that you've set up an equation, solve for x.

$$x + 400 - 60 = 3x$$
$$x + 340 = 3x$$
$$340 = 2x$$
$$170 = x$$

3. D

$$\text{Average} = \frac{\text{total sum}}{\text{number of items}}$$

Let x equal the unknown average

$$x = \frac{48}{10} = \$4.80$$

Notice that the information about how much is charged per item is extraneous. You don't need it to solve the problem.

4. C

Let x = the unknown number of coats in stock before the sale. Use the formula part = percent × whole

$$33 \text{ winter coats} = .30x$$

$$\frac{33}{.3} = 110$$

5. A

The key here is that while the value of the stock increases and decreases by the same amount, it doesn't increase and decrease by the same percent since the "whole" is different once the stock has lost value.

If it seems confusing, this is a good question to pick numbers for. Let's pick $100 for the price of the stock. If the price decreases by 20%, the price is now $80. For the price to return to its original value of $100, it must be increased by $20. What percent of 80 equals $20?

$$x\%(80) = 20$$

$$x\% = \frac{20}{80}$$

$$x\% = \frac{1}{4}$$

$\frac{1}{4}$ is equal to 25%.

6. B

Translate this question using the verbal clues provided.

Let the amount of money Mrs. Bailer has $= x$

Mrs. Bailer divides the amount of money she has between her 4 children: $\frac{x}{4}$

Mr. Bailer then adds $2 to the amount each one receives:

$\frac{x}{4} + 2$ so that each child now has a total of 5.25:

$\frac{x}{4} + 2 = 5.25$

7. C

This question has several steps. First, determine the amount of overtime dollars the worker earned. Do this by figuring how much she earned over a 40-hour work week. If she makes $16 for 40 hours, she would earn $16 \times \$40 = \$640$. However, she earned $60 more than that. ($700 − $640 = $60.) How many extra hours did she work to earn that $60 if she earns time and a half for each hour over 40? If she earned $16 per hour, then she made $16 \times 1.5 = \$24$ per hour in overtime. Therefore, $\frac{\$60}{\$24} = 2.5$ hours worked overtime.

8. A

This is a simple translation problem. You're told that Janice has B books. Lisa has 40 less than 3 times the number of books Janice has, which you can translate as $L = 3B − 40$. The total number they have together equals $B + 3B − 40$ or $4B − 40$ which is choice (A).

9. D

Let $x =$ the number of ties the Tigers had. It lost 5 times as many games as it tied, $5x$. It had no wins so the total number of games played by the Tigers $= 5x + x = 6x$. So, the number of games the Tigers played must be a multiple of 6; the only choice that is a multiple of 6 is choice (D).

10. C

Let $x =$ the part of the novel Ruth has finished.

$$x = \frac{3}{8} + \frac{1}{10}$$

Change these two fractions to a common denominator of 80 and add them.

$$\frac{30}{80} + \frac{8}{80} = \frac{38}{80}$$

Reduce the fraction to $\frac{19}{40}$

Chapter Ten: **Geometry**

You will definitely see some basic geometry on the COOP or HSPT test. You can count on seeing questions that test your knowledge of lines and angles, triangles, and circles. You'll also see a little coordinate geometry. You might also see geometry in word problems that don't include diagrams.

If you're concerned about your geometry skills, take some time to review this chapter, spending more time with the subjects that are less familiar to you. Make sure you do all of the problems in the practice set, and that you read and understand the answer explanations even for questions you answer correctly.

It's important to know that unless it's specified, diagrams that accompany geometry questions are NOT drawn to scale. Keep this in mind so that you don't just eyeball the diagram and come to a conclusion. In other words, don't judge the answer just by looking at the size of the diagram.

LINES AND ANGLES

There are 180 degrees in a straight line.

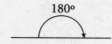

Line Segments

Some of the most basic geometry problems deal with line segments. A **line segment** is a piece of a line, and it has an exact measurable length. A question might give you a segment divided into several pieces, provide the measurements of some of these pieces, and ask you for the measurement of the remaining piece.

If $PR = 12$ and $QR = 4$, $PQ =$

$PQ = PR - QR$
$PQQ = 12 - 4$
$PQ = 8$

KAPLAN TIP

Don't assume figures or diagrams are drawn to scale.

The point exactly in the middle of a line segment, halfway between the endpoints, is called the midpoint of the line segment. To bisect means to cut in half, so the **midpoint** of a line segment bisects that line segment.

M is the midpoint of AB, so $AM = MB$.

ANGLES

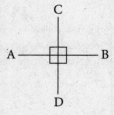

A **right angle** measures 90 degrees and is usually indicated in a diagram by a little box. The figure above is a right angle. Lines that intersect to form right angles are said to be **perpendicular.**

In the figure above, line AB and line CD are perpendicular.

Angles that form a straight line add up to 180 degrees. In the figure above, $a + b = 180°$.

The interior angle b is less than 90 degrees; it is an **acute angle**. The exterior angle, angle a is greater than 90 degrees. Angles greater than 90 degrees are called **obtuse**.

right angle = 90 degrees

acute angle < 90 degrees

obtuse angle > 90 degrees

When two lines intersect, adjacent angles are **supplementary**, meaning they add up to 180 degrees. In the figure above $a + b = 180°$.

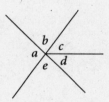

Angles around a point add up to 360 degrees. In the figure above $a + b + c + d + e = 360°$.

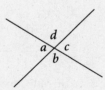

When lines intersect, angles across the vertex (the middle point) from each other are called vertical angles and are equal to each other. Above, $a = c$ and $b = d$.

PARALLEL LINES

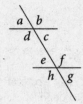

When parallel lines are crossed by a transversal:

- Corresponding angles are equal (for example $a = e$, $d = h$)
- Alternate interior angles are equal ($d = f$)
- Same side interior angles are supplementary ($c + f = 180$)
- All four acute angles are equal, as are all four obtuse angles (a, c, e, g are equal, b, d, f, h are equal)

TRIANGLES

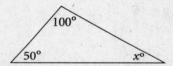

The three interior angles of any triangle add up to 180 degrees. In the figure above $x + 50° + 100° = 180°$, so $x = 30°$

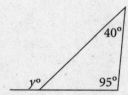
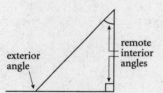

An exterior angle of a triangle is equal to the sum of the remote interior angles. In this figure, the exterior angle labeled y is equal to the sum of the remote interior angels $y = 40° + 95° = 135°$.

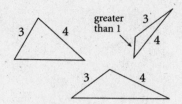

The length of one side of a triangle must be **greater than the positive difference** and **less than the sum** of the lengths of the other two sides. For example, if it is given that the length of one side is 3 and the length of another side is 4, then the length of the third side must be greater than $4 - 3 = 1$ and less than $4 + 3 = 7$.

Triangles—Area and Perimeter

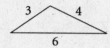

The **perimeter** of a triangle is the sum of the lengths of its sides. The perimeter of the triangle in the figure above is $3 + 4 + 6 = 13$.

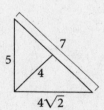

Area of triangle $= \frac{1}{2}$(base)(height) or $A = \frac{1}{2}bh$.

The height is the perpendicular distance between the side that is chosen as the base and the opposite vertex. In this triangle, 4 is the height when 7 is chosen as the base.

Area $= \frac{1}{2}bh = \frac{1}{2}(7)4 = 14$

Similar Triangles

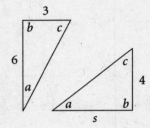

Similar triangles have the same shape: **corresponding angles are equal** and **corresponding sides are proportional**. The triangles above are similar because they have the same angles. The 3 corresponds (or relates to) the 4 and the 6 corresponds to the unknown *s*. Because the triangles are similar, therefore, you can set up a ratio to solve for *s*.

$$\frac{3}{4} = \frac{6}{s}$$
$$3s = 24$$
$$s = 8$$

Special Triangles

Isosceles Triangles

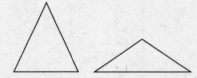

An isosceles triangle is a triangle that has **two equal sides**. Not only are two sides equal, but the angles opposite the equal sides, called base angles, are also equal to one another.

So, if you were asked to determine angle *a* in the isosceles triangle above, you could set up an equation. Since the sum of the degrees in a triangle is 180, and you are given 1 angle of 40 degrees: $2a = 180 - 40$, $2a = 140$, $\frac{2a}{2} = \frac{140}{2}$, $a = 70°$.

Equilateral Triangles

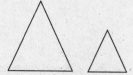

Equilateral triangles are triangles in which **all three sides are equal**. Since the sides are equal, all the angles are also equal. If all three angles are equal, and the sum of the angles in a triangle = 180, how much does each angle in an equilateral triangle equal?

$$\frac{180}{3} = 60.$$

60 degrees!

Right Triangles

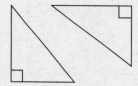

A right triangle is a triangle with a right angle. (Remember, a right angle equals 90 degrees.) Every right triangle has exactly two acute angles. The sides opposite the acute angles are called the legs. The side opposite the right angle is called the hypotenuse. Since it is opposite the largest angle, the hypotenuse is the longest side of a right triangle.

THE PYTHAGOREAN THEOREM

The Pythagorean theorem states the following.

$$leg^2 + leg^2 = (hypotenuse)^2$$

It is also sometimes written as

$$a^2 + b^2 = c^2$$

If one leg is 2 and the other leg is 3, then:

$$2^2 + 3^2 = c^2$$

Here is where your knowledge of squares and square roots will really come in handy.

QUADRILATERALS

A quadrilateral has 4 sides. The perimeter of a quadrilateral (or any polygon) is the sum of the lengths of its sides.

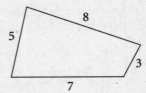

The perimeter of the quadrilateral in the figure above is: 5 + 8 + 3 + 7 = 23

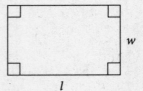

A **rectangle** is a parallelogram containing four right angles. Opposite sides are equal. The formula for the area of a rectangle is: Area = (length)(width), which is sometimes abbreviated as $A = lw$. In the diagram above, l = length and w = width, so area = lw and perimeter = $2(l + w)$

A **square** is a rectangle with four equal sides. The formula for the area of a square is: Area = (side)^2. Notice this can also be written as $A = lw$. However, since $l = w$ in a square, you can use the notation s^2.

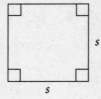

In the diagram above, s = length of a side, so area = s^2 and perimeter = $4s$.

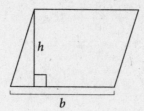

A parallelogram is a quadrilateral with two sets of parallel sides. Opposite sides are equal, as are opposite angles. The formula for the area of a parallelogram is:

$$\text{Area} = (\text{base})(\text{height}) \text{ or } A = bh$$

In the diagram above, h = height and b = base, so you can use the formula: $A = bh$.

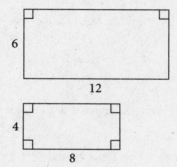

If two rectangles (or squares, since squares are special rectangles) are similar, then the corresponding angles are equal (90 degrees) and corresponding sides are in proportion. In the figures above, the two rectangles are similar because all the angles are right angles, and each side of the larger rectangle is $1\frac{1}{2}$ times the corresponding side of the smaller.

CIRCLES

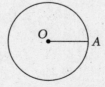

A **circle** is a figure in which each point is an equal distance from its center. In the diagram, O is the center of the circle.

The **radius** (r) of a circle is the direct distance from its center to any point on the circle. All radii of one circle have equal lengths. In the figure above, OA is the radius of circle O.

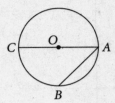

A **chord** is a line segment that connects any two points on a circle. Segments *AB* and *AC* are both chords. The largest chord that may be drawn in a circle is the diameter of that circle.

The **diameter** (*d*) of a circle is a chord that passes through the circle's center. All diameters are the same length and are equal to twice the radius. In the figure above, *AC* is a diameter of circle *O*.

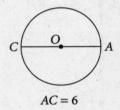

$$AC = 6$$

A **circumference** of a circle is the distance around it. It is equal to πd, or $2\pi r$. In this example
Circumference $= \pi d = 6\pi$

The **area** of a circle equals π times the square of the radius, or πr^2. In this example, since *AC* is the diameter, $r = \dfrac{6}{2} = 3$ and area $= \pi r^2 = \pi(3)^2 = 9\pi$.

COORDINATE GEOMETRY

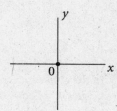

Coordinate geometry has to do with plotting points on a graph. The diagram above represents the coordinate axes—the perpendicular number lines in the coordinate plane. The horizontal line is called the x-axis. The vertical line is called the y-axis. In a coordinate plane, the point O at which the two axes intersect is called the **origin**, or (0, 0).

The pair of numbers, written inside parenthesis, specifies the location of a point in the coordinate plane. These are called coordinates. The first number is the x-coordinate, and the second number is the y-coordinate. The origin is the zero point of both axes, with coordinates (0, 0)

Starting at the origin:

*   To the right: x is positive
*   To the left: x is negative
*   Up: y is positive
*   Down: y is negative
*   The two axes divide the coordinate plane into 4 quadrants. When you know what quadrant a point lies in, you know the signs of its coordinates. A point in the upper left quadrant, for example, has a negative x-coordinate and a positive y-coordinate.

$$\begin{array}{c|c}
(-,+) \quad \text{II} & \text{I} \quad (+,+) \\
\hline
(-,-) \quad \text{III} & \text{IV} \quad (+,-)
\end{array}$$

If you were asked the coordinates of a given point, you would start at the origin, count the number of units given to the right or left on the x-axis, and then do the same up or down on the y-axis.

If you had to plot given points you would start at the origin, count the number of units given on the x-axis, and then on the y-axis. To plot (2, −3) for example, you would count 2 units to the right along the x-axis, then three units down along the y-axis.

GEOMETRY PRACTICE SET

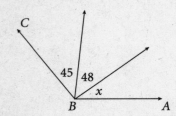

1. If the measure of angle *ABC* is 145 degrees, what is the value of *x*?

    (A) 39

    (B) 45

    (C) 52

    (D) 62

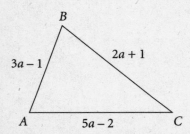

2. If the perimeter of triangle *ABC* is 28 meters, what is the number of meters in the length of *AC*?

    (A) 28

    (B) 13

    (C) 10

    (D) 12

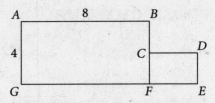

3. In the above diagram, *ABFG* and *CDEF* are rectangles, *C* bisects *BF*, and *EF* has a length of 2 cm. What is the area, in cm^2, of the entire figure?

    (A) 36

    (B) 32

    (C) 16

    (D) 72

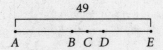

4. In the figure above, *AB* is twice the length of *BC*, *BC* = *CD*, and *DE* is three times the length of *CD*. If *AE* = 49 cm, what is the length, in cm, of *BD*?

    (A) 14

    (B) 20

    (C) 22

    (D) 29

5. What is the radius of a circle whose circumference is 18π in?

    (A) 3 in

    (B) 6 in

    (C) 18 in

    (D) 9 in

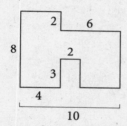

6. A square and a circle are drawn as shown above. The area of the square is 64 in². What is the area of the shaded region?

    (A) 16π in²

    (B) 8π in²

    (C) 4π in²

    (D) 32π in²

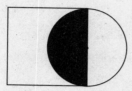

7. What is the area of the polygon above, in square units, if each corner of the polygon is a right angle?

    (A) 40

    (B) 62

    (C) 68

    (D) 74

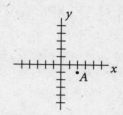

8. What are the coordinates of point A on the graph above?

    (A) (−1, 2)

    (B) (2, −1)

    (C) (−2, −1)

    (D) (−2, 1)

9. A bicycle rider travels 8 miles due north, then 6 miles due east. How many miles is she from her starting point?

    (A) 16

    (B) 12

    (C) 10

    (D) 14

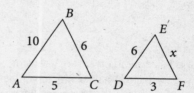

10. If triangle ABC is similar to triangle DEF, then EF =

    (A) 6

    (B) 3.6

    (C) 4.1

    (D) 5

ANSWERS AND EXPLANATIONS

1. C

This is a simple arithmetic problem if m∠ABD = 145 degrees, the $x = 145 - (48 + 45)$

$x = 145 - 93 = 52$ degrees.

2. B

The perimeter of triangle ABC is 28, so $AB + BC + AC = 28$. Plug in the algebraic expression given for the length of each side in meters:

$$(3a - 1) + (2a + 1) + (5a - 2) = 28$$
$$10a - 2 = 28$$
$$10a = 30$$
$$a = 3$$

The length of AC is represented by the expression $5a - 2$, so $AC = 5(3) - 2 = 13$.

3. A

To find the area of the entire figure, determine the area of each rectangle and add these values together. ABFG has an area of $8 \times 4 = 32$ square units.

CDEF has a length of 2, and, since C bisects BF which = 4, CDEF also has a width of 2. In other words, it is a square. If you eyeballed the diagram, rather than doing the math, you probably would not have arrived at the correct value. Remember, diagrams are not drawn to scale. The area of CDEF then is $2^2 = 4$ square cm.

The area of the entire figure = $32 + 4 = 36$ square cm.

4. A

Remember, don't rely on the diagrams, they are not drawn to scale. To solve this problem, set up an algebraic equation.

Let $BC = x$. AB is twice the length of BC, so it can be represented by $2x$. $BC = CD$, so $CD = x$. DE is three times the length of CD, or $3x$. Since $AE = 49$, $2x + x + x + 3x = 49$, $7x = 49$ and $x = 7$. BD is composed of segments BC and CD, so its length is $7 + 7 = 14$ units.

5. D

Circumference of a circle = $2\pi r$, where r is the radius of the circle. So, a circle with a circumference of 18π has a radius of $\frac{18\pi}{2\pi} = 9$ in.

6. B

The shaded region represents half the area of the circle. Find the length of the radius to determine this area. Notice that the diameter of the circle is equal to a side of the square. Since the area of the square is 64 in², it has a side length of 8 in. So, the diameter of the circle is 8, and its radius is 4. The area of a circle is πr^2, where r is the radius, so the area of this circle is $\pi(4)^2 = 16\pi$ in². This isn't the answer though; the shaded region is only half the circle, so its area is 8π in².

7. B

Think of the figure as a rectangle with two rectangular bites taken out of it. Sketch in lines to make one large rectangle as shown below.

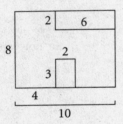

The area of a rectangle is length times width. If we call the length of the large rectangle 10, then its width is 8, so its area is $10 \times 8 = 80$ square units. The rectangle missing from the top right corner has dimensions of 6 and 2, so its area is $6 \times 2 = 12$ square units. The rectangle missing from the bottom has dimensions of 2 and 3, so its area is $2 \times 3 = 6$ square units. To find the area of the polygon, subtract the areas of the two missing shapes from the area of the large rectangle: $80 - (12 + 6) = 80 - 18 = 62$ square units, choice (B).

8. B

When giving coordinates, give the x-coordinate first, and then the y-coordinate second. Point A lies at 2 on the x-axis and −1 on the y-axis. Therefore, $(2, -1)$ is correct.

KAPLAN
Test Prep and Admissions

9. **C**

This is a geometry word problem. If you draw the path with the directions provided, you'll see a right triangle. The question is asking you how many miles the rider is from her starting point, or the hypotenuse of the triangle. Use the formula $leg^2 + leg^2 = hypotenuse^2$.

The legs are 8 and 6, so $8^2 + 6^2 = 64 + 36 = 100 =$ (hypotenuse)^2. $\sqrt{100} = 10$. The rider is 10 miles from her starting point.

10. **B**

Since the triangles are similar, set up a proportion to solve for the unknown side.

$$\frac{10}{6} = \frac{6}{x}$$

$$10x = 36$$

$$x = \frac{36}{10} = 3.6$$

Chapter Eleven: **Tables, Charts, Graphs, and Maps**

You are most likely to see some type of table, chart, graph, or map on the COOP or HSPT. You will have to gather information from these graphics and use them to solve accompanying questions.

Keep in mind that no matter which type of graphic representation you see, labels or keys must be given to identify the material. By carefully reading the labels, we can understand what information is contained and in what manner it is organized. Remember, a table, chart, or graph is a visual way of organizing information.

In this chapter, we will review various types of tables, charts, and graphs and then give you a systematic approach to answering the questions that are associated with them. Even if you feel familiar with tables, charts, or other graphic representations, you should read the material below. Be sure to do the practice set at the end of the chapter.

LINE GRAPHS

A line graph presents information by plotting points on an *x*- and *y*-axes, then connecting them with a line. Because you can plot more than one line, a line graph is widely used to communicate relationships. Also, since the lines clearly indicate rising or decreasing trends, a line graph is a great way to show growth or decline trends.

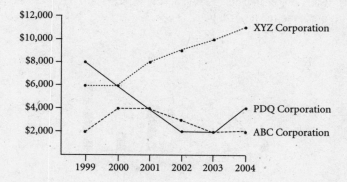

Notice that the previous graph is not titled. Charts, tables, and graphs on the COOP or HSPT may not have titles. However, we can use the information found on the *x*- and *y*-axes to decode or make sense of the graph. The *x*-axis is labeled 1999–2004. Therefore, each marking represents one year from 1999 to 2004. The *y*-axis is marked in units of increasing dollar value. Each unit going up the *y*-axis increases $2,000 dollars. The lines themselves are labeled ABC Corporation, PDQ Corporation, and XYZ Corporation. Therefore, we can see the dollar amount of each company at a particular point in time during the period of 1999–2004. A line connects these points to show an upward, or downward trend.

Though the individual charts may not be titled on the COOP or HSPT, the accompanying question will help you identify what the material is. Here is a sample question that might accompany a chart like the one above.

BAR GRAPHS

A bar graph is also called a histogram or histograph. In it, numerical values are shown in bars of varying length. This type of graph is also a good, clear way to show comparisons.

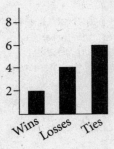

The bar graph above labels the various bars on the *x*-axis "win," "loss" or "tie." The *y*-axis shows units of 2. This bar graph represents the numerical value of a team's wins, losses, and ties. See how far each vertical bar extends on the *y*-axis. The bar representing wins is at the 2 unit; the team has 2 wins. The bar representing losses is at 4 units; the team has 4 losses. The bar representing ties is at 6 units; the team has 6 ties.

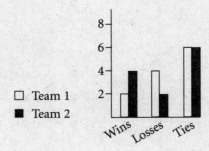

A bar graph has the added benefit of illustrating multiple comparisons in a way that is still visually clear. The previous bar graph includes a second set of bars. These bars, the shaded bars, represent the performance of another team. By placing the two sets of bars side by side, we can easily see that Team 2 won more games than Team 1, it lost fewer, and it tied the same number of games.

A bar graph can be vertical or horizontal. Decode it the same way you would a line graph, by reading the labels on the *x*- and *y*-axes which tell what the bars represent and the value of the units given.

PICTOGRAPHS

A pictograph uses simple drawings to depict quantities.

Each truck = 1,000 vehicles

Pictographs can make a point vividly, but they work best when there is a large number of items being shown. The key at the bottom lets us know that each truck represents 1,000 vehicles. Imagine if we really wanted to draw all 1,000 of them!

TABLES

Tables compare information in rows and columns. Because information appears side by side, tables are a good way to present detailed information to compare.

	Mon	Tues	Wed	Thurs	Fri
New York	70°	72°	65°	71°	80°
Boston	65°	70°	60°	63°	72°
L.A.	81°	82°	85°	80°	80°
Miami	80°	85°	86°	81°	84°

Labels in the far left column and on the top row will identify the information in the table. The left column in the table above, for example, contains the names of cities. The top row is labeled with days of the week. Let's say you were looking for the temperature in New York on Thursday. You would find the row labeled New York and the column labeled Thursday. The box that aligns with these two axes gives you the temperature in New York on Thursday, 71 degrees.

Tables may also use pictures rather than numbers. Either way, when you are looking for information in a table, find the row corresponding to the information you are looking for. Then, read across and find the vertical column that corresponds to the second detail you are looking for. The box at which these details meet will give you your data.

PIE CHARTS

A pie chart is a circle cut into parts. You can think of it as showing the pieces of a pie or how the pie is divided. Thus, a pie chart is a good chart to use when showing the distribution of a whole, or into which parts a whole is divided. On a pie chart, the portions or pieces of the pie will be labeled. The labels will explain what the different sections represent and the percentage of the whole each section comprises.

NOTE: The whole pie always equals 100%. That does not mean that the numbers shown in a pie chart will equal 100. However, you should think of a pie chart as 100% with each section representing a part (percentage) of the whole.

The pie chart above shows the various after school activities of students in a class. The whole pie represents the whole class. As the labels indicate, 40% of the students participate in sports, 40% participate in the drama club, and 20% participate in the band.

While pie charts are a great way to show how a whole is divided, they can be difficult to use if the pie is divided into sections that are too small.

The following pie chart shows an example of when NOT to use a pie chart. It is meant to show the after-school activities of an entire class, but breaking the sections down into such small pieces makes the chart difficult to use.

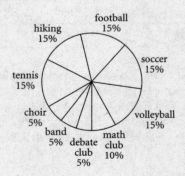

VENN DIAGRAMS

A Venn diagram is like a pie chart in that it uses circles to represent groups. Unlike a pie chart however, a Venn diagram contains more than one intersecting circle. The place at which the circles intersect shows elements or characteristics that the various wholes have in common.

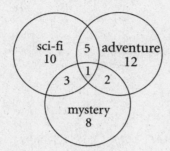

The Venn diagram above shows how many students in a class at Rosewood High read various types of novels. Notice that the circles are labeled according to each type. The number 10 indicates that 10 students read only science fiction novels. Twelve students make up the whole group of students that read only adventure novels. Eight students make up the whole group of students who read only mysteries. The fact that the circles intersect indicates that some students read more than one type of novel. Notice where the science fiction and adventure circles intersect. The number 5 in this section indicates that 5 students read both science fiction and adventure novels. The number 3 where the mystery and science fiction circles intersect indicates that three students read both these types of novels.

MAPS

Don't worry, no one is going to ask you for complicated directions to the corner store. Reading maps on the COOP or HSPT will be relatively simple. Actually, maps may more likely resemble a coordinate graph than a road map. We will review coordinates first, and then provide some additional map basics just in case.

Coordinates

Coordinates are given according to an *x*- and *y*-axes. The *x*-axis runs horizontally (across) and the *y*-axis runs vertically (up and down). The point where the axes meet is called the origin. Going right along the *x*-axis from the point of origin, numbers are positive and increase incrementally. Going left along the *x*-axis from the point of origin, numbers are negative and increase incrementally. Going up along the *y*-axis from the point of origin, numbers are positive. Going down along the *y*-axis numbers are negative. Remember, when giving coordinates, state the *x*-axis coordinate first, and the *y*-axis coordinate second.

Reading Directions

Directions on a map are always as follows:

north

northwest   northeast

west   east

southwest   southeast

south

HOW TO APPROACH DIAGRAM QUESTIONS

The tables, charts, and graphs you have just reviewed are valuable ways to organize information. Reading these will help you in everyday life. But, remember we have a goal here—preparing for the COOP or HSPT. So, while you make take your time examining a table, chart, graph, or map you encounter in everyday life, it's important to approach these materials a little differently on test day. You have to stay on track and approach these questions systematically to win the maximum number of points. The Kaplan Three-Step Method will help you do that.

THE KAPLAN THREE-STEP METHOD FOR DIAGRAM QUESTIONS

Step 1. Read the question.

Step 2. Decode the diagram.

Step 3. Find the answer.

Step 1—Read the Question

It may seem obvious, but the point here is not to spend any time examining the chart, graph, or table until you read the question. Think of the information in a diagram like detail questions on the reading comprehension section. You are given many details, but you don't know which ones the questions will ask about. It doesn't make sense to spend too much time reviewing all the details until you know what the questions are asking.

For example:

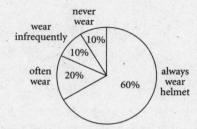

> The diagram above shows the safety habits of a group of 60 skateboarders. How many of the group always wear their helmets?

An essential element of reading the question includes reading exactly what the diagram illustrates. In the example above, we are told that the pie chart shows the **safety habits** of a group of **60 skateboarders**. The size of the group is important information you may chose to circle or underline.

Naturally, the other important part of reading the question is determining what the question is asking you. This question is asking how many of the group (the 60 total) always wear their helmets.

Step 2—Decode the Diagram

Now that you have read the question and know what you are looking for, refer to the diagram. Use the labels provided to decode it, or figure out what exactly it is illustrating.

The pie chart is divided into sections, showing parts of a whole. Each section is labeled with a percent amount and titled *always wear helmet, often wear, wear infrequently, never wear.* Thus, the sections represent how often the group of 60 skateboarders wears their helmets.

Step 3—Find the Answer

Now that we know what we are looking for and what the diagram means, we can look for our answer within the diagram and do any calculations necessary. Remember we want to know how many of the group always wear their helmets. The diagram shows a section labeled 60% as always wearing their helmets. We need a number, so we must convert the 60% into a number of skateboarders. 60% of 60 = .60 x 60 = 36

Once we have determined the answer, look for an answer choice that matches.

Let's use The Kaplan Three-Step Method to answer the question below.

New York State   Florida

1 raindrop = 2 inches of rain

The diagram above shows the average annual rainfall of two states. What is the annual average rainfall in Florida?

Step 1—Read the Question

What is the question asking you? What is the annual average rainfall in Florida?

Step 2—Decode the Diagram

The information before the question helps decode the diagram. It explains that the diagram represents the average annual rainfall of two states. The key at the bottom of the diagram is also essential. It tells us that 1 raindrop represents 2 inches of rainfall. If you don't read the key, you won't arrive at the correct answer.

Step 3—Find the Answer

The question is asking the annual average rainfall in Florida. There are 6 rain drops in the picture and we are told that each one represents 2 inches of rain. $6 \times 2 = 12$, so, an average of 12 inches of rain fell in Florida.

Now that we have an answer, we can look for the answer choice that matches.

THE BEST WAY TO SHOW INFORMATION

Some questions on the COOP or HSPT may ask you which is the best way to present information. Remember that certain types of tables, graphs, and charts lend themselves best to certain kinds of information.

Line Graphs: good for showing upward or downward trends over time

Bar Graphs: good for showing comparisons

Pie Charts: good for showing how a whole is divided into various parts

Venn Diagrams: good for showing how information intersects, or what is in common

Pictographs: good for large amounts, graphically showing large differences

Coordinate Graphs and Maps: good for showing location

Tables: good for large amounts of data and for comparison

Despite the pros and cons of various diagrams, the best way to present information is always the simplest way! It is also the clearest. When evaluating various diagrams and deciding which one best presents certain information, be sure to look at the labels provided. A good diagram will be clearly labeled to help the reader decode the information it provides.

Look at the example below.

Which of the following diagrams is the best way to compare various types of tables, charts, and graphs?

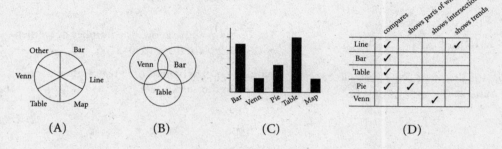

	compares	shows parts of whole	shows intersection	shows trends
Line	✓			✓
Bar	✓			
Table	✓			
Pie	✓	✓		
Venn			✓	

(A)   (B)   (C)   (D)

Choice (A), though it divides the pie into parts, doesn't *compare* the various types of diagrams. It doesn't answer the question!

Choice (B) shows various types of diagrams intersecting, but again, it doesn't do anything to *compare* them.

Though bar graphs are a good way to illustrate comparisons, the bar graph in answer choice (C) is not a good one since the *y*-axis contains no information to help us decode the chart. Why are some bars higher than others? What value does the *y*-axis represent? We don't know. Therefore, it's not a good chart.

Choice (D) clearly labels the rows and columns of the table. The rows represent the various types of diagrams and the columns represent characteristics of these diagrams. The checkmarks show in which area each diagram is successful. This is the best way to compare the various diagrams because it is clearest. Choice (D) is the correct answer.

TABLES, CHARTS, GRAPHS, AND MAPS PRACTICE SET

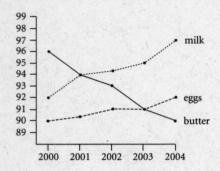

1. The graph above shows the price of milk and eggs between 2000–2004. What is the price of eggs in 2002?

    (A) 91 cents

    (B) 92 cents

    (C) 90 cents

    (D) 93 cents

2. What is the difference between the price of milk in 2004 and the price of milk in 2000?

    (A) 2 cents

    (B) 4 cents

    (C) 5 cents

    (D) 6 cents

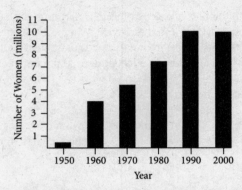

3. The diagram above shows the number of women in the workplace from 1950–2000.

    Which year experienced the greatest increase of women in the workplace?

    (A) 1960

    (B) 1950

    (C) 2000

    (D) 2010

Answer question 4 based on the table below.

Price of Different Tickets on Different Airlines

	First Class	Business Class	Economy Class
Happy Air	$301	$252	$108
Jet Stream Airways	$309	$250	$99
Lucky Travel Airline	$357	$312	$89

4. How much does a business class ticket cost on Lucky Travel Airline?

    (A) $357

    (B) $312

    (C) $99

    (D) $108

5. Examine the graph and find the best answer.

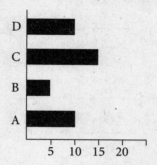

(A) D plus A are greater than C plus B

(B) A plus B equals C

(C) A and D are less than C and A

(D) B is greater than A

6. The pie chart below shows the lunch orders of a group of 150 junior high school students. How many students ordered lasagna?

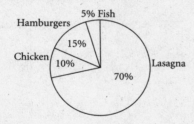

(A) 70

(B) 105

(C) 100

(D) 95

Answer question 7 based on the diagram below. The Venn diagram shows three categories involving the children of Garden Village.

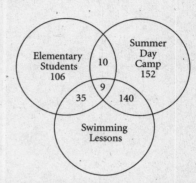

7. According to the diagram, how many children are attending summer day camp only?

(A) 9

(B) 10

(C) 140

(D) 152

8. The diagram below represents students who take the bus to school in 3 school districts.

Each bus = 54 students

How many students take the bus in Grandville?

(A) 54

(B) 216

(C) 200

(D) 108

9. At what coordinates is the location of the row-boat?

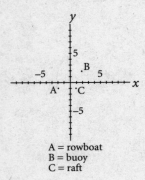

A = rowboat
B = buoy
C = raft

(A) (−2, −1)

(B) (2, 1)

(C) (−1, 2)

(D) (2, −1)

10. The map below shows a seating arrangement.

	A	B	C
1	Inessa	Tom	Geoff
2	Susan	Victoria	Don
3	Tori	Aarthi	Evan

Where is Tori seated?

(A) 1C

(B) 2B

(C) 2A

(D) 3A

ANSWERS AND EXPLANATIONS

1. A

Locate the line that shows the price of eggs, then find 2002 on the *x*-axis. Then, locate the coordinate on the *y*-axis, the price value where the line representing eggs is in 2002. It falls at 91 cents.

2. D

Locate the price of milk in 2000 on the *y*-axis. It is 92 cents. Then locate the price of milk in 2004. It is at 97 cents on the *y*-axis. The price of milk has gone up 5 cents.

3. A

The height at which the vertical bars reach on the *y*-axis represent the number of women in the workplace at a given year in millions. In order to find the year at which there was the greatest increase of women in the workplace, look for the greatest leap between the previous bar and the next. The bar at 1950 is at less than 1 million, while the bar at 1960 shows a dramatic rise to the 4 million mark. Therefore, the year 1960 experienced the greatest increase of women in the workplace. Choice (A) is the correct answer.

4. B

Find the row labeled "Lucky Travel Airline." Read across until you reach the corresponding column labeled business class. The box that aligns with these two labels will give you the price of a business class ticket on Lucky Airlines. It is $312, choice (B).

5. B

Don't be put off by the fact that this bar graph is arranged horizontally. Read it as you would any other bar graph, identifying the values at which each bar falls. Bar A is at the 10 mark. Bar B is at the 5 mark. Bar C is at the 15 mark, and bar D is at the 10 mark. Add the various combinations in the answer choices until you arrive at the correct answer. A + B = C; 10 + 5 = 15.

6. B

First, find the percent of students in the pie chart who ordered lasagna: 70%. Since there are 150 students in the whole group, 70% of 150 ordered lasagna; .7 x 150 = 105.

7. D

Read the labels on the various circles that make up the Venn diagram. The one to the right is labeled Summer Day Camp. That entire circle comprises all the children who are attending summer day camp. The number in the portion of the circle that does not intersect with any other is 152. That is the number of children who are attending summer day camp only.

8. B

There are 4 buses under the label Grandville. The key indicates that each bus represents 54 students; 54 × 4 students take the bus to Grandville = 216 students.

9. A

The key indicates that point A represents the row boat. Locate point A on the graph, then note its coordinates, giving the *x*-coordinate first, and the *y*-coordinate second. Point A, the rowboat, is at (−2, −1) on the graph.

10. D

Locate the name Tori on the chart. Note which row and column it falls under. It is in column A, row 3. Thus, answer choice (D) is the correct answer.

Chapter Twelve: **Quantitative Reasoning**

The Quantitative Reasoning test on the COOP is different than mathematics sections you will see on other tests. Because it's intended to test your reasoning ability, rather than learned math skills, it has several special question types.

Though they might seem strange at first, the more you practice, the more comfortable you'll feel with these questions. We'll review each of them here and give you some techniques for answering these question types.

Since the COOP changes from year to year, the breakdown may be slightly different in the year that you take the exam. At the time of printing, the section breaks down as follows:

The 20 quantitative reasoning questions are made up of three question types:
- Number Relationships—questions 1–6
- Visual Problems— questions 7–13
- Symbol Relationships— questions 14–20

Because you have to switch gears rapidly in the time you are allotted for this section, it is important to have a clear grasp on what each of the various question types requires you to do.

NUMBER RELATIONSHIPS

The instructions for number relationship questions instruct you to find the relationship between the two numbers in an expression. You'll see three expressions, in a vertical column. An arrow points from a number on the left to a blank box, then to a number on the right. The final set in the column has a blank in the right hand column. You have to figure out what number should go where the blank is.

$$3 \rightarrow \boxed{} \rightarrow 7$$

$$5 \rightarrow \boxed{} \rightarrow 9$$

$$1 \rightarrow \boxed{} \rightarrow \underline{}$$

5	6	10	4
(A)	(B)	(C)	(D)

To find the correct answer, look at each expression and think about what operation was performed on the number on the left to arrive at the number on the right.

$$3 \; + \; 4 \; = \; 7$$

$$5 \; + \; 4 \; = \; 9$$

The pattern is +4. Therefore, to find the missing number where the blank is, add 4 to 1; $1 + 4 = 5$. The correct answer is choice (A), 5

KAPLAN TIP

Be sure to work ACROSS from left to right, not up and down when you are looking for the pattern.

Because it is possible for more than one relationship or operation to fit in the missing box, always be sure to test your assumption on all the examples given.

Look at this example:

$$2 \rightarrow \boxed{} \rightarrow 4$$

$$3 \rightarrow \boxed{} \rightarrow 6$$

$$5 \rightarrow \boxed{} \rightarrow \underline{}$$

Look at the first row of numbers: 2 and 4. The operation being performed could be +2 or ×2. Note this, then look at the next row of numbers: 3 and 6; $3 \times 2 = 6$. The pattern is ×2, rather than +2. The number that belongs in the blank is 5×2, or 10.

When you approach number relationship questions, work through all the examples and predict the answer before reading the answer choices. This will help keep you from falling for trick answers or becoming confused.

VISUAL PROBLEMS

These problems ask you to look at a shaded shape and figure out how much of the whole is shaded. Basically, they are asking you to express a fraction of a whole. The key to doing well on this question type is taking the time to actually count the sections that make up the whole. Also, you should count the shaded sections rather than guess how much is shaded simply by eyeing the diagram.

Look at this problem:

(A) $\dfrac{2}{6}$

(B) $\dfrac{1}{2}$

(C) $\dfrac{1}{4}$

(D) 2

In this drawing, the rectangle is sectioned into 8 equal squares. Two are shaded and 6 are not. In other words 2 out of 8 are shaded. This can be expressed as a fraction thus: $\dfrac{2}{8}$. Reduced, $\dfrac{2}{8} =$ $\dfrac{1}{4}$. The correct answer is $\dfrac{1}{4}$, or choice (C).

Notice how the incorrect answers assume that you have made a mistake in counting the total number of sections, or the number of sections that are shaded. Choice (A) puts the shaded portion, 2, over the amount that are not shaded, 6, rather than the whole, which is 8.

You could rule out choice (B) since you can easily see that less than $\dfrac{1}{2}$ of the whole is shaded.

Choice (D) is incorrect because it fails to put the number of shaded squares as a numerator above the number of sections in the whole.

Sometimes in visual problems you may find it that you will have to create lines to divide a whole into equal parts so that you can count them. Doing this will help you work quickly and accurately.

In the drawing above, the square is sectioned into four equal smaller squares. A triangular region of one of these squares is shaded. The triangular region is $\frac{1}{2}$ of one square. Because the other three square regions are not divided in this way, you may be lead astray and tricked into counting the shaded portion or the whole incorrectly. To avoid this, divide the other three square regions in half as well.

By making all the sections the same, we can more easily count the sections that make up the whole: there are 8. How many are shaded? 1 of 8, or $\frac{1}{8}$.

SYMBOL RELATIONSHIPS

Symbol relationship questions use symbols or drawings of objects—such as cones or cubes—in the place of numbers. Each question contains a picture of a scale that shows how many of each of the symbols equal one another.

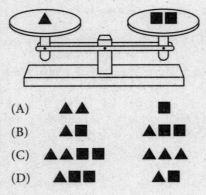

(A) ▲▲   ■

(B) ▲■   ▲■■

(C) ▲▲■■   ▲▲▲

(D) ▲■■   ▲■

Because the scale is balanced by one cone on the left and two cubes on the right, we can read it as a mathematical statement that says: 1 cone = 2 cubes.

Your job is to find the set of shapes from the answer choices that could also balance the scale. The easiest way to do this is to convert the symbols in each answer choice to either all cones or all cubes.

See how we've done this with the answer choices:

(A) ■■■■ (4) ≠ 1
    ▲ ▲   ■

(B) ■■ (2 + 1) ≠ ■■ (2 + 2)
    ▲ ■   ▲ ■ ■

(C) ■■■■ (4 + 2) = ■■■■■■ (6)
    ▲ ▲ ■ ■   ▲ ▲ ▲

(D) ■■ (2 + 2) ≠ ■■ (2 + 1)
    ▲ ■ ■   ▲ ■

In other words:

A: 4 cubes (1 cone = 2 cubes) ≠ 1 cube.

B: 2 cubes (1 cone = 2 cubes) + 1 cube ≠ 2 cubes (1 cone = 2 cubes) + 2 cubes

C: 4 cubes (1 cone = 2 cubes) + 2 cubes = 6 cubes (1 cone = 2 cubes)

D: 2 cubes (1 cone = 2 cubes) + 2 cubes ≠ 2 cubes (1 cone = 2 cubes) + 1 cube

It doesn't matter whether you choose to make the answer choices all cones or all cubes, but it is important to be consistent. Here's an example where we've changed all the symbols to cones.

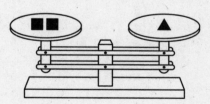

(A) ■ ▲ ▲ (2) = ■ ▲ ▲ (2)

(B) ■ ▲ ▲ ▲ (3) ≠ ▲ ■ ■ (2)

(C) ■ ▲ (1½) ≠ ▲ ■ ■ ▲ (2½)

(D) ■ ▲ ▲ ▲ (3½) ≠ ▲ ■ ■ ■ ▲ (2)

By changing all the cubes to cones we realize:

A: 1 cones (2 cubes = 1 cone) + 1 cone = 2 cones. This is the correct answer.

B: 1 cone (2 cubes = 1 cone) + 2 cones ≠ 1 cone + 1 cone (2 cubes = 1 cone)

C: $\frac{1}{2}$ cone (if 2 cubes = 1 cone, then 1 cube = $\frac{1}{2}$ cone) + 1 cone ≠ 1 cone (2 cubes = 1 cone) + $\frac{1}{2}$ cone (1 cube = $\frac{1}{2}$ cone) + 1 cone

C: $\frac{1}{2}$ cone (2 cubes = 1 cone, 1 cube = $\frac{1}{2}$ cone) + 3 cones ≠ 2 cones (2 cubes = 1 cone)

This method will help you work through symbol relationship problems efficiently and accurately. No matter how simple a symbol relationship question may look, it is better to take the time and work through answer choices in this way; in the end you'll save time you otherwise may waste if you try to answer by eyeballing the scale and moving on to the answer choices without a clear plan of action.

QUANTITATIVE REASONING PRACTICE SET

Directions: For questions 1–4, find the relationship of the numbers in the left column to the numbers in the right column. Choose the number that should replace the blank.

1. 172 → ☐ → 167

   58 → ☐ → 53

   47 → ☐ → —

43	42	40	44
(A)	(B)	(C)	(D)

2. 20 → ☐ → 38

   10 → ☐ → 18

   9 → ☐ → —

22	18	16	20
(A)	(B)	(C)	(D)

3. 99 → ☐ → 91

   7 → ☐ → -1

   12 → ☐ → —

0	4	5	-2
(A)	(B)	(C)	(D)

4. 4 → ☐ → 12

   9 → ☐ → 27

   1 → ☐ → —

9	3	42	4
(A)	(B)	(C)	(D)

Directions: For questions 5–8, find the fraction of the grid that is shaded.

5.

(A) $\frac{1}{6}$

(B) $\frac{1}{4}$

(C) $\frac{1}{8}$

(D) $\frac{1}{10}$

6.

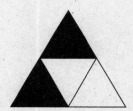

(A) $\frac{1}{4}$

(B) $\frac{2}{5}$

(C) $\frac{2}{3}$

(D) $\frac{1}{2}$

7.

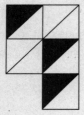

(A) $\frac{5}{10}$

(B) $\frac{3}{5}$

(C) $\frac{3}{10}$

(D) $\frac{4}{10}$

8.

(A) $\frac{1}{2}$

(B) $\frac{1}{50}$

(C) $\frac{10}{100}$

(D) $\frac{100}{100}$

Directions: For questions 9–10, the scale shows sets of shapes of equal weight. Find a pair of sets that would also balance the scale.

9.

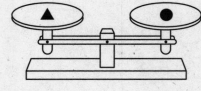

(A) ▲▲   ●

(B) ▲   ●●

(C) ▲▲▲   ●●●●

(D) ▲▲▲   ●●●

10.

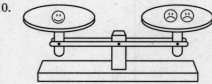

(A) ☺☺☹   ☹☹☹

(B) ☺☹☹   ☺☺

(C) ☺☹☹   ☺☺☺

(D) ☺☺☺   ☹☹☹☹

ANSWERS AND EXPLANATIONS

1.   B

The number in the right column is 5 less than the number in the left hand column. The relationship is −5. The missing number = 47 − 5 = 42.

2.   C

The number in the right column is 2 less than twice the number in the left hand column. The relationship is to multiply the term by 2, and then subtract 2. The missing number = (9 × 2) − 2 = 18 − 2 = 16.

3.   B

The number in the right column is 8 less than the number in the left hand column. The relationship is −8. The missing number = 12 − 8 = 4.

4.   B

The number in the right column is 3 times the number in the left column. In the final row, if 1 is the number on the left, then 3 is the number on the right.

5.   C

Count the total pieces of the circle and count the number of pieces shaded. There are 8 pieces and 1 is shaded; 1 part of 8 is shaded, or $\frac{1}{8}$.

6.   D

Count the total pieces of the triangle and count the number of pieces shaded. There are 4 pieces and 2 are shaded; 2 parts of 4 are shaded, or $\frac{2}{4}$ which reduces to $\frac{1}{2}$.

7.   C

Count the total pieces of the diagram and count the number of pieces shaded. There are 10 pieces and 3 are shaded; 3 parts of 10 are shaded, or $\frac{3}{10}$.

8.   A

Count the total pieces of the circle and count the number of pieces shaded. There are 2 pieces and 1 is shaded; 1 part of 2 is shaded, or $\frac{1}{2}$.

9.   D

The diagram shows that one triangle equals one circle. Therefore, 3 triangles must equal three circles.

10. B

1 smile = 2 frowns, thus, 1 smile + 2 frowns = 2 smiles.

Chapter Thirteen: **Reasoning Skills**

Naturally, all question types on the COOP or HSPT require you to use your reasoning skills. Not only do you need to have a good command of mathematics, geometry, algebra, and verbal skills, you also need to be able to work through questions methodically.

We have covered nearly every question type in the previous chapters, but there are a few more question types we have yet to review. These questions fall outside or between the bounds of the subject areas we have covered already. These are reasoning skills questions.

Reasoning skills questions include:

1. Sequence Questions—on the COOP and in the Mathematics section of the HSPT
2. Logic Questions—on both the COOP and the HSPT
3. Essential Element Questions—on the COOP only
4. Picture Analogy Questions—on the COOP only
5. Verbal Sequence Questions—on the COOP only

What do these five question types have in common? They each test your reasoning ability. You may find the question types challenging, or strange at first. However, working through this chapter, and the practice set at the end of the chapter will help you become accustomed to these five question types. Try to approach them as something fun, a puzzle that needs to be solved, or a code that needs to be cracked. Review each question type and become an expert.

QUESTION TYPE 1—SEQUENCE

A sequence is an arrangement of objects, numbers, or letters, coming one after the other in succession. In other words, the items in a sequence are *arranged* in some way.

Sequence questions are the first subtest on the COOP. You will also see one special type of sequence question, the number series question, on the Mathematics section of the HSPT.

Here are some examples of sequence questions:

(A)   (B)   (C)   (D)

aB   bC   dE   _____

(A) fG

(B) FG

(C) Gh

(D) eF

What is the next number in the following series:
44, 21, 20, 9, 8, ...

(A) 6

(B) 4

(C) 3

(D) 5

So, sequence questions arrange objects, numbers, or letters is some order. The *way* that the items are arranged may not be immediately obvious to you. Your job is to figure out the logic behind the arrangement of the items and select an answer choice that completes the sequence.

How do you do that?

THE KAPLAN THREE-STEP METHOD FOR SEQUENCE QUESTIONS

Step 1—Examine the building blocks and define the sequence.

Step 2—Predict the answer.

Step 3—Select the answer choice that best fits your prediction.

Step 1—Examine the Building Blocks and Define the Sequence

Define the sequence... Easier said than done you may say. Stay focused and remember that there always IS a relationship, an arrangement, a movement, or a progression of some sort between the items.

Figure out the progression by adding on one building block at a time.

1. Examine each building block by itself.
2. Examine the relationship, or movement from one building block to the next.

Don't try to define the progression until you have worked through each of the building blocks given. Look at the first example question and see how this is done.

Sequence Type 1—Picture Sequence Questions

Look carefully at the first building block of the sequence:

Define it. Your definition doesn't have to be a complete sentence, just something to help you bring the picture into focus mentally. Your definition might be "square with dot in center, line from dot to top corner."

Look at the next building block of the sequence:

We have "square with dot in center, line from dot to bottom corner." Now, define this second building block as it relates to the first building block. Notice how in the second building block of the pattern the line drawn from the dot goes to a different part of the square than it went to in the previous item. We can say then that the building blocks of the sequence are made up of a square with a dot in the center, and a line drawn from that dot to a corner of the square.

But wait! If we try to define our pattern now, we will be in trouble. According to our definition, the third building block should also contain a square with a line drawn from a dot in the center to a corner of the square. However, that is not the case. What happened?

If you feel like tossing up your hands here—don't. Do not get frustrated. Don't give up on breaking the code, and don't define the code until you have reached the end of the items given.

Before you jump to any conclusions, be sure to examine every piece of the pattern given to you. Look carefully at the third item given, the third square. What can we say about it by itself? In the third building block of the pattern, the line drawn from the dot in the center of the square is drawn to the center of the base, NOT to a corner.

So, we have recognized several important things about the sequence.

- Each item has a square with a dot in the center.
- A line is drawn from the dot in the center to some point of the square's perimeter.
- In each subsequent building block of the pattern, the line is drawn to a different place than in the previous one.

By analyzing each building block of the pattern separately, and then comparing each subsequent block to the one that went before it, we have defined the pattern.

Marking up the test booklet might help you do this more easily.

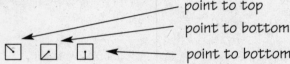

Step 2—Predict the Answer

If we were to continue the pattern, what would we have next?

The next item needs to be a square, with a point in the middle. The line drawn from the point should be in the opposite direction from the previous square. Since in the previous square the line was heading down, in this next one it needs to be heading up.

Drawn your picture in the answer book.

Now that you have a clear idea of what the correct answer should look like, you are ready for Step 3.

Step 3—Select the Answer Choice that Best Fits Your Prediction

Look at the answer choices again.

     (A)   (B)   (C)   (D)

There it is. Choice (D) matches your prediction. It's the right answer. But...what if no choice exactly matches your prediction? You have got to redefine, refocus, broaden or narrow your prediction.

What if these were the answer choices?

None of these choices has a line drawn from the dot, up. Choice (A) has a dot in the center but no line. In choice (B) the line is too long. Choice (C) has two lines that cross. However, the fourth one still does have a line drawn from the center dot of the square. The line, like those in the rest of the pattern is short. Choice (D) still best fits the prediction you made.

> **KAPLAN TIP**
>
> Look out for common patterns. The direction of lines, shapes, sizes, shading, and more or less detail are often elements of picture sequence patterns.

Common Patterns to Look Out For

Doing well on picture sequence questions has a lot to do with your powers of observation. Take your time, focus, and look for the details that make one building block different from the next. Some common differences to watch out for are:

Direction of lines: does one piece of the diagram point up, down, or sideways? Do pieces of the pattern point in opposite directions?

Shapes and size of shapes: Is the pattern made up of squares, circles, or other shapes? Do the shapes increase or decrease in size?

Shading: Are portions of the building blocks shaded? Is the shading increasing or decreasing as you progress through the sequence?

Increasing or decreasing detail: Does each subsequent building block have more or less detail than the one before it?

Sequence Type 2—Alphabet Sequence Questions

The same techniques you have just learned and practiced for picture sequence questions, also apply to alphabet sequence questions. (We have called this question type alphabet sequence, but you might also see letters of the alphabet mixed in with numbers.)

Let's take the example from the beginning of this chapter to work though.

aB   bC   dE   _____

(A) fG
(B) FG
(C) Gh
(D) eF

Step 1—Examine the Building Blocks and Define the Sequence

Look carefully at the first building block of the sequence: aB. Define it. Your definition might be "lowercase letter, capital of next letter"

Look at the next building block of the sequence: bC. Again we have "lowercase letter, capital of next letter."

Now, define this second building block as it relates to the first building block. Notice how the first letter in the pairing moved up one letter of the alphabet from a to b. The second letter also moved up a letter in the alphabet from B to C.

It seems as though the building blocks of the sequence are made up of two letters, a lowercase letter, followed by a capital letter. And each subsequent pair is beginning with the second letter of the previous pair.

If we tried to define our pattern now though, we would be wrong. According to our definition, the third building block should start with a lowercase letter, and move up one letter from b to c. The second letter of the pair should be a capital letter following c—it should be D. Thus, we expect the next pair to be cD.

However, that is not the case. The third building block is NOT cD, it is dE. What happened? What happened is we tried to define the code too soon. Remember, don't define the code until you have reached the end of the three items given.

Okay, we have to look at the third item given, dE. What can we say about it by itself? Well, dE is made up of a lowercase letter followed by a capital of the next letter of the alphabet.

Now that we have defined the pair, see how it relates to the previous item, bC. Instead of the first letter being THE SAME as the second letter of the previous pair, it is the NEXT letter. The first letter doesn't start with a lowercase c, it starts with a d.

The pattern then is: firstSECOND secondTHIRD fourthFIFTH or, two alike and one different.

By analyzing each separate building block, we defined the pattern. Marking up the test booklet might help you do this more easily.

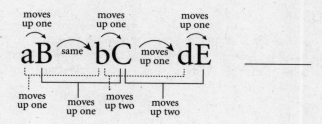

Step 2—Predict the Answer

If we were to continue the pattern, what would we have next?

The next pair needs to return to the "move up one" beginning of the pattern. Keep in mind that the pattern just completed itself with dE, so we know we need to return to the beginning of the formula—in which the first letter of the subsequent pair is the same as the second letter of the previous pair. dE should be followed by the next capital letter in the alphabet. So, we move from dE to eF.

Step 3—Select the Answer Choice that Best Fits Your Prediction

Of the choices provided, choice (D) fits our prediction.

        (A) fG

        (B) FG

        (C) Gh

        (D) eF

This was a not a particularly obvious sequence, but it does illustrate a couple of important points to remember when you approach alphabet sequence problems.

LOOK OUT FOR COMMON PATTERNS

There is only so much the test makers can do with the letters of the alphabet.

Look out for movement or changes in

- **Letters going up or down:** Does the pattern move toward Z? As in PQR…or does it move toward A as in LKJIH
- **Lowercase vs. capital letters:** BdBB, BDbb, BDBb, etc.
- **Patterns that skip letters:** A C E G (skips 1 letter) or A D G J (skips 2), etc.
- **Letters with numbers thrown in:** a1 b2 c3 $A^1B^2C^3$ AB3 BC2 CD1

Analyze these the way you would any other pattern: examine the details in the building block and look for changes as the sequence progresses.

BE TENACIOUS

That is, don't give up too easily. Stick with the pattern. Know that there IS a pattern. Analyze one building block at a time. Then, examine the movement from one block to another, trying to see what the difference between them is. Do this for every piece of the pattern. Use all the pieces given to you. Then, define the pattern.

KNOW YOUR ALPHABET

It may seem obvious, but the only way to find the pattern in an alphabet item is to know the alphabet inside out. If you find yourself getting confused, or just don't see it, write out the alphabet at the top of your test booklet. There is nothing wrong with having a clear list to refer to.

IF YOU ARE STUMPED, ELIMINATE WRONG ANSWERS AND GUESS

Let's say you did your best to define the pattern, and you just aren't clear on what it is. Maybe in the previous example you recognized that each of the first letters of the pair started with a lowercase letter followed by a capital letter. But, the difference between the second and third building block confused you.

Don't give up. Use the information to eliminate clearly incorrect answer choices. Remember, you know the next pair has to start with a lowercase letter.

aB	bC	dE	_____

(A) fG

(B) FG

(C) Gh

(D) eF

Right off the bat you can rule out choices (B) and (C) since they begin with capital letters. Take your best guess from between the remaining answer choices. By eliminating two of the answer choices, you have greatly improved the odds of choosing the correct one.

Defining the building blocks of each pattern, and examining the relationship between them is essential to solving sequence items. Let's practice a bit with both skills. Then, we will apply the Kaplan Three-Step Method.

Now that we have practiced with picture and letter sequences, there is one more type of sequence question to cover.

Sequence Type 3—Numerical Sequence/Series

On the COOP, numerical sequence items look like this:

> 3   7   11   2   6   10   8   12   ___

You will also see series questions on the Mathematics section of the HSPT. They are mixed in with the rest of the mathematical questions and they look like this:

> **What is the next number in the series: 2, 5, 8, 11…**

On both tests, each question will be followed by four answer choices.

Though the question formats on each exam look slightly different, the idea is basically the same. You need to come up with a missing number using the pattern established by the numbers given. How do you do that?

THE KAPLAN THREE-STEP METHOD FOR NUMERICAL SEQUENCE AND SERIES QUESTIONS

Step 1. Define the pattern.

Step 2. Predict the answer.

Step 3. Find an answer choice that fits your prediction.

Step 1—Define the Pattern

The nice thing about numerical sequence questions is that you already recognize the building blocks of the pattern—numbers.

You know that in order to make a pattern from one building block—one number—to the next, something mathematical procedure had to be performed on the first number. It was either added to, subtracted from, multiplied by, or divided by some other number.

How do you find the operation that was performed to create the pattern? Compare each subsequent number to the one before it.

Let's see how this works, using the first example. The sequence given is:

> 3   7   11   2   6   10   8   12   ___

1. Compare the first and second numbers given. What is the relationship between 3 and 7? 7 is 4 more than 3. What operation has been performed to the first number? +4

2. Compare the second and third number: What is the relationship between 7 and 11? 11 is 4 more than 3. Aha! A pattern of +4 emerges.

But wait, you're not finished yet.

3. Verify your pattern by checking the second group given. Treat this set as a completely different entity. Examine it by itself, *not in relation to the first set!* That is, don't look for any connection between the 3 in the first set and the 2 in the second. This is not the way sequence items are set up.

Okay, look at 2, 6, and 10. Look at them with an open mind, and go through the comparison process once more.

1. Compare the first and second numbers given. What is the relationship between 2 and 6? 6 is 4 more than 2. What operation has been performed to the first number? +4

2. Compare the second and third number: What is the relationship between 6 and 10? 10 is 4 more than 6. Our pattern of +4 applies here as well.

Now, we can say with confidence that the pattern is +4. However, you must still check this out using the pieces of the third pattern given to you. What is the relationship between 8 and 12? 12 is 4 more than 8; +4 is indeed our pattern.

Step 2—Predict the Answer

Now that you have uncovered the pattern (+4), the operation that makes up the series, to the missing number in the last set. 8 + 4 = 12, and 12 + 4 = 16.

The next number in the set or series must be 16.

Step 3—Find an Answer Choice that Fits Your Prediction

Review the answer choices. Which one best fits your prediction?

$$3 \quad 7 \quad 11 \qquad 2 \quad 6 \quad 10 \qquad 8 \quad 12 \quad \underline{\quad}$$

(A) 16

(B) 14

(C) 10

(D) 11

Choice (A) is the correct answer. You got it; fill in the answer bubble on your answer sheet and move on. There is no need to read through the rest of the answers and allow yourself to be distracted or confused by them.

On the other hand, *do* be careful when performing arithmetical operations to find a number of a missing pattern. Use the blank space in your answer booklet to work through the equation. You don't want to rush, do the math incorrectly in your head, and accidentally come up with a wrong answer.

Common Patterns

Since only so many mathematical procedures can be performed with numbers, you will see certain common patterns on the COOP or HSPT. Being familiar with these should help you recognize the pattern more quickly.

+

–

×

÷

Strange Patterns

A few additional mathematical operations that may lead to strange patterns are operations performed using the number 1, or the square root and square of a number.

1   1   1   2   4   8   3   9   ___

Can you figure out the pattern above?

Compare the first and second number in the first set; 1 and 1. These appear to be the same number. Hmm… This is strange.

Compare the second and third number in the first set; 1 and 1. Again, these appear to be the same number. Could the pattern be made up of repeating numbers?

We have to look at the next set given before we can determine our pattern. Compare the first and second number in the second set. 2 and 4; 2 + 2 is 4, or 2 × 2 is 4.

Compare the second and third number in the first set. 4 and 8; 8 is 4 plus 4, or 4 × 2. Since the pattern has to be the same, we look for some procedure the movements have in common. That is ×2. The pattern looks to be ×2.

Yet, a pattern of ×2 certainly didn't apply to the first grouping of the set. Move on to the third set and examine it for a pattern. Compare the first and second number in the second set; 3 and 9; 9 is the first number, 3, multiplied by itself.

This is an important clue which can help us refocus our understanding of the pattern; 3 is multiplied by itself. So was 2, the first number of the second set.

Therefore, we can say that the pattern is, first number multiplied by itself. Second number, again, multiplied by the first.

Now our 1, 1, 1 makes sense; 1 times itself is 1. Times itself again is still 1.

When the Blank Is in the Middle

Sometimes the missing number will be in the middle of a series, like this:

$$3 \quad 6 \quad 12 \qquad 2 \quad 4 \quad 8 \qquad 5 \quad \underline{\quad} \quad 20$$

(A) 10

(B) 12

(C) 8

(D) 2

The same rules for solving the question still apply.

Compare the first and second numbers of the first pattern 3 and 6; 6 is 3×2.

Compare the second and third numbers of the first pattern 6 and 12; 12 is 6×2.

Compare the first and second numbers of the next pattern 2 and 4; 4 is 2×2.

Compare the second and third numbers of the next pattern 4 and 8; 8 is 4×2.

Apply the pattern to the missing number, and check it, working backward.

$5 \times 2 = 10$.

Is $10 \times 2 = 20$? Yes. Our pattern is correct.

In fact, it doesn't matter where the missing number in the pattern. Examine the building blocks of each complete pattern first. Find the relationship between each preceding number and the one that follows it. Apply that operation to the missing number.

Double Operation Patterns

Series questions may contain double operation patterns, where the pattern may seem to be more than one operation. This is where the importance of examining each subsequent step in the sequence is really essential. Look at this example:

What is the next number in the set 1, 2, 4, 5, 10, ...

We compare the first and second numbers, 1 to 2, and realize that the second number is 1 more than the first. Write down +1. We compare 2 and 4 and realize that 4 is the second number +2, or ×2. Could be either. Write both down.

At this point, your analytical ability, and your patience really come into play. You might be asking yourself is the pattern +1, ×2, or +2? Rather than becoming frustrated, or annoyed, stay focused. Think of yourself as a detective. Your job is to remain skeptical and examine all the evidence before you jump to any conclusions.

Let's continue examining the series. The next number in the series is 5; 5 is 1 more than 4. Write down +1 again.

Don't stop yet. Use all the numbers given to you before you try to define the pattern. The next number in the series is 10; 10 is the previous number, 5, × 2. Look at all your observations. +1, ×2, +1, ×2.

Aha! The pattern is +1, ×2.

What is the next number in the series? We just finished with ×2, the next procedure needs to be +1; 10 + 1 = 11. That's your answer.

Look out for Combination Patterns

If the operation being performed isn't immediately obvious, suspect a combination pattern. Use the empty space in your test booklet to quickly write down relationships. This will help you stay focused, especially on series questions that use combination patterns.

Work Backward to Verify Missing Numbers in the Middle of a Sequence

Rather than finding the next number in a series, you may be asked to find a number missing from the middle of a series. In this case, you need to work backward.

What is the missing number in the set: 8, 10, _____, 8, 4, 6

Compare the first and second numbers: 10 is 2 more than 8. Write down +2.

The next number is missing, so move on and continue comparing numbers that are given to you.

Compare the fourth and fifth numbers in the set: 8 and 4; 4 is 8 − 4. Write down −4.

Compare the sixth and seventh numbers in the set: 4 and 6; 6 is 2 more than 4. Write down +2.

So, the pattern is +2, −4,,+2, −4.

The first and second numbers, 8 and 10, contain the +2, −4, +2, −4 element of the pattern, therefore the next operation should be −4; 10 − 4 = 6.

The missing number is 6. You got it.

QUESTION TYPE 2—LOGIC

Congratulations, you're almost there. We have worked through the various types of sequence questions and you are thinking methodically, scientifically, skeptically, in a step-by-step manner. You are relying on evidence, rather than jumping to conclusions.

These skills are essential in approaching our next question type—logic questions.

Logic questions are short statements that require you to reach a logical conclusion. You will find them mixed in with the rest of the verbal reasoning questions—synonyms, antonyms, analogies, and verbal classification—on the HSPT. On the COOP, these questions will appear on the Verbal Reasoning Subtest, in a group by themselves.

On the HSPT, logic questions are followed by only 3 answer choices. They are the only question type of the test with 3 rather than 4 answer choices. They look like this:

> Amy runs faster than Pete. Pete runs faster than Jack. If the first two statements are true, the third is

(A) true

(B) false

(C) uncertain

On the COOP, logic questions are followed by four answer choices. The statements themselves may be two sentences, or they could be longer.

Here's an example of a COOP logic question:

> The Grand Canyon is in Arizona. Mark has visited the Grand Canyon.

(A) Mark has been in Arizona.

(B) Mark is from Arizona.

(C) Mark's family likes to take road trips.

(D) The Grand Canyon is the largest canyon in the world.

Just the Facts

The key to solving logic questions is relying on the facts. Good logic employs factual information. Faulty logic, and incorrect answer choices, makes use of unfounded assumptions.

Approach logic questions with …

THE KAPLAN THREE-STEP METHOD FOR LOGIC QUESTIONS

Step 1. Read the statement for facts.

Step 2. Think about what the facts *are* and *are not* telling you.

Step 3. Predict the correct answer choice.

We will show you how the method works, then review some common logical problems and some common, avoidable, incorrect answer choices.

Step 1—Read the Statement for Facts

Because a logical deduction is based on facts, not assumptions, it is important to be able to tell what elements of each logic statement are indeed FACTS.

A FACT is something that exists. A fact is real or true.

Fact: The Grand Canyon is located in Arizona.

Fact: Ann runs faster than Jack.

Fact: The Declaration of Independence was signed in 1776.

Opinions, desires, assumptions are NOT FACTS.

Now that we are clear on this, read the following statement for facts. In fact, underline the facts.

> Katherine is the best violinist in the orchestra. Suzie plays
> cello.

Did you underline the facts? You should have underlined both sentences. Both are statements of fact.

Step 2—Think about What These Facts *Are* and *Are Not* Telling You

What do the facts in the previous statements tell us? The facts tell us:

- Katherine plays violin.
- Katherine is the best violin player in the orchestra.
- Suzie plays cello.

Notice how we teased apart this information from the two statements given. Notice also the information we are not given.

What the facts *do not* tell us:

- Whether Suzie is a good cellist
- Whether Suzie and Katherine play together
- Whether Suzie and Katherine are friends, relatives, or even know each other

What else don't we know about Suzie and Katherine? A whole lot of things!

We don't know what color hair they have, how old they are, or where they live...the list could go on and on. All we know for sure is the information we listed.

If the example about Katherine and Suzie was a logic question on the HSPT a third statement would follow the first two. The third statement tests your understanding of the first two. It would look like this:

> Katherine is the best violinist in the orchestra. Suzie plays cello. Katherine is a better musician than Suzie. If the first two statements are true, the third is
>
> (A) true
>
> (B) false
>
> (C) uncertain

Notice that the previous example *does not* say that the third statement is true. Rather, it is asking us to decide whether or not it could be true is the first two statements are indeed true. In other words, take the first two statements as fact. Then, based on those facts, decide whether or not the third statement could be proven true or false. If you don't have enough information to go on, select answer choice (C), uncertain.

Step 3—Predict the Correct Answer Choice

We already figured out that all we know for certain is that Katherine plays violin the best, and Suzie plays cello. We noted that there was no comparison given between the two.

So, based on the first two statements, do we have enough information to say whether or not Katherine is a better musician than Suzie? We don't! The answer is uncertain, choice (C).

Sometimes, on logic questions it can become difficult to see the connection between facts if a lot of information is given to you. Making diagrams can help you visualize the connection, or the lack of one.

For example:

> Bread is more expensive than rice, but less expensive than tuna. Rice is more expensive than beans, but less expensive than potatoes. Tuna is more expensive than rice. If the first two statements are true, the third is
>
> (A) true
>
> (B) false
>
> (C) uncertain

A question like this becomes a lot clearer if you plot it out.

According to the first statement: bread > rice and tuna > bread

Combine these two statements into one: tuna > bread > rice

According to the second statement: potatoes > rice > beans

Add this to the first statement and we see that: tuna > bread ≥ potatoes > rice > beans.

Notice how we made bread greater than or equal to potatoes. Although we know that bread is more expensive than rice and potatoes are more expensive than rice, we don't know the value of these items in relation to one another.

Finally, in the third statement, we are told that tuna is more expensive than rice. Is that true? Based on the information in the first two statements, is tuna more expensive than rice?

tuna > bread ≥ potatoes > rice > beans

Yes! It is. The third statement is true.

Now that we have a method in place for evaluating facts and selecting correct answer choices, let's discuss some common logic questions. We will examine each category and give you some important traps to avoid. To best illustrate our point, we will draw examples from COOP format type questions, since these ask you to select an answer choice that can be deduced from the information given.

Logic Type 1—Category

One type of logic question might ask you to base your conclusion on whether or not a item fits into the category defined. This example uses the COOP format; it is followed by four statements. You decide which one is correct based only on the information provided.

> Bees are attracted to bright flowers. Terry has a bouquet of yellow roses in a vase by her window.
>
> (A) Bees will fly into Terry's window.
> (B) Terry's favorite flowers are yellow roses.
> (C) Yellow roses are wildflowers.
> (D) Bees are attracted to yellow roses.

Remember our step-by-step method. First read the statements and think about what the facts do and do not tell us.

The facts tell us:

- Bees are attracted to bright flowers.
- Terry has a vase of yellow roses by her window.
- Terry is a female; the pronoun *she* is used to describe her.
- Terry has a window.

They do not tell us:

- What color Terry's vase is
- If the window is open
- What season it is
- Whether or not there are bees outside of Terry's window
- Where Terry lives

Keep these facts in mind as you read through the answer choices.

Which answer choice is the only conclusion we can make based just on the facts? Choice (D). Since yellow roses fall into the category of bright flowers, bees must be attracted to them.

Be sure to read each answer choice carefully before you select one based just on the facts given in the statements.

Logic Type 2—Cause/Effect

Another type of question you might see in the logic section of each exam is cause and effect reasoning.

In order to have a solid cause/effect relationship, the cause and effect must be clearly stated and clearly dependent on one another. One thing and only one thing must be the cause of an effect in order for the cause/effect relationship to be logical.

Facts, not feelings, have to bear out the cause/effect relationship.

Now that you have an idea of strong and weak cause/effect relationships, here's an example of a cause/effect question. Read the statements; think of what the facts do and do not tell us. Then, evaluate each answer choice.

> Mr. Brown usually drinks coffee every morning. Today Mr. Brown hasn't had his coffee and he has a headache.
>
> (A) Mr. Brown is drinking tea instead of coffee.
> (B) Mr. Brown isn't feeling well.
> (C) Mr. Brow is quitting drinking coffee.
> (D) Coffee gives Mr. Brown a headache.

Can we say that Mr. Brown is drinking tea instead of coffee? Not based on the information given.

Can we say that Mr. Brown isn't feeling well? Yes, the facts state that he has a headache.

Can we say that Mr. Brown is quitting drinking coffee? Not based on the statements given. We were not told the reason he missed his morning cup. Maybe he was just running late.

Can we say coffee gives Mr. Brown a headache? Not based on the information given. Besides, today he *hasn't* had his coffee and he *does have a headache*. This choice doesn't make sense.

The only thing we know for certain based on the facts is (B), Mr. Brown isn't feeling well.

Logic Type 3—All/Some/Most

This logic question type is a form of category question; solving it hinges on carefully attention to the use of the words *all*, *some*, or *most*. In other words, you want to find out whether or not someone or something belongs to a group and then draw conclusions.

Here's an example:

> Most people require between 7–10 hours of sleep each
> night. Joe has slept four hours.
>
> (A) Joe is sick.
> (B) Something was bothering Joe.
> (C) Joe has more energy than others.
> (D) Joe did not sleep much last night.

Examining the facts of the statement we know that *most* people require a certain number of hours sleep. Most people is not everyone. There are some people that require less sleep, and some people that require more.

The fact that Joe slept 4 hours only proves that Joe slept little. It does not say anything about his energy as compared with others or the reason he slept so little or even that he is sick today.

Here's another example. Pay attention to the words *all*, *some*, or *most*.

> All yurps warble. Blue yurps fly. Blue yurps fly and warble.
> If the first two statements are true, the third is
>
> (A) true
> (B) false
> (C) uncertain

Notice how the first statements said that *all yurps warble*. The second went on to state that *blue yurps fly*. Therefore, the third statement *blue yurps fly and warble* must be true since the group of *all yurps* include blue yurps.

On a question like this, you might find it helpful to draw a diagram.

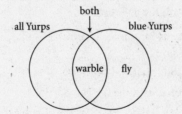

Four Traps to Avoid

Drawing sound logical conclusions depends on the facts and just the facts. Make sure you read, and understand the facts of each statement in the question before attempting to draw any conclusion. Quickly sketching a diagram may help you keep your facts straight. Know the limits of what the facts tell you and beware of these common traps.

Trap 1—Character Assumption

Don't select answer choices that make assumptions about a person or group not stated in the question.

> Thomas accepted a part-time job as a receptionist in the afternoons. Unfortunately, he lost the first telephone call that he tried to transfer to his boss. When the person called back and Thomas tried to transfer the call again, again he lost it and disconnected the caller.
>
> (A) Thomas's telephone is broken.
> (B) Thomas' boss will be angry with him.
> (C) Thomas is having trouble connecting calls.
> (D) Thomas should get another job.

The only thing we know for certain is that Thomas is having trouble connecting calls; he lost two of them. Thus, the answer is (C). We cannot speculate on the emotions of his boss, nor do we know whether or not his telephone is broken. Perhaps Thomas' performance will improve in time; he need not get another job yet.

Trap 2—Too Much Information

Some statements may deliberately try to throw you off the track of the correct answer by including too much information.

> The Dixon family eats dinner together three nights a week. On Monday night, Mrs. Dixon has pizza delivered from the Italian restaurant on Main Street. On Tuesday, night Joe Dixon makes hotdogs. On Wednesday night, the Dixons belong to a family bowling team.
>
> (A) The Dixons eat dinner together Monday, Tuesday, and Wednesday.
> (B) The Dixons are good bowlers.
> (C) Joe Dixon eats alone on Tuesday night.
> (D) There is an Italian restaurant on Main Street.

Despite all the information, we don't know which nights the Dixons eat together. Mrs. Dixon could eat the pizza all by herself. Joe Dixon, likewise could be cooking for one. Do the Dixons eat at the bowling alley together on Wednesday? We don't know. Don't be distracted from the facts by the amount of information given. The only thing we know for sue is that (D) there is an Italian Restaurant on Main Street. How do we know? It delivers pizza to Mrs. Dixon on Monday night!

Trap 3—No Relationship

This trap could also be called the "not enough information" trap. Although a lot of details are given, it is possible you still might not have enough information to draw a conclusion relating two distinct people or groups. Here's an example of a question that uses this trap.

> Danika is faster than Julio. Maribel is faster than Tanya.
> Danika is faster than Maribel. If the first two statements are
> true, the third is

(A) true

(B) false

(C) uncertain

Sketch a diagram to help you keep the facts straight. Remember, the first two statements are given, the third is in question.

The facts tell us:

  . D > J

  M > T

Notice that there is no relationship, or point of comparison given between the two different pairs. Based only on the information provided, we can't say whether Danika is faster than Maribel. The third statement is (C), uncertain.

Trap 4—Using Previous Knowledge to Answer a Question

While it is important to rely on facts, on these questions you can rely only on the facts you are given. For example, read the following question:

> Sacramento is in California. Albert has been to Sacramento.

(A) Sacramento is the capital of California.

(B) Albert has been to California.

(C) San Francisco is a city in California.

(D) Albert loved Sacramento.

If you are looking for facts, you might be tempted to choose (A) or (C) because they are facts. However, although these statements are true, they cannot be determined based only on the information given in the first two statements. You should NOT use previous knowledge to answer these questions. Remember, they are testing your ability to reason, not to memorize facts. In this example, the correct answer is (B).

You will have a chance to practice with all these types of logic questions at the end of this chapter. We still have a few more reasoning questions to review. One of them is similar to the logic questions, in that it requires you to focus on the facts, the facts, and just the facts!

QUESTION TYPE 3—ESSENTIAL ELEMENT

Essential element questions appear on the COOP. The directions instruct you to find the essential element or necessary part of an underlined word. Each underlined word is followed by four answer choices. For example:

<u>cookie</u>

(A) sweet

(B) round

(C) chocolate

(D) snack

If you look at the answer choices, you will notice that all of them have something to do with a cookie. Remember, the question isn't asking which answer is vaguely related to the underlined word. The question is asking what is the *essential element* or *necessary part of* the underlined word. How do you approach this question type then?

THE KAPLAN THREE-STEP METHOD FOR ESSENTIAL ELEMENT QUESTIONS

Step 1. Define the word.

Step 2. Find the answer choice that best fits your definition.

Step 3. If no choice fits, think of other definitions for the word and go through the choices again.

Step 1—Define the Word

The words in essential element questions will usually be words you know. Defining the word in this question type, means asking yourself: "What makes a cookie a cookie?"

Let's take the cookie example. You know cookies. You know they come in many shapes, sizes, and flavors. You could eat cookies for snack or for dessert, or even for breakfast.

But what is the one thing that makes a cookie a cookie and nothing else? *Cookies are sweet.*

Step 2—Find the Answer Choice that Best Fits Your Definition

Now that you have a sense of what makes a cookie a cookie and nothing else, you are ready to look at the answer choices. Happily, choice (A) fits your definition.

Step 3—If No Choice Fits, Think of Other Definitions for the Word and Go Through the Choices Again

Let's try another example to illustrate Step 3.

<u>tool</u>

(A) hammer

(B) twist

(C) assist

(D) break

First, define what makes a tool a tool. Let's say the word *tool* immediately made you think of a crowbar, a screwdriver, or a wrench. If so, your definition of a tool: *it helps you open*.

You would go to the answer choices and look for the word *open*. However, *open* is not among the answer choices. Since no choice fits your definition, you would have to think of other definitions of the word.

We have to rethink what a tool is, and what makes a tool a tool and nothing else. What do we know about tools? A hammer is a tool. So is a telephone. So is a car. Many, many things are tools. What do all of these things have in common? They *help people* accomplish tasks. So, our definition of the word tool becomes *something that helps*.

Go back to the answer choices and look for a choice that fits our refocused definition. Choice (C), assist, is closest to *help*. That's it!

Watch Out for Traps!

Like other question types, this one has common traps. Wrong answers will be concerned with one part, one expression, one situation, or one possible use of the word in question, rather than what makes it what it is. Avoid this trap by honing in on what makes this thing unique. Think about: What does it do? What is it used for? What makes it special or different from anything else?

With practice, essential element questions can be fun. Picture analogies can also be fun. Keep reading to learn more about them.

QUESTION TYPE 4—PICTURE ANALOGY

Twenty picture analogies questions make up the second subtest of the COOP. (You won't find these on the HSPT.) They are just like verbal analogy questions, only instead of words, they give you pictures. If you haven't done so yet, be sure to work through the analogy section in chapter four; it will help you understand how analogies work. All the techniques discussed apply to picture analogy questions as well.

A picture analogy question looks like this:

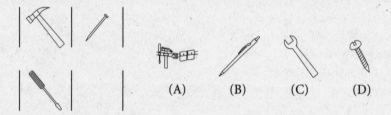

(A) (B) (C) (D)

Your job is to find the item that creates the same relationship in the bottom row, as the two pictures in the top row have.

The pictures may be cute, the pictures may be fun, but remember, time is of the essence. Don't waste time gazing at the pictures. DO look at them carefully, and make sure you are clear about what the picture represents. Stating the object to yourself, in your head, is a helpful way to keep focused. It is important to note exactly what the picture is, and not embellish it, elaborate on it, or add anything to it that is not there.

Once you have noted what the picture is, you are ready to solve the picture analogy question.

Work systematically using the Kaplan Three-Step Method.

THE KAPLAN THREE-STEP METHOD FOR PICTURE ANALOGY QUESTIONS

Step 1. Build a bridge.
Step 2. Predict your answer choice and select an answer.
Step 3. Adjust your bridge if necessary.

Step 1—Build a Bridge

Your first job is to connect the pictures on the top left and top right. You need to build a bridge or a link between them.

In the previous example you have a hammer and a nail. How are these items connected? Well, you could say a hammer bangs a nail into place. That's your bridge.

Step 2—Predict Your Answer Choice and Select an Answer

Now that we have our bridge, we can use it to predict an answer choice for the missing item.

We said the first item, the hammer, bangs the second one into place.

So... we use this bridge in the bottom row: A screwdriver bangs a _____ into place. Well, a screwdriver doesn't bang anything, so right away we know we have to move to Step 3.

Step 3—Adjust Your Bridge if Necessary

Since our bridge was a bit too specific, let's adjust it. Rather than bang, let's say a hammer is used to put a nail in place. Apply the bridge on the bottom to predict the missing word. A screwdriver puts a screw in place.

Now that we have predicted an answer, screw, we can look for the best fit from among the answer choices. Choice (D) fits our prediction. We got it.

Remember these important things about picture analogy questions:

- Read picture analogies ACROSS, not up and down. Connect the items in the top row with a bridge. Then, think of an item that completes the same relationship with the item in the bottom row.
- In every analogy question, there is a strong, definite connection between the two items pictured.
- Try to build a bridge that relates the items to each other by definition. This will help you avoid predicting, and choosing an incorrect answer choice.

Avoid the Traps!

Wrong answer choices will often remind you of something related to one of the items pictured. The best way to avoid trap answers is to build a strong, definite bridge. Review classic bridges in chapter four.

Congratulations, you are almost there. We just have one more question type to discuss, then you will have a chance to practice all your skills. This last type is a cross between analogies and sequences. We call it ...

QUESTION TYPE 5—VERBAL SEQUENCE

Verbal sequence questions look like this:

> Choose the word that best fits in the blank provided.
>
> warm   hot   _____
>
> (A) scalding
> (B) frozen
> (C) tepid
> (D) toasty

They could also look like this:

> Words in the top row are related in some way. The words in
> the bottom row are related in the same way. Find the word
> that completes the bottom row.
>
> | major | significant | large |
> |-------|-------------|-------|
> | minor | trivial | |
>
> (A) essential
> (B) mediocre
> (C) small
> (D) miniature

Your job is to find a word for the missing blank that completes the sequence.

As always, working methodically using the Kaplan Three-Step Method will help you hone in on the correct answer choice and avoid incorrect ones.

THE KAPLAN THREE-STEP METHOD FOR VERBAL SEQUENCE QUESTIONS

Step 1. Define the sequence.

Step 2. Predict the answer and select the answer choice that best fits.

Step 3. If necessary refocus. If no answer choice, or more than one answer choice fits, think of other definitions for the sequence and go through the choices again.

Let's use the first example to demonstrate how this works. Here it is again:

> warm   hot   _____
>
> (A) scalding
> (B) frozen
> (C) tepid
> (D) toasty

Step 1—Define the Sequence

In order to define the sequence, you have to read each word given and notice the direction they are moving in.

We have *warm* and *hot*. What direction are these words moving in? The second word, *hot* is greater in temperature than *warm*. We can say the sequence is *getting hotter*.

Step 2—Predict the Answer and Select the Answer Choice that Best Fits

If the sequence is *getting hotter*, what should the next word be? Something that means hotter than hot.

We can predict that the answer choice is hotter than hot. Don't worry about choosing a fancy word for your prediction. The important thing is to note that the next word in the sequence has to be very hot.

Now that we have made a prediction, we can look at the answer choices. Which one fits our prediction very hot? Choice (A), scalding, is the correct answer.

Step 3—If Necessary Refocus. If no Answer Choice, or More Than One Answer Choice Fits, Think of Other Definitions for the Sequence and Go Through the Choices Again.

The previous example fit our prediction very well. What happens if that's not the case? Let's use another example to show what to do if that's not the case. Look at this one. It's a two-row verbal sequence question. Remember, the words in the bottom row have to be related in the same way as the words in the top row.

petal	flower	bouquet
mound	hill	

(A) valley
(B) ditch
(C) mountain
(D) cliff

Define the sequence using the words given to you in the top row: petal, flower, bouquet.

A petal is a small piece of a flower, a bouquet is a bunch of flowers. Let's define our sequence, as a *group of*.

Now that we defined a sequence, we can predict an answer and select an answer choice. We need a word for the blank that completes the sequence below in the same way that the words on the top are related.

We said the relationship is a *group of*. Is a hill a *group of* a mound? Not exactly, though hill is a bigger mound. If we continued with the definition *group of*, what could be predict would come next? Something that means a *group of hills*.

Yet, when we go to the answer choices, none of them means *group of hills*. We have to refocus our definition then. We thought that *bigger* also worked, when we looked at the movement or progression between mound and hill.

Let's apply *bigger* to the top row and see if that works. Is a flower *bigger* than a petal? Yes. Is a bouquet *bigger* than a flower? Yes. *Bigger* works as a sequence.

Go back now and predict an answer choice using the sequence definition *bigger*. What would fit the blank? What's bigger than a hill? A mountain. Look at the answer choices, choice (C) fits our prediction. That's it!

THREE TYPICAL VERBAL SEQUENCES

Like analogies, there are typical relationships you will find again and again in verbal sequence questions. Being familiar with these will help you work through this question type at an improved pace.

Sequence 1—Degree of

One typical sequence will move from one degree to another. It will either get smaller or less in amount:

tiny	minute	miniscule
mansion	house	shack

Or larger or greater in amount:

large	great	grand
wordy	talkative	garrulous

Sequence 2—Members of a Group

In this type of sequence, the group or category is named.

flower	daisy	rose

The first word of the sequence, tells what the group is and the two words that follow are members of the group.

Sequence 3—Elements of an Unnamed Group

This type of sequence is not a sequence at all. Instead, the words are linked because they belong to the same, unnamed, category. These can be tricky, because the category is not immediately obvious. You have to figure out what it is.

star	planet	moon: Are all in the sky
winter	spring	summer: Are all seasons

If you are just not getting it…

GET RID OF TRICK ANSWERS

If you are finding it difficult to define the sequence or relationship and predict an answer choice for a verbal sequence question, you can still improve your odds of choosing the correct answer by eliminating bad answer choices. This works especially well on two-line verbal sequence questions.

On two-line verbal sequence questions bad answer choices will usually relate to the top row, rather than to the bottom.

Here's an example:

cleat	boot	slipper
uniform	coat	

(A) robe
(B) sandal
(C) heel
(D) vest

Let's say this question caused you difficulty, and you are running very low on time. Notice that two of the choices relate to shoes, the elements of the top row. These must be incorrect since we are looking to complete the bottom row. Eliminate them.

Now that you have narrowed down your choices to (A) *shorts* and (D) *coat*, take your best guess based on the definition you came up with for your sequence.

Did you have trouble defining the sequence because you were uncertain about the meaning of the word *cleat*? Perhaps you guessed that it was a type of shoe because it is in a group with other things you put on your feet. Or, maybe you took a hunch since you heard *cleat* in context of a soccer cleat.

In that case, you could say that the sequence moves from something you wear in sports, to something you wear in cold weather, to something you wear at home.

BACKSOLVE

Since the items in a sequence must be related in a strong and definite way, the word that fills in the blank must have a strong, definite relationship to the word that precedes it.

Plug in answer choices and see if they have a strong relationship to the preceding word in the sequence. In the previous example, ask yourself:

- Could a robe be related to a coat? Yes. A robe is a casual coat.
- Could a sandal be related to a coat? No. Neither or these items help define the other.
- Could a heel be related to a coat? No. Neither or these items help define the other.
- Could a vest be related to a coat? No. Although a vest may go under a coat, neither or these items help define the other.

Choice (A) is the only one with a strong and definite relationship to the preceding word in the sequence. Select this answer choice.

CONGRATULATIONS!

We have covered a lot of ground in this chapter. Give yourself a big pat on the back for working through some difficult material.

Spend some time revisiting the questions in this chapter that you found most challenging. Review the Kaplan Method for these question types and go through sample questions and answers again. With each new pass you will find that your pacing and facility will improve.

REASONING SKILLS PRACTICE SET

Directions: For questions 1–3, choose the element that would continue the pattern or sequence.

1. △○   ⊙□   ▫△   _____

   △○   ▫▫   △⊙   □▭
   (A)   (B)   (C)   (D)

2. 2 7 9   3 8 10   4 ___ 11
   - (A) 6
   - (B) 9
   - (C) 8
   - (D) 12

3. ZAB   XCD   VEF   _____
   - (A) UGH
   - (B) WFG
   - (C) YHI
   - (D) TGH

4. What is the next number in the following series: 9, 7, 10, 8, 11, …
   - (A) 13
   - (B) 10
   - (C) 9
   - (D) 11

Directions: For questions 5 and 6, look at the two pictures on top. Then, choose the picture that belongs in the space so that the bottom two pictures are related the same way that the top two are related.

5.

   (A)   (B)   (C)   (D)

6.

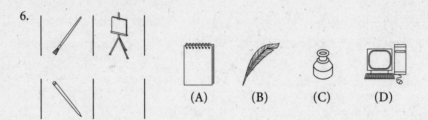

(A)   (B)   (C)   (D)

Directions: Read the statement in question 7. Based on the information in the statement, select the answer choice that is true.

7. The bus costs $1.50 for adults and is free for students traveling to school in the morning and returning home from school in the afternoon until 4 P.M. It is now 4:30 P.M. and Karen does not have enough money to take the bus.

(A) Karen usually gets home before 3 P.M.

(B) Karen is coming home late from school.

(C) Karen is a student.

(D) Karen has less than $1.50.

Directions: Read the statements and based on the information, select true, false, or uncertain.

8. Elissa has scored more baskets than Tina. Tina has scored more baskets than Gail. Elissa has scored more baskets than Gail. If the first two statements are true, the third is

(A) true

(B) false

(C) uncertain

Directions: For question 9, find the answer choice that names an essential element of the underlined word.

9. <u>transportation</u>

(A) driving

(B) commuting

(C) sitting

(D) paying

Directions: For question 10, find the word that completes the bottom row of words so that it is related in the same way as the words in the top row.

10.

crayon	marker	pen
house	apartment	

(A) shutter

(B) door

(C) cabin

(D) cave

ANSWERS AND EXPLANATIONS

1. A

Examine the building blocks of each section that makes up the sequence. The first shape has a hole in the middle of it, and the second one is whole. Notice that the second shape is always different from the first. The shapes are either circles, squares, or triangles. Therefore, the next element in the pattern has to begin with a shape with a hole in it, followed by a circle, triangle, or square. Only choice (A) fits this pattern.

2. B

The pattern is +5, +2. The missing number must be 4 + 5 = 9.

3. D

The first letter of each sequence moves toward A, skipping a letter of the alphabet. Notice that we move from Z to X, having skipped Y. We move from X to V having skipped W. The second and third letters of each sequence move toward Z. AB, CD, EF. The next part of the sequence should move from V to T, skipping U and followed by GH. Writing down the alphabet somewhere in the blank margins of your test booklet would help you map out the sequence and see the skipped letters on a question like this one.

4. C

The pattern is −2, +3. Writing down the progression from one number to the next will help keep you focused and make sure that you don't accidentally perform the wrong operation next. The next number must be
11 − 2 = 9.

5. B

Make sure you are clear on what each picture represents. You have a broom, a dust pan, a mop, and a missing item. Build a bridge between *broom* and *dustpan*. You use a dustpan with a broom to clean. *Use with* is our bridge. Apply it to *mop* to predict an answer. You use a mop with a bucket to clean. Bucket is choice (B). Notice how the incorrect answers are related to cleaning, but do not have the relationship defined by our bridge.

6. A

We have a paintbrush, painter's canvas, and pen. Build a bridge between paintbrush and canvas. You use a paintbrush to perform a task (paint) on a canvas. What do you use with a pen to perform a task? The task is writing, so in order to write, you would also need a piece of paper. Which answer choice best fits our prediction? Choice (A), the notepad, is correct.

7. D

Although we are told the price of riding the bus for adults and students traveling to and from school, no mention is made of Karen's age. Even if Karen is a student, it is after 4 P.M., so she would have to pay $1.50 to ride the bus. All we can tell for certain is that Karen has less that $1.50.

8. A

Draw a diagram, or write down the initials of each girl in order of baskets scored to help you see this more clearly.

E > T > G

Since the first two statements are true, the third is true as well according to the order given.

9. B

Before looking at the answer choices, ask yourself what makes this thing special. What defines it? Transportation is the act of *taking people from one place to another*. The answer choice that is closest to our definition is (B) which conveys the idea of traveling. Notice how the incorrect answer choices are things we might associate with transportation, such as driving in a car, or sitting on a plane, or even paying a toll. However, they do not define what transportation is—getting from one place to another.

10. C

First, define the sequence in the top row. Crayon, marker, and pen are all types of writing implements. *Types of* is your sequence. Predict an answer choice for the missing element of the bottom row. Houses and apartments are types of homes. The missing word should be another type of home. Choice (C), cabin, is the closest to our prediction.

| SECTION FOUR |

Practice Tests

COOP Practice Test 1
Answer Sheet

Remove (or photocopy) this answer sheet and use it to complete the practice test.

Sequences

1. Ⓐ Ⓑ Ⓒ Ⓓ   5. Ⓐ Ⓑ Ⓒ Ⓓ   9. Ⓐ Ⓑ Ⓒ Ⓓ   13. Ⓐ Ⓑ Ⓒ Ⓓ   17. Ⓐ Ⓑ Ⓒ Ⓓ
2. Ⓕ Ⓖ Ⓗ Ⓙ   6. Ⓕ Ⓖ Ⓗ Ⓙ   10. Ⓕ Ⓖ Ⓗ Ⓙ   14. Ⓕ Ⓖ Ⓗ Ⓙ   18. Ⓕ Ⓖ Ⓗ Ⓙ
3. Ⓐ Ⓑ Ⓒ Ⓓ   7. Ⓐ Ⓑ Ⓒ Ⓓ   11. Ⓐ Ⓑ Ⓒ Ⓓ   15. Ⓐ Ⓑ Ⓒ Ⓓ   19. Ⓐ Ⓑ Ⓒ Ⓓ
4. Ⓕ Ⓖ Ⓗ Ⓙ   8. Ⓕ Ⓖ Ⓗ Ⓙ   12. Ⓕ Ⓖ Ⓗ Ⓙ   16. Ⓕ Ⓖ Ⓗ Ⓙ   20. Ⓕ Ⓖ Ⓗ Ⓙ

Analogies

1. Ⓐ Ⓑ Ⓒ Ⓓ   5. Ⓐ Ⓑ Ⓒ Ⓓ   9. Ⓐ Ⓑ Ⓒ Ⓓ   13. Ⓐ Ⓑ Ⓒ Ⓓ   17. Ⓐ Ⓑ Ⓒ Ⓓ
2. Ⓕ Ⓖ Ⓗ Ⓙ   6. Ⓕ Ⓖ Ⓗ Ⓙ   10. Ⓕ Ⓖ Ⓗ Ⓙ   14. Ⓕ Ⓖ Ⓗ Ⓙ   18. Ⓕ Ⓖ Ⓗ Ⓙ
3. Ⓐ Ⓑ Ⓒ Ⓓ   7. Ⓐ Ⓑ Ⓒ Ⓓ   11. Ⓐ Ⓑ Ⓒ Ⓓ   15. Ⓐ Ⓑ Ⓒ Ⓓ   19. Ⓐ Ⓑ Ⓒ Ⓓ
4. Ⓕ Ⓖ Ⓗ Ⓙ   8. Ⓕ Ⓖ Ⓗ Ⓙ   12. Ⓕ Ⓖ Ⓗ Ⓙ   16. Ⓕ Ⓖ Ⓗ Ⓙ   20. Ⓕ Ⓖ Ⓗ Ⓙ

Quantitative Reasoning

1. Ⓐ Ⓑ Ⓒ Ⓓ   5. Ⓐ Ⓑ Ⓒ Ⓓ   9. Ⓐ Ⓑ Ⓒ Ⓓ   13. Ⓐ Ⓑ Ⓒ Ⓓ   17. Ⓐ Ⓑ Ⓒ Ⓓ
2. Ⓕ Ⓖ Ⓗ Ⓙ   6. Ⓕ Ⓖ Ⓗ Ⓙ   10. Ⓕ Ⓖ Ⓗ Ⓙ   14. Ⓕ Ⓖ Ⓗ Ⓙ   18. Ⓕ Ⓖ Ⓗ Ⓙ
3. Ⓐ Ⓑ Ⓒ Ⓓ   7. Ⓐ Ⓑ Ⓒ Ⓓ   11. Ⓐ Ⓑ Ⓒ Ⓓ   15. Ⓐ Ⓑ Ⓒ Ⓓ   19. Ⓐ Ⓑ Ⓒ Ⓓ
4. Ⓕ Ⓖ Ⓗ Ⓙ   8. Ⓕ Ⓖ Ⓗ Ⓙ   12. Ⓕ Ⓖ Ⓗ Ⓙ   16. Ⓕ Ⓖ Ⓗ Ⓙ   20. Ⓕ Ⓖ Ⓗ Ⓙ

Verbal Reasoning—Words

1. Ⓐ Ⓑ Ⓒ Ⓓ   5. Ⓐ Ⓑ Ⓒ Ⓓ   9. Ⓐ Ⓑ Ⓒ Ⓓ   13. Ⓐ Ⓑ Ⓒ Ⓓ   17. Ⓐ Ⓑ Ⓒ Ⓓ
2. Ⓕ Ⓖ Ⓗ Ⓙ   6. Ⓕ Ⓖ Ⓗ Ⓙ   10. Ⓕ Ⓖ Ⓗ Ⓙ   14. Ⓕ Ⓖ Ⓗ Ⓙ   18. Ⓕ Ⓖ Ⓗ Ⓙ
3. Ⓐ Ⓑ Ⓒ Ⓓ   7. Ⓐ Ⓑ Ⓒ Ⓓ   11. Ⓐ Ⓑ Ⓒ Ⓓ   15. Ⓐ Ⓑ Ⓒ Ⓓ   19. Ⓐ Ⓑ Ⓒ Ⓓ
4. Ⓕ Ⓖ Ⓗ Ⓙ   8. Ⓕ Ⓖ Ⓗ Ⓙ   12. Ⓕ Ⓖ Ⓗ Ⓙ   16. Ⓕ Ⓖ Ⓗ Ⓙ   20. Ⓕ Ⓖ Ⓗ Ⓙ

Verbal Reasoning—Context

1. Ⓐ Ⓑ Ⓒ Ⓓ   5. Ⓐ Ⓑ Ⓒ Ⓓ   9. Ⓐ Ⓑ Ⓒ Ⓓ   13. Ⓐ Ⓑ Ⓒ Ⓓ   17. Ⓐ Ⓑ Ⓒ Ⓓ
2. Ⓕ Ⓖ Ⓗ Ⓙ   6. Ⓕ Ⓖ Ⓗ Ⓙ   10. Ⓕ Ⓖ Ⓗ Ⓙ   14. Ⓕ Ⓖ Ⓗ Ⓙ   18. Ⓕ Ⓖ Ⓗ Ⓙ
3. Ⓐ Ⓑ Ⓒ Ⓓ   7. Ⓐ Ⓑ Ⓒ Ⓓ   11. Ⓐ Ⓑ Ⓒ Ⓓ   15. Ⓐ Ⓑ Ⓒ Ⓓ   19. Ⓐ Ⓑ Ⓒ Ⓓ
4. Ⓕ Ⓖ Ⓗ Ⓙ   8. Ⓕ Ⓖ Ⓗ Ⓙ   12. Ⓕ Ⓖ Ⓗ Ⓙ   16. Ⓕ Ⓖ Ⓗ Ⓙ   20. Ⓕ Ⓖ Ⓗ Ⓙ

Reading and Language Arts

1. Ⓐ Ⓑ Ⓒ Ⓓ   9. Ⓐ Ⓑ Ⓒ Ⓓ   17. Ⓐ Ⓑ Ⓒ Ⓓ   25. Ⓐ Ⓑ Ⓒ Ⓓ   33. Ⓐ Ⓑ Ⓒ Ⓓ

2. Ⓕ Ⓖ Ⓗ Ⓙ   10. Ⓕ Ⓖ Ⓗ Ⓙ   18. Ⓕ Ⓖ Ⓗ Ⓙ   26. Ⓕ Ⓖ Ⓗ Ⓙ   34. Ⓕ Ⓖ Ⓗ Ⓙ

3. Ⓐ Ⓑ Ⓒ Ⓓ   11. Ⓐ Ⓑ Ⓒ Ⓓ   19. Ⓐ Ⓑ Ⓒ Ⓓ   27. Ⓐ Ⓑ Ⓒ Ⓓ   35. Ⓐ Ⓑ Ⓒ Ⓓ

4. Ⓕ Ⓖ Ⓗ Ⓙ   12. Ⓕ Ⓖ Ⓗ Ⓙ   20. Ⓕ Ⓖ Ⓗ Ⓙ   28. Ⓕ Ⓖ Ⓗ Ⓙ   36. Ⓕ Ⓖ Ⓗ Ⓙ

5. Ⓐ Ⓑ Ⓒ Ⓓ   13. Ⓐ Ⓑ Ⓒ Ⓓ   21. Ⓐ Ⓑ Ⓒ Ⓓ   29. Ⓐ Ⓑ Ⓒ Ⓓ   37. Ⓐ Ⓑ Ⓒ Ⓓ

6. Ⓕ Ⓖ Ⓗ Ⓙ   14. Ⓕ Ⓖ Ⓗ Ⓙ   22. Ⓕ Ⓖ Ⓗ Ⓙ   30. Ⓕ Ⓖ Ⓗ Ⓙ   38. Ⓕ Ⓖ Ⓗ Ⓙ

7. Ⓐ Ⓑ Ⓒ Ⓓ   15. Ⓐ Ⓑ Ⓒ Ⓓ   23. Ⓐ Ⓑ Ⓒ Ⓓ   31. Ⓐ Ⓑ Ⓒ Ⓓ   39. Ⓐ Ⓑ Ⓒ Ⓓ

8. Ⓕ Ⓖ Ⓗ Ⓙ   16. Ⓕ Ⓖ Ⓗ Ⓙ   24. Ⓕ Ⓖ Ⓗ Ⓙ   32. Ⓕ Ⓖ Ⓗ Ⓙ   40. Ⓕ Ⓖ Ⓗ Ⓙ

Mathematics

1. Ⓐ Ⓑ Ⓒ Ⓓ Ⓔ   9. Ⓐ Ⓑ Ⓒ Ⓓ   17. Ⓐ Ⓑ Ⓒ Ⓓ   25. Ⓐ Ⓑ Ⓒ Ⓓ   33. Ⓐ Ⓑ Ⓒ Ⓓ

2. Ⓕ Ⓖ Ⓗ Ⓙ Ⓚ   10. Ⓕ Ⓖ Ⓗ Ⓙ   18. Ⓕ Ⓖ Ⓗ Ⓙ   26. Ⓕ Ⓖ Ⓗ Ⓙ   34. Ⓕ Ⓖ Ⓗ Ⓙ

3. Ⓐ Ⓑ Ⓒ Ⓓ Ⓔ   11. Ⓐ Ⓑ Ⓒ Ⓓ   19. Ⓐ Ⓑ Ⓒ Ⓓ   27. Ⓐ Ⓑ Ⓒ Ⓓ   35. Ⓐ Ⓑ Ⓒ Ⓓ

4. Ⓕ Ⓖ Ⓗ Ⓙ Ⓚ   12. Ⓕ Ⓖ Ⓗ Ⓙ   20. Ⓕ Ⓖ Ⓗ Ⓙ   28. Ⓕ Ⓖ Ⓗ Ⓙ   36. Ⓕ Ⓖ Ⓗ Ⓙ

5. Ⓐ Ⓑ Ⓒ Ⓓ Ⓔ   13. Ⓐ Ⓑ Ⓒ Ⓓ   21. Ⓐ Ⓑ Ⓒ Ⓓ   29. Ⓐ Ⓑ Ⓒ Ⓓ   37. Ⓐ Ⓑ Ⓒ Ⓓ

6. Ⓕ Ⓖ Ⓗ Ⓙ Ⓚ   14. Ⓕ Ⓖ Ⓗ Ⓙ   22. Ⓕ Ⓖ Ⓗ Ⓙ   30. Ⓕ Ⓖ Ⓗ Ⓙ   38. Ⓕ Ⓖ Ⓗ Ⓙ

7. Ⓐ Ⓑ Ⓒ Ⓓ Ⓔ   15. Ⓐ Ⓑ Ⓒ Ⓓ   23. Ⓐ Ⓑ Ⓒ Ⓓ   31. Ⓐ Ⓑ Ⓒ Ⓓ   39. Ⓐ Ⓑ Ⓒ Ⓓ

8. Ⓕ Ⓖ Ⓗ Ⓙ Ⓚ   16. Ⓕ Ⓖ Ⓗ Ⓙ   24. Ⓕ Ⓖ Ⓗ Ⓙ   32. Ⓕ Ⓖ Ⓗ Ⓙ   40. Ⓕ Ⓖ Ⓗ Ⓙ

COOP Practice Test 1

TEST 1: SEQUENCES

Directions: For questions 1–20, choose the answer that best continues the sequence.

1. ꟸꟸꟸ ꟸꟸꟸ ꟸꟸꟸ ___

   ꟸꟸꟸ ꟸꟸꟸ ꟸꟸꟸ ꟸꟸꟸ
   (A)   (B)   (C)   (D)

2. ▲▲▲◨ ▲▲▲◻ ▲▲▲◨ _____

   ▲▲▲◻ ▲▲◨▲ ▲▲◨◻ ▲▲▲◻
   (F)   (G)   (H)   (J)

3. ✕✕✕ ✕✕✕ ✕✕✕ ✕✕__

   ✕   ✕   ✕   ✕
   (A)   (B)   (C)   (D)

4. ☆★★★ ★★★☆ ★★★☆ ★★★__

   ☆   ★   ★   ☆
   (F)   (G)   (H)   (J)

5.

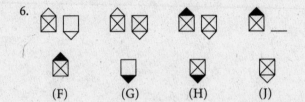

(A)   (B)   (C)   (D)

6.

(F)   (G)   (H)   (J)

7. 2   5   10   3   7   21   4   9   ___

(A) 13

(B) 36

(C) 27

(D) 5

8. 1   2   6   3   6   18   5   10 ___

(F) 30

(G) 20

(H) 25

(J) 22

9. 100 10 7   64 8   5   49 7   ___

(A) 2

(B) 4

(C) 3

(D) 1

10. 64 51 13   52 40 8   33 22 ___

(F) 11

(G) 9

(H) 5

(J) 10

11. 2   8   0   4   16   8   7   28   ___

(A) 15

(B) 21

(C) 20

(D) 16

12. 6   7   9   8   9   11   12   13   ___

(F) 15

(G) 18

(H) 20

(J) 19

13. 72   67   65   87   82   80   91   86   ___

(A) 79

(B) 82

(C) 84

(D) 80

14. 100   90   25   80   70   20   40   30   ___

(F) 23

(G) 10

(H) 30

(J) 5

15. A1B0C1   A2B1C2   _____   A4B3C4

(A) A3B2C3

(B) A4B3C3

(C) A3B3C3

(D) A4B4C3

16. $X^1Y^9Z^2$ $X^2Y^7Z^4$ _____ $X^4Y^2Z^8$

(F) $X^3Y^2Z^6$

(G) $X^3Y^3Z^5$

(H) $X^1Y^3Z^4$

(J) $X^3Y^5Z^6$

17. lfg   mgh   _____   oij

  (A) hgm

  (B) nhi

  (C) ngh

  (D) mhi

18. BxY   cXy   DxY   _____

  (F) ExY

  (G) eXy

  (H) exy

  (J) Dxy

19. ZAB   YBC   _____   WDE

  (A) WDC

  (B) XCD

  (C) XAE

  (D) XCF

20. ABE   BCF   CDG   _____

  (F) DFG

  (G) DEF

  (H) DFH

  (J) DEH

TEST 2: ANALOGIES

Directions: For questions 1–20, look at the two pictures on top. Then, choose the picture that belongs in the space so that the bottom two pictures are related the same way that the top two are related.

1.

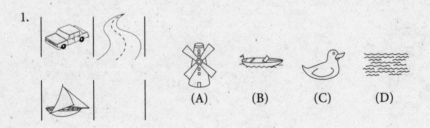

        (A)   (B)   (C)   (D)

2.

(F)   (G)   (H)   (J)

3.

(A)   (B)   (C)   (D)

4.

(F)   (G)   (H)   (J)

5.

(A)   (B)   (C)   (D)

6.

(F)   (G)   (H)   (J)

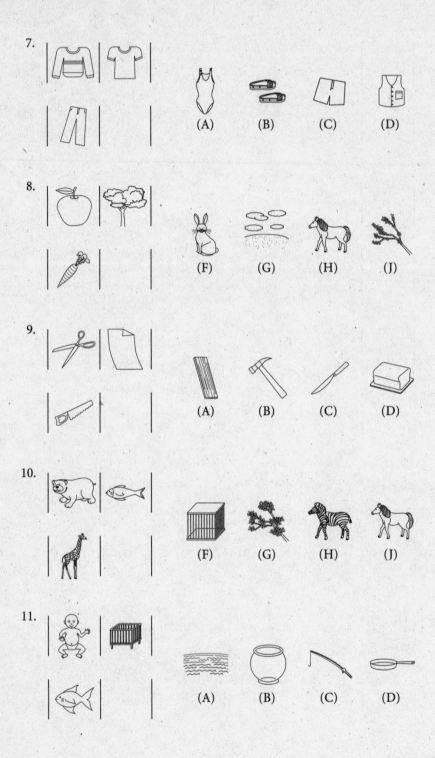

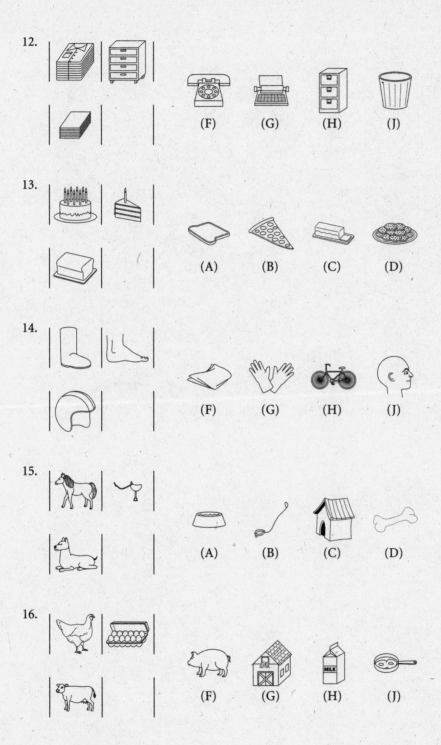

12.   (F)   (G)   (H)   (J)

13.   (A)   (B)   (C)   (D)

14.   (F)   (G)   (H)   (J)

15.   (A)   (B)   (C)   (D)

16.   (F)   (G)   (H)   (J)

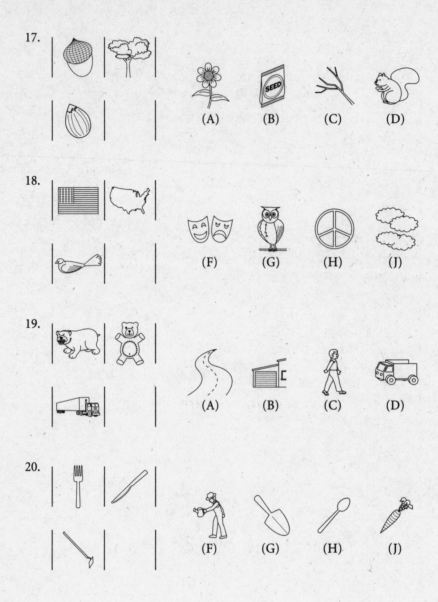

17.

18.

19.

20.

TEST 3: QUANTITATIVE REASONING

Directions: For questions 1–6, find the relationship of the numbers in the left column to the numbers in the right column. Choose the number that should replace the blank.

1. $3 \rightarrow \square \rightarrow 9$

   $1 \rightarrow \square \rightarrow 7$

   $2 \rightarrow \square \rightarrow \_\_$

5	4	8	9
(A)	(B)	(C)	(D)

2. $4 \rightarrow \square \rightarrow 6$

   $1 \rightarrow \square \rightarrow 3$

   $5 \rightarrow \square \rightarrow \_\_$

7	5	4	8
(F)	(G)	(H)	(J)

3. $\frac{1}{2} \rightarrow \square \rightarrow 1\frac{1}{2}$

   $\frac{1}{3} \rightarrow \square \rightarrow 1\frac{1}{3}$

   $2 \rightarrow \square \rightarrow \_\_$

3	$2\frac{1}{4}$	1	$1\frac{1}{2}$
(A)	(B)	(C)	(D)

4. $12 \rightarrow \boxed{} \rightarrow 3$

    $20 \rightarrow \boxed{} \rightarrow 5$

    $8 \rightarrow \boxed{} \rightarrow \underline{}$

4	2	1	3
(F)	(G)	(H)	(J)

5. $9 \rightarrow \boxed{} \rightarrow 4$

    $4 \rightarrow \boxed{} \rightarrow -1$

    $10 \rightarrow \boxed{} \rightarrow \underline{}$

−2	4	7	5
(A)	(B)	(C)	(D)

6. $.5 \rightarrow \boxed{} \rightarrow .05$

    $1.0 \rightarrow \boxed{} \rightarrow .1$

    $10.0 \rightarrow \boxed{} \rightarrow \underline{}$

1.0	10	100	.01
(F)	(G)	(H)	(J)

Directions: For questions 7–13, find the fraction of the grid that is shaded.

7.

   (A) $\dfrac{1}{4}$ (B) $\dfrac{1}{8}$ (C) $\dfrac{1}{6}$ (D) $\dfrac{1}{10}$

8.

   (F) 2   (G) $\dfrac{1}{16}$ (H) $\dfrac{1}{8}$ (J) $\dfrac{2}{10}$

9.

   (A) 1   (B) $\dfrac{1}{4}$ (C) $\dfrac{2}{1}$ (D) $\dfrac{1}{2}$

10.

   (F) $\dfrac{1}{8}$ (G) $\dfrac{1}{2}$ (H) $\dfrac{2}{3}$ (J) $\dfrac{1}{4}$

11.

   (A) $\dfrac{1}{8}$ (B) $\dfrac{1}{2}$ (C) $\dfrac{3}{8}$ (D) $\dfrac{1}{5}$

12.

(F) $\frac{1}{2}$ (G) $\frac{1}{3}$ (H) $\frac{1}{4}$ (J) $\frac{2}{7}$

13.

(A) 2 (B) $\frac{2}{3}$ (C) $\frac{1}{3}$ (D) $\frac{1}{2}$

Directions: For questions 14–20, the scale shows sets of shapes of equal weight. Find a pair of sets that would also balance the scale.

14.

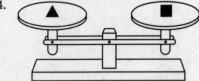

15.

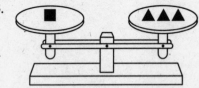

16.

(F)

(G)

(H)

(J)

17.

(A)

(B)

(C)

(D)

18.

(F)

(G)

(H)

(J)

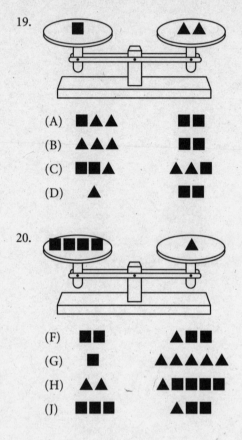

19.

(A) ■▲▲   ■■
(B) ▲▲▲   ■■
(C) ■■▲   ▲▲■
(D) ▲   ■■

20.

(F) ■■   ▲■■
(G) ■   ▲▲▲▲▲
(H) ▲▲   ▲■■■■
(J) ■■■   ▲■■

TEST 4: VERBAL REASONING—WORDS

Directions: For questions 1–9, find the word that names a necessary part of the underlined word.

1. <u>cage</u>

    (A) captivity
    (B) security
    (C) display
    (D) door

2. <u>megaphone</u>

    (F) hearing
    (G) yelling
    (H) listening
    (J) announcing

3. <u>oven</u>

   (A) coal
   (B) heat
   (C) aroma
   (D) food

4. <u>carpet</u>

   (F) comfort
   (G) pattern
   (H) fringe
   (J) thread

5. <u>concert</u>

   (A) stage
   (B) audience
   (C) seats
   (D) conductor

6. <u>trial</u>

   (F) objection
   (G) witness
   (H) verdict
   (J) courtroom

7. <u>message</u>

   (A) letter
   (B) writing
   (C) communication
   (D) telephone

8. <u>fish</u>

   (F) gills
   (G) ocean
   (H) lake
   (J) tail

9. <u>leash</u>

    (A) walk

    (B) control

    (C) drag

    (D) encircle

Directions: For questions 10–13, the words in the top row are related in some way. The words in the bottom row are related in the same way. Find the word that competes the bottom row of words.

10. content   happy   ecstatic

    ruffled   annoyed

    (F) peaceful

    (G) agitated

    (H) controlled

    (J) emotional

11. tree   trunk   leaf

    flower   stem

    (A) petal

    (B) branch

    (C) root

    (D) bouquet

12. umbrella   rainhat   galoshes

    sunglasses   sunhat

    (F) parasol

    (G) nature

    (H) sandals

    (J) hammock

13. daughter   mother   grandmother

                    father   grandfather

    (A) brother

    (B) son

    (C) cousin

    (D) uncle

Directions: For questions 14–17, find the word that does *not* belong with the others.

14. Which word does *not* belong with the others?

    (F) bottle
    (G) diaper
    (H) crib
    (J) slide

15. Which word does *not* belong with the others?

    (A) rooster
    (B) mare
    (C) bull
    (D) stallion

16. Which word does *not* belong with the others?

    (F) data
    (G) evidence
    (H) opinion
    (J) fact

17. Which word does *not* belong with the others?

    (A) wink
    (B) grimace
    (C) frown
    (D) smile

Directions: For questions 18–20, find the word that is most like the underlined words.

18. <u>calm</u>   <u>peaceful</u>   <u>tranquil</u>

    (F) clean
    (G) boring
    (H) relaxing
    (J) restless

19. <u>moral</u>   <u>honest</u>   <u>loyal</u>

    (A) true
    (B) brave
    (C) verbose
    (D) durable

20. <u>tidy</u>   <u>neat</u>   <u>orderly</u>

   (F) cozy

   (G) disorderly

   (H) cute

   (J) spotless

TEST 5: VERBAL REASONING—CONTEXT

Directions: For questions 1–20, find the statement that is true according to the given information.

1. The Statue of Liberty is in New York City. Christine has climbed to the top of the Statue of Liberty.

   (A) Many tourists visit the Statue of Liberty.

   (B) The Statue of Liberty was a gift from the French.

   (C) Christine has been to New York City.

   (D) Christine is in good physical condition.

2. Marcia is older than Jan. Jan is 5 feet 2 inches tall.

   (F) Marcia is taller than Jan.

   (G) Jan is taller than Marcia.

   (H) Jan is younger than Marcia.

   (J) Marcia and Jan are sisters.

3. A slice of white bread is 100 calories a slice. A slice of wheat bread is 150 calories a slice.

   (A) Wheat bread is fattening and white bread is not.

   (B) White bread is tastier than wheat bread.

   (C) More people buy white bread than wheat bread.

   (D) There is more caloric energy in a slice of wheat bread than in a slice of white bread.

4. Jean sold 6 used cars in March. No one sold more cars than Jean in March.

   (F) Jean also sold the most cards in April.

   (G) Jean was employee of the month in March.

   (H) No one other than Jean sold cars in March.

   (J) Jean sold the most cars in March.

5. Dogs often bark to protect their territory from intruders. Fluffy the dog is inside the house barking.

   (A) Someone is threatening his owner.

   (B) Someone may be trying to break into Fluffy's owner's home.

   (C) Fluffy is too high strung.

   (D) Fluffy is tired of being locked up and he needs to go outside.

6. Lisa sent an email her friend Amy. Amy hasn't written Lisa back yet.

   (F) Lisa hasn't received a reply from Amy yet.

   (G) Amy is too busy to write Lisa.

   (H) Lisa likes to write letters.

   (J) Amy is probably angry at Lisa.

7. Rare coins are worth a lot of money. Jim has a rare 1942 copper penny.

   (A) Jim collects coins.

   (B) Jim has a valuable coin.

   (C) Silver dollars are rare coins.

   (D) Copper pennies are no longer made.

8. Mercedes Brown lives at #2 Front Street. Yesterday she found a letter in her mailbox addressed to Mercedes Brow at #3 Front Street.

   (F) A woman with a similar name lives next door to Mercedes Brown.

   (G) The mail carrier made a mistake when he delivered the letter to Mercedes Brown.

   (H) The person addressing the letter probably made a mistake.

   (J) A woman with a similar name lived in Mercedes Brown's house before she did.

9. John's computer suddenly turns off. His lights, television, and radio are still running.

   (A) There is a blackout.

   (B) There is a problem with John's computer.

   (C) John's computer is unplugged.

   (D) John does not know how to use a computer.

10. Romero's offers a free pizza to any delivery customer who waits longer than 30 minutes to receive their order. Samina ordered a large pepperoni pizza from Romero's.

    (F) Samina is a customer of Romero's.

    (G) Samina likes pepperoni pizza.

    (H) Romero's always delivers on time.

    (J) Romero's is faster than the competitor.

11. Joseph would like to attend Minetta Music School. The school only accepts students who can read music.

    (A) Joseph is a talented musician.

    (B) Joseph must read music in order to attend Minetta Music School.

    (C) Joseph cannot read music.

    (D) Minetta Music School is the best in Joseph's town.

12. Polar bears live in Alaska. There are two polar bears at the Bronx Zoo in New York.

    (F) Polar bears also live in New York.
    (G) The polar bear at the zoo is unhappy.

    (H) It is too warm in New York for a polar bear.

    (J) Polar bears are threatened with extinction.

13. Maria lives in New Jersey. Monday through Friday she commutes to New York City for work. On Saturday and Sunday afternoon she pitches for a softball team. On Sunday evening she cooks dinner for the entire week.

    (A) Maria works in New York City five days a week.

    (B) Maria shares her cooking with players on her team.

    (C) Softball players are good cooks.

    (D) Maria has a microwave oven.

14. Zookeepers in Seattle brought a black bear from Kodiak Island to share a cage with another black bear. Yesterday, the black bear from Kodiak Island gave birth to a baby bear. Zookeepers were overjoyed and threw a little birthday party for the baby bear.

    (F) Black bears prefer salmon to birthday cake.

    (G) Zookeepers like to have birthday parties.

    (H) Black bears are friendly.

    (J) The bear from Kodiak Island is female.

15. Brandon was looking for his car keys all morning. He looked under the bed, in the kitchen cabinet, and in his coat pocket. Finally, he looked in the ignition of the car and shouted "Aha!"

    (A) Brandon is always absentminded.

    (B) The lost keys were in the car.

    (C) Brandon left the car running.

    (D) Brandon was late to work.

16. Mr. Sloan wears reading glasses. He can't find his glasses.

 (F) Mr. Sloan likes to read.

 (G) He won't be able to find his glasses.

 (H) Mr. Sloan probably won't be able to read without his glasses.

 (J) Mr. Sloan reads the paper every morning.

17. On its way uptown, the local train stops every ten blocks, starting at 10th Street. The express train also starts at 10th Street, but after that it stops only at every other station. The #6 train is an express train.

 (A) The local train is very slow.

 (B) The #6 train does not stop at 40th Street.

 (C) The #6 train stops at 20th Street.

 (D) The #6 train is faster than the #5 train.

18. Lunch is served in the cafeteria Monday through Friday between 12 P.M. and 2 P.M. It is now 11:55 A.M. on Thursday.

 (F) Lunch is being served early today.

 (G) The cafeteria food is not good.

 (H) Lunch is served every day of the week.

 (J) Lunch will be served in five minutes.

19. You must be 16 years old to get a driver's permit. John's birthday is in March.

 (A) No one under the age of 16 is allowed to get a driver's permit.

 (B) John will apply for a driver's permit this year.

 (C) John is looking forward to driving.

 (D) All 16 year olds apply for driver's permits.

20. Mount Everest is the highest mountain in the world. Mount Everest is in Nepal.

 (F) Mount Everest is in the Himalayas.

 (G) The highest mountain in the world is in Nepal.

 (H) The Rocky Mountains are the highest mountain range in the United States.

 (J) Mount Everest is hard to climb.

TEST 6: READING AND LANGUAGE ARTS

Directions: Follow the directions for questions 1–40.

Read the following passage and answer questions 1–5.

It's a beautiful spring day. There has been a brief shower, and now, with the sun shining brightly again, a brilliant rainbow appears in the sky. It feels as though the entire world is celebrating the reappearance of the sun. Yet, there is a <u>precise</u> scientific reason why rainbows can only be seen on particular types of day, at particular times of day, and from particular vantage points. For example, have you ever noticed that the sun is always behind you when you face a rainbow? Or, have you noticed that when you face a rainbow the center of its arc is opposite the sun?

French philosopher and scientist Rene Descartes studied and discussed the basis for this marvelous phenomenon in 1637. Descartes reasoned that since rainbows only appear in the sky when there are drops of water illuminated by the sun, the rainbow must be caused by the way in which the rays of light act on water drops and pass from them to our eyes. As sunlight hits a raindrop it is refracted, or bent, by the drop in such a way that the light appears as a spectrum of colors. Traditionally, the rainbow is described as containing seven colors—red, orange, yellow, green, blue, indigo, and violet. In reality, the rainbow is a whole continuum of colors from red to violet, including colors on either end of the spectrum that the eye cannot even see.

The colors are only apparent however, when the angle of reflection between the sun, the drop of water, and the observer's line of sight is an angle between 40 and 42 degrees. The lower the sun is in the sky, the higher the rainbow appears. As the sun rises higher, the rainbow appears lower, thus keeping the essential 40 to 42 degree angle. When the sun is more than 42 degrees above the horizon line, we can no longer see the rainbow, because the required angle is then over our heads.

1. The word <u>precise</u> most nearly means

   (A) true

   (B) exact

   (C) precious

   (D) difficult

2. Rainbows are caused by

   (F) light acting on water

   (G) the angle of the sun in the sky

   (H) warm air currents

   (J) a spectrum of colors

3. A rainbow is made up of

   (A) white light

   (B) a continuum of colors

   (C) seven colors

   (D) sunlight

4. Rainbows disappear when

   (F) the sun sets

   (G) you stand in front of them

   (H) the sun is higher than 42 degrees

   (J) the sun rises

5. In a rainbow, water drops affect light by

   (A) absorbing it

   (B) refracting it

   (C) making it visible

   (D) illustrating it

Here is a story a student wrote about seeing a rainbow one spring afternoon. There are a few mistakes that need correcting. Read the story, then answer questions 6–8.

(1) Yesterday afternoon was a sunny, Spring Day. (2) Janet and me were outside riding our bicycles around the block. (3) It began to rain. (4) Janet's mother called, "Come inside girls." (5) It only rained a few minutes. (6) So we kept riding. (7) When the rain finished, we looked up in the sky and saw the most beautifulest rainbow.

6. Which sentence contains a capitalization error?

   (F) Sentence 1

   (G) Sentence 2

   (H) Sentence 3

   (J) Sentence 4

7. Choose the best way to combine sentences 5 and 6.

   (A) It only rained a few minutes and so we kept riding.

   (B) It only rained a few minutes, and so we kept riding.

   (C) It only rained a few minutes, so we kept riding.

   (D) It only rained a few minutes so we kept riding.

8. Choose the best way to rewrite sentence 7.

(F) When the rain finished, we looked up in the sky and saw the more beautifuller rainbow.

(G) When the rain finished, we looked up in the sky and saw the beautifulest rainbow.

(H) When the rain finished, we looked up in the sky and saw the most beautiful rainbow.

(J) Best as is.

Read the following passage and answer questions 9–12.

The alarm clock rings, we rush out of bed, we throw on our clothes, maybe grab a quick breakfast and run out the door. Maybe we get stuck in a traffic jam on our way to work or school. As we wait, trapped in the middle of a sea of automobiles, our pulse quickens, our breath grows shallow, we growl at the other drivers, who we blame for our predicament. This is a typical morning for many Americans. Not only is it stressful, it is also unhealthy.

The constant pressures of everyday life take a toll on the physical and mental well-being of millions of people each year. Medical research indicates that common illnesses such as high blood pressure, heart disease, stomach ulcers, and headaches are related to stress. Stress is also an underlying factor in emotional and behavioral problems including difficulty concentrating, aggressive behavior, and difficulty sleeping or eating. While these are the "positive" effects of stress, there are "negative" ones as well, which we often fail to link to their true cause. Instead of nervousness and aggression, people who manifest these reactions to stress find themselves lethargic, sleeping too much, overeating, or becoming anti-social.

What's the solution? Relax! It sounds simple, but many people find it incredibly difficult. True relaxation is more than getting away from the regular routine. It is the experience of finding peace of mind, self-awareness, and thoughtful reflection. Find small ways to build relaxation into your day-to-day routine. Exercise to relieve stress. Walk, bicycle, dance, or swim a little bit each day. For physically fit people, strenuous exercise, which allows them to work up a sweat, can give a tremendous feeling of relaxation when it is finished. The deep breathing necessitated by exercise can help calm the anxious body. Deep breathing in general is a great way to relax. Participate in creative activities such as painting, drawing, knitting, or cooking. Try some mental exercises to relieve stress, such as imagining a special place where you enjoy going. Most importantly, try to build relaxation into every day.

9. Relaxation is essential because it

(A) keeps us physically fit

(B) prevents us from becoming aggressive

(C) helps us to lead healthy lives

(D) is difficult to do

10. According to this article

    (F) people become aggressive under pressure

    (G) people don't eat enough breakfast

    (H) stress allows us to accomplish many things

    (J) stress may cause health problems

11. In this article, the term "negative" response to stress means

    (A) any bad reactions to stress

    (B) ulcers, headaches, high blood pressure

    (C) reactions that show low energy

    (D) emotional reactions

12. All of the following are mentioned as possible ways to relax EXCEPT

    (F) mental exercise

    (G) denying worries or concerns

    (H) physical movement

    (J) pursuing an artistic endeavor

13. Here are two sentences related to the passage:

    Regular exercise is a good way to stay healthy.

    Regular exercise can reduce blood pressure and help maintain a stable weight.

    Select the answer choice that best combines the two sentences into one.

    (A) There are two reasons why regular exercise is a good way to stay healthy; it can reduce blood pressure and help maintain a stable weight.

    (B) Regular exercise is a good way to stay healthy; it can reduce blood pressure and help maintain a stable weight.

    (C) Regular exercise can reduce blood pressure and help maintain a stable weight that is why it's a good way to stay healthy.

    (D) Regular exercise is a good way to stay healthy and it can reduce blood pressure and help maintain a stable weight.

14. Choose the sentence that would be the best conclusion to the article.

    (F) Relax, but don't fall asleep.

    (G) Remember, relaxation can help you stay in good shape.

    (H) Some athletes practice relaxation techniques before a competition.

    (J) Remember, it's essential to relax in order to be in good shape to meet the demands of a busy lifestyle.

Read the following passage and answer questions 15–18.

It was part of her nefarious plot! Of that I had no doubt. She would slowly deprive me of my delicious slumber until finally, exhausted, I gave in to her wretched demands. She could claw her way into my dreams, she could growl and complain, but no, I would not give in. I pulled the covers close over my head and rolled over. I was the stronger of we two. I was the determined one. I was the human, and she the beast. She must have understood my determination, for mercifully, the whining stopped. My breathing grew deeper and I returned to my wonderful sleep. Until moments later a crash awakened me. I bolted out of bed and there she was, in the kitchen guiltily lapping kitty treats off the floor. The mischievous beast had jumped onto the countertop and knocked the bag of food onto the floor. "Bad kitty!" I scolded, pushing her away from the mess of chow. But that sweet face, that little sandpaper tongue licking her chops somehow softened me.

15. Probably the next thing that will happen is that the author will

   (A) lock the kitten out of the bedroom
   (B) let the kitten eat the treats
   (C) bring the kitten to bed
   (D) go back to sleep

16. The action described in this selection could *not* be part of

   (F) a children's television show
   (G) a situation comedy
   (H) an digest magazine
   (J) a science fiction

17. The author's attitude toward the kitten is

   (A) reluctant indulgence
   (B) total animosity
   (C) patient resolve
   (D) complete annoyance

18. The reader is *not* told

   (F) the kitten's tactics
   (G) why the author is annoyed at the kitten
   (H) where the author got the kitten
   (J) what the kitten's plot is

Here is a story a student wrote about her own kittens. There are a few mistakes that need correcting. Read the story, then answer questions 19–21.

(1) I have three kittens named Orange, Apple, and Nana. (2) To take care of them is a lot of work. (3) I have to make sure they have water every day. (4) And food. (5) There's also cleaning their litter box.

19. Which is the best way to write Sentence 1?

(A) I have three kittens. And they are named Orange, Apple, and Nana.

(B) I have three kittens. They are named Orange, Apple, and Nana.

(C) Three kittens that I have are named Orange, Apple, and Nana.

(D) Best as is.

20. What is the best way to combine sentences 3 and 4?

(F) I have to make sure they have water and food every day.

(G) Everyday, I am having to make sure they have water and food

(H) Having to make sure they have water and food every day.

(J) Water and food every day is what I have to make sure they have.

21. Choose the best way to write Sentence 5.

(A) There is also the litter box to clean.

(B) Cleaning the litter box there is also.

(C) I also have to clean their litter box.

(D) Best as is.

Read the following passage and answer questions 22–26.

When we think of elephants, we generally conjure images of Africa and India because that is where they live today. But in the very recent past, elephants, or their close relative, the woolly mammoth, inhabited every continent except Australia and South America. Although the mammoth became extinct at least 10,000 years ago, some mammoths continued to populate Wrangel Island near Siberia until as recently as 4,000 years ago. In the United States, woolly mammoth remains have been found in Wisconsin, Indiana, and Alaska.

Closely related to existing African and Asian species, the woolly mammoth most likely originated in Eurasia about a quarter of a million years ago. They migrated to the Americas over the Bering land bridge. Thanks to numerous cave paintings in Europe, and the discovery of well-preserved mammoth body parts in the permafrost of Alaska and Siberia, the mammoth's appearance is well-known today.

Mammoths stood nine to eleven feet tall and weighed four to six tons. The great beasts were covered with long, shaggy hair and had a high, domed head, a hunched back, and long, twisted tusks. However, since the trunks were composed of soft tissue, they did not survive in fossil form. Scientists are convinced of the mammoth's appear-ance due to the cave paintings, and a large cavity in the skull of mammoth remains precisely where the trunks would have been. The great mammoth's skulls, with one massive opening, may have been the basis for the myth of the Cyclopes, the imaginary one-eyed giant. Perhaps ancient people, observing mammoth remains, mistook the trunk opening in the mammoth's skull for an eye socket.

22. Woolly mammoths came to the Americas from

(F) India
(G) Eurasia
(H) Africa
(J) Europe

23. We know the appearance of woolly mammoths because

(A) legends have been passed down
(B) paintings of them have been discovered
(C) they resemble elephants in India
(D) they disappeared during the ice age

24. Mammoths lived

(F) during the time of the pharaohs of Egypt
(G) until Alaska became a state
(H) at the same time as the Cyclops
(J) about a quarter of a century ago

25. Mammoth trunks are not found among their remains because

(A) North American mammoths did not have trunks
(B) they were carried away by ancient peoples
(C) they were not fossilized
(D) they were composed of bone

26. Compared with modern elephants, the mammoth

(F) traveled longer distances
(G) lived in warmer climates
(H) had a longer trunk
(J) had more natural habitats

Here is a paragraph related to the passage. Read the paragraph, then answer questions 27–28.

The Asian elephant has a large domed head with small ears, an arched back and a single finger-like protrusion at the tip of the trunk. An Asian elephant has five toes on the front feet and four toes on the back. The African elephant has a straight back, enormous ears, and two trunk "fingers" instead of one. African elephants live in family groups headed by a female cow. The African elephant has only four toes on the front feet and three on the back. African elephants are also much larger than Asian elephants.

27. Choose the best topic sentence for this paragraph.

   (A) Asian elephants are completely different than African elephants.

   (B) *Elephas Maximus* is the species name for the Asian elephant.

   (C) Asian and African elephants have some noticeable differences.

   (D) Elephants can weigh between 4 and 7 tons.

28. Which sentence does NOT belong in the paragraph?

   (F) African elephants are also much larger than Asian elephants.

   (G) The African elephant has a straight back, enormous ears, and two trunk "fingers" instead of one.

   (H) African elephants live in family groups headed by a female cow.

   (J) An Asian elephant has five toes on the front feet and four toes on the back.

Read the following passage and answer questions 29–33.

Today we planted the first seeds of our very own victory garden. How wonderful it felt to know that we were part of the effort, supporting our brave troops fighting overseas. Such a small step—this little garden of ours, but still it makes me proud that we are doing our part to help the American war effort against Hitler's tyranny and oppression. I can almost imagine that as our seeds take root and grow, so does democracy root out the evil weed spreading through Europe.

Meanwhile, George complains about the gasoline rationing. He hates not being able to drive that spiffy new car of his. I personally could never stand our little pleasure drives over the bumpy back roads and I find it no sacrifice at all to forgo a tank of gasoline if it will help the war effort. It is doing without silk stockings that bothers me. Though I am ashamed to admit it, I do love my little luxuries. And though I do admire our many "Rosie the Riveters" I myself can't imagine taking up work in a factory. Who knows, maybe I'd feel differently with my first paycheck in hand. But all that remains speculation, for now there are four little boys to feed, bathe, and tuck in for the night. When we receive next month's ration coupons, I plan to bake all manner of cakes. Until then, unfortunately the pantry is out of sugar and George has to make do with unsweetened coffee. Though the coffee too is almost finished and we most certainly will run out before the next book of ration coupons arrives.

29. This passage takes place during

    (A) futuristic times
    (B) the Korean War
    (C) World War II
    (D) World War I

30. George is most likely

    (F) the author's son
    (G) the author's husband
    (H) the author
    (J) a soldier

31. The author of this selection is most probably a

    (A) baker
    (B) "Rosie the Riveter"
    (C) homemaker
    (D) farmer

32. According to the passage, all of the following must be rationed EXCEPT

    (F) vegetables
    (G) sugar
    (H) gasoline
    (J) silk stockings

33. Why do you think the author felt her garden was helping the war effort?

    (A) It meant more canned food would be available for the troops.
    (B) She was going to send the food she grew to the troops in Europe.
    (C) She was earning money which she would give to support the soldiers.
    (D) By gardening, she was promoting peaceful activity.

34. Here are two sentences related to the passage:

    Certain items such as metal, gasoline, and silk were not available.

    They were needed for the war effort.

    Select the answer choice that best combines the two sentences into one.

    (F) Certain items such as metal, gasoline, and silk were not available and they were needed for the war effort.

    (G) Metal, gasoline, and silk were not available and they were needed for the war effort.

    (H) Certain items such as metal, gasoline, and silk were not available; they were needed for the war effort.

    (J) Because they were needed for the war effort, certain items such as metal, gasoline, and silk were not available.

35. Choose the sentence that is written correctly.

    (A) Many rationed items people were able to get on the black market.

    (B) Although many items were rationed, people still managed to get them on the black market.

    (C) Getting many items on the black market people managed although they were rationed.

    (D) Although they were rationed, people still managed to get many items on the black market.

Read the following passage and answer questions 36–40.

The state lottery is unfair because it steals from the poor and gives to the rich. Every study available shows that the lottery is played more often by poor people than by rich people. Since the state takes a percentage of every dollar bet on the lottery, this amounts to a greater tax on poor people than on rich. We all know the odds of winning the lottery are horrendously bad. It is common knowledge that a person has more chance of being hit by lightening than winning the lottery. Thus, the lottery is nothing more than an elaborate excuse to separate a fool from his money. It is shameful that the government, whose function should be to protect the public good, administers and even advertises this sham. Let's say Joe Schmoe has the astoundingly good fortune to win a grand prize of a million dollars. Paid out over twenty years, this amounts to only $50,00 per year for twenty years. While Joe receives his annual $50,000, the balance of Joe's jackpot remains in the bank. The government collects on the interest, not Joe. Plus, Joe has to pay taxes on his winnings. Joe's relatives crawl out of the woodwork, looking for a piece of the pie. He argues with his family over how to spend his winnings. Or, he blows all the money living beyond his means and finds himself alone and miserable a year later. When you do the math, there is no question who the real winner of the lottery is.

36. According to the author, the main problem with the lottery is

   (F) winners often find they are unhappy a year later
   (G) it is unfair because it steals from the poor
   (H) the government taxes winnings
   (J) not enough people win

37. The author argues against

   (A) the happiness of the winners
   (B) government support of the lottery
   (C) using taxes to pay for public good
   (D) taxing a lottery winner's jackpot

38. The name *Joe Schmoe* is used to

   (F) make the reader jealous of one winner
   (G) make fun of people who play the lottery
   (H) give an example of a specific winner
   (J) represent the common man

39. In this selection, the author

   (A) illustrates why the lottery is unfair
   (B) tells people to stop buying lottery tickets
   (C) asks the government to ban the lottery
   (D) shows how the lottery fails to help education

40. According to the passage all of these are benefits to the government for lottery EXCEPT

   (F) collecting tax on winnings
   (G) keeping interest on winnings
   (H) paying out lump sum winnings
   (J) receiving tax on each ticket purchased

TEST 7: MATHEMATICS

Directions: For questions 1–40, read each problem and find the answer.

1. $3^3 \times 3^4 =$

   (A) 312

   (B) 3^7

   (C) $3 \times 3 \times 3 \times 3 \times 3 \times 3$

   (D) 1,260

   (E) None of these.

2. $6.2 - .4 =$

   (F) 2.8

   (G) 6.5

   (H) 2.2

   (J) 5.8

   (K) None of these.

3. 0.04% is equal to

   (A) 4

   (B) 40

   (C) $\dfrac{1}{4}$

   (D) $\dfrac{4}{10,000}$

   (E) None of these.

4. $\dfrac{16}{35}$ is greater than

   (F) $\dfrac{7}{8}$

   (G) $\dfrac{5}{6}$

   (H) $\dfrac{12}{61}$

   (J) $\dfrac{43}{45}$

   (K) None of these.

5. .875 − .625 =

 (A) .5

 (B) .375

 (C) .25

 (D) .125

 (E) None of these.

6. .3 × 19.95 =

 (F) 5.985

 (G) 5.895

 (H) 5.85

 (J) .5895

 (K) None of these.

7. −6(3 − 4 × 3) =

 (A) −66

 (B) −54

 (C) −12

 (D) 18

 (E) None of these.

8. $\dfrac{3}{4}$ + 7.55 =

 (F) 8.2

 (G) 8.3

 (H) 7.25

 (J) 5.6

 (K) None of these.

9. Lisa's drive to work each day takes her forty-five minutes. If she travels at an average speed of 60 miles per hour, how far is her home from her place of work?

 (A) 450 miles

 (B) 270 miles

 (C) 2,700 miles

 (D) 45 miles

10. In a recent board meeting, the executives of Company X decided that 10% of their operating budget should go to advertising, 50% to operating expenses, 25% to salaries, and the rest to developing new products. What fraction of the budget will be used for developing new products?

    (F) $\dfrac{5}{100}$

    (G) $\dfrac{3}{20}$

    (H) $\dfrac{4}{10}$

    (J) $\dfrac{1}{7}$

11. In the number 215,602 what is the value of the digit 1?

    (A) 10,000
    (B) 1,000
    (C) 1
    (D) 10

12. If a birthday cake is divided into 5 slices, one slice is what percent of the whole cake?

    (F) 10%
    (G) 2%
    (H) 20%
    (J) .2%

13. Alexis earns $350 a week as a salesperson, plus 6% commission on her sales. What will she earn this week if she has sold $2,500 worth of merchandise?

    (A) $350
    (B) $400
    (C) $500
    (D) $550

14. A health club has 5 treadmills, 12 stationary bicycles, and 4 stair-climbing machines. When $\dfrac{2}{3}$ of all the machines are occupied, how many people are using the machines?

    (F) 14
    (G) 12
    (H) 15
    (J) 7

15. Which of the following sets of numbers may be placed in the blank to make the sentence below true?

    $5 > \underline{\quad} > 0$

    (A) {5, 4, 3, 2, 1, 0}
    (B) {5, 4, 3, 2, 1}
    (C) {4, 3, 2, 1}
    (D) {4, 3, 2, 1, 0}

16. One inch is what part of one yard?

    (F) $\dfrac{1}{12}$

    (G) $\dfrac{1}{100}$

    (H) $\dfrac{1}{3}$

    (J) $\dfrac{1}{36}$

17. A luncheonette serves 56 burgers a day. $\dfrac{7}{8}$ of these burgers are ordered with cheese. How many cheeseburgers are ordered?

    (A) 56
    (B) 49
    (C) 50
    (D) 42

18. Which of the following are the prime factors of 72?

    (F) $2^2, 3^3$
    (G) $2^2, 3^2$
    (H) 2, 3, 5
    (J) 2, 36

19. Complete the following statement:

    $2(5 \times \underline{\quad}) + 4 = 54$

    (A) 5
    (B) 6
    (C) 10
    (D) 4

20. Find the area of a triangle whose base is 12 inches and whose height is 5 inches.
    - (F) 34 square inches
    - (G) 60 square inches
    - (H) 30 square inches
    - (J) 36 square inches

21. Which of the following is equivalent to *five hundred fifty thousand sixty nine*?
    - (A) 500,069
    - (B) 550,069
    - (C) 500,690
    - (D) 55,690

22. A quadrilateral is ALWAYS a
    - (F) four-sided polygon
    - (G) polygon with four equal sides
    - (H) five-sided polygon
    - (J) polygon with four right angles

23. A clothing store made $120,650 in sales during the month of August. Two of its six salespeople made 50% of the sales. How much did the other four salespeople sell altogether?
    - (A) $24,130
    - (B) $60,325
    - (C) $15,081
    - (D) $25,300

24. The set of common factors for 50 and 250 is
    - (F) {2, 5, 10, 25}
    - (G) {2, 5, 10, 25, 50}
    - (H) {2, 5, 10, 25, 50, 100}
    - (J) {2, 5, 10, 20, 25, 50}

25. If $-1 < x < 2$, which of the following must NOT be true?
    - (A) $x > -3$
    - (B) $x = 0$
    - (C) $x = 1$
    - (D) $x > 2$

26. Which of these points on the number line represents 5×10^3?

A	B	C	D	E	F
0	500	5,000	25,000	50,000	100,000

 (F) Point E

 (G) Point B

 (H) Point C

 (J) Point F

27. If one glass of lemonade costs x dollars and y cents, what is the cost of 3 glasses of lemonade?

 (A) $3(x + y)$

 (B) $3x(y)$

 (C) $3x - 3y$

 (D) $3(xy)$

28. Ken and Keisha disagree about how to solve the problem below. Ken thinks that the first thing to do is add all the terms. Keisha thinks they should perform the operations within the parenthesis first.

 $(8 + 5 + 4) \times (12 + 3 + 2)$

 (F) Only Ken is correct.

 (G) Only Keisha is correct.

 (H) They are both correct.

 (J) Neither Ken nor Keisha is correct.

29. An importer reasons that in order to make a profit on each item that she sells, she must mark it up to 200% of the original cost. If she imports a scarf for $6, including her shipping costs, how much must she sell it for in order to be profitable?

 (A) $12

 (B) $6

 (C) $9

 (D) $60

30. Which coordinates show most clearly the location of Rosewood City?

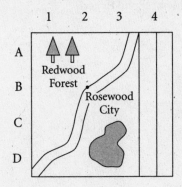

(F) C3

(G) B3

(H) B2

(J) C4

31. The product of a negative integer and a positive integer is

(A) zero

(B) negative

(C) positive

(D) 1

32. Reesa is deciding which telephone company offers her the best day, evening, and weekend rates. Which chart or graph below would be most helpful to her?

(F)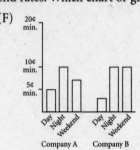
Company A   Company B

(G)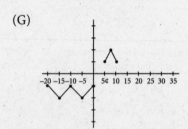

(H)

	Company A	Company B
Day	5¢	3¢
Night	10¢	10¢
Weekend	7¢	10¢

(J)

33. What is the circumference of circle below?

2 units

(A) 16π units

(B) 4π units

(C) 8π units

(D) 6π units

34. A right angle measures

    (F) 45 degrees

    (G) 80 degrees

    (H) 180 degrees

    (J) 90 degrees

35. All of the following are quadrilaterals EXCEPT

    (A) rhombus

    (B) square

    (C) rectangle

    (D) pentagon

36. Mr. Strong took out a bank loan for $2,500 to repair his roof. The interest is 12%. What is the total amount he owes the bank?

    (F) $3,000

    (G) $2,600

    (H) $2,800

    (J) $300

37. If $x > -3$, and $y < 1$, and x and y are integers, then which of the following sets represent all values that would satisfy both x and y?

    (A) {0, 1}

    (B) {0, −1}

    (C) {−1, 0, 1}

    (D) {−2, −1, 0, 1}

38. What is the value of x if $2(3 + x) = 46$?

    (F) 41

    (G) 40

    (H) 46

    (J) 20

39. What are the coordinates of point *A* on the graph?

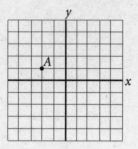

(A) (2, –1)

(B) (2, 1)

(C) (–2, 1)

(D) (1, –2)

40. A certain county has experienced 39 inches of rainfall this year—twelve more inches than last year. What is this year's monthly average rainfall?

(F) $\dfrac{39}{12}$ inches

(G) $39 - \dfrac{12}{12}$ inches

(H) $39 + \dfrac{12}{12}$ inches

(J) $\dfrac{12}{12}$ inches

ANSWER KEY

Test 1: Sequences

1. D
2. J
3. C
4. J
5. A
6. H
7. B
8. F
9. B
10. F
11. C
12. F
13. C
14. G
15. A
16. J
17. B
18. G
19. B
20. J

Test 2: Analogies

1. D
2. G
3. D
4. G
5. B
6. F
7. C
8. G
9. A
10. G
11. C
12. H

13. A
14. J
15. B
16. H
17. A
18. H
19. D
20. G

Test 3: Quantitative Reasoning

1. C
2. F
3. A
4. G
5. D
6. F
7. B
8. H
9. D
10. G
11. C
12. H
13. D
14. J
15. B
16. J
17. A
18. H
19. A
20. H

Test 4: Verbal Reasoning— Words

1. A
2. F
3. B
4. J
5. B
6. H
7. C
8. F
9. B
10. G
11. A
12. F
13. B
14. J
15. B
16. H
17. A
18. H
19. A
20. J

Test 5: Verbal Reasoning— Context

1. C
2. H
3. D
4. J
5. B
6. F
7. B
8. H
9. B
10. F

11. B
12. F
13. A
14. J
15. B
16. H
17. B
18. J
19. A
20. G

Test 6: Reading and Language Arts

1. B
2. F
3. B
4. H
5. B
6. F
7. D
8. H
9. C
10. J
11. C
12. G
13. B
14. J
15. B
16. J
17. A
18. H
19. B
20. F
21. C
22. G
23. B
24. F
25. C

26. J
27. C
28. H
29. C
30. G
31. C
32. F
33. A
34. J
35. B
36. G
37. B
38. J
39. A
40. H

Test 7: Mathematics

1. B
2. J
3. D
4. H
5. C
6. F
7. E
8. G
9. D
10. G
11. A
12. H
13. C
14 F
15. C
16. J
17. B
18. G
19. A
20. H

21. B
22. F
23. B
24. G
25. D
26. H
27. A
28. H
29. A
30. H
31. B
32. H
33. B
34. J
35. D
36. H
37. B
38. J
39. C
40. F

ANSWERS AND EXPLANATIONS

Test 1: Sequences

1.   D

Each set is made up of four arrows. The first, second, and fourth arrow alternate between pointing up or down. The third arrow always points up. The next set should start with an arrow pointing down, followed by one pointing up, the third arrow always points up, and the fourth should point up.

2.   J

The pattern is made up of three triangles and a square. The first triangle always has a solid dot in the center, though the second and third triangle alternate between having a solid or an empty dot in the middle. The square also alternates between having a solid or empty dot in the center. Therefore, the next set should include a triangle with a solid dot, a triangle with an open dot, a triangle with a solid dot, and a square with an open dot.

3.   C

Each set is made up of three X's. In the first set, two small v's are inside the vertex of each of the X's. In the second set, a third v is added to all the X's. In the next set a third v is added to the X's. In the last set, another detail is added; the ends of the X's are now arrows. Since in all three sets each X has the same amount of detail, the missing X in the last set should also have arrow points on the ends of the rays of the X and should have 4 v's inside the vertex of the X like the other X's in its set.

4.   J

The sets are made up of four stars; two are filled in and two are not. The missing star in the last set should be empty so that the balance of two filled in and two empty remains the same. There is no reason to believe the star would be only partially filled in.

5.   A

The elements in each set are either the bottom part of a triangle, the mid-section of a triangle, or the top section of the triangle. The only answer choice that has one of these elements is choice (A).

6.   H

Each set is made up of two "houses." One points up, the next points down. In each subsequent set, the second house gains a detail that was present previously in the first house. Therefore, the missing house should point down (as the second one always does) and it should gain the shading in the top triangle that the first house had in the preceding set.

7.   B

The first two numbers of each set are multiplied to get the third number of each set. For example, $2 \times 5 = 10$, $3 \times 7 = 21$, and finally, $4 \times 9 = 36$.

8.   F

In each set, the first number is multiplied by 2 to obtain the second number, and the second number is multiplied by 3 to obtain the third number; $10 \times 3 = 30$.

9.   B

In each set, the second number is the square root of the first number, and the third number is that square root minus 3; $7 - 3 = 4$.

10. F

In this sequence, the third number in each set is the difference between the first and second number in each set. For example, $64 - 51 = 13$, $52 - 40 = 8$, and $33 - 22 = 11$.

11. C

In each set, the first number is multiplied by 4 to obtain the second number and the second number is reduced by 8 to obtain the third number; $28 - 8 = 20$.

12. F

In each set, the second number is 1 more than the first number, and the third number is 2 more than the second number; $13 + 2 = 15$.

13. C

In each set, the difference between the first two numbers is 5 and the difference between the second and third number is 2; $86 - 2 = 84$.

14. G

In each set, the second number is 10 less than the first number, and the third number is $\frac{1}{4}$ of the first number.

15. A

Note the pattern as shown below.

A1B0C1   A2B1C2   A3B2C3   A4B3C4

In other words, B is 1 behind A and C.

16. J

As you move from left to right the superscript of X is increased by 1; the superscript of Y is decreased by 2 and the superscript of Z is increased by 2.

$X^1Y^9Z^2$ $X^2Y^7Z^4$ $X^3Y^5Z^6$ $X^4Y^3Z^8$

17. B

The first letter of each set goes up by one letter: l, m, n, o. The last two letters are also increase by one letter, but the last letter is repeated: fg, gh, hi, ij. So the missing set is nhi.

18. G

Notice that in the first and third sets, the first letter is capitalized, the second letter is lowercase, and the last letter is capitalized. In the second set, the first letter is lowercase, the second letter is capitalized, and the last letter is also lowercase. The last 2 letters are always x and y, and the first letter increases by one letter: b, c, d. So, to follow the pattern, you are looking for a set beginning with a lowercase e, followed by a capital X, followed by a lowercase y. The correct answer is choice (B).

19. B

As we move from left to right, the first letters are arranged in decreasing alphabetical order, and the second letters and third letters are arranged in increasing alphabetical order.

ZAB   YBC   XCD   WDE

20. J

Note the pattern of the first and second letter of each group: AB, BC, CD, DE. Also note the pattern of the third letter of each group: E, F, G, H.

ABE   BCF   CDG   DEH

Test 2: Analogies

1. D

A car travels on a road. A boat travels on water.

2. G

A rectangle is an elongated version of a square. An oval is an elongated version of a circle.

3. D

An umbrella protects against the rain. Sunglasses protect against the sun.

4. G

A flower is displayed in a vase. A photo is displayed in a picture frame.

5. B

A parachute is used to escape from an airplane. A lifeboat is used to escape from a boat.

6. F

A computer is the modern version of a feather pen; they are both used to write. A cell phone is the modern version of a regular phone.

7. C

A sweater is worn in winter; a T-shirt is worn in summer. Long pants are worn in winter; shorts are worn in summer.

8. G

An apple grows in a tree. A carrot grows in the ground.

9. A

Scissors are used to cut paper. A saw is used to cut wood.

10. G

A bear eats fish. A giraffe eats foliage.

11. C

A playpen is an enclosure that holds a baby. A fishbowl is an enclosure that holds a goldfish.

12. H

Clothes are kept in a dresser. Papers are kept in a file cabinet.

13. A

A slice of cake is a portion of the whole cake. A slice of bread is a portion of the whole loaf.

14. J

Boots protect the feet. A helmet protects the head.

15. B

A bridle and saddle are used to control a horse, and a collar and leash are used to control a dog.

16. H

A chicken produces eggs. A cow produces milk.

17. A

An acorn grows into a tree. A seed grows into a flower.

18. H

A flag is a symbol of a country. A dove is a symbol of peace.

19. D

A teddy bear is a toy figure of a real bear. A toy truck is a smaller figure of a real 18-wheeler truck.

20. G

A fork and knife are both implements used to eat. A hoe and trowel are both implements used to garden.

Test 3: Quantitative Reasoning

1. C

Figure out what operation is being done to the number in the left column. What is done to 3 to make it 9? 6 is added. What is done to 1 to make it 7? 6 is added. The pattern is +6; 2 + 6 = 8, choice (C).

2. F

In this set, 2 is added to 4 to make 6; 2 is added to 1 to make three. The pattern is +2; 5 + 2 = 7, choice (F).

3. A

1 is added to $\frac{1}{2}$ to make $1\frac{1}{2}$. 1 is added to $\frac{1}{3}$ to make $1\frac{1}{3}$. The pattern is +1. 2 + 1 = 3, choice (A).

4. G

What is done to 12 to make 3? It is divided by 4. What is done to 20 to make 5? It is divided by 4. The pattern is ÷4. 8 ÷ 4 = 2.

5. D

First, figure out what operation is being performed to the number on the left; 9 − 5 = 4; 4 − 5 = −1. The operation is −5; 10 − 5 = 5.

6. F

Each number on the left is divided by 10 to arrive at the number on the right. Therefore, 0.5 divided by 10 = .05; 1.0 divided by 10 = 0.1; 10 divided by 10 = 1.

7. B

There are 4 equal segments. If you were to divide each of these 4 segments with a diagonal line you would have 8 segments making up the whole.

Count the shaded segments. There is 1. The fraction of the grid that is shaded is $\frac{1}{8}$.

8. **H**

There are 16 squares and 2 are shaded; $\frac{2}{16}$ reduces to $\frac{1}{8}$.

9. **D**

There are 4 sections and 2 are shaded. That is 2 parts out of 4, or $\frac{2}{4}$, which reduces to $\frac{1}{2}$.

10. **G**

There are 4 parts and 2 are shaded. That is 2 parts out of 4, or $\frac{2}{4}$, which reduces to $\frac{1}{2}$.

11. **C**

Count the number of triangular sections. There are 8 triangular sections and 3 of these 8 sections are shaded. The answer is $\frac{3}{8}$.

12. **H**

There are 8 sections and 2 are shaded; $\frac{2}{8}$ reduces to $\frac{1}{4}$.

13. **D**

There are 4 sections and 2 are shaded. That is 2 parts out of 4, or $\frac{2}{4}$, which reduces to $\frac{1}{2}$.

14. **J**

Use the information to evaluate each answer choice.

You are told that 1 cone is equal to 1 cube. Therefore:

F: 1 cone ≠ 1 cone + 1 cone (remember, the cube equals 1 cone)

G: 1 cone (1 cube = 1 cone) ≠ 2 cones

H: 2 cones ≠ 1 cone (remember, 1 cube is equal to 1 cone)

J: 1 cone + 1 cone (1 cube = 1 cone) = 1 cone + 1 cone (the cube = a cone).

15. **B**

One cube is equal to three cones. Convert the answer choices to either all cones or all cubes to more readily see the equation.

A: 3 cones ≠ 9 cones (since each cube equals 3 cones and there are three cubes)

B: 3 cones + 3 cones (the cube) = 6 cones

C: 2 cones + 3 cones (since the cube equals 3 cones) ≠ 12 cones (since each cube equals 3 cones)

D: 1 cone ≠ 4 cones (1 cone + 1 cube which equals 3 cones)

16. **J**

2 cones = 1 cube. Convert the answer choices to either all cones or all cubes to more readily see the equation.

F: 4 cones (the 2 cubes) ≠ 3 cones (1 cube = 2 cones + 1 more cone)

G: 2 cones + (2 cones (the cube) ≠ 3 cones

H: 1 cone + 2 cones (the cube) ≠ 4 cones (1 cube = 2 cones + 2 more cones)

J: 3 cones = 1 cone + 2 cones (1 cube = 2 cones)

17. **A**

1 cone = 2 cubes. Convert the answer choices to either all cones or all cubes to more readily see the equation.

A: 2 cones = 1 cone (the two cubes) + 1 cone

B: 1 cone (the 2 cubes) + 1 cone ≠ 2 cones (the 4 cubes)

C: $\frac{1}{2}$ cone (1 cube) + 1 cone ≠ 3 cones

D: 1 cone ≠ $\frac{1}{2}$ cone (the 1 cube)

18. **H**

3 cones = 1 cube. Convert the answer choices to either all cones or all cubes to more readily see the equation.

F: 3 cones (1 cube) ≠ 2 cones

G: 6 cones (2 cubes) ≠ 3 cones (1 cube) + 2 cones

H: 3 cones (1 cube) + 1 cone = 4 cones

J: 6 cones (2 cubes) ≠ 3 cones (1 cube) + 1 cone

19. A

3 cones = 1 cube. Convert the answer choices to either all cones or all cubes to more readily see the equation.

A: 2 cones (the 1 cube) + 2 cones = 4 cones (the 2 cubes)

B: 3 cones ≠ 4 cones (the 2 cubes)

C: 4 cones (the 2 cubes) + 1 cone ≠ 2 cones + 2 cones (the 1 cube)

D: 2 cones ≠ 4 cones (the 2 cubes)

20. H

4 cubes = 1 cone. Convert the answer choices to either all cones or all cubes to more readily see the equation.

F: $\frac{1}{2}$ cone (the two cubes) ≠ 1 cone + $\frac{1}{2}$ cone (the two cubes)

G: $\frac{1}{4}$ cone (the 1 cube) ≠ 5 cones

H: 2 cones = 1 cone + 1 cone (the 4 cubes)

J: $\frac{3}{4}$ cone (the 3 cubes) ≠ 1 cone + $\frac{1}{2}$ cone (the 2 cubes)

Test 4: Verbal Reasoning—Words

1. A

A cage is intended for captivity, not security or display. Although it may have a door, the essential element is that it keeps something or someone inside.

2. F

A megaphone amplifies the speaker's voice so that it may be heard more readily.

3. B

While food is cooked in an oven a pleasant aroma may result, but the essential element of an oven is that it cooks food because it contains heat.

4. J

A carpet is woven of thread. Although it may have fringe, or a pattern, or provide comfort, a carpet must be woven of thread.

5. B

A concert is given to an audience. It may take place without a stage, seats, or a conductor, but there must be a group of people to hear a concert.

6. H

A trial reveals guilt or innocence; it must result in a verdict regardless of whether or not there is a witness, or an objection, or an actual courtroom.

7. C

A message is a communication between two people. It can take any form—a letter, a telephone conversation, or an email. However, the essential idea is to communicate something.

8. F

A fish is unique because it has gills and can breathe in water. Though it has a tail, so do other animals. The essential element of a fish is its ability to live and breathe in water which gills allow it to do. A fish can live in a lake, ocean, pond, or river, so these are not essential elements.

9. B

A leash's function is to control. Though it does encircle an animal's neck, the essential thing about a leash is that it is used to control, not to drag or walk, an animal.

10. G

This relationship is one of degree. The items above the line are increasingly joyful; those below the line are increasingly bothered.

11. A

The items above the line are parts of a tree, and they are moving from general (tree) to specific (leaf). The items above the line are parts of a flower. They are moving from general (flower) to specific (petal).

12. F

The items above the line are all related to protection from rain. Those below the line are all related to protection from sun.

13. B

The items above the line express increasing age in family generations. The items below the line show the same relationship. Therefore, the correct answer is son.

14. J

The items in (F), (G), and (H) are all related to babies. A slide is used by children at a playground.

15. B

A mare is a female animal (a female horse). Roosters, bulls, and stallions are all male.

16. H

Data, evidence, and fact are all indisputable truths, an opinion is not.

17. A

Grimace, frown, and smile are facial expressions of the mouth. A wink is a facial expression of the eye.

18. H

Before looking at the answer choices, think about what the three words have in common. All three are adjectives with the same meaning—they all mean calm. Now look at the answer choices for a word that is most similar to calm. The most similar word is *relaxing*.

19. A

The three words have to do with good moral character and mean honest or trustworthy. Now evaluate the answer choices. Is *true* trustworthy? Yes it is. This is the correct answer. But, be sure to look at all the other choices to make sure you have selected the best one. Is *brave* trustworthy? No, it is not. Is *verbose* trustworthy? It is not (it means *wordy*). If you don't know the meaning of the word, leave it in. Is *durable* trustworthy? No, it is not. It is long lasting. You now must choose between (A) and (C)— a word you know is correct and one you may not be sure of. Choose the word you know is correct—*true*.

20. J

Before looking at the answer choices, think about what the three words have in common. All three are adjectives with the same meaning—they all mean clean. Now look at the

answer choices for a word that is most similar to clean. The most similar word is *spotless*.

Test 5: Verbal Reasoning—Context

1. C

The only thing known for certain is that Christine has been to New York City. Although (A) and (B) may be true, there is nothing in the two statements to support either of these conclusions. There is no way to verify choice (D).

2. H

Based on the two statements the only one of these answer choices that we can conclude is correct is that Jan is younger than Marcia (since Marcia is older than Jan.) No mention is made of Marcia's height, so rule out choices (F) and (G). We also do not know if the girls are sisters.

3. D

Based on the two statements the only one of these answer choices that is correct is that wheat bread contains more caloric energy (50 calories more) than white bread. There is no point of comparison to allow us to judge whether either of these types of bread is fattening. We also have no information on people's buying habits. Choice (C) is an opinion, unsupported by the facts stated.

4. J

Based only on the information given, you do not know if Jean sold the most cars in April, nor if she was employee of the month. Although no one sold more cars than Jean, you do not know for certain that no one else sold a car. The only statement that is true based solely on the passage is that Jean sold the most cars in March.

5. B

The key here is the word *often* in the first statement and *may* in choice (B). There are many reasons dogs bark; the first statement offers one. Someone could be threatening Fluffy's owner, but this sentence is not tempered with *may* or *might be*. Choices (C) and (D), though possibly true, do not relate to the information given in the statements. Remember, you are choosing the statement that is true according to the information given.

6. F

Based on the two statements the only thing we know for sure is that Amy hasn't written Lisa back yet (since Lisa hasn't received a reply). We do not know why Amy hasn't written back, only that she hasn't. We also cannot say based only on the information given whether or not Lisa likes to write letters.

7. B

Since Jim has a rare coin and rare coins are worth a lot of money, Jim has a valuable coin. Based on the information given, we cannot say with certainty whether or not Jim collects coins. Regardless of whether or not it is true, the information in (C) and (D) is not related to the information given and is incorrect.

8. H

It is most reasonable to assume that the person addressing the letter probably made a mistake since the details are so similar to Mercedes Brown's real name and address. The mail carrier probably also made this reasonable assumption.

9. B

Based on the information given, the only thing we know for sure is that there is a problem with John's computer. Although being unplugged may be a reason for the problem, we do not have the information to arrive at this conclusion. (If the statement included the phrase *probably unplugged* this would be a stronger answer choice.) There is clearly not a blackout since the other electric appliances are working. We cannot make a judgment about John's ability based solely on the information given.

10. F

Based on the information given, the only thing known for sure is that Samina is a customer of Romero's. The statements do not tell us whether Samina herself likes pepperoni pizza—she may have ordered it for her family or friends. Although Romero's offers a free pizza to customers who wait longer than 30 minutes to receive their order, we do not know how often Romero's delivers late or how they compare to the competition.

11. B

Based on the information given, all that we know is that Minetta Music School requires its students to read music. We do not know whether it is the best school in town. Think about what information we have on Joseph. We do not know whether or not he is a talented musician, or whether he reads music at all. All we know is that Joseph *would like to attend*. The sentence tells us that he does not yet attend. If Joseph would like to attend the school, based on the school's requirements, he must read music.

12. F

Based only on the information given, we know that polar bears also live in New York. Based on the statements, we can say that polar bears live in New York. Choice (G) is a value judgment that we cannot affirm based only on the statements. Choice (H) must not be true, since there are polar bears in New York. Choice (J) depends on outside information to draw a conclusion and remember, you are only allowed to use the statements given to come to a conclusion.

13. A

The only thing we can be sure of is that Maria works five days a week in New York City. We do not know whether she shares the food she cooks with her team, or if she is a good cook. We also do not know if she has a microwave.

14. J

The black bear from Kodiak Island gave birth; therefore, she must be female. Although the zookeepers were happy and threw a party we cannot generalize that they like to have parties. The paragraph gives no information about what black bears eat or if they are friendly.

15. B

The car keys must have been in the ignition, since when Brandon finally looked there he shouted "Aha!" Keys can be in an ignition while the car is off; therefore, we cannot assume that the car was running. We do not know if Brandon is always absentminded or if he was late to work that morning.

16. H

Based only on the information, the only statement that you can verify is that Mr. Sloan probably won't be able to read without his glasses. He has glasses for reading, so you can assume that he probably needs them in order to read. The other statements might be true, but you do not know for certain based on the information provided.

17. B

Express trains skip every other station. That is, they start at 10th Street, skip 20th Street, go to 30th Street, skip 40th Street, etc. The #6 train is an express, so it follows this pattern. That makes choice (B) correct, but choice (C) incorrect. We do not know the relative speed of the local train since it is not mentioned, nor do we know how slow the local train is.

18. J

Before looking at the answer choices, think about what the information does and does not tell you. You know that it is 11:55 A.M., five minutes to 12 on Thursday. Lunch is served Monday through Friday between 12 P.M. and 2 P.M. Eliminate choice (F), nothing is said about lunch being served early. Choice (G) is a guess, no information is given about the quality of the food. Choice (H) is wrong because lunch is only served Monday through Friday.

19. A

The statements tell how old one must be in order to drive and tell us when John's birthday is. They say nothing about how old John is and whether or not he can, can't, or would like to drive. Based on the information given, all we can conclude is that no one under the age of 16 may get a permit. You can eliminate choices (B) and (C)—we do not know these details about John. You can also eliminate choice (D) because it is a sweeping generalization. We cannot say that all 16 year olds apply for driver's permits.

20. G

If Mount Everest is the highest mountain in the world and it is in Nepal, the highest mountain in the world is in Nepal. Though (F) and (H) and (J) are true, remember that you are asked to draw a conclusion based *only* on the information given.

Test 6: Reading and Language Arts

1. B

You should use context clues to answer this question. The passage says there is a *precise scientific reason why rainbows can only be seen*. Precise is describing the scientific reason. Is a scientific reason sharp? Or exact? Or precious? Or difficult? The word *exact* makes the most sense in the context of this passage.

2. F

For the answer, see paragraph 2, sentence 2: *...the rainbow must be caused by the way in which the rays of light act on water drops and pass from them to our eyes.*

3. B

To find the correct answer, see the last sentence of paragraph 2.

4. H

When the sun is more than 42 degrees above the horizon line, we can no longer see the rainbow, because the required angle is now over our heads. See the last sentence of the passage.

5. B

This is a detail question. Paragraph 2, sentence 3 says: *As sunlight hits a raindrop it is refracted, or bent, by the drop in such a way that the light appears as a spectrum of colors.*

6. F

Sentence 1 contains the capitalization error. *Spring Day* does not need to be capitalized.

7. D

These sentences can be combined by simply adding the conjunction *so*. The word *and* in choice (A) is not necessary, nor are any commas necessary.

8. H

Most beautifulest is incorrect. The correct superlative is *most beautiful*.

9. C

Relaxation is important for mental and physical well-being. That is, it is an essential element of a healthy life.

10. J

Although some people may become aggressive under pressure, others do not. Choice (G) is also a generalization and may not be true of all people. The fact that stress allows us to accomplish things is not mentioned. A main idea of the article is that stress may cause health problems.

11. C

Reread the section where the term "negative" is used. It refers to reactions that do not demonstrate high energy such as sleeping too much or withdrawing socially.

12. G

Paragraph 3 mentions all of the answer choices except denying worries or concerns.

13. B

Since the second sentence supports the main idea of the first, the best way to combine these sentences is to arrange for it to follow the first. Choice (A) accomplishes this but *there are two reasons why* is unnecessarily wordy. Choices (C) and (D) are also too wordy.

14. J

The best conclusion sums up ideas presented in the entire article. Choice (J) accomplishes this. Choice (F) introduces a new idea. Choice (G) adds to one detail discussed in the first paragraph rather than the article as a whole. Choice (H) introduces a new idea.

15. B

The kitten just knocked the bag of treats off the counter. The next logical thing to happen would be related to the treats; the author will probably let the kitten eat them.

16 J

The selection is a humorous story. The only medium that would not contain this type of story is a science fiction movie, since science fiction is about the future.

17. A

The author initially describes the kitten as an enemy and a monster, but his or her tone is humorous. In truth, the author loves the kitten and indulges it, as we see from his or her reaction at the end of the story when the author writes about *that sweet little face.*

18. H

Through the course of the selection we learn that the kitten is trying to get kitten treats. That is her plot. Her tactics have been to whine, growl, and otherwise wake the author. Thus, the author is annoyed. The only thing we don't know is where the author got the kitten.

19. B

The sentence is unclear. It implies the three kittens all have one name. Breaking the information into two sentences makes it more clear. Choice (A) does this as well, but it is incorrect to start a sentence with the conjunction *and.*

20. F

The best way to combine these sentences is to add the conjunction *and.* There is no reason to change every tense or make the structure of the sentence more complicated.

21. C

This sentence extends the idea that the writer has a lot of responsibilities. Using the subject pronoun *I* and an active verb makes this idea clearer.

22. G

This is a detail question. The answer is located in the second paragraph.

23. B

Paragraph 2 explains that we know how mammoths looked thanks to cave paintings and the discovery of mammoth remains.

24. F

Mammoths lived a quarter of a million years ago. (Not a quarter of a century.) They inhabited some parts of Siberia until as recently as 4,000 years ago. That means they would have existed during the time of the Egyptian pharaohs. The Cyclops was an imaginary beast. Alaska became a state in modern times.

25. C

Paragraph 3, sentence 3 explains that the mammoth's trunk was composed of soft tissue, and was not fossilized. That is, it decomposed and was not preserved.

26. J

The woolly mammoth inhabited five continents, while the elephant only natural habitats are in India and Africa. Although we are told that the mammoth migrated over the Bering land bridge, no mention is made of the or distance either animal traveled. Relative trunk size is not mentioned either. Mammoths were found in Siberia, which is colder than Africa, ruling out choice (G).

27. C

The paragraph gives some details about Asian and African elephants for the purpose of comparison. A good topic sentence should introduce this idea. Choice (A), although it contains the idea of comparison, is not the best choice because it states that the two species are *completely different* which is not correct based on the information in the paragraph.

28. H

The information about family groups is not related to the rest of the paragraph, which discusses details about the physical characteristics of African and Asian elephants.

29. C

The author mentions Hitler. This is related to World War II.

30. G

From the author's tone it seems that George is the author's husband. We know that the author is a woman because she mentions wearing silk stockings. We have no clue that George is younger than she, and since George owns a car (which he misses being able to drive), and she does not include when talking about the boys she must feed, bathe, and tuck in for the night.

31. C

Although she mentions baking, there is no reason to believe that is her occupation. And, though she writes that she admires the "Rosie the Riveters" she goes on to say that she is not among them. She does discuss needing to

care for four children which implies that she is a homemaker. She only planted the garden that particular day, which does not make her a full-time farmer.

32. F

The author mentions not being able to drive because her family cannot receive gasoline; thus, it must be rationed. Likewise, she is waiting for her ration book in order to buy more sugar. She misses silk stockings because they are not available and must be rationed. The only thing not mentioned as rationed is vegetables.

33. A

The author discusses her garden and rationing in the same passage. Therefore, the garden and rationing are related. America was undergoing a period of increased demand because of the war effort. Therefore, supplies that might normally be available for civilians were needed for the troops. By growing her own food, she ensures that supplies of canned food would be available for the troops.

34. J

These two sentences are related by cause/effect. Therefore, the best way to combine them expresses this relationship. Only choice (J) which contains the word *because* makes clear the cause/effect.

35. B

This sentence expresses the idea clearly and correctly using the conjunction *although* to show how the clauses related to one another. Choice (D) also uses *although* but the way the sentence is constructed it conveys that people were rationed rather than the items.

36. G

The main problem is expressed in the introductory sentence: *The state lottery is unfair because it steals from the poor and gives to the rich.*

37. B

Although the author does not feel that playing the lottery is a good choice, his or her main argument concerns government support of the lottery. The author is not opposed to using taxes to pay for public works, nor does he or she argue whether or not it is fair to tax a winner's jackpot.

38. J

Though the author uses Joe as one example of a winner, the term *Joe Schmoe* refers to the common Joe, the common man on the street. The description of what happens to Joe after he wins does not inspire the reader's jealousy. Despite the silly sound of Joe's name, the term is not used to make fun of people who play the lottery.

39. A

The author makes the main point that the lottery is unfair and then goes on to illustrate why. He or she does not tell people to stop buying lottery tickets. Although the author does argue against government involvement, nowhere is a ban mentioned. Nor, is the connection made between the lottery and education.

40. H

The passage does not mention paying out lump sum winnings. It does however explain that the lottery takes a tax on each ticket purchased, that it taxes winnings, and that it benefits by collecting interest on portions of jackpots held in the bank for winners who only receive a portion of their winnings, annually.

Test 7: Mathematics

1. B

When multiplying numbers to a power, add the powers. Thus, $3^3 \times 3^4 = 3^7$.

2. J

Line up the decimal points and subtract:

$$\begin{array}{r} 6.2 \\ -.4 \\ \hline 5.8 \end{array}$$

3. D

A percent is a part of 100. Thus, .04% is $\frac{.04}{100}$, or $\frac{4}{10,000}$.

4. H

Notice that $\frac{16}{35}$ is just slightly greater than $\frac{16}{32}$, or $\frac{1}{2}$. Answers (A) and (B) are (D) are far greater than $\frac{1}{2}$.

5. C

Subtract the decimals and you get .25, choice (C).

6. F

Be careful when you multiply decimals that you put the decimal in the correct place; .3 × 19.95 = 5.985.

7. E

According to the order of operations, start in the parentheses. Perform multiplication before subtraction: $-6(3-12)$. After the subtraction: $-6(-9)$. Since a negative times a negative is a positive, the answer is 54. Because that is not one of the answer choices, the correct answer is (E).

8. G

First, change the fraction to a decimal; $\frac{3}{4} = .75$. Now, add the two decimals: .75 + 7.55 = 8.3.

9. D

Distance = Rate × Time; 60 mph × $\frac{3}{4}$ hour = 45 miles.

10. G

First, total the percent going to everything but new products: 10 + 50 + 25 = 85.

100% − 85% = 15% left over for developing new products. To express this as a fraction of the whole budget, write $\frac{15}{100}$, which reduces to $\frac{3}{20}$.

11. A

The 1 is in the ten thousand's place.

12. H

One slice out of five can be written as $\frac{1}{5}$, which is equal to 20%.

13. C

$0.06 \times 2{,}500 = 150 + 350$ (her salary) $= 500$.

14. F

First, determine the total number of machines:

$5 + 12 + 4 = 21$

$21 \times \dfrac{2}{3} = \dfrac{42}{3} = 14$ people using the machines.

15. C

The sentence reads: $5 > \underline{\hspace{1cm}} > 0$. Thus, the numbers that may be placed in the blank must be less than 5 but greater than 0; 4, 3, 2, 1 are less than 5 but greater than 0.

16. J

A yard is 3 feet. One foot is 12 inches; 1 yard $= 36$ inches.

Thus, one inch $= \dfrac{1}{36}$ of a yard.

17. B

$56 \times \dfrac{7}{8} = 49$

18. G

A prime number is a whole number whose only factors are 1 and itself. The prime factors of 72 are the prime numbers whose product is equal to 72; 2 and 3 are both prime numbers and $2^3 = 8$ and $3^2 = 9$. Since the product of 8 and 9 is 72, choice (G) is the answer.

19. A

Let x equal the unknown number.

$$2(5x) + 4 = 54$$
$$10x + 4 = 54$$
$$10x = 50$$
$$x = 5$$

20. H

The formula for area of a triangle is: $A = \dfrac{1}{2}bh$

$A = \dfrac{1}{2}(12 \times 5) = \dfrac{1}{2}(60) = 30$ square inches.

21. B

five hundred thousand	500,000
fifty thousand	50,000
sixty-nine	69
	550,069

22. F

A quadrilateral is always polygon with four sides.

23. B

First, find how much money the two top salesmen made.

50% of $120{,}650 = .50 \times 120{,}650 = \$60{,}325$.

Since 50% is half of the total sales, the other four sales people together made $60,325.

24. G

50 and 250 are both divisible by the factors 2, 5, 10, 25 and 50.

25. D

The sentence states that x is greater than -1 but less than 2. Only choice (D) does not support this range of numbers, since if x is greater than 2 it will not be contained in the interval.

26. H

$5 \times 10^3 = 5 \times (10 \times 10 \times 10) = 5 \times 1{,}000 = 5{,}000$

27. A

One glass of lemonade $= x$ dollars $+ y$ cents. Three glasses $= 3(x + y)$.

28. H

In this case, both Ken and Keisha are essentially saying the same thing. Ken wants to add the terms in parenthesis; Keisha also wants to perform the operations within the parentheses first. This is the correct order of operations.

29. A

100% equals 1 whole; 200% $= 2$ wholes; $\$6 \times 2 = \$12$.

30. **H**

Rosewood City is horizontally across from the section labeled B and below the section labeled 2. Therefore, it falls under coordinates B2.

31. **B**

A negative integer times a positive one results in a negative integer.

32. **H**

The table demonstrates most clearly the rates the various phone companies offer.

33. **B**

Circumference = diameter × π

diameter = 2 × radius = 2 × 2 = 4

circumference = 4π units

34. **J**

A right angle measures 90 degrees.

35. **D**

A quadrilateral has 4 sides; a pentagon has five sides.

36. **H**

Add the interest to the original loan amount.

$2500 × .12 = $300

$300 + $2,500 = $2,800 total

37. **B**

Organize these two sentences in ascending value.

$x > -3$; $x = -2, -1, 0$ and all positive integers.
$y < 1$; $y = 0, -1$, and all negative integers.

Therefore, the set of numbers in common with both x and y is {0, −1}.

38. **J**

Solve for x.

$$2(3 + x) = 46$$
$$6 + 2x = 46$$
$$2x = 46 - 6$$
$$2x = 40$$
$$x = 20$$

39. **C**

When plotting points on a coordinate graph, list the x-axis first, and the y axis second. In order to get to the indicated point on the graph, move two units over to the left on the x-axis and then one unit up parallel to the y-axis. This gives the coordinates of (−2, 1).

40. **F**

The comparison to last year is irrelevant in determining this year's monthly average.

$$\text{The average} = \frac{\text{number of inches total}}{\text{months}} ; \frac{39}{12}.$$

COOP Practice Test 2
Answer Sheet

Remove (or photocopy) this answer sheet and use it to complete the practice test.

Sequences

1. Ⓐ Ⓑ Ⓒ Ⓓ   5. Ⓐ Ⓑ Ⓒ Ⓓ   9. Ⓐ Ⓑ Ⓒ Ⓓ   13. Ⓐ Ⓑ Ⓒ Ⓓ   17. Ⓐ Ⓑ Ⓒ Ⓓ
2. Ⓕ Ⓖ Ⓗ Ⓙ   6. Ⓕ Ⓖ Ⓗ Ⓙ   10. Ⓕ Ⓖ Ⓗ Ⓙ   14. Ⓕ Ⓖ Ⓗ Ⓙ   18. Ⓕ Ⓖ Ⓗ Ⓙ
3. Ⓐ Ⓑ Ⓒ Ⓓ   7. Ⓐ Ⓑ Ⓒ Ⓓ   11. Ⓐ Ⓑ Ⓒ Ⓓ   15. Ⓐ Ⓑ Ⓒ Ⓓ   19. Ⓐ Ⓑ Ⓒ Ⓓ
4. Ⓕ Ⓖ Ⓗ Ⓙ   8. Ⓕ Ⓖ Ⓗ Ⓙ   12. Ⓕ Ⓖ Ⓗ Ⓙ   16. Ⓕ Ⓖ Ⓗ Ⓙ   20. Ⓕ Ⓖ Ⓗ Ⓙ

Analogies

1. Ⓐ Ⓑ Ⓒ Ⓓ   5. Ⓐ Ⓑ Ⓒ Ⓓ   9. Ⓐ Ⓑ Ⓒ Ⓓ   13. Ⓐ Ⓑ Ⓒ Ⓓ   17. Ⓐ Ⓑ Ⓒ Ⓓ
2. Ⓕ Ⓖ Ⓗ Ⓙ   6. Ⓕ Ⓖ Ⓗ Ⓙ   10. Ⓕ Ⓖ Ⓗ Ⓙ   14. Ⓕ Ⓖ Ⓗ Ⓙ   18. Ⓕ Ⓖ Ⓗ Ⓙ
3. Ⓐ Ⓑ Ⓒ Ⓓ   7. Ⓐ Ⓑ Ⓒ Ⓓ   11. Ⓐ Ⓑ Ⓒ Ⓓ   15. Ⓐ Ⓑ Ⓒ Ⓓ   19. Ⓐ Ⓑ Ⓒ Ⓓ
4. Ⓕ Ⓖ Ⓗ Ⓙ   8. Ⓕ Ⓖ Ⓗ Ⓙ   12. Ⓕ Ⓖ Ⓗ Ⓙ   16. Ⓕ Ⓖ Ⓗ Ⓙ   20. Ⓕ Ⓖ Ⓗ Ⓙ

Quantitative Reasoning

1. Ⓐ Ⓑ Ⓒ Ⓓ   5. Ⓐ Ⓑ Ⓒ Ⓓ   9. Ⓐ Ⓑ Ⓒ Ⓓ   13. Ⓐ Ⓑ Ⓒ Ⓓ   17. Ⓐ Ⓑ Ⓒ Ⓓ
2. Ⓕ Ⓖ Ⓗ Ⓙ   6. Ⓕ Ⓖ Ⓗ Ⓙ   10. Ⓕ Ⓖ Ⓗ Ⓙ   14. Ⓕ Ⓖ Ⓗ Ⓙ   18. Ⓕ Ⓖ Ⓗ Ⓙ
3. Ⓐ Ⓑ Ⓒ Ⓓ   7. Ⓐ Ⓑ Ⓒ Ⓓ   11. Ⓐ Ⓑ Ⓒ Ⓓ   15. Ⓐ Ⓑ Ⓒ Ⓓ   19. Ⓐ Ⓑ Ⓒ Ⓓ
4. Ⓕ Ⓖ Ⓗ Ⓙ   8. Ⓕ Ⓖ Ⓗ Ⓙ   12. Ⓕ Ⓖ Ⓗ Ⓙ   16. Ⓕ Ⓖ Ⓗ Ⓙ   20. Ⓕ Ⓖ Ⓗ Ⓙ

Verbal Reasoning—Words

1. Ⓐ Ⓑ Ⓒ Ⓓ   5. Ⓐ Ⓑ Ⓒ Ⓓ   9. Ⓐ Ⓑ Ⓒ Ⓓ   13. Ⓐ Ⓑ Ⓒ Ⓓ   17. Ⓐ Ⓑ Ⓒ Ⓓ
2. Ⓕ Ⓖ Ⓗ Ⓙ   6. Ⓕ Ⓖ Ⓗ Ⓙ   10. Ⓕ Ⓖ Ⓗ Ⓙ   14. Ⓕ Ⓖ Ⓗ Ⓙ   18. Ⓕ Ⓖ Ⓗ Ⓙ
3. Ⓐ Ⓑ Ⓒ Ⓓ   7. Ⓐ Ⓑ Ⓒ Ⓓ   11. Ⓐ Ⓑ Ⓒ Ⓓ   15. Ⓐ Ⓑ Ⓒ Ⓓ   19. Ⓐ Ⓑ Ⓒ Ⓓ
4. Ⓕ Ⓖ Ⓗ Ⓙ   8. Ⓕ Ⓖ Ⓗ Ⓙ   12. Ⓕ Ⓖ Ⓗ Ⓙ   16. Ⓕ Ⓖ Ⓗ Ⓙ   20. Ⓕ Ⓖ Ⓗ Ⓙ

Verbal Reasoning—Context

1. Ⓐ Ⓑ Ⓒ Ⓓ   5. Ⓐ Ⓑ Ⓒ Ⓓ   9. Ⓐ Ⓑ Ⓒ Ⓓ   13. Ⓐ Ⓑ Ⓒ Ⓓ   17. Ⓐ Ⓑ Ⓒ Ⓓ
2. Ⓕ Ⓖ Ⓗ Ⓙ   6. Ⓕ Ⓖ Ⓗ Ⓙ   10. Ⓕ Ⓖ Ⓗ Ⓙ   14. Ⓕ Ⓖ Ⓗ Ⓙ   18. Ⓕ Ⓖ Ⓗ Ⓙ
3. Ⓐ Ⓑ Ⓒ Ⓓ   7. Ⓐ Ⓑ Ⓒ Ⓓ   11. Ⓐ Ⓑ Ⓒ Ⓓ   15. Ⓐ Ⓑ Ⓒ Ⓓ   19. Ⓐ Ⓑ Ⓒ Ⓓ
4. Ⓕ Ⓖ Ⓗ Ⓙ   8. Ⓕ Ⓖ Ⓗ Ⓙ   12. Ⓕ Ⓖ Ⓗ Ⓙ   16. Ⓕ Ⓖ Ⓗ Ⓙ   20. Ⓕ Ⓖ Ⓗ Ⓙ

Reading and Language Arts

1. Ⓐ Ⓑ Ⓒ Ⓓ	9. Ⓐ Ⓑ Ⓒ Ⓓ	17. Ⓐ Ⓑ Ⓒ Ⓓ	25. Ⓐ Ⓑ Ⓒ Ⓓ	33. Ⓐ Ⓑ Ⓒ Ⓓ
2. Ⓕ Ⓖ Ⓗ Ⓙ	10. Ⓕ Ⓖ Ⓗ Ⓙ	18. Ⓕ Ⓖ Ⓗ Ⓙ	26. Ⓕ Ⓖ Ⓗ Ⓙ	34. Ⓕ Ⓖ Ⓗ Ⓙ
3. Ⓐ Ⓑ Ⓒ Ⓓ	11. Ⓐ Ⓑ Ⓒ Ⓓ	19. Ⓐ Ⓑ Ⓒ Ⓓ	27. Ⓐ Ⓑ Ⓒ Ⓓ	35. Ⓐ Ⓑ Ⓒ Ⓓ
4. Ⓕ Ⓖ Ⓗ Ⓙ	12. Ⓕ Ⓖ Ⓗ Ⓙ	20. Ⓕ Ⓖ Ⓗ Ⓙ	28. Ⓕ Ⓖ Ⓗ Ⓙ	36. Ⓕ Ⓖ Ⓗ Ⓙ
5. Ⓐ Ⓑ Ⓒ Ⓓ	13. Ⓐ Ⓑ Ⓒ Ⓓ	21. Ⓐ Ⓑ Ⓒ Ⓓ	29. Ⓐ Ⓑ Ⓒ Ⓓ	37. Ⓐ Ⓑ Ⓒ Ⓓ
6. Ⓕ Ⓖ Ⓗ Ⓙ	14. Ⓕ Ⓖ Ⓗ Ⓙ	22. Ⓕ Ⓖ Ⓗ Ⓙ	30. Ⓕ Ⓖ Ⓗ Ⓙ	38. Ⓕ Ⓖ Ⓗ Ⓙ
7. Ⓐ Ⓑ Ⓒ Ⓓ	15. Ⓐ Ⓑ Ⓒ Ⓓ	23. Ⓐ Ⓑ Ⓒ Ⓓ	31. Ⓐ Ⓑ Ⓒ Ⓓ	39. Ⓐ Ⓑ Ⓒ Ⓓ
8. Ⓕ Ⓖ Ⓗ Ⓙ	16. Ⓕ Ⓖ Ⓗ Ⓙ	24. Ⓕ Ⓖ Ⓗ Ⓙ	32. Ⓕ Ⓖ Ⓗ Ⓙ	40. Ⓕ Ⓖ Ⓗ Ⓙ

Mathematics

1. Ⓐ Ⓑ Ⓒ Ⓓ Ⓔ	9. Ⓐ Ⓑ Ⓒ Ⓓ	17. Ⓐ Ⓑ Ⓒ Ⓓ	25. Ⓐ Ⓑ Ⓒ Ⓓ	33. Ⓐ Ⓑ Ⓒ Ⓓ
2. Ⓕ Ⓖ Ⓗ Ⓙ Ⓚ	10. Ⓕ Ⓖ Ⓗ Ⓙ	18. Ⓕ Ⓖ Ⓗ Ⓙ	26. Ⓕ Ⓖ Ⓗ Ⓙ	34. Ⓕ Ⓖ Ⓗ Ⓙ
3. Ⓐ Ⓑ Ⓒ Ⓓ Ⓔ	11. Ⓐ Ⓑ Ⓒ Ⓓ	19. Ⓐ Ⓑ Ⓒ Ⓓ	27. Ⓐ Ⓑ Ⓒ Ⓓ	35. Ⓐ Ⓑ Ⓒ Ⓓ
4. Ⓕ Ⓖ Ⓗ Ⓙ Ⓚ	12. Ⓕ Ⓖ Ⓗ Ⓙ	20. Ⓕ Ⓖ Ⓗ Ⓙ	28. Ⓕ Ⓖ Ⓗ Ⓙ	36. Ⓕ Ⓖ Ⓗ Ⓙ
5. Ⓐ Ⓑ Ⓒ Ⓓ Ⓔ	13. Ⓐ Ⓑ Ⓒ Ⓓ	21. Ⓐ Ⓑ Ⓒ Ⓓ	29. Ⓐ Ⓑ Ⓒ Ⓓ	37. Ⓐ Ⓑ Ⓒ Ⓓ
6. Ⓕ Ⓖ Ⓗ Ⓙ Ⓚ	14. Ⓕ Ⓖ Ⓗ Ⓙ	22. Ⓕ Ⓖ Ⓗ Ⓙ	30. Ⓕ Ⓖ Ⓗ Ⓙ	38. Ⓕ Ⓖ Ⓗ Ⓙ
7. Ⓐ Ⓑ Ⓒ Ⓓ Ⓔ	15. Ⓐ Ⓑ Ⓒ Ⓓ	23. Ⓐ Ⓑ Ⓒ Ⓓ	31. Ⓐ Ⓑ Ⓒ Ⓓ	39. Ⓐ Ⓑ Ⓒ Ⓓ
8. Ⓕ Ⓖ Ⓗ Ⓙ Ⓚ	16. Ⓕ Ⓖ Ⓗ Ⓙ	24. Ⓕ Ⓖ Ⓗ Ⓙ	32. Ⓕ Ⓖ Ⓗ Ⓙ	40. Ⓕ Ⓖ Ⓗ Ⓙ

COOP Practice Test 2

TEST 1: SEQUENCES

Directions: For questions 1–20, choose the answer that best continues the sequence.

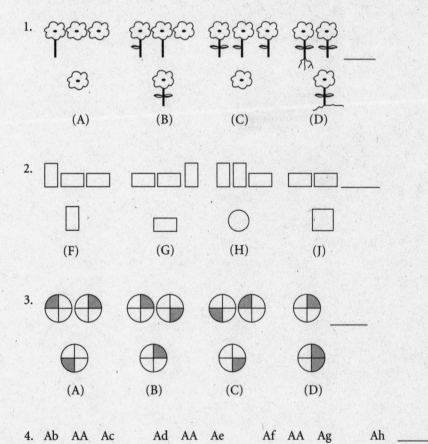

1.

(A) (B) (C) (D)

2.

(F) (G) (H) (J)

3.

(A) (B) (C) (D)

4. Ab AA Ac   Ad AA Ae   Af AA Ag   Ah _____ Ai

AA   Ai   Aj   Ak
(F)   (G)   (H)   (J)

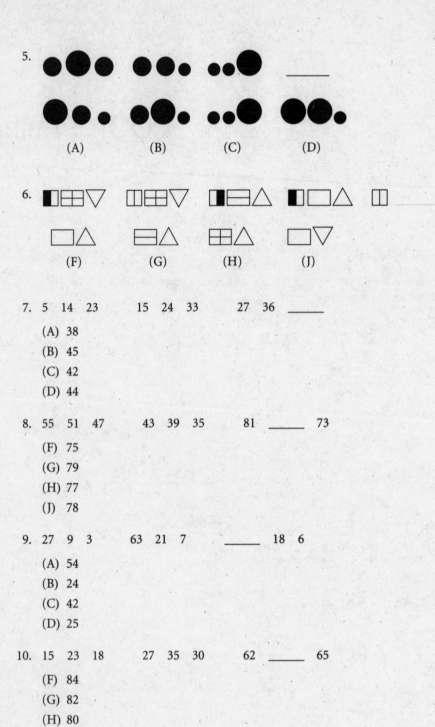

7. 5 14 23   15 24 33   27 36 _____

(A) 38

(B) 45

(C) 42

(D) 44

8. 55 51 47   43 39 35   81 _____ 73

(F) 75

(G) 79

(H) 77

(J) 78

9. 27 9 3   63 21 7   _____ 18 6

(A) 54

(B) 24

(C) 42

(D) 25

10. 15 23 18   27 35 30   62 _____ 65

(F) 84

(G) 82

(H) 80

(J) 70

11. 5 20 10   8 32 16   7 28 _____

    (A) 10

    (B) 12

    (C) 20

    (D) 14

12. 6 7 13   9 7 16   8 _____ 15

    (F) 7

    (G) 10

    (H) 9

    (J) 13

13. 1 1 1   3 9 81   2 _____ 8

    (A) 6

    (B) 4

    (C) 5

    (D) 1

14. $A_6B_5C_4$ $A_5B_4C_3$ $A_4B_3C_2$ _____

    (F) $A_4B_3C_2$

    (G) $A_3B_2C_1$

    (H) $A_5B_3C_2$

    (J) $A_4B_3C_3$

15. $2X^1Y_5$ $2X^2Y_4$ $2X^3Y_3$ _____

    (A) $2X_4Y_2$

    (B) $2X^3Y_3$

    (C) $2X^4Y_2$

    (D) $2X^4Y_1$

16. $A^1B^1C^2$ $B^2B^3C^3$ _____ $D^4B^7C^5$

    (F) $C^3B^5C^4$

    (G) $C^3B^3C^5$

    (H) $C^3B^4B^3C^4$

    (J) $C^3B^4C^6$

17. BOB   MOM   _____   PIP

 (A) POP
 (B) MOP
 (C) BOP
 (D) BIP

18. CDAI   FGEO   HJUA   _____

 (F) IJKO
 (G) IJEA
 (H) JKOP
 (J) KLOA

19. Yxx   Wvv   _____   Srr

 (A) Zyy
 (B) Qrr
 (C) Utt
 (D) Tuu

20. AABA   BACB   CADC   _____

 (F) ACAE
 (G) ACDC
 (H) DAED
 (J) DADE

TEST 2: ANALOGIES

Directions: For questions 1–20, look at the two pictures in the top boxes. Then, choose the picture that belongs in the empty box so that the bottom two pictures are related the same way that the top two are related.

1.

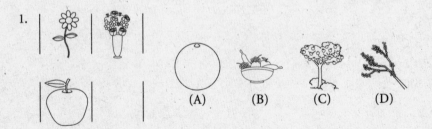

(A)   (B)   (C)   (D)

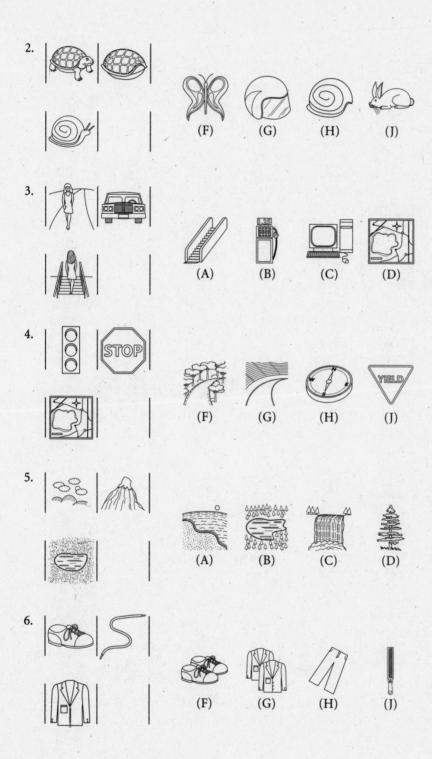

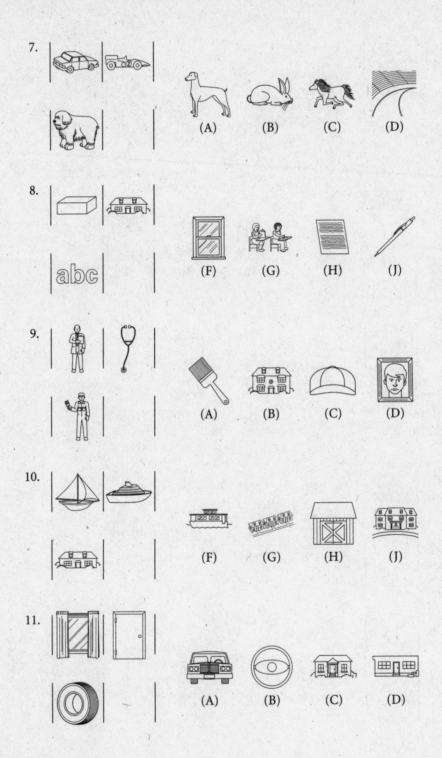

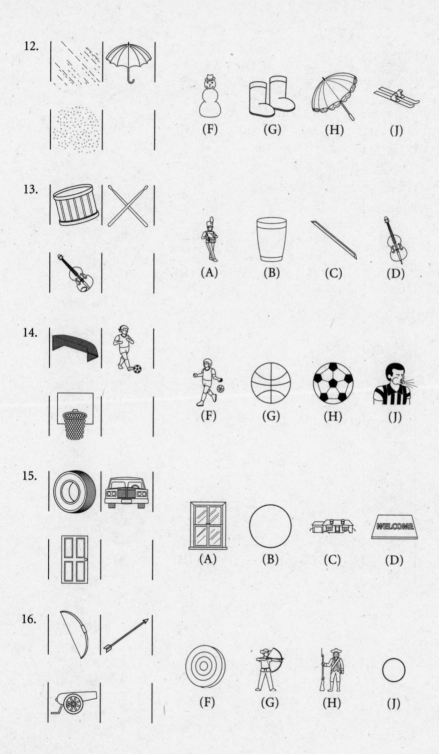

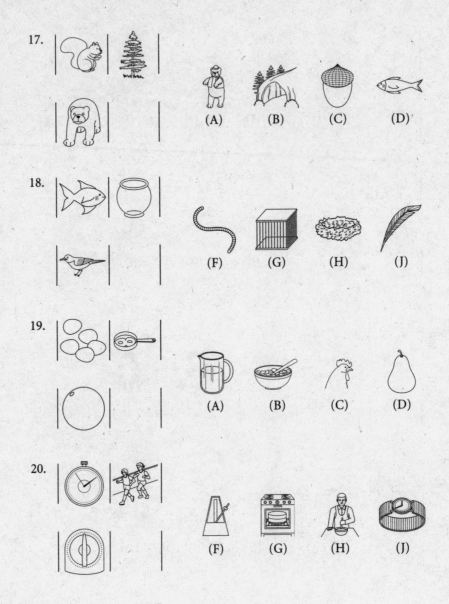

17.

18.

19.

20.

TEST 3: QUANTITATIVE REASONING

Directions: For questions 1–6, find the relationship of the numbers in the left column to the numbers in the right column. Choose the number that should replace the blank.

1. $2 \rightarrow \square \rightarrow 12$

   $1 \rightarrow \square \rightarrow 6$

   $3 \rightarrow \square \rightarrow \underline{\quad}$

4	18	9	24
(A)	(B)	(C)	(D)

2. $15 \rightarrow \square \rightarrow 8$

   $16 \rightarrow \square \rightarrow 9$

   $11 \rightarrow \square \rightarrow \underline{\quad}$

3	10	12	4
(F)	(G)	(H)	(J)

3. $12 \rightarrow \square \rightarrow 19$

   $2 \rightarrow \square \rightarrow 9$

   $5 \rightarrow \square \rightarrow \underline{\quad}$

12	15	13	10
(A)	(B)	(C)	(D)

4. $\frac{1}{3} \rightarrow \square \rightarrow \frac{4}{3}$

   $\frac{1}{4} \rightarrow \square \rightarrow \frac{5}{4}$

   $\frac{1}{5} \rightarrow \square \rightarrow \underline{\quad}$

$\frac{5}{5}$	1	$\frac{6}{5}$	$\frac{7}{5}$
(F)	(G)	(H)	(J)

5. $2 \rightarrow \square \rightarrow 1$

   $1 \rightarrow \square \rightarrow 0$

   $3 \rightarrow \square \rightarrow \underline{\quad}$

2	$\frac{1}{3}$	1	−1
(A)	(B)	(C)	(D)

6. $17 \rightarrow \square \rightarrow 22$

   $9 \rightarrow \square \rightarrow 14$

   $3 \rightarrow \square \rightarrow \underline{\quad}$

9	6	8	10
(F)	(G)	(H)	(J)

Directions: For questions 7–13, find the fraction of the grid that is shaded.

7.

   (A) $\frac{1}{2}$ (B) $\frac{1}{4}$ (C) $\frac{1}{8}$ (D) $\frac{1}{16}$

8.

   (F) 2   (G) $\frac{1}{6}$ (H) $\frac{2}{3}$ (J) $\frac{1}{3}$

9.

   (A) $\frac{1}{2}$ (B) $\frac{1}{5}$ (C) 5   (D) $\frac{5}{12}$

10.

    (F) $\frac{1}{4}$ (G) 12   (H) $\frac{2}{9}$ (J) $\frac{2}{7}$

11.

    (A) $\frac{3}{8}$ (B) $\frac{1}{3}$ (C) $\frac{1}{4}$ (D) $\frac{1}{2}$

12.

    (F) $\frac{1}{3}$ (G) $\frac{1}{12}$ (H) $\frac{3}{10}$ (J) $\frac{1}{4}$

13.

(A) $\frac{1}{4}$ (B) $\frac{1}{3}$ (C) $\frac{1}{2}$ (D) $\frac{2}{3}$

Directions: For questions 14–20, the scale shows sets of shapes of equal weight. Find a pair of sets that would also balance the scale.

14.

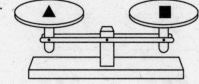

(F) ▲   ▲▲
(G) ▲■   ■▲
(H) ■▲   ■
(J) ▲▲■   ■

15.

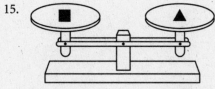

(A) ▲   ▲■
(B) ▲■   ▲▲
(C) ■▲   ■
(D) ▲▲   ■

16.

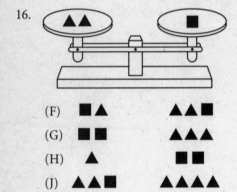

(F) ■ ▲   ▲ ▲ ■

(G) ■ ■   ▲ ▲ ▲

(H) ▲   ■ ■

(J) ▲ ▲ ■   ▲ ▲ ▲ ▲

17.

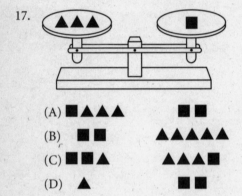

(A) ■ ▲ ▲ ▲   ■ ■

(B) ■ ■   ▲ ▲ ▲ ▲ ▲ ▲

(C) ■ ■ ▲   ▲ ▲ ▲ ■

(D) ▲   ■ ■

18.

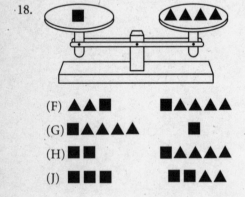

(F) ▲ ▲ ■   ■ ▲ ▲ ▲ ▲

(G) ■ ▲ ▲ ▲ ▲   ■

(H) ■ ■   ■ ▲ ▲ ▲ ▲

(J) ■ ■ ■   ■ ■ ▲ ▲

19.

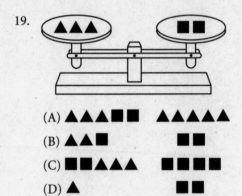

(A) ▲ ▲ ▲ ■ ■   ▲ ▲ ▲ ▲ ▲ ▲

(B) ▲ ▲ ■   ■ ■

(C) ■ ■ ▲ ▲ ▲   ■ ■ ■ ■

(D) ▲   ■ ■

20.

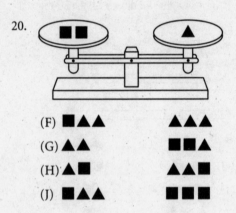

(F) ■ ▲ ▲   ▲ ▲ ▲

(G) ▲ ▲   ■ ■ ▲

(H) ■ ■   ▲ ▲ ■

(J) ■ ▲ ▲   ■ ■ ■

TEST 4: VERBAL REASONING—WORDS

Directions: For questions 1–9, find the word that names a necessary part of the underlined word.

1. <u>wedding</u>

   (A) invitation
   (B) party
   (C) dress
   (D) bride

2. <u>controversy</u>

   (F) disagreement
   (G) aggression
   (H) truce
   (J) resolution

3. <u>drum</u>

   (A) cymbals
   (B) sticks
   (C) rhythm
   (D) rhyme

4. <u>agriculture</u>

   (F) seasons
   (G) livestock
   (H) garden
   (J) crops

5. <u>candidate</u>

   (A) politics
   (B) choice
   (C) freedom
   (D) poll

6. <u>optimist</u>

   (F) joy
   (G) love
   (H) hope
   (J) emotion

7. <u>flower</u>

   (A) garden
   (B) petal
   (C) daisy
   (D) bee

8. <u>guitar</u>

   (F) strings
   (G) concert
   (H) electric
   (J) bass

9. <u>ticket</u>

   (A) window
   (B) stadium
   (C) expense
   (D) entry

Directions: For questions 10–13, the words in the top row are related in some way. The words in the bottom row are related in the same way. Find the word that competes the bottom row of words.

10. drizzle   rain   downpour

     warm   hot

     (F) scorching
     (G) sun
     (H) tepid
     (J) heat

11. car   truck   motorcycle

     jet   hot air balloon

     (A) helicopter
     (B) scooter
     (C) horse
     (D) sky

12. word   sentence   paragraph

     chapter   book

     (F) magazine
     (G) title
     (H) series
     (J) author

13. snail   worm   turtle

     cheetah   greyhound

     (A) horse
     (B) race
     (C) snake
     (D) spots

Directions: For questions 14–17, find the word that does not belong with the others.

14. Which word does *not* belong with the others?

    (F) approve
    (G) scorn
    (H) condemn
    (J) mock

15. Which word does *not* belong with the others?

    (A) license
    (B) visa
    (C) permit
    (D) regulation

16. Which word does *not* belong with the others?

    (F) kick
    (G) draw
    (H) bounce
    (J) throw

17. Which word does *not* belong with the others?

    (A) nose
    (B) aroma
    (C) odor
    (D) scent

Directions: For questions 18–20, find the word that is most like the underlined words.

18. <u>land</u>   <u>earth</u>   <u>dirt</u>

    (F) soil
    (G) island
    (H) muddy
    (J) garden

19. <u>exercise</u>   <u>sports</u>   <u>workout</u>

    (A) athletics
    (B) gym
    (C) tennis
    (D) sweat

20. <u>work</u>   <u>job</u>   <u>occupation</u>

(F) employment

(G) boss

(H) salary

(J) promotion

TEST 5: VERBAL REASONING—CONTEXT

Directions: For questions 1–20, find the statement that is true according to the given information.

1. Cherry trees bloom in the spring. The cherry tree in Alonso's backyard is blooming.

(A) Alonso has a cherry tree in his yard.

(B) It is March.

(C) It is not April.

(D) Alonso lives in the country.

2. Today is a windy day. Sailboats need wind in order to move.

(F) It is fall.

(G) It is November.

(H) Today is a good day to sail.

(J) It is easy to sail.

3. "Hola" means hello in Spanish. Marco just told Lena "hello" in French.

(A) Marco speaks French well.

(B) Marco probably did not say "hola."

(C) Lena speaks French.

(D) Marco does not speak Spanish.

4. At an auction, the highest bidder wins the item. Rachel bid $100 on an antique chair.

(F) Someone will probably outbid Rachel.

(G) Rachel is the auctioneer.

(H) Rachel will win the chair.

(J) Rachel is at an auction.

5. Mr. and Mrs. Bowden have a two-year old son and a five-year old daughter. Clarissa is eight years old.

    (A) Clarissa is not Mr. and Mrs. Bowden's daughter.

    (B) Clarissa is Mr. and Mrs. Bowden's niece.

    (C) Clarissa is younger than Mr. and Mrs. Bowden's daughter.

    (D) Clarissa lives next door to the Bowdens.

6. There is a tasty smell coming from the kitchen. David is in the kitchen.

    (F) David is baking cookies.

    (G) Something is in the oven.

    (H) David is making a sandwich.

    (J) Someone is in the kitchen.

7. The flowers in the front yard need to be watered twice a day. The flowers in the front yard are wilting.

    (A) The flowers need more water.

    (B) Someone is watering the flowers too much.

    (C) The flowers are not healthy.

    (D) There are flowers in the backyard.

8. Adina is watching television. She is smiling.

    (F) Adina is probably happy.

    (G) Adina loves to watch television.

    (H) Adina is watching a comedy.

    (J) Adina is sitting down.

9. A cookie is missing from Sarah's cookie jar. Seung Hee loves cookies.

    (A) Seung Hee took the missing cookie.

    (B) The cookie jar is easy to open.

    (C) Sarah bakes cookies.

    (D) Sarah keeps cookies in a cookie jar.

10. Suzie received 10 Valentine's Day cards. One card was signed "from your secret admirer."

    (F) Suzie's secret admirer sent her only one card.

    (G) Suzie sent a card to her secret admirer.

    (H) Suzie received fewer than a dozen Valentine's Day cards.

    (J) Suzie's secret admirer is in her class.

11. All soldiers in boot camp must be able to run the camp's obstacle course. Elise is in boot camp.

    (A) Elise is in good physical condition.

    (B) Elise is able to run the camp's obstacle course.

    (C) Elise is stronger than the men in boot camp.

    (D) Elise is a drill sergeant.

12. Hope and Joey went fishing. Hope caught 3 fish and Joey caught 5.

    (F) Joey is a better fisher than Hope.

    (G) Hope used different bait than Joey.

    (H) Hope and Joey are best friends.

    (J) Hope caught fewer fish than Joey.

13. Babies cry if they are tired or hungry. Baby X is crying. Her parents just fed her.

    (A) Baby X doesn't like to eat.

    (B) Baby X does not sleep enough at night.

    (C) Baby X is confusing her parents.

    (D) Baby X needs to take a nap.

14. The Bailer family lives in an apartment complex with a swimming pool and a communal tennis court. The tennis court can get very crowded on Saturdays and they must make a reservation if they want to play.

    (F) The Bailers like to swim.

    (G) The Bailers do not live in a house.

    (H) The people in the complex are good tennis players.

    (J) Everyone likes to play tennis.

15. Bobby Lee tried out for the fall production and won the lead role. In the spring he only landed a bit part. Bobby Lee is joining the town football league in the summer.

    (A) Bobby Lee has given up acting.

    (B) Bobby Lee is a better actor than football player.

    (C) Bobby Lee's acting is improving.

    (D) Bobby Lee enjoys various activities.

16. Karl and Karla Cooper watch television in the evenings. Karl sits on the sofa and changes channels frequently. Karla sits in the armchair and does the crossword puzzle.

    (F) Karla Cooper is good at the crossword puzzle.

    (G) Karla Cooper would like to watch just one show.

    (H) Karl Cooper does not like to watch only one show.

    (J) Karl and Karla Cooper are married.

17. Rene's grandmother calls her every Sunday from Paris. Rene is always happy to hear from her grandmother.

    (A) Rene has a good relationship with her grandmother.

    (B) Rene understands French.

    (C) Rene has been to Paris.

    (D) Rene's grandmother speaks French.

18. The special of the day at Kelly's Diner is fried chicken. All the employees at Kelly's can eat the special of the day for free.

    (F) All the employees at Kelly's will eat fried chicken

    (G) The cooks cannot eat fried chicken for free today.

    (H) The employees at Kelly's do not have to pay for the special of the day.

    (J) The employees at Kelly's love fried chicken.

19. Jason is taking a ferry to New Hope Island. The ferry ride to New Hope Island takes 1 hour.

    (A) Jason cannot swim to New Hope Island.

    (B) Jason likes the ferry ride.

    (C) Jason will be at New Hope Island in an hour.

    (D) New Hope Island is an hour ferry ride from shore.

20. There is a "buy one get one free" sale at Shoe Shack. Sam left Shoe Shack with two pairs of sneakers.

    (F) Sam should get two more pairs of sneakers for free.

    (G) Sam always buys his sneakers at Shoe Shack.

    (H) Shoe Shack has the best deal in town.

    (J) Sam only paid for one pair of sneakers.

TEST 6: READING AND LANGUAGE ARTS

Directions: Follow the directions for questions 1–40.

Read the following passage and answer questions 1–4.

Say the word "Dada." It may sound like gibberish, baby talk, or just plain nonsense. That's what the creators of the Dada art movement wanted. The ideas these artists put forth, and the artwork they created intentionally mocked mature, rational culture. In reaction to the brutality of World War I, the Dadaists rejected the values that they believed led to the war—nationalism, militarism, and rational philosophy. Instead they stressed child-like creativity and the triumph of life in the face of war and destruction.

The Dadaists did not acquire their name until 1916, but the work of several artists years earlier sparked the spirit of the movement. In 1913, French artist Marcel Duchamp made the first of his *ready-mades*, in which he selected everyday objects, such as a bicycle wheel or a toilet seat, and raised them to the status of art by signing them and exhibiting them in art galleries. Duchamp also had the gall to take the world famous Leonardo DaVinci painting, the Mona Lisa, and draw a moustache on Mona Lisa's face. He then declared the painting his own. Every musician today who "samples" tunes from other sources owes a debt of gratitude to Marcel Duchamp.

The artist Francis Picabia was also an important "father" of the Dada movement. Working in New York City in 1915, Picabia created playful paintings, drawings, and sculptures that depicted human figures in the form of machines—a joking stab at new technology. Picabia and Duchamp's work drew the attention of a small but active circle of American patrons, writers, and artists who helped them gain notoriety.

The official—if Dadaism can be called official—launch of Dada took place in 1916 with the opening of the nightclub, the Cabaret Voltaire in Zurich, Switzerland. As a neutral country, Switzerland attracted artists and intellectuals opposed to the war. The exact genesis of the name Dada is debated, but Romanian-born French poet, Tristan Tzara claims to have created it. Some argue that Dada means rocking horse in French but Tzara proclaimed "Dada means nothing!" arguing for the absurdity of the movement and its art.

1. According to this article

    (A) the Dadaists were children

    (B) Dadaists were reacting to the war

    (C) Dadaists were not good artists

    (D) Dadaism was started by Marcel Duchamp

2. All of the following were mentioned as qualities of Dadaism EXCEPT

    (F) love of nonsense

    (G) making fun of rational thought

    (H) joking about technology

    (J) patriotic demonstrations

3. Dadaism officially began

   (A) when Cabaret Voltaire opened in Zurich.

   (B) when Marcel Duchamp began to create ready-mades

   (C) when World War I began

   (D) when Tristan Tzara declared "Dada means nothing!"

4. Duchamp probably drew a moustache on the Mona Lisa

   (F) because he didn't like the painting

   (G) to insult the original artist

   (H) to mock the establishment

   (J) to make himself famous

Here is a paragraph a student wrote about the Dada movement. There are a few mistakes that need correcting. Read the story, then answer questions 5–7.

(1) The Dada art movement was an interesting, exciting, and original movement. (2) It was also very creative. (3) These artists believed it was important not to take life too seriously. (4) They thought that War was caused by too much seriousness and since they were against War, they wanted to act differently. (5) They behaved childish and made childish artwork.

5. Which is the best way to combine sentences 1 and 2?

   (A) The Dada art movement was an interesting, exciting, and original, and creative movement.

   (B) The Dada art movement was an interesting, exciting, original movement and it was also very creative.

   (C) The Dada art movement was an interesting, exciting, and original and creative movement.

   (D) The Dada art movement was interesting, exciting, original, and creative.

6. Which sentence contains a capitalization error?

   (F) Sentence 1

   (G) Sentence 2

   (H) Sentence 3

   (J) Sentence 4

7. Which is the best way to write Sentence 5?

   (A) They behaved childish and childishly made artwork.

   (B) They were behaving childish and were making childish artwork.

   (C) They behaved childishly and made childish artwork.

   (D) Best as is.

Read the following passage and answer questions 8–11.

"A rose by any other name would smell as sweet," said Shakespeare's Romeo to Juliet. Meaning, he would love her no matter what her name was. Juliet was still Juliet to Romeo no matter whether she was a Capulet (from the enemy family), a Montague, or a Smith.

But, is Romeo's declaration true? Would a rose by any other name smell as sweet? Linguists have been asking this question for many years. They wonder does someone or something's name contribute to how we see that person or thing? If Juliet were called Barney would Romeo still feel romantic about her? If a rose were called a stinkweed, would we still consider it beautiful and fragrant? What if we called the rose George? Or, what if we used the word *kurchup* to signify a rose? Is it still a rose?

The French linguist Ferdinand Saussure said no. In a series of lectures Saussure delivered in 1910, he rejected the idea that words have a relationship to real, concrete objects. Words, according to Saussure, exist in relation to one another. A rose is a rose because it is **not** a daisy, a violet, a peony, or an ant. Words, or the sounds we make that become words, are randomly selected and take on meaning only because we give them meaning. This theory makes sense when you realize that the word for rose is different in many of the world's hundreds of languages. The group of sounds that make up the word *rose* have come to mean that particular flower because we all have agreed to let them mean that thing. The words that make up a language come about because they are mutually agreed on by a group, rather than from any special character of the object they describe.

8. A good title for this selection would be

   (F) Romeo and Juliet

   (G) All About Roses

   (H) A Theory of Language

   (J) Shakespeare's Drama

9. The author's tone in this selection is

   (A) enthusiastic

   (B) biased

   (C) matter of fact

   (D) poetic

10. The author uses questions in this selection to

    (F) inspire the reader to think about a complicated idea

    (G) show that no one has answers to these difficult questions

    (H) prove that Saussure had answers to all these questions

    (J) demonstrate that Shakespeare is confusing

11. Which of the following BEST demonstrates Saussure's theory?

    (A) one person making up his own word to describe a flower

    (B) a group of people agreeing to call a flower a *blurp*

    (C) a pet owner naming her cat Mittens

    (D) a flower having a different name in 10 different languages

12. Here are two sentences related to the passage:

    Saussure was a French linguist.

    Saussure changed the way people thought about language.

    Select the answer choice that best combines the two sentences into one.

    (F) Saussure was a French linguist and he changed the way people thought about language.

    (G) Saussure was a French linguist, which changed people's thinking about language.

    (H) Saussure, a French linguist, changed the way people thought about language.

    (J) Saussure changed the way people thought about language, and was a French linguist.

13. Choose the sentence that is written correctly.

    (A) Linguists study the origins, evolution, and roots of languages.

    (B) Linguists are people whom are skilled in languages.

    (C) Saussure discussed many new ideas when he lectures in 1910.

    (D) Speaking many languages, are necessary to a linguist.

Read the following passage and answer questions 14–16.

It's 9 o'clock on a dark, moonlit night and you're rowing a boat over the calm waters of a bay. You slip your oar into the water and notice a curious thing. A glowing green light shines from the waters below. You raise your oar out of the water and the light vanishes. What is this strange phenomenon? The glow you're seeing is caused by a bioluminescent creature, an animal able to emit it's own light. Many marine animals possess this amazing quality—from microscopic bacteria to the five meter-long 'Megamouth' shark.

Despite their tremendous diversity, all bioluminescent organisms create light by the same process. Bioluminescence occurs as a result of a chemical reaction between a protein (luciferin) and an enzyme (luciferase) in the presence of oxygen. If you've ever accidentally touched a light bulb when it's on, you know that most light sources give off a lot of heat. This reduces the amount of free energy that can be converted into light. Another source of energy loss is the production of sound—think of the humming noise that same light bulb makes. Bioluminescence however is almost 100% efficient. Practically all of the energy generated by the luciferin-luciferase reaction is converted into light without being lost in heat or sound production. Bioluminescence is amazingly a 'cold fire.'

14. Bioluminescent organisms create light by

   (F) a chemical reaction

   (G) converting free energy into light

   (H) producing sound

   (J) touching other organisms

15. Bioluminescent light differs from other light sources because

   (A) it takes place in the presence of oxygen

   (B) it loses heat in light production

   (C) it is more efficient

   (D) it is a type of fire

16. According to the passage, all of the following are true of bioluminescent creatures EXCEPT

   (F) there are a wide variety of bioluminescent creatures

   (G) all bioluminescent creatures make light the same way

   (H) many bioluminescent creatures are marine animals

   (J) it may be painful to touch a bioluminescent creature

Here is a paragraph related to the passage. Read the paragraph, then answer questions 17–18.

The first category of bioluminescent creatures includes animals equipped with 'photophores.' These are organs similar to eye structures located deep within the skin. In photophores, light is produced by specialized cells and reflected through a lens or clear outer covering. The second category of bioluminescent animal uses the luminosity of bacteria that live within it. The host cannot control the amount of light produced by the bacteria, and so those organisms with bacterial symbionts have developed some interesting ways to "turn out the light" when necessary.

17. Choose the best topic sentence for this paragraph.

(A) Bioluminescent creatures can be classified into two basic categories.

(B) Bioluminescent creatures often use their light to stun or confuse predators.

(C) Some bioluminescent creatures are photophores.

(D) Many deep-sea creatures migrate toward the surface nightly, following their prey.

18. What might you expect the next paragraph to be about?

(F) how symbionts get inside the host animal

(G) how bioluminescence can help an animal

(H) what are some ways bioluminescent animals can control their symbionts

(J) why host organisms may need to "turn out the light"

Read the following passage and answer questions 19–22.

As the saying goes, Rome wasn't built in a day. Writing a top-notch essay takes time, planning, and careful revision. In order to revise, you must first have something down on paper. Many students feel that this is the most difficult part of the composition process. When faced with an assignment, they suffer from writer's block.

Brainstorming is often a helpful way to overcome writer's block. Sit quietly somewhere with a piece of blank paper and your chosen topic. Jot down all the things that occur to you on that topic. For example, if you were writing an essay about horses, you might jot down *fast, beautiful, Arabian Stallion, work horses,* or anything else that jars your imagination. Once you have some ideas down on paper, you can begin to organize them.

19. You might expect the next paragraph to be about

(A) organizing your essay

(B) the topic sentence

(C) overcoming writer's block

(D) work horses

20. Where would you most likely find this selection?

(F) a teacher's edition of an English textbook

(G) a book about horses

(H) a manual for students

(J) a magazine for poets

21. The saying *Rome wasn't built in a day* is intended to do all of the following EXCEPT

(A) encourage students

(B) tell the reader to study Romans

(C) create interest in the passage

(D) introduce the topic

22. A good title for this passage would be

(F) An Essay about Horses

(G) Things Take Time

(H) How to Write an Essay

(J) Overcoming Writer's Block

Here is part of an essay a student contributed to the school magazine. There are a few mistakes that need correcting. Read the story, then answer questions 23–26.

(1) Some of the people don't like to write papers. (2) I do. (3) I enjoy putting my ideas down on paper and to share them with my audience. (4) I never have a problem with writer's block because I think of my writing as a conversation I am having with my reader. (5) If you imagine someone reading what you write, you wouldn't have any problem coming up with ideas.

23. Which is the best way to write Sentence 1?

(A) Some of the people doesn't like to write papers.

(B) Some people don't like to write papers.

(C) Some people doesn't like to write papers.

(D) Best as is.

24. What would be the best way to combine sentences 1 and 2?

(F) I do like to write papers, unlike those people.

(G) Some of the people don't like to write papers, but I do.

(H) Some of the people don't like to write papers. But I do.

(J) Writing papers is not liked by other people except for me.

25. Which is the best way to write Sentence 3?

    (A) I am enjoying putting my ideas down on paper and to share them with my audience.

    (B) I enjoy to put my ideas down on paper and to share them with my audience.

    (C) I enjoy putting my ideas down on paper and sharing them with my audience.

    (D) Best as is.

26. Which is the best way to write Sentence 5?

    (F) If you could imagine that someone is reading what you write, you wouldn't have any problem coming up with ideas.

    (G) If you imagine someone reading what you write, then you wouldn't have any problem to come up with ideas.

    (H) If you imagine someone reading what you write, you won't have any problem coming up with ideas.

    (J) Best as is.

Read the following passage and answer questions 27–31.

By the late 1800s, many native peoples were being pushed off their lands to make way for American expansionism. There were numerous battles of resistance, and many brave tribal leaders led the fight to keep their ancestral homes. Chief Joseph of the Nez Perce, a peaceful nation that spread from Idaho to Northern Washington, was one such leader. He became well known for his courageous resistance and his eloquent speeches.

Chief Joseph, known by his people as In-mut-too-yah-lat-lat (Thunder coming up over the land from the water), assumed the role of tribal leader from his father, Old Joseph. Old Joseph was on friendly terms with the American government and had signed a treaty that allowed his people to retain much of their land.

In 1863 however, following the discovery of gold in Nez Perce territory, the federal government took back almost 6 million acres of territory. Old Joseph argued that his people had never agreed to this second treaty and he refused to move them.

A showdown over the second "non-treaty" came after Old Joseph died in 1871 and the young Chief Joseph assumed his place. Chief Joseph resisted all efforts to relocate his people to a small reservation in Idaho. The Nez Perce tribe was terribly outnumbered though.

After months of fighting and forced marches, many of the Nez Perce were sent to a reservation in what is now Oklahoma. Many died from malaria and starvation. Chief Joseph tried every possible appeal to the federal authorities to return the Nez Perce to their land. He explained, "All men were made brothers. The earth is the mother of all people, and all people should have equal rights upon it. You might as well expect the rivers to run backward as that any man who was born free should be contented when penned up and denied liberty to go where he pleases." Despite his appeals, Chief Joseph was sent to a reservation in Washington where, according to the reservation doctor, he later died of a broken heart.

27. A showdown between the federal authorities and the Nez Perce began

   (A) when Old Joseph died
   (B) when gold was discovered in Nez Perce territory
   (C) when Chief Joseph refused to move his people
   (D) in 1871

28. The federal government probably wanted to move the Nez Perce

   (F) so they could take possession of gold-rich lands
   (G) to protect the Nez Perce from gold diggers
   (H) to teach them how to farm on settled land
   (J) to punish Chief Joseph for resisting

29. Chief Joseph was different from his father because

   (A) he was an eloquent speaker
   (B) he was a more courageous hunter
   (C) he helped his people move to new land
   (D) he led his people in battle against the government

30. Chief Joseph probably died of a broken heart because

   (F) he missed his father
   (G) he missed his freedom
   (H) he was wounded in battle
   (J) he was upset about losing the gold

31. The author includes the quote at the end of the passage to show

   (A) why Chief Joseph died
   (B) what a good speaker Chief Joseph was
   (C) how Chief Joseph felt about the U.S. government
   (D) what a good leader Chief Joseph was

32. Choose the sentence that is written correctly.

   (F) Chief Joseph appealed to the U.S. government and asking to stay on his land.
   (G) If he would of moved his people, the government wouldn't have fought the Nez Perce.
   (H) When gold was discovered on Nez Perce land, the government broke its treaty.
   (J) In Oklahoma, was the Nez Perce reservation.

33. Here are two sentences related to the passage:

    Chief Joseph was a courageous leader.

    Chief Joseph fought for the rights of his people.

    Select the answer choice that best combines the two sentences into one.

    (A) Chief Joseph was a courageous leader who fought for the rights of his people.

    (B) Chief Joseph was a courageous leader and he also fought for the rights of his people.

    (C) Chief Joseph, a courageous leader, was fighting for the rights of his people.

    (D) Chief Joseph was a courageous leader; who fought for the rights of his people.

Read the following passage and answer questions 34–37.

Sight, taste, touch, hearing, and sight—these are the five senses we all know about. But did you know that some creatures have a sixth sense? What is this sixth sense and what animal possesses it? The shark, the most efficient hunter on Earth, is endowed with a sensitivity to electric fields that help it to pinpoint any animal, even in dark waters.

Special receptors located around the shark's head and snout enable it to detect the electric vibrations that all animals, even human beings, give off. This sense works best at close range and helps the shark zero in on its prey. However, the shark cannot tell the difference between electrical signals given off by animals, and those made by objects such as metal and wire. This is why sharks may sometimes attack boats, docks, or underwater divers in steel cages. The shark's amazing sensory system has earned it the nickname, the perfect predator. However, only a few shark species are dangerous to humans. Most sharks shy away from people and avoid large animals whenever possible.

34. This passage is mostly about

    (F) how sharks hunt

    (G) the five senses

    (H) why sharks attack people

    (J) the shark's special sense

35. As it is used in the passage, *efficient* most nearly means

    (A) capable

    (B) slow

    (C) unskilled

    (D) sensitive

36. All of the following are true of the sharks sixth sense EXCEPT

   (F) it helps the shark detect electric vibrations

   (G) it works best at far range

   (H) it cannot tell the difference between certain types of vibrations

   (J) it helps the shark find its prey

37. According to this passage, sharks may attack divers in steel cages people because

   (A) the divers are in their territory

   (B) they mistake the diver for a boat

   (C) they think the cage is an animal

   (D) the cage is vibrating

Here is a story a student wrote about seeing a shark and other animals at an aquarium. There are a few mistakes that need correcting. Read the story, then answer questions 38–40.

(1) Every saturday my family tries to do something special. (2) Last week we visited a museum. (3) This weekend, we went to Sea Life Park. (4) Swimming around in the tanks, I saw lots of fish. (5) There was even a bottlenose shark. (6) He was pretty scary looking but we were behind the glass. (7) You're not supposed to tap on the glass but somebody next to us did anyway.

38. Which sentence contains a capitalization error?

   (F) Sentence 1

   (G) Sentence 2

   (H) Sentence 3

   (J) Sentence 5

39. Which sentence does not belong within this paragraph?

   (A) Sentence 1

   (B) Sentence 2

   (C) Sentence 5

   (D) Sentence 7

40. Which of the following is the best way to rewrite sentence 4?

   (F) I saw lots of fish swimming around in the tanks.

   (G) Swimming around in the tanks; I saw lots of fish.

   (H) Swimming around in the tanks there were lots of fish that I saw.

   (J) Best as is.

TEST 7: MATHEMATICS

Directions: For questions 1–40, read each problem and find the answer.

1. $4(-4) - 3 =$
   - (A) -16
   - (B) -19
   - (C) -3
   - (D) 48
   - (E) None of these.

2. $\dfrac{15 \times 7 \times 3}{9 \times 5 \times 2} =$
   - (F) $\dfrac{2}{7}$
   - (G) $\dfrac{3}{5}$
   - (H) 7
   - (J) $7\dfrac{1}{2}$
   - (K) None of these.

3. $-2^3(1-2)^3 + (-2)^3 =$
   - (A) -12
   - (B) -4
   - (C) 0
   - (D) 4
   - (E) None of these.

4. $\sqrt{1500} =$
   - (F) $10 + \sqrt{15}$
   - (G) $10\sqrt{15}$
   - (H) 25
   - (J) $100 + \sqrt{15}$
   - (K) None of these.

5. $4^2 \times 4^3 =$
   - (A) 120
   - (B) 4^6
   - (C) $4 \times 4 \times 4 \times 4 \times 4$
   - (D) 4×8
   - (E) None of these.

6. $13.254 - 1.04 =$
   - (F) 12.251
   - (G) 13.214
   - (H) 12.214
   - (J) 13.114
   - (K) None of these.

7. $6\% =$
   - (A) $\dfrac{60}{100}$
   - (B) $\dfrac{6}{100}$
   - (C) 6
   - (D) $\dfrac{1}{6}$
   - (E) None of these.

8. The number 100,000 is equivalent to
   - (F) 10^6
   - (G) 10^4
   - (H) 10^5
   - (J) 10^3
   - (K) None of these.

9. In the number 328,567 what is the value of the digit 8?
   - (A) $8,000$
   - (B) 8
   - (C) $80,000$
   - (D) 80

10. In a recent poll, 10% of voters were in favor of a new bill, 42% were against it, and 18% were undecided. The rest did not vote. What is the ratio of voters to non-voters?

(F) $\dfrac{7}{3}$

(G) 70%

(H) $\dfrac{7}{100}$

(J) $\dfrac{3}{7}$

11. Which of the following represents {2, 3, 5, 6, 7} ∩ {3, 4, 5, 8, 10}?

(A) {2, 3, 4, 5}

(B) {3, 4, 5}

(C) {3, 5}

(D) {3}

12. An office contains 40 cubicles. When the cubicles are $\dfrac{1}{5}$ full, how many cubicles are full?

(F) 8

(G) 9

(H) $\dfrac{1}{8}$

(J) $\dfrac{1}{9}$

13. A centimeter is what part of a meter?

(A) $\dfrac{1}{10}$

(B) $\dfrac{1}{1000}$

(C) $\dfrac{1}{100}$

(D) $\dfrac{1}{12}$

14. The express train travels from Boston to New York City in 3 hours. Boston and New York City are 216 miles apart. How fast does the train travel?

(F) 120 mph

(G) 72 mph

(H) 642 mph

(J) 64 mph

15. Which of the following shows all integer values that may replace the blank to make the sentence true?

$7 >$ ____ > 4

(A) 5

(B) 7, 6, 5, 4

(C) 6, 5, 4

(D) 6, 5

16. Which of the following represents $\{5, 6, 8, 9, 10\} \cap \{3, 4, 8, 9\}$?

(F) $\{8, 9, 10\}$

(G) $\{8\}$

(H) $\{3, 8\}$

(J) $\{8, 9\}$

17. What are the prime factors of 230?

(A) 2, 5, 10

(B) 2, 5, 23

(C) 10, 23

(D) 2, 3, 4

18. If a pizza is cut into 9 equal pieces and Joe eats $\frac{2}{3}$ of the pie, approximately what percent did Joe eat?

(F) 30%

(G) 40%

(H) 60%

(J) 67%

19. Carpet salespeople at Cover Up Carpets do not earn a base salary. Instead, they receive a commission of 7.5% on all of their sales. How many dollars worth of carpets will Max have to sell if he wants to bring home $600 a week?

(A) $900

(B) $1200

(C) $8,000

(D) $7,000

20. Which of the following is equivalent to "three million, one hundred and seventy eight thousand forty two"?

    (F) 3,100,742
    (G) 3,178,042
    (H) 3,170,842
    (J) 3,078,420

21. An equilateral triangle has

    (A) three equal angles
    (B) one right angle
    (C) two equal sides and one right angle
    (D) angles that each equal 80 degrees

22. The set of all common factors of 62 and 84 is

    (F) {2, 3, 6, 8}
    (G) {2, 3, 4, 8}
    (H) {2, 3}
    (J) {2}

23. A group of eight girl guides raised $590 for their group by selling cookies. Three of the guides collectively raised 90% of the money. How much did the other five girls raise together?

    (A) $590
    (B) $49
    (C) $59
    (D) $159

24. Children play in a rectangular sandbox that is 3 feet wide by 16 feet long. What is the perimeter of the sandbox?

    (F) 19 feet
    (G) 48 feet
    (H) 24 feet
    (J) 38 feet

25. Check-It-Out Motors charged Mr. Franco $97 to replace a faulty part in his car plus $42 per hour for each hour that a mechanic worked on his car. The total charge was $230. About how long did the mechanic work on Mr. Franco's car?

    (A) 1 hour
    (B) 2 hours
    (C) 3 hours
    (D) 4 hours

26. Find the area of the triangle below.

    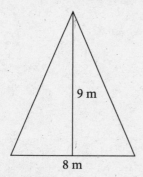

    9 m

    8 m

    (F) 36 m^2
    (G) 30 m^2
    (H) 72 m^2
    (J) 35 m^2

27. Complete the following statement
    $$7(2 \times \underline{\quad}) + 6 = 4,206$$

    (A) 3,000
    (B) 30 × 10
    (C) 3 × 10^2
    (D) 3 × 10^3

The salespeople at Sit Down Furniture Store had their best month of sales ever. The chart below shows the dollar amount each salesperson sold of each item. Answer questions 28–30 based on the chart.

	Chairs	Sofas	Ottomans	Sofa and loveseat sets
John	$400	$10,330	$0	$4,050
Marina	$1,800	$6,800	$400	$7,620
Leslie	$200	$5,450	$150	$9,170
Total	$2,400	$22,580	$550	$20,840

28. If 20 sofas were sold, what was the average price of each sofa?

(F) $1,000

(G) $1,240

(H) $1,128

(J) $1,129

29. What percentage of chair sales was Marina responsible for?

(A) 66%

(B) 33%

(C) 75%

(D) 80%

30. The manager of Sit Down Furniture Store is designing a graph to show the fraction of total sales revenues that were made in each item that the store sells. Which of these is the best graph for him to use?

(F)   Sales Revenues
         by Item

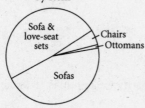

(G)   Sales Revenues by Item

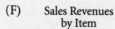

(H)   Sales Revenues by Item

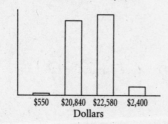

(J)   Sales Revenues by Item

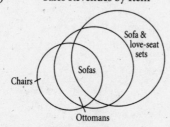

31. Which of these points on the number line represents 4×10^4?

A	B	C	D
400	4,000	40,000	400,000

(A) Point A
(B) Point B
(C) Point C
(D) Point D

32. 1.6 kilometers equals approximately 1 mile. If a charity walkathon is 18 kilometers, about how many miles is it?

(F) 18
(G) 10
(H) 12
(J) 11

33. A 20-ounce bottle of soda costs x cents while a 12-ounce can of the same soda costs 10 cents less. What is the cost of 2 cans of soda?

(A) $2x - 10$
(B) $2(x - 10)$
(C) $2(x + 10)$
(D) $2x - 2(x - 10)$

34. If $-4 < x < -2$, which of the following could be a value of x?

(F) 1
(G) −1
(H) −3
(J) −4

35. A football team won 22 games and tied 2. This was 60% of its season. How many games did the team lose?

(A) 12
(B) 10
(C) 6
(D) 16

36. In which case are the numbers arranged in ascending order with the smallest value listed first?

(F) 40%, .04, $\frac{1}{2}$

(G) $\frac{3}{100}$, $\frac{1}{3}$, $\frac{2}{3}$

(H) $\frac{1}{5}$, .22, 2%

(J) .4, 20%, 30%

37. Which of the following is an example of the distributive property of multiplication over addition?

(A) $a(b + c) = ab + ac$

(B) $a(b + c) = abc$

(C) $a(bc) = \frac{a}{bc}$

(D) $a(b - c) = ab + ac$

38. David has $200 to spend on new, winter clothes. However there is 8% sales tax on items over $100. Which combination of items below allows him to buy the greatest number of items without going over his $200 limit?

(F) $60 shoes, $42 sweater, $10 shirt, $100 boots

(G) $100 boots, $20 sweater, $50 shirt

(H) $110 coat, $40 pants, $50 sweater

(J) $12 socks, $100 coat, $85 suit

39. The gym teacher at Hollingsworth High wants to show her principal a graph illustrating that students who chose to play on varsity football often join other varsity teams as well. Which of the graphs below best achieves that goal?

(A)

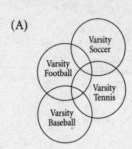

(B)

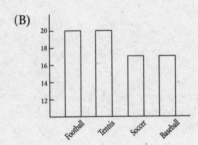

(C)

(D)

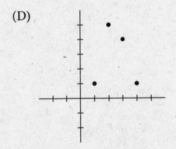

40. What is the circumference of the wheel whose spoke is 15 inches long?

(F) 30π in

(G) 15π in

(H) 7.5π in

(J) 225π in

ANSWER KEY

Test 1:
Sequences

1. B
2. F
3. C
4. F
5. D
6. J
7. B
8. H
9. A
10. J
11. D
12. F
13. B
14. G
15. C
16. F
17. A
18. J
19. C
20. H

Test 2:
Analogies

1. B
2. H
3. A
4. H
5. B
6. J
7. A
8. H
9. A
10. J

11. B
12. G
13. C
14. F
15. C
16. J
17. B
18. G
19. C
20. G

Test 3:
Quantitative Reasoning

1. B
2. J
3. A
4. H
5. A
6. H
7. A
8. J
9. A
10. F
11. C
12. F
13. C
14. G
15. B
16. J
17. A
18. H
19. C
20. G

Test 4:
Verbal Reasoning—Words

1. D
2. F
3. C
4. J
5. B
6. H
7. B
8. F
9. D
10. F
11. A
12. H
13. A
14. F
15. D
16. G
17. A
18. F
19. A
20. F

Test 5:
Verbal Reasoning—Context

1. A
2. H
3. B
4. J
5. A
6. J
7. C
8. F
9. D
10. H

11. B
12. J
13. D
14. G
15. D
16. H
17. A
18. H
19. D
20. J

Test 6:
Reading and Language Arts

1. B
2. J
3. A
4. H
5. D
6. J
7. C
8. H
9. C
10. F
11. B
12. H
13. A
14. F
15. C
16. J
17. A
18. H
19. A
20. H
21. B
22. H
23. B
24. G

25. C
26. H
27. C
28. F
29. D
30. G
31. B
32. H
33. A
34. J
35. A
36. G
37. C
38. F
39. D
40. F

Test 7:
Mathematics Concepts and Applications

1. B
2. K
3. C
4. G
5. C
6. H
7. B
8. H
9. A
10. F
11. C
12. F
13. C
14. G
15. D
16. J
17. B

18. J
19. C
20. G
21. A
22. J
23. C
24. J
25. C
26. F
27. C
28. J
29. C
30. F
31. C
32. J
33. B
34. H
35. D
36. G
37. A
38. G
39. A
40. F

ANSWERS AND EXPLANATIONS

Test 1: Sequences

1. B

In each set of the pattern, the first flower has more detail than the second two. The second two flowers are the same. The missing flower should be the same as the one in the middle and have a stem and two leaves.

2. F

Each set of the pattern contains three rectangles, either on their side (horizontal) or standing up (vertical). Two are of the same orientation, the third is of another. Since in the last set two rectangles are already horizontal, the third should be vertical. There is no reason to believe the missing shape should be anything other than a rectangle.

3. C

Notice how the shading is moving clockwise from its position in the first circle of each set to the second circle of each set. Therefore, the missing circle should be shaded in the quadrant below where the shading is located in the first circle. There is no reason to believe that two segments of the circle should be shaded.

4. F

Look at the sequence and see what is missing. Every set has "AA" in the middle. That is what is missing from the last set.

5. D

Each set is made up of three circles. They are either small, medium, or large. Notice that the size of the last circle in each set dictates number of circles of that particular size in the next set. In the first set a medium size circle is last. There are two medium size circles in the next set, followed by a small circle. The small circle is the last element of this second set. Therefore, there are two small circles in the third set. These are followed by a large circle. Therefore, there should be two large circles in the missing set. These may be followed by a circle of any size. Only choice (D) has the two large circles necessary to begin the set.

6. J

Each set is made up of a square, a rectangle, and a triangle. When the square is shaded, the triangle points up. When the square is not shaded, it points down. The number of lines in the rectangle has no bearing on this. So, since the square is not shaded in the last set, the missing triangle must point down. Only choice (J) has the downward pointing triangle.

7. B

The pattern in this series is +9. Within each set, each number is 9 more than the preceding number; $36 + 9 = 45$.

8. H

The pattern in this series is −4. Thus, from the first number in the last set, we subtract 4; $81 − 4 = 77$.

9. A

The pattern in this series is ÷3. Since we know this, multiply the second number in the last set by 3 to arrive at the missing first number; $18 \times 3 = 54$.

10. J

Within each set the pattern is +8, −5. Thus, the middle number must be 8 more than the preceding one; $62 + 8 = 70$.

11. D

The pattern is ×4, ÷2. Divide 28 by 2 to arrive at the next number in the sequence.

12. F

The pattern in this series is +7. The number 7 in the middle remains constant.

13. B

If the first set doesn't help you recognize the sequence, look at the second set. It has a number (3), its square ($3 \times 3 = 9$), and its cube ($3 \times 3 \times 3 = 9$). So, you are looking for the square of 2, or 2×2. The answer is 4.

14. **G**

Isolate the subscript and the letters in order to see the pattern more readily.

The subscripts are decreasing, while the letters are always A, B, and C.

15. **C**

The numeral 2 remains the same in each set. Each number always has an X and a Y attached. The Xs have superscripts, the Ys have subscripts. The superscripts attached to the Xs are increasing, while the subscripts attached to the Ys decreasing.

16. **F**

As we move from left to right, the first letter ascends alphabetically: A, B, __, D. The second letters are always B and C. The superscript attached to the first letter is increased by 1; the superscript B is increased by 2 and the superscript C is increased by 1.

17. **A**

The series consists of palindromes—words that are the same spelled backwards and forwards. Only POP is a palindrome.

18. **J**

The pattern consists of two consonants and two vowels. The consonants are two letters of the alphabet in ascending order. The vowels are random. Thus, the next part of the series must begin with the consonants KL. It can end in any two vowels.

19. **C**

The pattern is, a capitalized letter, followed by the lowercase of the previous letter listed twice. What comes before the letter v? The next set should begin with a capital U and be followed by tt.

20. **H**

Note that in each set, the first and last letter are the same and are increasing, AA, BB, CC... Therefore, the missing sequence should begin and end with the letter D. Next, you should focus on the 2 letters in the middle of each set. The letters in the middle are always A followed by an increasing letter in the alphabet, for example, AB, AC, AD. Its middle letters should be A and E. So, the next set should be: DAED.

Test 2: Analogies

1. **B**

The bouquet is a combination of various flowers. The bowl of fruit is a combination of various fruits.

2. **H**

A turtle is protected by its shell. A snail is protected by its shell.

3. **A**

A car helps the woman travel more easily. The escalator helps the woman go up more easily.

4. **H**

Both the traffic light and the stop sign serve the same function, they instruct people how to drive. Both the map and compass serve the same function, they help people find their way.

5. **B**

The mountain is a larger version of the hill. The lake is a larger version of the pond.

6. **J**

The lace is used to close the shoe. The zipper is used to close the jacket.

7. **A**

A race car is a fast car. A greyhound is a fast dog.

8. **H**

Bricks make up a house. The letters of the alphabet make up a letter.

9. **A**

The stethoscope is tool of the doctor. The paintbrush is a tool of the painter.

10. **J**

The yacht is a luxurious boat. The mansion is a luxurious house.

11. B

The window and door are parts of a house. The tire and steering wheel are parts of a car.

12. G

The umbrella protects against the rain. The snow boots protect against the snow.

13. C

Drumsticks are used to play a drum. A bow is used to play a violin.

14. F

The soccer player's goal is to shoot a goal. The basketball player's goal is to shoot a hoop.

15. C

A tire is a component of a car. A door is a component of a house.

16. J

An arrow is shot from a bow. A cannon ball is shot from a cannon.

17. B

A squirrel lives in a tree. A bear lives in a cave

18. G

A goldfish is kept in a fishbowl. A bird is kept in a cage.

19. C

Eggs are used to make sunny-side-up eggs. Oranges are used to make orange juice.

20. G

The stopwatch times a race. The egg timer times a cake baking.

Test 3: Quantitative Reasoning

1. B

First, determine what operation is being performed to the number on the left; 2 is multiplied by 6 to make 12; 1 is multiplied by 6 to make 6; $3 \times 6 = 18$, choice (B).

2. J

First, figure out the pattern; $15 - 7 = 8$; $16 - 7 = 9$. The pattern is -7; $11 - 7 = 4$, choice (J).

3. A

What operation is done to 12 to make 19? 7 is added. What is done to 2 to make 9? 7 is added. Add 7 to 5; the result is 12, choice (A).

4. H

What is done to $\frac{1}{3}$ to make $\frac{4}{3}$? 1, or $\frac{3}{3}$ is added. What is done to $\frac{1}{4}$ to make $\frac{5}{4}$? 1, or $\frac{4}{4}$ is added. Add 1 or $\frac{5}{5}$ to $\frac{1}{5}$ and the result is $\frac{6}{5}$, choice (H).

5. A

What operation is performed to 2 to arrive at 1? 1 is subtracted; $1 - 1 = 0$; $3 - 1 = 2$, choice (A).

6. H

First, determine the pattern. What is done to 17 to arrive at 22? 5 is added; $9 + 5 = 14$. The pattern is $+5$; $3 + 5 = 8$, choice (H).

7. A

There are two rectangles. If you were to divide the rectangles into triangular sections,

there would be 8 equal sections. 4 of these are shaded; $\frac{4}{8} = \frac{1}{2}$.

8. J

Count the number of segments that make up the whole. There are 6 segments and 2 of these are shaded. $\frac{2}{6}$ reduces to $\frac{1}{3}$.

9. A

Count the number of segments that make up the whole. There are 10 segments and 5 of these are shaded. Turn this into a fraction to determine the amount of the whole that is shaded; $\frac{5}{10}$ reduces to $\frac{1}{2}$.

10. F

The square is made up of 4 equal segments; 1 of these is shaded, or $\frac{1}{4}$.

11. C

Count the number of segments that make up the whole. There are 4; 1 of these is shaded, or $\frac{1}{4}$.

12. F

There are 6 rectangular segments that make up the whole. Draw a diagonal line down each segment to divide it in half and you have 12 equal segments.

Count the number of triangular segments that are shaded; there are 4 or $\frac{4}{12}$ which reduces to $\frac{1}{3}$.

13. C

There are 4 equal segments that make up the whole circle. Draw a diagonal line through each segment to divide it in half and you have 8 equal segments.

Count the number of segments that are shaded; there are 4 or $\frac{4}{8}$ which reduces to $\frac{1}{2}$.

14. G

Although it might be tempting, don't try to solve these by eyeballing the scales. Even on these simpler ones, it is a bad habit to get into. Instead, use the information to evaluate each answer choice. This is easiest if you convert all the choices to either cones or cubes.

You are told that 1 cone is equal to one cube. Therefore:

F: 1 cone ≠ 2 cones

G: 1 cone + 1 cone (1 cube = 1 cone) does equal 1 cone + 1 cone (1 cube = 1 cone) This is the correct answer.

H: 2 cones ≠ 1 cone (1 cube = 1 cone)

J: 1 cone + 1 cone (1 cube = 1 cone) ≠ 1 cone (1 cube = 1 cone)

15. B

1 cube = 1 cone. Convert the answer choices to either all cones or all cubes to more readily see the equation.

A: 1 cone ≠ 1 cone + 1 cone (1 cube = 1 cone)

B: 1 cone + 1 cone (the cube) = 2 cones. This is the correct answer.

C: 1 cone + 1 cone (the cube) ≠ 1 cone (the cube)

D: 2 cones ≠ 1 cone (the cube)

16. J

2 cones = 1 cube. Convert the answer choices to either all cones or all cubes to more readily see the equation.

F: 2 cones (1 cube = 2 cones) + 1 cone ≠ 2 cones + 2 cones (1 cube = 2 cones)

G: 4 cones (1 cube = 2 cones) ≠ 3 cones.

H: 1 cone ≠ 4 cones (1 cube = 2 cones)

J: 2 cones + 2 cones (1 cube = 2 cones) = 4 cones. This is the correct answer.

17. A

3 cone = 1 cube. Convert the answer choices to either all cones or all cubes to more readily see the equation.

A: 3 cones (1 cube = 3 cones) + 3 cones = 6 cones (1 cube = 3 cones). This is the correct answer.

B: 6 cones (1 cube = 3 cones) ≠ 5 cones.

C: 6 cones (1 cube = 3 cones) + 1 cone ≠ 3 cones + 3 cones

D: 1 cone ≠ 6 cones (1 cube = 3 cones)

18. **H**

1 cube = 4 cones. Convert the answer choices to either all cones or all cubes to more readily see the equation.

F: 4 cones (1 cube = 4 cones) + 2 cones ≠ 4 cones (1 cube = 4 cones) + 4 cones

G: 4 cones (1 cube = 4 cones) + 4 cones ≠ 4 cones

H: 8 cones (1 cube = 4 cones) = 4 cones (1 cube = 4 cones) + 4 cones. This is the correct answer.

J: 12 cones (1 cube = 4 cones) ≠ 8 cones (1 cube = 4 cones) + 2 cones

19. **C**

3 cones = 2 cubes. Convert the answer choices to either all cones or all cubes to more readily see the equation.

A: 3 cones + 3 cones (2 cubes = 3 cones) ≠ 5 cones

B: 2 cones + 1$\frac{1}{2}$ cones (2 cubes = 3 cones) ≠ 3 cones

C: 3 cones + 3 cones = 6 cones. This is the correct answer.

D: 1 cone ≠ 3 cones. This is one of the rare answer choices you could have eliminated just by looking at, since the scale in the question indicated that it takes 3 cones to balance 2 cubes.

20. **G**

The scale indicates that 2 cubes = 1 cone. Convert all the answer choices to cones to more easily evaluate them.

F: $\frac{1}{2}$ cone (2 cubes = 1 cone) + 2 cones ≠ 3 cones

G: 2 cones = 1 cone (2 cubes = 1 cone) + 1 cone

H: 1 cone + $\frac{1}{2}$ cone (if 2 cubes = 1 cone, then 1 cube must equal $\frac{1}{2}$ cone) ≠ 2 cones + $\frac{1}{2}$ cone (1 cube = $\frac{1}{2}$ cone)

J: $\frac{1}{2}$ cone (if 2 cubes = 1 cone, then 1 cube must equal $\frac{1}{2}$ cone) + 2 cones ≠ 1$\frac{1}{2}$ cones.

Test 4: Verbal Reasoning—Words

1. **D**

In order for there to be a wedding, there must be a bride (and groom). The other elements are not necessary elements.

2. **F**

A controversy is a hotly debated topic. There must be two sides in a controversy, which disagree. Truce, resolution, and aggression are not the essential elements of controversy.

3. **C**

A drum provides rhythm. Cymbals and (drum)sticks are used as rhythmic instruments though they do not convey the essential element of what a drum is. Rhyme is not an essential element of a drum.

4. **J**

The intention of agriculture is to grow crops. A garden may grow crops, or flowers. Livestock are animals on a farm. Seasons, though necessary to farming, does not convey the essential element of producing food to eat.

5. **B**

A candidate is chosen, which necessitates choice. A poll asks public opinion. Politics is related, but not the essential element of a candidate. Freedom reminds us of democracy, but again is not the essential element of the word candidate.

6. **H**

An optimist is full of hope; that is what defines him or her.

7. **B**

What makes a flower a flower? It has petals. It need not be in a garden, so you can eliminate (A). There are many types of flowers, so you can eliminate (B). A bee, though related to the idea of flowers and gardens, is a distracter and not the essential element of what defines a flower.

8. F

Before looking at the answer choices think about what defines a guitar. It is a musical instrument with strings. Choice (F) fits this definition. You don't have to play guitar at a concert. A guitar doesn't have to be electric. A bass, though a related instrument, does not name an essential element of a guitar.

9. D

A ticket gains you admittance to someplace. Look for the answer choice that has to do with gaining admittance. Window, stadium and expense are not essential elements that define what a ticket is. The ticket may or may not be purchased at a window. It may be used to enter a stadium, or a train. It may or may not be an expense. Maybe it is free. Only choice (D) defines the purpose of a ticket.

10. F

The words in the top row are increasing in degree. For example, a downpour is more severe than a drizzle. So, you are looking for something that is more severe than warm. The best choice is scorching.

11. A

The words in the top row are all types of vehicles on land. The words in the bottom row are all types of vehicles for the air. Only a helicopter is a type of airborne vehicle.

12. H

Items above and below the line are ordered in increasingly larger sizes.

13. A

The items above the line are slow animals; those below the line are fast.

14. F

Approve is the opposite of the other words which are all verbs meaning to criticize or judge in a negative manner.

15. D

A regulation is a rule, while the other choices are all grants of permission.

16. G

Kick, bounce, and throw are all actions that can be performed on a ball. Draw is not.

17. A

Although you need a nose to smell, it does not belong in this list. The words aroma, odor, and scent, are other ways of referring to a smell.

18. F

The underlined words are all ways of referring to dirt, or the soil. Don't be tempted by choice (J), garden. Although a garden does have dirt in it, it is not the closest in meaning to the underlined words.

19. A

The underlined words all have to do with physical activity. Although these may take place in a gym, a gym is not the same as a physical activity. You may have been tempted to choose (C) tennis, but that is too specific to be the correct answer.

20. F

You are looking for a word that is similar in meaning to a job, or work. Although choices (G), (H), and (J) are tempting, the correct answer is employment.

Test 5: Verbal Reasoning—Context

1. A

Read the statements carefully and think about what they tell you: cherry trees bloom in spring. Alonso has a blooming cherry tree in his backyard. Also consider what the statements **do not** tell you: which month it is, where Alonso lives, how old Alonso is, or anything else about Alonso or his yard. Now, read each answer choice carefully. The only one that is true based solely on the information given is (A).

2. H

Read the statements and consider the facts. It is windy and sailboats need wind. What conclusion can you draw? Will it be possible to sail today? Yes. That's all the statements help you conclude. They say nothing about the time of year or how easy or difficult it is to sail.

3. **B**

What do we know based on the statements? "Hola" means hello in Spanish. Fact: Marco told Lena "hello" in French. What can we conclude? Marco speaks at least one word of French (he said "hello" in French.) What don't we know? What that word for "hello" is in French. (Remember, you cannot apply any outside knowledge, you can only use the statements given to draw a conclusion.) We also don't know whether or not Marco knows any other words in French or any other languages. We also don't know whether Lena understands Marco or not. Eliminate choices (A), (C), and (D). Choice (B) is the best answer choice. Since Marco did not say hello in Spanish (he said hello in French) it is safe to assume *he probably did not say "hola."*

4. **J**

Based on the two statements, the only thing we can conclude for certain is that Rachel is attending an auction. Therefore, we do not know whether or not she will be outbid and win or lose the chair. She is *not* the auctioneer because she is bidding.

5. **A**

The two statements tell about Mr. and Mrs. Bowden's children (who are 2 and 5). Clarissa is 8 years old. She cannot be one of the Bowden's children—that's clear. We are not told whether she is another member of the family (a niece or a cousin) or what if any relationship she has to them. Don't be led astray just because the two statements are next to one another. They are unrelated facts.

6. **J**

Based on the statements given, all that we know is that David is in the kitchen. We do not know (based only on the statements) what the nice smell is, what is being cooked or baked, or who is making it.

7. **C**

The flowers need water twice a day and they are wilting. Why are they wilting? We don't know why based on the statements. Maybe they are getting too much water, or too little. Or maybe they need more sun or less. The only conclusion we can draw is that the flowers are not healthy. We are not told whether or not there are also flowers in the backyard.

8. **F**

Based on the statements given, we can conclude that Adina is probably happy—smiling is a generally accepted sign of happiness. We do not know why she is smiling or whether or not it is related to the program she is watching. We do not know whether she likes to watch television or whether she is watching sitting, standing, or lying down.

9. **D**

Someone took a cookie from the cookie jar—we do not know who. Although Seung Hee loves cookies, there is no evidence to lead us to the conclusion that she took the missing cookie—no cookie crumbs on her face, for example. We do not know whether the cookie jar was easy or difficult to break into and open, or that Sarah bakes cookies. We do know that Sarah has a cookie jar and keeps cookies in it.

10. **H**

Suzie received 10 cards and 1 was signed by a secret admirer. Did he send any of the other nine? Perhaps. Perhaps she also unknowingly sent one to him, not realizing that this person was her secret admirer. Based on the information stated, we can only conclude that Suzie received fewer than a dozen Valentine's Day cards. No mention is given of whether or not Suzie is a schoolgirl or whether the cards were from classmates; therefore, we can't determine whether the admirer is in her class.

11. **B**

Elise is in boot camp and the first statements says that all soldiers in boot camp must be able to run the camp's obstacle course. Therefore, you can conclude that Elise is able to run the course. You cannot conclude for certain that the other statements are true.

12. **J**

The statements only tell us that Joey caught more fish than Hope. We do not know whether this is because of talent or luck or the quality of their bait, hooks, or style. The only certain thing is that Hope caught fewer fish than Joey. (The fact that they went fishing does not make them best friends or even friends at all.)

13. D

We are told that babies cry if they are tired or hungry. Baby X is crying but she was just fed. Therefore, she must be tired (in need of a nap).

14. G

The only thing we know for certain is that the Bailers live in an apartment complex. Although we are told many details about their apartment complex we do not know if they like to swim. Nor can we make a generalization about whether everyone likes to play tennis. We only know that they do not live in a house.

15. D

Bobby Lee has acted, and now he is joining the football league. He must enjoy various activities. We do not know from the passage whether or not he will continue to act next year, or which activity he is better at. Nor do we know why he won the lead role and then later a bit part; we cannot assume that his acting is improving nor getting worse.

16. H

The only thing we can be sure of is that Karl Cooper does not like to watch only one show because he changes channels frequently. We know that Karla does the crossword puzzle, but not whether she is good at it. Nor do we know whether or not she would like to watch just one show. Furthermore, we are not told whether or not Karl and Karla are married, they could be brother and sister.

17. A

We are told that Rene is happy to hear from her grandmother; thus, you can say that the two have a good relationship.

18. H

The statements tell us that today's special at Kelly's Diner is fried chicken and that all of the employees at the diner can eat the special (fried chicken) for free. That is, they do not have to pay if they order the special. However, the statements do not tell us if all the employees will eat fried chicken, or even if they like the fried chicken.

19. D

Think of what the information does and does not tell you. We know where Jason is and where he is going. We know how long the complete ferry ride takes, but not how long Jason's been on the ferry so far or whether or not he likes the ferry. We also are not told about his swimming abilities. Only choice (D) is correct based on the limited information given.

20. J

The sale is *buy one get one free*. So, for every pair he buys Sam gets one free—that means if he left the store with 2 pairs, he only paid for one. This is the only thing that is true based on the information given.

Test 6: Reading and Language Arts

1. B

Dadaism, although preferring childish style, was not a movement of children. Paragraph 1 states *the Dadaists rejected the values that they believe led to the war*. The passage does not comment as to whether or not they were good artists. The movement was not actually started by Duchamp, but sparked by his work. Be sure to take notes in the margins and jot down the main idea of each paragraph to help you locate information later.

2. J

The passage mentions all of the qualities of the Dada movement except patriotism. Paragraph 1 states that the Dadaists rejected nationalism and militarism, or patriotism.

3. A

This is a detail question. Paragraph 4 begins with the following sentence: *The official—if Dadaism can be called official—launch of Dada took place in 1916 with the opening of the nightclub, the Cabaret Voltaire in Zurich, Switzerland*. While you read, be sure to underline or circle important information in the passage as well as jot down the main idea of paragraphs in the margins to help you locate the information you need to answer questions later.

4. H

This is an inference question. Based on what the passage stated about Dada goals of making fun of established culture, this is the best answer choice. Although Duchamp started working before the Dada movement officially began, we know that Dadaists admired him. Therefore, it makes sense that his style and message were the same as those of the Dadaists.

5. D

Simplest is best. Choice (D) combines the sentences concisely by adding one more adjective to the list. Choices (A) and (C) contain a redundant *and*. Choice (B) is a run-on sentence.

6. J

In sentence 4, *war* should not be capitalized because it is not naming a specific war, such as World War II. In sentence 1, *Dada* should be capitalized since it is the name of the movement. Sentences 2 and 3 are correct; they do not contain any proper nouns to capitalize.

7. C

After the verb *behaved* the adverb *childishly* should be used. The simplest way to fix this error is exhibited in choice (C). There is no reason to change the verb tense.

8. H

The title of the selection should reflect the main idea discussed in the selection. Because the selection is mainly about one theory of language, choice (H) is the best answer. Choice (G) is too vague, choice (J) and (F) are details within the selection, but not the main idea of the selection.

9. C

The author states opinions and presents theories in a matter of fact manner. Although the author says that Saussure's theories make sense, she does not write in a biased manner, nor does she gush enthusiastically. There is no poetic language used in this selection.

10. F

The questions are a device, intended to get the reader to think about the ideas presented in the article. The questions are answered, which eliminates choice (G). Although Saussure does have answers to the questions, they are not included to prove that. Though the questions do show that the topic is complicated, they are not included to demonstrating that the issue is confusing.

11. B

According to the Saussure, *the words that make up a language come about because they are mutually agreed on by a group…* Putting ideas from the passage into your own words will help you arrive at the answer more readily. Make a habit of paraphrasing and jotting down ideas in the margin of each reading.

12. H

The modifying clause *a French linguist* correctly sets off additional information about Saussure. Choice (F) is a run-on sentence. Choice (G) incorrectly uses *which* rather than *who* to describe a person and it includes an unnecessary comma. Choice (J) also contains an unnecessary comma and does not succinctly combine the two sentences.

13. A

Choice (A) correctly lists items, separating them with a comma. Choice (B) uses *whom* incorrectly; it should be the subject pronoun *who*. Choice (C) contains an incorrect verb tense—*lectures* should be *lectured* since it is in the past.

14. F

This is a detail question. To answer this question, locate and reread the part of the passage that discusses how bioluminescent organisms create light. The beginning of paragraph 2 clearly states that *bioluminescence occurs as a result of a chemical reaction between a protein (luciferin) and an enzyme (luciferase) in the presence of oxygen.*

KAPLAN
Test Prep and Admissions

15. C

Paragraph 2 explains how bioluminescence differs from other light sources: *Bioluminescence however is almost 100% efficient.* Circle key words like *however, although, despite* when reading. They indicate a change of direction and may help you locate important information within a passage that is asked about. Choice (B) is not true of bioluminescence. Choices (A) and (D), though correct, are details taken out of context and not the reason bioluminescent light differs from other light sources.

16. J

The passage discussed the diversity of bioluminescent creatures, that many of them are marine animals, and that they all make light the same way. Nothing was stated in the passage about whether or not touching these creatures would be painful. Be sure to circle important key words while you are reading. *Marine animals, diversity,* and *same process* would be important words to circle. Doing this can help you focus on the information and locate details more readily later.

17. A

A good topic sentence should introduce the ideas to be discussed in the paragraph. Since the paragraph is about two different categories of bioluminescent creatures choice (A) is the best choice. Choices (B) and (D) are unrelated to the paragraph. Choice (C) introduces the idea of photophores, but not the other category of bioluminescent creatures also discussed in the paragraph.

18. H

The ideas within a well-organized essay should flow logically from one to the next. Since the last idea developed in the preceding paragraph claimed that *organisms with bacterial symbionts have developed some interesting ways to "turn out the light" when necessary* you would expect a discussion of these techniques to follow. While (F), (G), and (J) may be interesting ideas to discuss, they wouldn't logically follow the idea that symbionts have interesting ways to turn out the light.

19. A

The paragraph ends *once you have some ideas down on paper, you can begin to organize them.* Therefore, the logical continuation would be a paragraph about organizing. Writer's block was already dealt with. The passage is not about horses. And, while the topic sentence is an important element of essay writing, it wouldn't flow smoothly to discuss it next, after the introduction of the topic of organization.

20. H

This paragraph is about essay writing and would be most helpful to students who need to write essays. Therefore, you could expect to find it in a student's manual.

21. B

This saying is intended to create an interesting introduction to the passage. It also means that doing something well takes time. Therefore, it is used here to encourage students who may struggle with writing.

22. H

A title should let the reader know what the piece is generally about. This piece is a guide about how to write an essay. The part about horses is meant to serve as an example and is not the main idea of the essay. The part about overcoming writer's block is just one element of the essay, not the whole process. The quote about time is an introduction to the idea that writing a good essay takes time, but again, it is not the main idea of the paragraph.

23. B

The subject of the sentence is *some* not *people*. Therefore, *some* should have the singular verb *don't*.

24. G

Choices (F) and (J) are unclear. *But I do* is not correct as a sentence, so choice (G) is the best way to combine the two sentences.

25. C

Parallelism demands that the verbs be in the same tense. Because the correct idiom is *enjoy putting* the verbs must be *putting* and *sharing*.

26. H

Before reading the answer choices, reread the sentence in question. Look carefully at the placement of commas, verb agreement, and verb tense. Identify the error before reading the answer choices to avoid becoming confused by them. The correct modal of the verb after an *if* clause is the future *won't*. If you imagine…you *won't have* any problem.

27. C

This is a detail question. Reread the order of events described after the word *showdown*. Be sure to read a few sentences before and after the key word so as not to take details out of context. The passage explains that the showdown came after Old Joseph died and Chief Joseph refused to relocate his people.

28. F

This is an inference question. The passage explains that the government broke its original treaty once gold was discovered in Nez Perce territory. Thus, it makes sense that the federal government wanted to move the tribe in order to take possession of the gold-rich lands.

29. D

The passage does not go into detail about the character of Old Joseph. However, it does say that Old Joseph was on good terms with the U.S. government. Chief Joseph was different because he led his people in battle against the federal government in order to try to keep the land.

30. G

The quotation at the end of the passage shows how much Chief Joseph valued his freedom. He died on the reservation, without his freedom.

31. B

The introductory paragraph of the passage indicates that Chief Joseph was known for being a brave leader and an *eloquent* speaker. Even if you did not know what *eloquent* means, you could guess that it was something positive, since the passage has a positive tone about Chief Joseph. Therefore, the quote is included to prove that Chief Joseph was a good speaker. Although the quote mentions freedom and may explain indirectly why he died and how he felt about the government, it is used as a device to back up the initial claim out his speaking ability. Because it does not mention how this speech motivated people, it does not show what a good leader he was.

32. H

Read each answer choice carefully, looking for common errors. You can expect to find mistakes in comma usage, subject-verb agreement, and verb tense. Choice (F) has a problem with verb tense—since the first verb is *appealed*, a simple past tense verb, the second verb should also be simple past—*asked* rather than *asking*. Choice (G) has a mistake in usage. The correct phrase is *would have* not *would of*. Choice (H) correctly uses a comma to separate an adverbial clause from the main clause. Choice (J) incorrectly inserts a comma where none is necessary. It is also a convoluted sentence and would be more clearly stated as: *The Nez Perce reservation was in Oklahoma.*

33. A

The best answer choice is clearest and most succinct—that is, it doesn't add unnecessary words. Choice (A) combines the sentences with a adjective phrase describing Chief Joseph. Choice (B) is not incorrect, but rather more wordy than necessary—it is not the best choice. Choice (C) unnecessarily changes verb tense and alters the meaning of the sentences. However, setting the adjective phrase between commas is correct. Choice (D) would be correct (though not the best and simplest way to combine the two sentences) if the semicolon were followed by *he* rather than *who*. As is, the *who* makes the sentence unclear.

34. J

The first and last sentences of the first paragraph are the best place to look for the main topic of the passage. They discuss the shark's special abilities. Choices (G) and (H) are details taken out of context from the passage. Choice (F) is incorrect since the passage is not about how sharks hunt, but rather about one of their particular skills.

35. A

Reread the sentences in and around where the word *efficient* is found. They describe how the shark is a good hunter, able to find it's prey. *Efficient* must be a positive word, having to do with ability. *Capable* is the best answer choice. However, even if you are unsure of the answer, you can use word charge to help you eliminate poor answer choices. *Slow* and *unskilled* are both negative—eliminate these. *Sensitive* is taken out of context, and is meant to mislead you since the following phrase discusses the shark's sensitivity. However, the sensitivity is just one more detail that makes the shark an *efficient* or capable hunter.

36. G

Underlining or circling important information in the passage will help you answer this type of question more easily. You should have circled *sixth sense* and then the phrase that defines it as an ability to detect electric vibrations. The details within the passage explain that it works best *at close range*. The passage also explains that sharks cannot distinguish between vibrations given off by humans or those by electrical fences. However, this is one of the abilities that makes the shark a great hunter.

37. C

Reread the section that explains why sharks attack steel cages. It explains that sharks cannot tell the difference between vibrations made by metal and those made by animals. They attack the cages not only because it is vibrating (choice D), but also because they mistakenly think the cage is an animal, or possible prey. Choice (A) is not mentioned in the passage, choice (B) is an incorrect paraphrase of details in the passage.

38. F

Capitalize proper names, days of the week, months, and holidays. *Saturday* must be capitalized in sentence 1.

39. D

All the sentences in a well-written paragraph should concern the same topic or theme. This sentence does not follow the topic of Sea Life Park.

40. F

Because of the dangling modifier, the original sentence implies that the writer was actually swimming around in the tanks. Choice (F) makes the subject of the sentence clear and uses a simple verb. Choice (G) is not correct because the first phrase is not a complete sentence, it lacks a pronoun. Who was swimming around in the tanks? Choice (H) is a run-on sentence.

Test 7: Mathematics Concepts and Applications

1. B

Remember the order of operations: PEMDAS. In this equation, you should complete the multiplication first; $4 \times -4 = -16$. Now, you need to subtract 3 from -16; $-16 - 3 = -19$.

2. K

Before you do the multiplication, see which common factors in the numerator and denominator can be canceled. Cancelling a 3 from the 3 in the numerator and the 9 in the denominator leaves $\frac{15 \times 7 \times 1}{3 \times 5 \times 2}$. Cancelling a 5 from the 15 in the numerator and the 5 in the denominator leaves $\frac{3 \times 7 \times 1}{3 \times 1 \times 2}$. Cancelling the 3 in the numerator and the 3 in the denominator leaves $\frac{7 \times 1}{1 \times 2} = \frac{7}{2} = 3\frac{1}{2}$. Because this is not one of the choices, the answer is (K).

3. C

A negative number raised to an odd power is negative. Using PEMDAS,

$$-2^3(1-2)^3 + (-2)^3$$
$$= -2^3(-1)^3 + (-2)^3$$
$$= -8(-1) + (-8)$$
$$= 8 + (-8)$$
$$= 8 - 8$$
$$= 0$$

4. G

To simplify the square root of a large number, break the number down int two or more factors and write the number as the product of the square roots of those factors. This is especially useful when one of the factors is a perfect square. In this case, break 1,500 down into two factors; $1,500 = 15 \times 100$, and 100 is a perfect square. So, $1,500 = \sqrt{100 \times 15} = \sqrt{100} \times \sqrt{15} + 10\sqrt{15}$.

5. C

$4^2 = 4 \times 4$, and $4^3 = 4 \times 4 \times 4$.
Thus, $4^2 \times 4^3 = 4 \times 4 \times 4 \times 4 \times 4$.

6. H

Line up the decimal points and subtract

13.254
− 1.040
12.214

7. B

A percent is a part of 100. Thus, 6% is equivalent to $\frac{6}{100}$.

8. H

$10^1 = 10$, $10^2 = 100$, $10^3 = 1,000$, $10^4 = 10,000$, $10^5 = 100,000$

9. A

The eight is in the thousand's place, so the value is 8,000.

10. F

First, find the total the percentage of voters: 10 + 42 + 18 = 70%. Of 100% of the people polled, 70% voted and 30% did not. The ratio of voters to non-voters is $\frac{70}{30}$, which reduces to $\frac{7}{3}$.

11. C

The symbol ∩ represents intersection. The intersection of two sets consists of the elements that are common to both sets; 3 and 5 are common elements of both sets.

12. F

$40 \times \frac{1}{5} = 8$ cubicles are full

13. C

One hundred centimeters make up 1 meter. Thus, one centimeter is $\frac{1}{100}$ of a meter.

14. G

Rate × Time = Distance. Since we are looking for rate, we make the equation

Rate = $\frac{\text{Distance}}{\text{Time}}$

Rate = $\frac{216}{3}$ = 72 miles per hour

15. D

The sentence reads: 7 > ____ > 4. Thus, the numbers that may be placed in the blank must be less than 7 but greater than 4; 6 and 5 are less than 7 but greater than 4.

16. J

The symbol ∩ represents intersection. The intersection of two sets consists of the elements that are common to both sets; 8 and 9 are common elements of both sets.

17. B

2, 5, and 23 are prime numbers and are also factors of 230.

18. J

$\frac{2}{3} = 0.6666... = 67\%$.

19. C

You can set this up as an algebraic equation. Let x be the amount Max needs to sell.

$x(.075) = 600$

$x = \frac{600}{.075} = 8,000$

20. G

Convert each part of the number:

three million	3,000,000
one hundred seventy eight thousand	178,000
forty two	42
	3,178,042

21. A

An equilateral triangle has equal sides and equal angles. The angles in a triangle have a sum of 180 degrees. Therefore, each angle in an equilateral triangle would equal 60 degrees.

22. J

The only factor common to both 62 and 84 is 2.

23. **C**

First, find how much money the three guides raised.

$90\% \times (590) = .9 \times 590 = \$531$.

Subtract that amount from the whole to determine how much the other five girls raised.

$590 - 531 = \$59$

24. **J**

perimeter = width $\times$ 2 + length $\times$ 2

$(3 \times 2) + (16 \times 2) = 6 + 32 = 38$ feet

25. **C**

Subtract $97 for the part from the total 230 to find the charge for the labor; $230 - 97 = 133$. The problem then asks you to estimate *about how many hours* the mechanic worked on the car. Start your estimation by multiplying $42 \times 2 = 84$; 133 is 49 more than 84, so the mechanic definitely worked more than 2 hours. Try $42 \times 3 = 136$. Since 136 is only 3 dollars more than 133 we know that the mechanic worked about 3 hours.

26. **F**

The formula for area of a triangle is: $A = \frac{1}{2}bh$

$\frac{1}{2}(8 \times 9) = \frac{1}{2}(72) = 36$ m²

27. **C**

Let x equal the unknown number.

$7(2x) + 6 = 4,206$

$14x + 6 = 4,206$

$14x = 4,200$

$\frac{4200}{14} = 300$ or 3×10^2

28. **J**

Average $= \dfrac{\text{total amount}}{\text{number of items}}$

$\dfrac{\$22,580}{20} = \$1,129$

29. **C**

The total amount of chair sales = 2,400. Marina sold 1,800. You can express this as a ratio: $\dfrac{1,800}{2,400} = \dfrac{3}{4}$;

$\dfrac{3}{4} = 75\%$.

30. **F**

The manager wants to show the fraction of total sales revenue that each item brought in. The clearest way to demonstrate this needs to show parts of a whole. A pie chart does this best since it clearly shows parts of a whole. The bar graph allows you to compare the revenues of each item, but doesn't allow you to compare them to the whole amount. Choice (H) is confusing and indecipherable. Choice (J) does represent how many of the items were sold, but it is not clear how many each chair or star stands for—there's no key.

31. **C**

$4 \times 10^4 = 4 \times (10 \times 10 \times 10 \times 10) = 4 \times 10,000 = 40,000$.

32. **J**

1.6 kilometers = 1 mile

Divide the number of kilometers by 1.6 to find the number of miles.

$\dfrac{18 \text{ kilometers}}{1.6} = 11.25$. Round off to 11 miles for the closest approximation.

33. **B**

One can of soda costs 10 cents less than a bottle which costs x cents.

One can $= x - 10$; 2 cans $= 2(x - 10)$

34. **H**

The sentence states that x is greater than -4, but less than -2. Only choice (H) supports this.

35. **D**

$0.60x = 24$; $x = 40$ games total in the season. If the team won and tied 24 games out of 40 total, they lost 16.

36. **G**

By writing all the numbers are decimals, we can more readily compare.

F: .4, .04, .5—the smallest one is not first

G: .03, .33, .66—the smallest one is first. This is the correct answer.

H: .2, .22, .02—the smallest one is not first

J: .4, .2, .3—the smallest one is not first.

37. A

The distributive property of multiplication over addition states that when multiplying a value that is a quantity, the multiplier is distributed to each number in the parentheses.

38. G

Add each combination of items, don't forget to add sales tax to each item over $100.

Boots = 100 + 100(.08) = 100 + 8 = $108

Sweater = 20 + 20(.08) = 20 + 1.60 = $21.60

Shirt = 50 + 50 (.08) = 50 + 4 = $54

This results in a total of $108 + $21.60 + $54 = $183.60. All answer choices but (G) put David over $200.

39. A

The Venn diagram achieves the gym teacher's goal; it shows an intersection between the students who play football and other varsity sports. None of the other charts show the intersection. Choice (B) is a good way to show how many students play each sport. Notice that choice (C) is unclear—there is no label on either axis to explain what the peaks and lows on the chart is. Choice (D) is also unclear. A coordinate graph would be best to map points in a quadrant, such as to show where things are located on a map.

40. F

circumference = π × diameter

diameter = 2 × radius = 2 × 15 = 30. C = 30π in

HSPT Practice Test 1
Answer Sheet

Remove (or photocopy) this answer sheet and use it to complete the practice test.

Verbal Skills

1. Ⓐ Ⓑ Ⓒ Ⓓ 13. Ⓐ Ⓑ Ⓒ Ⓓ 25. Ⓐ Ⓑ Ⓒ Ⓓ 37. Ⓐ Ⓑ Ⓒ Ⓓ 49. Ⓐ Ⓑ Ⓒ Ⓓ
2. Ⓐ Ⓑ Ⓒ Ⓓ 14. Ⓐ Ⓑ Ⓒ Ⓓ 26. Ⓐ Ⓑ Ⓒ Ⓓ 38. Ⓐ Ⓑ Ⓒ Ⓓ 50. Ⓐ Ⓑ Ⓒ Ⓓ
3. Ⓐ Ⓑ Ⓒ Ⓓ 15. Ⓐ Ⓑ Ⓒ Ⓓ 27. Ⓐ Ⓑ Ⓒ Ⓓ 39. Ⓐ Ⓑ Ⓒ Ⓓ 51. Ⓐ Ⓑ Ⓒ Ⓓ
4. Ⓐ Ⓑ Ⓒ Ⓓ 16. Ⓐ Ⓑ Ⓒ Ⓓ 28. Ⓐ Ⓑ Ⓒ Ⓓ 40. Ⓐ Ⓑ Ⓒ Ⓓ 52. Ⓐ Ⓑ Ⓒ Ⓓ
5. Ⓐ Ⓑ Ⓒ Ⓓ 17. Ⓐ Ⓑ Ⓒ Ⓓ 29. Ⓐ Ⓑ Ⓒ Ⓓ 41. Ⓐ Ⓑ Ⓒ Ⓓ 53. Ⓐ Ⓑ Ⓒ Ⓓ
6. Ⓐ Ⓑ Ⓒ Ⓓ 18. Ⓐ Ⓑ Ⓒ Ⓓ 30. Ⓐ Ⓑ Ⓒ Ⓓ 42. Ⓐ Ⓑ Ⓒ Ⓓ 54. Ⓐ Ⓑ Ⓒ Ⓓ
7. Ⓐ Ⓑ Ⓒ Ⓓ 19. Ⓐ Ⓑ Ⓒ Ⓓ 31. Ⓐ Ⓑ Ⓒ Ⓓ 43. Ⓐ Ⓑ Ⓒ Ⓓ 55. Ⓐ Ⓑ Ⓒ Ⓓ
8. Ⓐ Ⓑ Ⓒ Ⓓ 20. Ⓐ Ⓑ Ⓒ Ⓓ 32. Ⓐ Ⓑ Ⓒ Ⓓ 44. Ⓐ Ⓑ Ⓒ Ⓓ 56. Ⓐ Ⓑ Ⓒ Ⓓ
9. Ⓐ Ⓑ Ⓒ Ⓓ 21. Ⓐ Ⓑ Ⓒ Ⓓ 33. Ⓐ Ⓑ Ⓒ Ⓓ 45. Ⓐ Ⓑ Ⓒ Ⓓ 57. Ⓐ Ⓑ Ⓒ Ⓓ
10. Ⓐ Ⓑ Ⓒ Ⓓ 22. Ⓐ Ⓑ Ⓒ Ⓓ 34. Ⓐ Ⓑ Ⓒ Ⓓ 46. Ⓐ Ⓑ Ⓒ Ⓓ 58. Ⓐ Ⓑ Ⓒ Ⓓ
11. Ⓐ Ⓑ Ⓒ Ⓓ 23. Ⓐ Ⓑ Ⓒ Ⓓ 35. Ⓐ Ⓑ Ⓒ Ⓓ 47. Ⓐ Ⓑ Ⓒ Ⓓ 59. Ⓐ Ⓑ Ⓒ Ⓓ
12. Ⓐ Ⓑ Ⓒ Ⓓ 24. Ⓐ Ⓑ Ⓒ Ⓓ 36. Ⓐ Ⓑ Ⓒ Ⓓ 48. Ⓐ Ⓑ Ⓒ Ⓓ 60. Ⓐ Ⓑ Ⓒ Ⓓ

Quantitative Skills

61. Ⓐ Ⓑ Ⓒ Ⓓ 72. Ⓐ Ⓑ Ⓒ Ⓓ 83. Ⓐ Ⓑ Ⓒ Ⓓ 93. Ⓐ Ⓑ Ⓒ Ⓓ 103. Ⓐ Ⓑ Ⓒ Ⓓ
62. Ⓐ Ⓑ Ⓒ Ⓓ 73. Ⓐ Ⓑ Ⓒ Ⓓ 84. Ⓐ Ⓑ Ⓒ Ⓓ 94. Ⓐ Ⓑ Ⓒ Ⓓ 104. Ⓐ Ⓑ Ⓒ Ⓓ
63. Ⓐ Ⓑ Ⓒ Ⓓ 74. Ⓐ Ⓑ Ⓒ Ⓓ 85. Ⓐ Ⓑ Ⓒ Ⓓ 95. Ⓐ Ⓑ Ⓒ Ⓓ 105. Ⓐ Ⓑ Ⓒ Ⓓ
64. Ⓐ Ⓑ Ⓒ Ⓓ 75. Ⓐ Ⓑ Ⓒ Ⓓ 86. Ⓐ Ⓑ Ⓒ Ⓓ 96. Ⓐ Ⓑ Ⓒ Ⓓ 106. Ⓐ Ⓑ Ⓒ Ⓓ
65. Ⓐ Ⓑ Ⓒ Ⓓ 76. Ⓐ Ⓑ Ⓒ Ⓓ 87. Ⓐ Ⓑ Ⓒ Ⓓ 97. Ⓐ Ⓑ Ⓒ Ⓓ 107. Ⓐ Ⓑ Ⓒ Ⓓ
66. Ⓐ Ⓑ Ⓒ Ⓓ 77. Ⓐ Ⓑ Ⓒ Ⓓ 88. Ⓐ Ⓑ Ⓒ Ⓓ 98. Ⓐ Ⓑ Ⓒ Ⓓ 108. Ⓐ Ⓑ Ⓒ Ⓓ
67. Ⓐ Ⓑ Ⓒ Ⓓ 78. Ⓐ Ⓑ Ⓒ Ⓓ 89. Ⓐ Ⓑ Ⓒ Ⓓ 99. Ⓐ Ⓑ Ⓒ Ⓓ 109. Ⓐ Ⓑ Ⓒ Ⓓ
68. Ⓐ Ⓑ Ⓒ Ⓓ 79. Ⓐ Ⓑ Ⓒ Ⓓ 90. Ⓐ Ⓑ Ⓒ Ⓓ 100. Ⓐ Ⓑ Ⓒ Ⓓ 110. Ⓐ Ⓑ Ⓒ Ⓓ
69. Ⓐ Ⓑ Ⓒ Ⓓ 80. Ⓐ Ⓑ Ⓒ Ⓓ 91. Ⓐ Ⓑ Ⓒ Ⓓ 101. Ⓐ Ⓑ Ⓒ Ⓓ 111. Ⓐ Ⓑ Ⓒ Ⓓ
70. Ⓐ Ⓑ Ⓒ Ⓓ 81. Ⓐ Ⓑ Ⓒ Ⓓ 92. Ⓐ Ⓑ Ⓒ Ⓓ 102. Ⓐ Ⓑ Ⓒ Ⓓ 112. Ⓐ Ⓑ Ⓒ Ⓓ
71. Ⓐ Ⓑ Ⓒ Ⓓ 82. Ⓐ Ⓑ Ⓒ Ⓓ

Reading

113. (A) (B) (C) (D)
114. (A) (B) (C) (D)
115. (A) (B) (C) (D)
116. (A) (B) (C) (D)
117. (A) (B) (C) (D)
118. (A) (B) (C) (D)
119. (A) (B) (C) (D)
120. (A) (B) (C) (D)
121. (A) (B) (C) (D)
122. (A) (B) (C) (D)
123. (A) (B) (C) (D)
124. (A) (B) (C) (D)
125. (A) (B) (C) (D)

126. (A) (B) (C) (D)
127. (A) (B) (C) (D)
128. (A) (B) (C) (D)
129. (A) (B) (C) (D)
130. (A) (B) (C) (D)
131. (A) (B) (C) (D)
132. (A) (B) (C) (D)
133. (A) (B) (C) (D)
134. (A) (B) (C) (D)
135. (A) (B) (C) (D)
136. (A) (B) (C) (D)
137. (A) (B) (C) (D)
138. (A) (B) (C) (D)

139. (A) (B) (C) (D)
140. (A) (B) (C) (D)
141. (A) (B) (C) (D)
142. (A) (B) (C) (D)
143. (A) (B) (C) (D)
144. (A) (B) (C) (D)
145. (A) (B) (C) (D)
146. (A) (B) (C) (D)
147. (A) (B) (C) (D)
148. (A) (B) (C) (D)
149. (A) (B) (C) (D)
150. (A) (B) (C) (D)
151. (A) (B) (C) (D)

152. (A) (B) (C) (D)
153. (A) (B) (C) (D)
154. (A) (B) (C) (D)
155. (A) (B) (C) (D)
156. (A) (B) (C) (D)
157. (A) (B) (C) (D)
158. (A) (B) (C) (D)
159. (A) (B) (C) (D)
160. (A) (B) (C) (D)
161. (A) (B) (C) (D)
162. (A) (B) (C) (D)
163. (A) (B) (C) (D)
164. (A) (B) (C) (D)

165. (A) (B) (C) (D)
166. (A) (B) (C) (D)
167. (A) (B) (C) (D)
168. (A) (B) (C) (D)
169. (A) (B) (C) (D)
170. (A) (B) (C) (D)
171. (A) (B) (C) (D)
172. (A) (B) (C) (D)
173. (A) (B) (C) (D)
174. (A) (B) (C) (D)

Mathematics

175. (A) (B) (C) (D)
176. (A) (B) (C) (D)
177. (A) (B) (C) (D)
178. (A) (B) (C) (D)
179. (A) (B) (C) (D)
180. (A) (B) (C) (D)
181. (A) (B) (C) (D)
182. (A) (B) (C) (D)
183. (A) (B) (C) (D)
184. (A) (B) (C) (D)
185. (A) (B) (C) (D)
186. (A) (B) (C) (D)
187. (A) (B) (C) (D)

188. (A) (B) (C) (D)
189. (A) (B) (C) (D)
190. (A) (B) (C) (D)
191. (A) (B) (C) (D)
192. (A) (B) (C) (D)
193. (A) (B) (C) (D)
194. (A) (B) (C) (D)
195. (A) (B) (C) (D)
196. (A) (B) (C) (D)
197. (A) (B) (C) (D)
198. (A) (B) (C) (D)
199. (A) (B) (C) (D)
200. (A) (B) (C) (D)

201. (A) (B) (C) (D)
202. (A) (B) (C) (D)
203. (A) (B) (C) (D)
204. (A) (B) (C) (D)
205. (A) (B) (C) (D)
206. (A) (B) (C) (D)
207. (A) (B) (C) (D)
208. (A) (B) (C) (D)
209. (A) (B) (C) (D)
210. (A) (B) (C) (D)
211. (A) (B) (C) (D)
212. (A) (B) (C) (D)
213. (A) (B) (C) (D)

214. (A) (B) (C) (D)
215. (A) (B) (C) (D)
216. (A) (B) (C) (D)
217. (A) (B) (C) (D)
218. (A) (B) (C) (D)
219. (A) (B) (C) (D)
220. (A) (B) (C) (D)
221. (A) (B) (C) (D)
222. (A) (B) (C) (D)
223. (A) (B) (C) (D)
224. (A) (B) (C) (D)
225. (A) (B) (C) (D)
226. (A) (B) (C) (D)

227. (A) (B) (C) (D)
228. (A) (B) (C) (D)
229. (A) (B) (C) (D)
230. (A) (B) (C) (D)
231. (A) (B) (C) (D)
232. (A) (B) (C) (D)
233. (A) (B) (C) (D)
234. (A) (B) (C) (D)
235. (A) (B) (C) (D)
236. (A) (B) (C) (D)
237. (A) (B) (C) (D)
238. (A) (B) (C) (D)

Language

239. (A) (B) (C) (D)   251. (A) (B) (C) (D)   263. (A) (B) (C) (D)   275. (A) (B) (C) (D)   287. (A) (B) (C) (D)

240. (A) (B) (C) (D)   252. (A) (B) (C) (D)   264. (A) (B) (C) (D)   276. (A) (B) (C) (D)   288. (A) (B) (C) (D)

241. (A) (B) (C) (D)   253. (A) (B) (C) (D)   265. (A) (B) (C) (D)   277. (A) (B) (C) (D)   289. (A) (B) (C) (D)

242. (A) (B) (C) (D)   254. (A) (B) (C) (D)   266. (A) (B) (C) (D)   278. (A) (B) (C) (D)   290. (A) (B) (C) (D)

243. (A) (B) (C) (D)   255. (A) (B) (C) (D)   267. (A) (B) (C) (D)   279. (A) (B) (C) (D)   291. (A) (B) (C) (D)

244. (A) (B) (C) (D)   256. (A) (B) (C) (D)   268. (A) (B) (C) (D)   280. (A) (B) (C) (D)   292. (A) (B) (C) (D)

245. (A) (B) (C) (D)   257. (A) (B) (C) (D)   269. (A) (B) (C) (D)   281. (A) (B) (C) (D)   293. (A) (B) (C) (D)

246. (A) (B) (C) (D)   258. (A) (B) (C) (D)   270. (A) (B) (C) (D)   282. (A) (B) (C) (D)   294. (A) (B) (C) (D)

247. (A) (B) (C) (D)   259. (A) (B) (C) (D)   271. (A) (B) (C) (D)   283. (A) (B) (C) (D)   295. (A) (B) (C) (D)

248. (A) (B) (C) (D)   260. (A) (B) (C) (D)   272. (A) (B) (C) (D)   284. (A) (B) (C) (D)   296. (A) (B) (C) (D)

249. (A) (B) (C) (D)   261. (A) (B) (C) (D)   273. (A) (B) (C) (D)   285. (A) (B) (C) (D)   297. (A) (B) (C) (D)

250. (A) (B) (C) (D)   262. (A) (B) (C) (D)   274. (A) (B) (C) (D)   286. (A) (B) (C) (D)   298. (A) (B) (C) (D)

HSPT Practice Test 1

VERBAL SKILLS

Questions 1–60
16 Minutes

Directions: For questions 1–60, choose the best answer.

1. Which word does *not* belong with the others?

    (A) argue
    (B) debate
    (C) angry
    (D) disagree

2. Which word does *not* belong with the others?

    (A) hopeful
    (B) optimistic
    (C) cordial
    (D) confident

3. Giant is to large as miniature is to

    (A) small
    (B) size
    (C) big
    (D) cute

4. Allan lives closer to the bus stop than Mark. Pat lives closer to the bus stop than Allan. Pat lives farther from the bus stop than Mark. If the first two statements are true, the third is

    (A) true
    (B) false
    (C) uncertain

5. Permit most nearly means

   (A) forgive
   (B) allow
   (C) forbid
   (D) give

6. Ink is to pen as paint is to

   (A) brush
   (B) bucket
   (C) wall
   (D) painter

7. Which word does *not* belong with the others?

   (A) event
   (B) affair
   (C) occasion
   (D) accident

8. Lake is to water as glacier is to

   (A) ice
   (B) snow
   (C) mountain
   (D) cold

9. Which word does *not* belong with the others?

   (A) weather
   (B) rain
   (C) snow
   (D) fog

10. A spider is a(n)

    (A) feline
    (B) reptile
    (C) arachnid
    (D) phobia

11. Conceited most nearly means

(A) arrogant

(B) inferior

(C) worthy

(D) hardworking

12. Button is to jacket as lace is to

(A) shoe

(B) zipper

(C) sweater

(D) foot

13. Water is to flower as birdseed is to

(A) garden

(B) fertilizer

(C) plant

(D) bird

14. Optimist is to hope as sage is to

(A) creativity

(B) fear

(C) talent

(D) wisdom

15. Christine is shorter than Louise. Louise is shorter than Joon. Christine is shorter than Joon. If the first two statements are true, the third is

(A) true

(B) false

(C) uncertain

16. An abridged book is

(A) short

(B) difficult

(C) thick

(D) published

17. Complex most nearly means

(A) intricate

(B) simple

(C) delicate

(D) double

18. Corrode most nearly means

    (A) destroy
    (B) rusty
    (C) dishonest
    (D) cheat

19. Ring is to bell as knock is to

    (A) door
    (B) alarm
    (C) hammer
    (D) ring

20. Actors is to director as players is to

    (A) coach
    (B) team
    (C) soccer
    (D) fan

21. Variation most nearly means

    (A) comparison
    (B) classification
    (C) support
    (D) difference

22. Frank is more outgoing than Joe. Joe is more outgoing than Rob. Rob is more outgoing than Frank. If the first two statements are true, the third is

    (A) true
    (B) false
    (C) uncertain

23. A postponed appointment

    (A) necessary
    (B) long
    (C) late
    (D) delayed

24. A is longer than B. B is longer than C. C is longer than D. If the first two statements are true, the third is

    (A) true
    (B) false
    (C) uncertain

25. A <u>unanimous</u> vote

    (A) complete
    (B) correct
    (C) undisputed
    (D) controversial

26. A <u>practical</u> person

    (A) normal
    (B) kind
    (C) sensible
    (D) silly

27. Which word does *not* belong with the others?

    (A) assembly
    (B) team
    (C) choir
    (D) director

28. Abandon most nearly means

    (A) adopt
    (B) realize
    (C) leave
    (D) litter

29. A <u>dynamic</u> speaker

    (A) energetic
    (B) loud
    (C) unstoppable
    (D) timid

30. A <u>penniless</u> person

    (A) thoughtless
    (B) poor
    (C) unkind
    (D) helpful

31. Folder is to paper as drawer is to

    (A) clothes
    (B) lamp
    (C) furniture
    (D) desk

32. Which word does *not* belong with the others?

    (A) hearing
    (B) sight
    (C) touch
    (D) sense

33. All googles are moogles. No googles wear glasses. No moogles wear glasses. If the first two statements are true, the third statement is

    (A) true
    (B) false
    (C) uncertain

34. Which word does *not* belong with the others?

    (A) coin
    (B) bill
    (C) check
    (D) money

35. Reduce means the *opposite* of

    (A) enlarge
    (B) relate
    (C) allot
    (D) react

36. Ladle is to soup as shovel is to

    (A) garage
    (B) hole
    (C) sand
    (D) beach

37. Disperse means the *opposite* of

    (A) gather
    (B) display
    (C) reverse
    (D) handle

38. Hiking trail L is longer than hiking trail K. Trail K is longer than trail J. Trail L is longer than trail J. If the first two statements are true, the third is

    (A) true
    (B) false
    (C) uncertain

39. Hamper means the *opposite* of

    (A) relax
    (B) hinder
    (C) seize
    (D) assist

40. Aptitude means the *opposite* of

    (A) inability
    (B) height
    (C) peak
    (D) talent

41. Agenda is to meeting as program is to

    (A) television
    (B) plan
    (C) play
    (D) detail

42. Which word does *not* belong with the others?

(A) hood

(B) trunk

(C) wheel

(D) car

43. Sturdy means the *opposite* of

(A) flimsy

(B) stout

(C) slender

(D) solid

44. Gullible means the *opposite* of

(A) dirty

(B) cosmopolitan

(C) incredulous

(D) immaculate

45. Which word does *not* belong with the others?

(A) gaunt

(B) thin

(C) svelte

(D) rotund

46. Which word does *not* belong with the others?

(A) pail

(B) bucket

(C) container

(D) rag

47. Genuine most nearly means

(A) real

(B) friendly

(C) original

(D) intelligent

48. Content is the *opposite* of

    (A) restless
    (B) happy
    (C) argumentative
    (D) static

49. Magazines are longer than catalogues but not as long as books. Dictionaries are longer than magazines but not as long as encyclopedias. Magazines are the shortest of the types of writing. If the first two statements are true, the third is

    (A) true
    (B) false
    (C) uncertain

50. Which word does *not* belong with the others?

    (A) canoe
    (B) yacht
    (C) kayak
    (D) submarine

51. Replenish is the *opposite* of

    (A) reward
    (B) supply
    (C) increase
    (D) deplete

52. Fatima blocks more goals than Maria. Maria blocks more goals than Ellen. Jaylene blocks more goals than Ellen. If the first two statements are true, the third is

    (A) true
    (B) false
    (C) uncertain

53. Enlist is the *opposite* of

    (A) join
    (B) quit
    (C) enter
    (D) elect

54. Which word does *not* belong with the others?

    (A) fragile
    (B) breakable
    (C) brittle
    (D) robust

55. The idividual pizza is smaller than the small pizza. The regular pizza is larger than the small pizza but not as big as the jumbo. The jumbo is not as big as the small pizza. If the first two statements are true, the third is

    (A) true
    (B) false
    (C) uncertain

56. Which word does *not* belong with the others?

    (A) cup
    (B) mug
    (C) saucer
    (D) glass

57. Renovate most nearly means

    (A) build
    (B) renew
    (C) create
    (D) remove

58. Which word does *not* belong with the others?

    (A) diamond
    (B) ruby
    (C) sapphire
    (D) gem

59. Which word does *not* belong with the others?

    (A) pacific
    (B) lively
    (C) playful
    (D) spirited

60. Mr. Thomas has more grandchildren than Mr. Blake. Mr. Smith has more grandchildren than Mr. Walter, but not as many as Mr. Thomas. Mr. Blake has the most grandchildren. If the first two statements are true, the third is

    (A) true
    (B) false
    (C) uncertain

QUANTITATIVE SKILLS

Questions 61–112
30 Minutes

Directions: For questions 61–112, choose the best answer.

61. What number is 7 more than 10% of 100?

    (A) 10
    (B) 17
    (C) 3
    (D) 18

62. What is the next number in the following series: 21, 27, 33, ...

    (A) 37
    (B) 35
    (C) 39
    (D) 36

63. What is the next number in the following series: 51, 46, 41, 36, ...

    (A) 28
    (B) 29
    (C) 32
    (D) 31

64. Examine (a), (b), and (c) and select the correct answer.

    (a) two nickels
    (b) two quarters
    (c) two pennies and one dime

    (A) (a) plus (c) is greater than (b)
    (B) (b) is equal to (a)
    (C) (a) is more than (c)
    (D) (b) minus (a) is greater than (c)

65. Examine (a), (b), and (c) and select the correct answer.

(a) .75

(b) $\frac{5}{8}$

(c) .26 × 3.4

(A) (a) plus (b) is less than (c)

(B) (a) is greater than (c)

(C) (a) is equal to (b)

(D) (c) is greater than (b)

66. What number is the cube of 4 divided by 8?

(A) 64

(B) 24

(C) 3

(D) 8

67. What number is $\frac{1}{2}$ of the average of 12, 8, 15, 6 and 29?

(A) 7

(B) 14

(C) 70

(D) 9

68. Examine (a), (b), and (c) and select the correct answer.

(a)　　　　(b)　　　　(c)

(A) (a) is shaded more than (b)

(B) (a) and (b) are equally shaded and both are shaded more than (c)

(C) (c) is shaded more than (a) and shaded less than (b)

(D) (a), (b), and (c) are equally shaded

69. What is the missing number in the following series: 88, 85, ___, 79, 76

(A) 84

(B) 82

(C) 78

(D) 81

70. Examine (a), (b), and (c) and select the correct answer.

    (a) 20% of 60
    (b) 60% of 20
    (c) 60% of 20%

    (A) (b) is greater than (a) or (c)

    (B) (a), (b), and (c) are equal

    (C) (a) is greater than (c)

    (D) (b) is equal to (c) and smaller than (a)

71. What is the next number in the following series: 240, 120, 60, 30, ...

    (A) 20

    (B) 10

    (C) 15

    (D) 12

72. What are the next three numbers in the following series: 1, 7, 5, 6, ...

    (A) 12, 10, 11

    (B) 13, 11, 12

    (C) 12, 9, 10

    (D) 14, 11, 12

73. What number subtracted from 62 leaves 3 more than $\frac{3}{5}$ of 75?

    (A) 48

    (B) 41

    (C) 45

    (D) 14

74. What number is 8 more than $\frac{3}{4}$ of 24?

    (A) 12

    (B) 18

    (C) 22

    (D) 26

75. Examine (a), (b), and (c) and select the correct answer.

  (a) $(2 \times 7) - 4$
  (b) $(5 \times 6) + 1$
  (c) $(6 \times 6) - 15$

  (A) (c) is greater than (b)

  (B) (b) is less than (a) and (c)

  (C) (a) plus (c) is equal to (b)

  (D) (a) is greater than (c) and less than (b)

76. What is the next number in the following series: 228, 236, 244, 252 ...

  (A) 260

  (B) 262

  (C) 258

  (D) 256

77. Examine (a), (b), and (c) and select the correct answer.

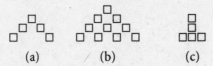

(a) (b) (c)

  (A) (a) has more squares than (c)

  (B) (a) and (b) each have more squares than (c)

  (C) (b) and (c) each have more squares than (a)

  (D) (a) and (c) each have fewer squares than (b)

78. Examine (a), (b), and (c) and select the correct answer.

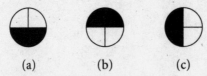

(a) (b) (c)

  (A) (a) is more shaded than (b)

  (B) (a) and (b) are equally shaded, and each have less shaded than (c)

  (C) (b) is more shaded than (c) and less shaded than (a)

  (D) (a), (b), and (c) are equally shaded

79. What is the next number in the following series: 110, 105, 101, 98, 96, ...

    (A) 95

    (B) 96

    (C) 94

    (D) 91

80. What number divided by 6 is $\frac{1}{5}$ of 80?

    (A) 420

    (B) 96

    (C) 16

    (D) 300

81. What is the next number in the following series: 6, X, 14, ...

    (A) IV

    (B) 18

    (C) IX

    (D) 16

82. Examine (a), (b), and (c) and select the correct answer.

    (a) $\frac{1}{3}$ of 9

    (b) $\frac{2}{3}$ of 12

    (c) $\frac{2}{5}$ of 15

    (A) (b) and (c) are equal

    (B) (a) and (b) are each greater than (c)

    (C) (c) is greater than (a)

    (D) (a), (b), and (c) are equal

83. $\frac{1}{2}$ of what number is 5 times 4?

    (A) 20

    (B) 22

    (C) 40

    (D) 41

84. Examine (a), (b), and (c) and select the correct answer.

     (a)   (b)   (c)

(A) (a) is shaded less than (b)

(B) (b) is shaded more than (c) and less than (a)

(C) (a), (b), and (c) are equally shaded

(D) (c) is less shaded than (a)

85. What number added to 7 is 2 times the product of 5 and 3?

(A) 29

(B) 14

(C) 15

(D) 23

86. What is the next number in the following series: 17, 13, 16, 12...

(A) 15

(B) 16

(C) 13

(D) 17

87. Examine (a), (b), and (c) and select the correct answer.

(a) 25%

(b) $\frac{1}{4}$

(c) .25

(A) (a) is greater than (b) which is greater than (c)

(B) (a), (b), and (c) are equal

(C) (c) is greater than (b) but less than (a)

(D) (a) and (b) are each more than (c)

88. $\frac{2}{5}$ of what number is 2 times 20?

(A) 10

(B) 6

(C) 40

(D) 100

89. What is the missing number in the following series: 1, 5, 3, ___, 13

    (A) 12
    (B) 15
    (C) 4
    (D) 6

90. What is the next number in the following series: 6, 11, 12, 13, 18, 19, 20,...

    (A) 23
    (B) 24
    (C) 25
    (D) 26

91. Examine the square *ABCD* and select the correct answer.

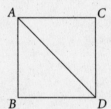

    (A) *AB* is greater than *AC*
    (B) *AC* and *AB* are each less than *AD*
    (C) *AC* is greater than *AB*
    (D) *AB* is equal to *AC* plus *CD*

92. What number multiplied by 6 is 2 less than 20?

    (A) 18
    (B) 3
    (C) 24
    (D) 12

93. What is the missing number in the following series: 12, 24, 25, 50, ___, 102...

    (A) 51
    (B) 52
    (C) 74
    (D) 54

94. Examine (a), (b), and (c) and select the correct answer.

    (a) $(15 \div 3) \times 2$
    (b) $(3 \div 1) \times 2$
    (c) $(25 \div 5) \times 2$

    (A) (a), and (c) are equal

    (B) (a) is greater than (b) and less than (c)

    (C) (b) and (c) are equal to (a)

    (D) (b) is less than (c) but greater than (a)

95. What are the next two numbers in the following series: 75, 77, 74, 76, 73,...

    (A) 71, 74

    (B) 74, 75

    (C) 75, 72

    (D) 76, 73

96. Examine the cube and select the correct answer.

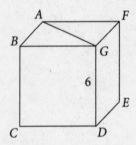

    (A) $AG < AB$

    (B) $AB + BG < AG$

    (C) $AG > DE$

    (D) $CG > AG$

97. What number divided by 6 leaves 3 more than 9?

    (A) 72

    (B) 12

    (C) 9

    (D) 3

98. Examine (a), (b), and (c). If both *a* and *b* are greater than zero, select the correct answer.

   (a) $6(a + b)$
   (b) $6a + 6b$
   (c) $6(a + b) + b$

   (A) (a) and (b) are greater than (c)

   (B) (b) and (c) are equal to (a)

   (C) (c) is greater than (a) and (b) which are equal

   (D) (a), (b), and (c) are equal

99. What is the next number in the following series: 2, 5, 10, 13, 26,...

   (A) 29

   (B) 28

   (C) 42

   (D) 52

100. What number subtracted from 12 leaves $\frac{1}{5}$ of 40?

   (A) 4

   (B) 6

   (C) 12

   (D) 7

101. What is the next term in the following series: A2, b4, C6, d8,...

   (A) F10

   (B) e9

   (C) E8

   (D) E10

102. Examine the bar graph and select the correct answer.

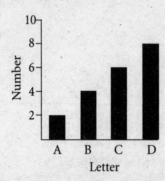

(A) Height of A plus height of B is equal to height of D

(B) Height of C minus height of A equals height of B

(C) Height of D is less than height of A but more than height of C

(D) Height of A minus height of B equals height of C plus height of D

103. What number is 7 less than $\frac{2}{3}$ of 15?

(A) 3

(B) 7

(C) 10

(D) 2

104. What is the next number in the following series: 3, 12, 4, 16, 8, …

(A) 32

(B) 8

(C) 60

(D) 12

105. Examine (a), (b), and (c) and select the correct answer.

(a) 2 squared

(b) 3 cubed

(c) 4 cubed

(A) (c) > (a) > (b)

(B) (a) > (b) > (c)

(C) (b) > (a) > (c)

(D) (c) > (b) > (a)

106. What is the next number in the following series: $9, \frac{3}{4}, 6\frac{1}{2}, 5\frac{1}{4}, \ldots$

    (A) $3\frac{1}{2}$

    (B) $4\frac{1}{4}$

    (C) 4

    (D) $\frac{1}{4}$

107. What number is 6 times $\frac{1}{4}$ of 60?

    (A) 80

    (B) 15

    (C) 90

    (D) 300

108. What are the next three numbers in the following series: 15, 16, 19, 17, 18, 21, 19...

    (A) 20, 23, 22

    (B) 21, 24, 22

    (C) 21, 19, 18

    (D) 20, 23, 21

109. $\frac{1}{8}$ of what number added to 6 is 2 times 7?

    (A) 14

    (B) 16

    (C) 8

    (D) 64

110. Examine the square and select the correct answer.

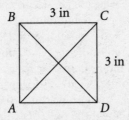

    (A) The area of triangle ABC is greater than the area of triangle ABD.

    (B) The area of the square is 9 inches.

    (C) The perimeter of the square is 12 inches.

    (D) The perimeter of triangle ABC is equal to the perimeter of the square.

111. What number is 8 more than $\frac{4}{5}$ of 10?

(A) 18

(B) 16

(C) 40

(D) 14

112. What number is 4 less than 3 cubed?

(A) 27

(B) 23

(C) 22

(D) 31

READING

Questions 113–174

25 Minutes

Comprehension

Directions: Read the passages and answer questions 113–152.

Read the following passage and answer questions 113–122.

Insects can be classified into fourteen separate groupings, or orders. Butterflies and moths belong to the Lepidoptera order. Lepidoptera means "scale wings," from the Greek word "lepido," which means "scales" and "ptera" which means "wing."

Lepidoptera is one of the largest and most <u>diverse</u> insect orders. The only order with more different species is Coleoptera, that of beetles. So far, scientists have observed approximately 150,000 different species of butterflies and moths. Each species is distinguished by the <u>unique</u> arrangement, color, and pattern of its scales. Worldwide, there are about 28,000 butterfly species. The rest of the species comprising Lepidoptera are species of moths. Though butterflies and moths both have scaled wings, there are some important differences between them. Butterflies are <u>distinguished</u> by their brightly colored wings. Moth's wings are usually less bright. Butterflies are usually active during the day, while moths are active at night. A butterfly's antennae are swollen at the tip while a moth's antennae are feathery.

113. The largest order of insects is

(A) Lepidoptera

(B) Butterfly

(C) Moth

(D) Coleoptera

114. How many insect orders are there?

    (A) 2
    (B) 14
    (C) 3
    (D) 150

115. Which of the following is true?

    (A) Butterflies and moths belong to different orders.
    (B) Butterflies and moths are both Lepidoptera.
    (C) Butterflies are insects, while moths are not.
    (D) Butterflies fly faster than other Lepidoptera.

116. You would expect to find the kind of information in this passage in

    (A) a scientific journal
    (B) a social studies text
    (C) neither of these
    (D) both of these

117. According to the passage, how many species of butterflies are there worldwide?

    (A) 14
    (B) 28
    (C) 28,000
    (D) 150,000

118. As used in the passage, the word <u>diverse</u> most nearly means

    (A) multiple
    (B) flying
    (C) winged
    (D) varied

119. Which of the following is true?

    (A) Scientists know the exact number of Lepidoptera species.
    (B) Scientists have not identified all Lepidoptera.
    (C) Scientists have already observed all Lepidoptera species.
    (D) Scientists are debating how to classify butterflies and moths

120. In comparing butterflies and moths, you would find that butterflies

    (A) are more friendly
    (B) are not attracted to sunlight
    (C) are more colorful
    (D) are more aggressive

121. As used in the passage, the word <u>distinguished</u> most nearly means

    (A) recognizable
    (B) respectable
    (C) similar
    (D) organized

122. As used in the passage, the word <u>unique</u> most nearly means

    (A) lonely
    (B) different
    (C) beautiful
    (D) order

Read the following passage and answer questions 123–132.

The man catches a glimpse of a redcoat emerging from the woods. His heart beats faster as first, one British soldier steps into the open, then another, then another. Soon, a line of redcoats fills the field. They far outnumber the man's own regiment. Surely, the rebel soldiers will be defeated. A general gives the command, and the man lowers his musket to aim. So do his comrades, standing beside him.

A sharp crackle rips through the quiet morning air. It is the first gunshot of the battle. In moments, the battlefield is crackling with the sound of bullets. A pungent aroma fills the air. The man's eyes <u>smart</u> and his vision dims from the thick cloud of gun smoke. His comrade beside him falls wounded.

But the man is only feigning injury. He will lie on the field until smoke clears and the war reenactment is finished. Then, he will get up, dust himself off, and join the rest of the soldiers for a picnic. This is not a real <u>skirmish</u>, but rather a carefully planned and orchestrated recreation of a revolutionary war battle. The redcoats and the rebels are members of a club, who reenact the battles of the Revolutionary War each fourth of July.

Reenactors feel that demonstrating what the War for Independence was really like is not only an enjoyable way to spend a morning, but also a way to bring history alive.

123. The first two paragraphs of this passage describe a battle's

    (A) sights and sounds
    (B) soldiers and commanders
    (C) weapons and soldiers
    (D) costumes and actors

124. As used in the passage, the word <u>skirmish</u> most nearly means

    (A) picnic
    (B) battle
    (C) soldier
    (D) wound

125. The author of this passage is most likely a

    (A) historian
    (B) reenactor
    (C) redcoat
    (D) soldier

126. The battle the man was reenacting was probably

    (A) won by the British
    (B) won by the rebels
    (C) the final battle of the war
    (D) a secret attack

127. According to this passage, why did the rebel soldier lower his musket?

    (A) He was afraid.
    (B) His general gave an order.
    (C) The British began to fire.
    (D) His friend was injured.

128. The man's heart beat when the British took the field because he was

    (A) motivated
    (B) afraid
    (C) surprised
    (D) elated

129. As used in the passage, the word <u>smart</u> most nearly means

    (A) intelligent
    (B) see
    (C) hurt
    (D) fog

130. According to this passage, reenactors enjoy

(A) fighting

(B) history

(C) picnics

(D) skirmishes

131. A good title for this passage would be

(A) History Comes Alive

(B) A Fallen Soldier

(C) Muskets Ready

(D) The War for Independence

132. According to this passage, which word would most nearly describe reenacting?

(A) courageous

(B) rebellious

(C) studious

(D) fun

Read the following passage and answer questions 133–142.

A garbage dump is a place for things we consider useless, but garbage dumps can provide a useful source of energy.

Garbage dumps, also called landfills, give off a small amount of energy. Wastes in the dump, such as apple cores, egg shells, and banana peels create methane gas as they <u>decompose</u>. At large dumps, the methane gas is burned, in order to prevent a hazardous gas buildup. Although landfill gas is generally a pollutant, it can also be a valuable source of fuel. Methane is the same gas sold by natural gas utility companies. At garbage dumps, the methane is either sold to commercial industries, or collected and used to power electric generators.

Depending on the size and age of the landfill, a <u>significant</u> amount of energy can collected. For example, a five-megawatt generator could produce 42 million kilowatt-hours per year. That's enough electricity to supply about 3,200 homes with power.

There's an added benefit of recovering methane gas from garbage dumps too. Methane that is released directly into the atmosphere can contribute to global warming. So you see, there's treasure in the trash.

133. The creation of methane gas in a garbage dump is caused by

(A) pollution

(B) fires

(C) electricity

(D) decomposition

134. Although the author of this passage describes garbage dumps as useless, her feeling toward garbage dumps is one of

(A) appreciation

(B) affection

(C) sarcasm

(D) disgust

135. Which of the following is true?

(A) Garbage dumps are clean.

(B) Garbage dumps produce electricity.

(C) Garbage dumps can be useful.

(D) Garbage dumps power automobiles.

136. According to this passage, a five-megawatt generator can power

(A) thousands of homes

(B) a small city

(C) a large factory

(D) forty-two garbage dumps

137. As used in the passage, the word <u>significant</u> most nearly means

(A) sizeable

(B) polluted

(C) electric

(D) small

138. Methane gas is

(A) dirty

(B) natural

(C) useless

(D) dangerous

139. A good title for this passage might be

(A) Don't Throw It Away

(B) How to Recycle

(C) Treasure in the Trash

(D) The Science of Decomposition

140. This passage implies that an added benefit of recovering methane gas from garbage dumps is that it

(A) prevents the contribution to global warming

(B) supplies all our electricity

(C) decrease the amount of trash we throw away

(D) provides an endless supply of power

141. As used in the passage, the word <u>decompose</u> most nearly means

(A) smell

(B) rot

(C) burn

(D) build

142. Based on the passage, it could be said that garbage dumps cause the

(A) decomposition of minerals

(B) reduction of global warming

(C) pollution of the oceans

(D) production of methane

Read the following passage and answer questions 143–148.

The practice of bloodletting, misguided by modern standards, was a popular cure of Medieval medicine. During medieval times, the body was viewed as part of the larger universe. People believed that the four elements of nature—earth, air, water, and fire—were related to four elements in the human body. Those elements were <u>respectively</u>, black bile, blood, phlegm, and yellow bile. Medieval doctors believed that illness was caused by an <u>imbalance</u> of one of these four elements. For example, too much black bile could make be the cause of a sad person's melancholy. These disease-causing imbalances were commonly treated with herbal remedies, meditation, and bloodletting.

Specialized medical books of the day, called leech books, contained description of various ailments and methods for treating them. These antique physician's desk references detailed where to apply bloodsucking leeches to a patient, or how much blood to drain from an individual to cure him or her. For despite the dangers obvious to us now, Medieval doctors and barbers believed they were helping their patients by causing them to bleed.

As modern doctors know, draining a person's blood does not have restorative powers. In spite of that, bloodletting persisted as a common cure well until the 18th century. In fact, George Washington, the father of the United States, eventually died as a result of improper bloodletting intended to cure him of a common cold.

143. This passage was probably printed in

    (A) a medical journal

    (B) a history book

    (C) a letter to a friend

    (D) an instructional booklet

144. According to this passage, the technique of bloodletting is

    (A) successful as a cure

    (B) still in practice

    (C) unused in current times

    (D) the beginning of modern medicine

145. With which of the following would the author of this passage most likely agree?

    (A) medieval medicine is unparalleled

    (B) George Washington was murdered

    (C) modern doctors are more aware of the causes of diseases

    (D) leeches are extinct

146. According to the passage, which group had members that practiced bloodletting?

    (A) herbalists

    (B) midwives

    (C) politicians

    (D) barbers

147. This passage calls bloodletting *misguided*. Which of these would also be misguided?

    (A) Wearing small shoes to keep your feet from growing.

    (B) Drinking tea to cure a sore throat.

    (C) Washing your hands to prevent spreading germs.

    (D) Saying "good luck," to someone about to compete in a race.

148. It is implied that modern doctors think bloodletting is

    (A) harmless

    (B) common

    (C) curative

    (D) unsafe

Read the following passage and answer questions 149–152.

Almost everyone enjoys hearing some kind of live music. But few of us realize the complex process that goes into designing the acoustics of concert and lecture halls. In the design of any building where the audibility of sound is a major considerations, architects have to carefully match the space and materials they use to the intended purpose of the venue. One problem is that the intensity of sound may build too quickly in an enclosed space. Another problem is that only part of the sound we hear in any large room or auditorium comes directly from the source. Much of it reaches us a fraction of a second later after it has been reflected off the walls, ceiling, and floor as reverberated sound. How much each room reverberates depends upon both its size, and the ability of its contents to absorb sound. Too little reverberation can make music sound thin and weak; too much reverberation can blur the listener's sense of where one note stops and the next begins.

Consequently, the most important factor in acoustic design is the time it takes for these reverberations to die down altogether, called the reverberation time.

149. Which of the following is the main topic of this passage?

    (A) the challenges of an architect's job
    (B) the differences between speech and music
    (C) the experience of hearing live music
    (D) the role of reverberation in acoustic design

150. The passage suggests that the *complex process* of acoustic design is

    (A) not widely appreciated by the public
    (B) really a matter of listener sensitivity
    (C) an engineer's problem, not an architect's
    (D) most difficult in concert hall construction

151. According to the passage, too little reverberation in a concert hall can result in

    (A) a rapid increase in the volume of sound
    (B) the blurring of details in a piece of music
    (C) a quiet and insubstantial quality of sound
    (D) confusion among a listening audience

152. Which of the following does the author regard as the most significant consideration in the design of a concert hall?

    (A) an appreciation for music
    (B) an understanding of reverberation time
    (C) the choice of building materials
    (D) the purpose of the venue

Vocabulary

Directions: For questions 153–174, choose the word that is closest in meaning to the underlined word.

153. to <u>predict</u> the future

    (A) change

    (B) prevent

    (C) foretell

    (D) control

154. <u>mutual</u> respect

    (A) strong

    (B) understandable

    (C) common

    (D) lost

155. a <u>gap</u> in logic

    (A) break

    (B) mistake

    (C) theory

    (D) grab

156. a <u>frank</u> response

    (A) honest

    (B) masculine

    (C) cold

    (D) lengthy

157. to <u>allege</u>

    (A) allow

    (B) arrest

    (C) imply

    (D) inspect

158. an important <u>consequence</u>

    (A) coincidence

    (B) effect

    (C) circumstance

    (D) point

159. to <u>confine</u>

    (A) restrict

    (B) reduce

    (C) separate

    (D) polish

160. to <u>delete</u> information

    (A) add

    (B) erase

    (C) edit

    (D) avoid

161. a <u>glossy</u> brochure

    (A) influential

    (B) glib

    (C) interesting

    (D) shiny

162. an <u>outrageous</u> remark

    (A) extraordinary

    (B) false

    (C) political

    (D) respectful

163. a <u>sophisticated</u> woman

    (A) learned

    (B) cosmopolitan

    (C) fashionable

    (D) wealthy

164. an interesting <u>proposal</u>

    (A) engagement

    (B) invention

    (C) suggestion

    (D) result

165. a <u>radical</u> idea

   (A) subversive

   (B) superb

   (C) novel

   (D) scientific

166. to <u>interrogate</u> a prisoner

   (A) interrupt

   (B) release

   (C) question

   (D) inspect

167. a <u>plausible</u> theory

   (A) proven

   (B) economic

   (C) extensive

   (D) valid

168. public <u>access</u>

   (A) park

   (B) tax

   (C) entrance

   (D) ramp

169. to <u>compose</u>

   (A) write

   (B) review

   (C) erase

   (D) send

170. an <u>ostentatious</u> person

   (A) skillful

   (B) conspicuous

   (C) bossy

   (D) pretentious

171. an <u>essential</u> element

   (A) necessary

   (B) elementary

   (C) elated

   (D) pure

172. a challenging <u>obstacle</u>

   (A) exam

   (B) track

   (C) difficulty

   (D) task

173. a <u>precise</u> instrument

   (A) musical

   (B) complicated

   (C) accurate

   (D) automotive

174. a <u>gracious</u> host

   (A) forgetful

   (B) unwelcome

   (C) useful

   (D) warm

MATHEMATICS

Questions 175–238

45 Minutes

Directions: For questions 175–238, choose the best answer.

Concepts

175. Which of the following is *not* a type of triangle?

    (A) isosceles

    (B) equilateral

    (C) obtuse

    (D) rhomboid

176. $\{1, 6, 11, 16\} \cap \{1, 2, 6, 10, 14\} =$

    (A) $\{1, 6\}$

    (B) $\{1, 2, 6\}$

    (C) $\{1, 2, 3, 4\}$

    (D) $\{6, 12, 14\}$

177. To the nearest tenth, 75.891 is written

    (A) 75.8

    (B) 75.9

    (C) 75

    (D) 75.91

178. Simplify: $3(-3^2)$

    (A) 9

    (B) 27

    (C) 18

    (D) 12

179. As a fraction, .12 can be written as

    (A) $\frac{1}{12}$

    (B) $\frac{12}{100}$

    (C) $\frac{1}{10}$

    (D) $\frac{100}{12}$

180. The measure of the angle labeled *x* is

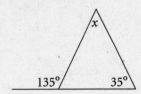

(A) 65°

(B) 35°

(C) 100°

(D) 95°

181. To multiply a number by 1,000, move the decimal point

(A) two places to the right

(B) three places to the right

(C) three places to the left

(D) four places to the right

182. Which of the following is a pair of consecutive numbers?

(A) 4, 5

(B) −4, +4

(C) 3, 6

(D) $\frac{1}{3}, \frac{3}{1}$

183. The diameter of this circle is

(A) 4π m

(B) 4 m

(C) 8 m

(D) 2π m

184. One centimeter is equal to how many meters?

    (A) $\frac{1}{100}$

    (B) $\frac{1}{1,000}$

    (C) $\frac{1}{10}$

    (D) $\frac{1}{10,000}$

185. How many integers are between $\frac{25}{3}$ and 12.3?

    (A) 12

    (B) 3

    (C) 5

    (D) 4

186. Which of the following is always true?

    (A) adding two negative numbers results in a positive number

    (B) multiplying one negative and one positive number results in a positive number

    (C) multiplying one negative and one positive number results in a negative number

    (D) subtracting a negative from a positive number results in zero.

187. The square root of 122 is between

    (A) 11 and 12

    (B) 12 and 13

    (C) 100 and 130

    (D) 120 and 130

188. Which of these statements is true?

    (A) $.042 = 4.2 \times \left(\frac{1}{10}\right)^2$

    (B) $420 = 4.2 \times 10^3$

    (C) $.42 = 4.2 \times 10$

    (D) $4,200 = 4.2 \times 10^4$

189. Two numbers are in the ratio 3:1. The sum of the two numbers is 52. What is the larger number?

    (A) 39

    (B) 52

    (C) 13

    (D) 3

190. Which of the following fractions has a value between $\frac{1}{5}$ and $\frac{4}{9}$?

    (A) $\frac{1}{8}$

    (B) $\frac{3}{5}$

    (C) $\frac{2}{3}$

    (D) $\frac{1}{3}$

191. If the measure of angle $AOB = 60$ degrees, what fractional part of the circle shown below is shaded?

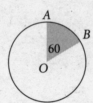

    (A) $\frac{1}{6}$

    (B) $\frac{1}{5}$

    (C) $\frac{1}{3}$

    (D) $\frac{2}{10}$

192. A recent poll showed that 42% of people polled favored a new bill, 28% were opposed to it, 20% were neither for nor against it and the rest did not vote at all. What fractional part of the whole did not vote at all?

    (A) $\frac{1}{9}$

    (B) $\frac{9}{10}$

    (C) $\frac{1}{10}$

    (D) $\frac{2}{10}$

193. One week, a child spent 40% of her allowance on soft drinks. If her allowance is 5 dollars, how much did she spend on soft drinks?

    (A) $4

    (B) $1.20

    (C) $20

    (D) $2

194. Which of the following is *not* a type of quadrilateral?

    (A) trapezoid

    (B) parallelogram

    (C) square

    (D) pythagorean

195. If triangle *ADE* is similar to triangle *ABC*, which of the following proportions is true?

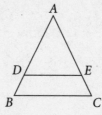

    (A) $\dfrac{AD}{AB} = \dfrac{DE}{BC}$

    (B) $\dfrac{AD}{AE} = \dfrac{AB}{AD}$

    (C) $\dfrac{AB}{BC} = \dfrac{AC}{EC}$

    (D) $\dfrac{DB}{DE} = \dfrac{AD}{EC}$

196. Which of the following is *not* a prime factor of 30?

    (A) 7

    (B) 3

    (C) 2

    (D) 5

197. The least common multiple of 3 and 4 is

    (A) 12

    (B) 6

    (C) 4

    (D) 3

198. Which of the following is an example of the associative property of addition?

    (A) $\dfrac{2}{3} + \dfrac{1}{3} + 3 = 2\left(\dfrac{1}{3} + \dfrac{2}{3}\right)$

    (B) $\dfrac{1}{3} + \dfrac{1}{2} + \dfrac{1}{4} = 1$

    (C) $\left(\dfrac{1}{3} + \dfrac{2}{3}\right) + 3 = \dfrac{1}{3} + \left(\dfrac{2}{3} + 3\right)$

    (D) $\dfrac{2}{3} + \dfrac{1}{3} = 3\dfrac{1}{3}$

Problem Solving

199. Solve the following equation for x:

    $12 + 3x = x + 40$

    (A) 4
    (B) 14
    (C) 28
    (D) 12

200. An artist bought 5 tubes of paint at $2.25 each and 3 paintbrushes at $4.30 each. How much did she spend?

    (A) 24.35
    (B) 25.00
    (C) 24.25
    (D) 24.15

201. Find the difference between $2\frac{1}{3}$ and $1\frac{1}{4}$.

    (A) $1\frac{1}{3}$
    (B) $1\frac{1}{2}$
    (C) $\frac{3}{4}$
    (D) $1\frac{1}{12}$

202. Mr. Brown paid $850 for bus tickets this year. How much did he pay, on the average, each month?

    (A) $70.80
    (B) $70.08
    (C) $85.00
    (D) $75.00

203. Solve: $1\frac{1}{2} \times 2\frac{1}{4} \times \frac{2}{3} =$

    (A) $5\frac{2}{8}$
    (B) $2\frac{1}{4}$
    (C) $2\frac{1}{2}$
    (D) 3

204. Simplify: $-5 + 6 + (-4) + (-8) =$

    (A) -8

    (B) -9

    (C) -17

    (D) -11

205. Ruth has saved 3 dollars less than 2 times the amount Mona has. If Mona has \$102, how much does Ruth have?

    (A) 35

    (B) 201

    (C) 99

    (D) 45

206. The formula $F = \frac{9}{5}C + 32$ converts temperature from Centigrade to Fahrenheit. What is the Fahrenheit temperature equivalent to 5 degrees Centigrade?

    (A) 32

    (B) 40

    (C) 41

    (D) 37

207. Solve: $9 + (-3) + 4 + (-5) =$

    (A) 6

    (B) 5

    (C) 12

    (D) 13

208. If the sum of two numbers is a and one of the numbers is 4, then two times the other number is

    (A) $2(a \times 4)$

    (B) $2(a + 4)$

    (C) $2a$

    (D) $2(a - 4)$

209. If a man can mow 3 acres in an hour, how many acres can he mow in 12 hours?

    (A) 36 acres

    (B) 12 acres

    (C) 6 acres

    (D) 38 acres

210. Martin has 4 dollars less than 2 times the amount his sister has. If his sister has $36, how much does Martin have?

    (A) $66
    (B) $32
    (C) $68
    (D) $72

211. A deli charges $2 per pound for items on its salad bar. What is the cost of a salad that weighs 1 pound 2 ounces?

    (A) $2.75
    (B) $2.25
    (C) $2.50
    (D) $3.00

212. If $a + 4 = b + 6$, then

    (A) $a < b$
    (B) $a = b$
    (C) $a > b$
    (D) $a = 2b$

213. If $3a - 2 > 10$, then a^2 must be

    (A) more than 16
    (B) less than 16
    (C) less than 10
    (D) equal to 16

214. In one year, Mrs. Daly paid $35.50 interest on a loan that had a 5% simple interest rate. How much did she borrow?

    (A) $177.5
    (B) $7,100
    (C) $700
    (D) $710

215. Find the value of $x^3 + 3y + 2$ if $x = 3$ and $y = \frac{1}{2}$.

    (A) 20
    (B) 30
    (C) $30\frac{1}{2}$
    (D) $12\frac{1}{2}$

216. What is the volume of this rectangular solid?

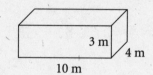

(A) 37 m³

(B) 74 m³

(C) 240 m³

(D) 120 m³

217. Suzanne would like to put wall-to-wall carpeting in her living room. At $4.00 a square foot, how much will it cost her to carpet a room that measures 12 ft by 15 ft?

(A) $240

(B) $720

(C) $170

(D) $108

218. If the 6% tax on a pair of roller blades was $4.50, how much were the roller blades, not including tax?

(A) $65

(B) $75

(C) $80

(D) $85

219. If $X = 2$, $Y = 3$, and $Z = 4$, then $2XYZ =$

(A) 48

(B) 24

(C) 11

(D) 96

220. Solve: $5.31\overline{)2.7633} =$

(A) .31

(B) 31

(C) 52

(D) .52

221. Solve: $42.13 \times .082 =$

   (A) 34.5466
   (B) 345.466
   (C) .345466
   (D) 3.45466

222. If $2x - 7 > 9$, then x^2 must be

   (A) 16
   (B) 64
   (C) 8
   (D) 7

223. Solve: $.354 + 7.9 + 2.03 =$

   (A) 9.444
   (B) 9.284
   (C) 10.284
   (D) 8.457

224. If $8x + 2 = 3x + 5$, then $x =$

   (A) $\frac{3}{5}$
   (B) $\frac{3}{4}$
   (C) $\frac{2}{5}$
   (D) $\frac{1}{6}$

225. A soccer player scores 4 goals in 10 games played. How many goals will she score in 15 games if she continues to score at the same rate?

   (A) 5
   (B) 7
   (C) 6
   (D) 4.5

226. If x is an even integer and $-1 > x > -4$, what is the value of x?

   (A) -2
   (B) 0
   (C) -1
   (D) 4

227. What is the value of *a* in the equation $3a - 6 = b$, if $b = 18$?

    (A) 4

    (B) 6

    (C) 8

    (D) 10

228. If it costs $22.75 to dry-clean 7 shirts, how much will it cost to dry-clean 4 shirts at the same price?

    (A) $9.75

    (B) $6.50

    (C) $13.00

    (D) $13.50

229. Ellen earns $30 a week babysitting. She puts 20% of everything she earns in a bank account earmarked for college. How much does she put in her college savings account each month?

    (A) 240

    (B) 24

    (C) 6

    (D) 60

230. Solve: $534 \times 32 =$

    (A) 17,088

    (B) 17,188

    (C) 17,988

    (D) 18,088

231. If the square root of $a + 6 = 12$, then $a =$

    (A) 136

    (B) 132

    (C) 138

    (D) 116

232. What is the area of the figure shown in the diagram?

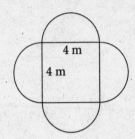

4 m
4 m

(A) $(16 + 8\pi)$ m^2

(B) $(16 + 64\pi)$ m^2

(C) $(16 + 16\pi)$ m^2

(D) $(16 + 4\pi)$ m^2

233. If $\frac{3}{4}x = 30$, find the value of $\frac{5}{8}x$.

(A) 90

(B) 25

(C) 120

(D) 40

234. A supervisor earns $25 an hour more than her coworker. The two, working together, earn $600 for an 8-hour work day. How much does the supervisor earn per hour?

(A) $36

(B) $500

(C) $400

(D) $50

235. The ratio of $\frac{2}{3}$ to $\frac{3}{8}$ is

(A) $\frac{2}{1}$

(B) $\frac{3}{1}$

(C) $\frac{16}{3}$

(D) $\frac{16}{9}$

236. Mark has saved three times as much money as his younger brother. If Mark gives his brother $10, the two will have equal amounts of money. How much money does Mark have?

(A) $30

(B) $5

(C) $15

(D) $20

237. If $6 > y > 3$ and y is an odd integer, then $y =$

  (A) 6

  (B) 5

  (C) 3

  (D) 7

238. If the square root of $a + 12 = 7$, then $a =$

  (A) 36

  (B) 7

  (C) 47

  (D) 37

LANGUAGE

Usage

Questions 239–298

25 Minutes

Directions: For questions 239–278 choose the sentence that contains an error in punctuation, capitalization, or usage. If there is no error, select choice (D).

239. (A) Suzie said, "I'm going to the store."

  (B) The president gave a speech last night.

  (C) Martina arrived on Tuesday February 8.

  (D) No mistake.

240. (A) What time is it?

  (B) Independence day is July 4.

  (C) Howard's aunt is 50 years old.

  (D) No mistake.

241. (A) We hope to visit the Museum of history.

  (B) Dave takes the bus every morning.

  (C) The teacher asked Jane to close the window.

  (D) No mistake.

242. (A) We watched *Treasure Island* yesterday afternoon.
 (B) My sister told me, "Mail the letter."
 (C) Where is the bus stop? Jose asked.
 (D) No mistake.

243. (A) You may have dessert after you eat your dinner.
 (B) Please carry these books for me.
 (C) Bob and Aarthi are the best singers in the choir.
 (D) No mistake.

244. (A) Miss Larson asked us to remain seated.
 (B) One of the puppies is smaller than the others.
 (C) Jerry and me will stay after school.
 (D) No mistake.

245. (A) Copenhagen is in Denmark.
 (B) Teresa asked, "Would you like a soda?"
 (C) May you pass the salt?
 (D) No mistake.

246. (A) Carol asked, "How are you feeling?"
 (B) The flock of birds was singing this morning.
 (C) San Diego is a beautiful city.
 (D) No mistake.

247. (A) Who is going to bring cups to the picnic?
 (B) Did you request two tickets?
 (C) The girl threw the ball.
 (D) No mistake.

248. (A) I told them I was going to be late.
 (B) You and I are on the class government.
 (C) Hello, Nancy said, how are you?
 (D) No mistake.

249. (A) The Girl Scouts are hiking in the mountains.
 (B) Their going to the beach this afternoon.
 (C) Dr. Hysmith gave a lecture at the university.
 (D) No mistake.

250. (A) Alex said, "I'm getting bored."
     (B) May I go out?
     (C) What will happen next, I wonder?
     (D) No mistake.

251. (A) I prefer apples to pears; they are sweeter.
     (B) Janet asked if she might play with the puppy.
     (C) The program begins at 8:00, right?
     (D) No mistake.

252. (A) Don't lay down on the sofa.
     (B) Have you met the new coach?
     (C) Winter recess starts on Thursday.
     (D) No mistake.

253. (A) Jamal exclaimed, "That's a great book!"
     (B) How much is your monthly bus pass?
     (C) Who's shoe is this?
     (D) No mistake.

254. (A) Kevin is the oldest person in our class.
     (B) The duty was given to Frank and I.
     (C) Let's visit the museum on our field trip.
     (D) No mistake.

255. (A) Lisa's grandparents live in Alabama.
     (B) George remarked, "she is the best player on the team."
     (C) The Redwood Forest is a beautiful place to visit.
     (D) No mistake.

256. (A) My mother is a lawyer.
     (B) What time did Roberto leave?
     (C) How are you feeling today.
     (D) No mistake.

257. (A) The Browns bought a new car.
     (B) How old is your cousin Mark?
     (C) The dog lied down in the corner.
     (D) No mistake.

258. (A) The teacher asked we to bring our projects home.
   (B) Did you notice the flowers blooming in the yard?
   (C) How long have you been working in the garage?
   (D) No mistake.

259. (A) Amy said, "I love reading to my little sister."
   (B) Cats sometimes catch mice.
   (C) It was the first time he had ever went horseback riding.
   (D) No mistake.

260. (A) Mayor Rivera has an office near the park.
   (B) Laura, please keep your dog on a leash.
   (C) Uncle Dan told us to wait in the car.
   (D) No mistake.

261. (A) There is a bicycle path along the river.
   (B) Everyone did their homework.
   (C) Veronica will join the Navy in November.
   (D) No mistake.

262. (A) We're all going to the Rocky Mountains this summer.
   (B) Have you ever seen the sunset?
   (C) Helen asked, "What are we having for dinner?"
   (D) No mistake.

263. (A) When the show was over, everyone leaves.
   (B) Our neighbor helped us shovel the driveway.
   (C) It's time for the show to start.
   (D) No mistake.

264. (A) Neither Kate nor Rachel has walked the dog.
   (B) You should of brought your lunch.
   (C) I have many more books than you.
   (D) No mistake.

265. (A) Jane asked, "How much did you pay for that pen?"
   (B) The womens' notebooks are on the table.
   (C) The sun rose at 5:00 this morning.
   (D) No mistake.

266. (A) The football players wear uniforms.
     (B) Mrs. Kahn is learning the children to swim.
     (C) I am glad that you're feeling better.
     (D) No mistake.

267. (A) Thomas is attending the University of california.
     (B) Ellen asked me to help her with her errands.
     (C) Everyone wants her drawing to win the prize.
     (D) No mistake.

268. (A) David didn't know whether he should call his mother or his father.
     (B) Dad put to much detergent in the washing machine.
     (C) If I wanted to go, I would have bought a ticket
     (D) No mistake.

269. (A) Charles asked Greg and me to play catch with him.
     (B) When we go camping, we can see the Big Dipper.
     (C) Dinner is ready, but the children are not home yet.
     (D) No mistake.

270. (A) When will the cake be ready?
     (B) Before the blizzard stopped, our car was covered in snow.
     (C) Me and Christine are skateboarding in the park.
     (D) No mistake.

271. (A) The baby is drinking her milk now.
     (B) If you would like to go, please tell me.
     (C) Shawn ran home quick.
     (D) No mistake.

272. (A) May I open my presents now?
     (B) Actually, Jim doesn't like to go to the beach.
     (C) I can't do nothing about it now.
     (D) No mistake.

273. (A) There are too many people on the subway.
     (B) Nelson is more talkative than Ramon.
     (C) The concert is Saturday, May 5.
     (D) No mistake.

274. (A) If you would like to go, please let me know.
     (B) Pamela is the faster of the three athletes.
     (C) I do not agree that Mike is stronger.
     (D) No mistake.

275. (A) When the bell rings, please turn off the oven.
     (B) Most cats like to drink milk.
     (C) He has fewer money than his brother.
     (D) No mistake.

276. (A) Herself has gone to the library.
     (B) Kim has more toys than Fran.
     (C) Joseph will leave for West Point tomorrow.
     (D) No mistake.

277. (A) We arrived on time at grand central station in New York City.
     (B) There is a spot on the glass.
     (C) My sister-in-law is coming to visit this week.
     (D) No mistake.

278. (A) The dog growled angrily at the letter carrier.
     (B) Alice said; "Let's all watch the movie tonight."
     (C) They would have waited, if they had known you were coming.
     (D) No mistake.

Spelling

Directions: For questions 279–288, choose the sentence that contains a spelling error. If there is no error, select choice (D).

279. (A) Our school cafateria always opens at 8:00 in the morning.
     (B) His proposal for a new park was very interesting.
     (C) The secretary typed very quickly.
     (D) No mistake.

280. (A) She described the circus in great detail.
     (B) Please turn in your composation on time.
     (C) If you work efficiently, you will finish on time.
     (D) No mistake.

281. (A) Do not criticize what you do not understand.
    (B) We waited impatiently for an answer.
    (C) The plane departed at 9:00.
    (D) No mistake.

282. (A) I think that author is a genius.
    (B) Dr. Alvarez is very successful.
    (C) The jury promised not to be prejediced.
    (D) No mistake.

283. (A) I wish it were possible to live forever.
    (B) Turn in your assignment imediately.
    (C) We visit the lake frequently.
    (D) No mistake.

284. (A) The art exhibition is downtown.
    (B) Each player has a speciffic role.
    (C) Tom and Sam argued about the election.
    (D) No mistake.

285. (A) The nurse said Mary is running a temperture.
    (B) General Radisson is the commander.
    (C) The tickets are inexpensive.
    (D) No mistake.

286. (A) I hope the delivery will arrive by noon.
    (B) Do you recognize that girl?
    (C) The sports arena is gigantic.
    (D) No mistake.

287. (A) The submarine rose to the surfice.
    (B) Oil is a natural resource.
    (C) The scientist examined the data.
    (D) No mistake.

288. (A) Please try not to interupt me when I'm speaking.
    (B) Are you sure this information is accurate?
    (C) This knitting pattern is very complicated.
    (D) No mistake.

Composition

Directions: For questions 289–298, follow the directions for each question.

289. Choose the best word to join the thoughts together.

I would like to take a walk; _____ I'm afraid
it is going to rain.

(A) however,

(B) moreover,

(C) also,

(D) none of these

290. Choose the words that best complete the following sentence.

The museum's new exhibit is _____

(A) a display dating back from the 12th century of antique armor.

(B) from the 12th century of display of antique armor dating back to then.

(C) dating back from the 12th century a display of antique armor.

(D) a display of antique armor dating back from the 12th century.

291. Choose the group of words that best completes the sentence.

When we have enough time, _____.

(A) swimming is what we do.

(B) we like to swim.

(C) we are swimming.

(D) to swim is what we like.

292. Which of these best fits under the topic "Bicycle Maintenance"?

(A) You should care for your bicycle if you want it to perform at its best.

(B) Henry Ford's first invention was a bicycle with an engine.

(C) It is easiest to change bicycle gears when you are pedaling.

(D) none of these

293. Choose the word to begin the following sentence.

_____ some feel that the high cost of space exploration is not worth the expense, others argue that it is an important expression of humankind's desire for knowledge.

(A) However,

(B) Importantly,

(C) Therefore,

(D) Although

294. Which of these expresses the idea most clearly?

    (A) Before leaving the house, we must turn off the lights.

    (B) Leaving the house, first we must turn off the lights.

    (C) To turn off the lights before leaving the house.

    (D) Turning off the lights before leaving the house is what we must do.

295. Choose the best word or words to join the thoughts together.

    Skiing is not an easy sport; _____ it requires skill, dexterity and talent.

    (A) but also

    (B) in addition

    (C) and moreover

    (D) none of these

296. Which sentence does *not* belong in the paragraph?

    (1) Though his brother liked to sleep late, Tom preferred to wake early. (2) He enjoyed the quiet calm of early morning. (3) He would often slip downstairs while the rest of the family was sleeping, stretch out on the sofa, and stare out the window while the sun came up. (4) Sometimes, he would make pancakes for dinner.

    (A) sentence 1

    (B) sentence 2

    (C) sentence 3

    (D) sentence 4

297. Which topic is best for a one paragraph theme?

    (A) The Politics of Western Africa

    (B) How to Make a Great Cup of Tea

    (C) Flowers of North America

    (D) None of these

298. Where should the following sentence be placed in the paragraph below?

    These lava spills, in addition to volcanic eruptions may have together killed off the dinosaurs.

    (1) Scientists have long argued over the causes leading to the extinction of the dinosaurs. (2) One common view holds that a combination of catastrophic events doomed the dinosaurs. (3) For example, a meteor shower hitting the Earth could have cracked the Earth's crust and allowed molten lava to spill across the land.

    (A) between sentences 1 and 2

    (B) between sentences 2 and 3

    (C) before sentence 1

    (D) after sentence 3

ANSWER KEY

Verbal Skills		Quantitative Skills
1. C	34. D	61. B
2. C	35. A	62. C
3. A	36. C	63. D
4. B	37. A	64. D
5. B	38. A	65. D
6. A	39. D	66. D
7. D	40. A	67. A
8. A	41. C	68. A
9. A	42. D	69. B
10. C	43. A	70. C
11. A	44. C	71. C
12. A	45. D	72. A
13. D	46. D	73. D
14. D	47. A	74. D
15. A	48. A	75. C
16. A	49. B	76. A
17. A	50. D	77. D
18. A	51. D	78. D
19. A	52. C	79. A
20. A	53. B	80. B
21. D	54. D	81. B
22. B	55. B	82. C
23. D	56. C	83. C
24. C	57. B	84. C
25. C	58. D	85. D
26. C	59. A	86. A
27. D	60. B	87. B
28. C		88. D
29. A		89. B
30. B		90. C
31. A		91. B
32. D		92. B
33. C		93. A
		94. A

95. C
96. C
97. A
98. C
99. A
100. A
101. D
102. B
103. A
104. A
105. D
106. C
107. C
108. D
109. D
110. C
111. B
112. B

READING
Comprehension

113. D
114. B
115. B
116. A
117. C
118. D
119. B
120. C
121. A
122. B
123. A
124. B
125. B
126. A
127. B
128. B
129. C

130. B
131. A
132. D
133. D
134. A
135. C
136. A
137. A
138. B
139. C
140. A
141. B
142. D
143. B
144. C
145. C
146. D
147. A
148. D
149. D
150. A
151. C
152. B

Vocabulary

153. C
154. C
155. A
156. A
157. C
158. B
159. A
160. B
161. D
162. A
163. B
164. C
165. A

166. C
167. D
168. C
169. A
170. B
171. A
172. C
173. C
174. D

MATHEMATICS
Concepts

175. D
176. A
177. B
178. B
179. B
180. C
181. B
182. A
183. B
184. A
185. D
186. C
187. A
188. A
189. A
190. D
191. A
192. C
193. D
194. D
195. A
196. A
197. A
198. C

Problem Solving

199. B
200. D
201. D
202. A
203. B
204. D
205. B
206. C
207. B
208. D
209. A
210. C
211. B
212. C
213. A
214. D
215. C
216. D
217. B
218. B
219. A
220. D
221. D
222. B
223. C
224. A
225. C
226. A
227. C
228. C
229. B
230. A
231. C
232. A
233. B
234. D
235. D
236. A
237. B
238. D

LANGUAGE

Usage

239. C
240. B
241. A
242. C
243. D
244. C
245. C
246. D
247. D
248. C
249. B
250. D
251. D
252. A
253. C
254. B
255. B
256. C
257. C
258. A
259. C
260. D
261. B
262. D
263. A
264. B
265. B
266. B
267. A
268. B
269. D
270. C
271. C
272. C
273. D
274. B
275. C
276. A
277. A
278. B

Spelling

279. A
280. B
281. D
282. C
283. B
284. B
285. A
286. D
287. A
288. A

Composition

289. A
290. D
291. B
292. A
293. D
294. A
295. D
296. D
297. B
298. D

ANSWERS AND EXPLANATIONS

Verbal Skills

1. C

Angry is an emotion. The other choices are verbs with similar meanings.

2. C

Hopeful, optimistic, and confident are synonyms. Cordial means gracious or friendly.

3. A

Giant means extremely large, miniature means extremely small.

4. B

Because the first two statements are true and Pat lives closer to the bus stop than Allan, Pat cannot live farther from the bus stop than Mark.

5. B

To permit means to give permission or to allow.

6. A

Create a bridge to link the first pair of words, then use it to think of the missing word in the second pair. A pen is a tool that uses ink. What is a tool that uses paint? A paint-brush. Look at the answer choices. Choice (A), *brush*, fits.

7. D

While all four terms are occurrences, accident is the only term that means an unfortunate or unforeseen occurrence. Event, affair, and occasion are planned occurrences.

8. A

A lake is made up of water and a glacier is made up of ice.

9. A

Weather is the general classification. The other choices are specific types of weather.

10. C

A spider is an arachnid. Even if you are not familiar with the term arachnid, you could make an intelligent guess by eliminating the other answer choices. Is a spider a feline? Well, a feline is a cat, so the answer would be no. Is a spider a reptile? Snakes and lizards are reptiles, but not spiders, so this can be eliminated. Is a spider a phobia? A phobia is a huge fear. You might have a huge fear of spiders, but a spider itself is not a phobia. So, the only answer left is (C), arachnid.

11. A

Conceited means proud in an unfriendly manner, so *arrogant* is the correct answer.

12. A

A button is used to close a jacket and a lace is used to close or secure a shoe.

13. D

Water feeds a flower and birdseed feeds a bird.

14. D

Optimistic means full of hope; sage means full of wisdom.

15. A

From the first two statements it is certain that Christine is shorter than Joon.

16. A

Abridged means shortened, so an abridged book is short.

17. A

Complex means intricate or complicated.

18. A

Although rusty is an adjective you might use to describe corrosion, corrode most nearly means destroy.

19. **A**

We ring a bell to attract attention and we knock on a door to attract attention.

20. **A**

Actors are led by a director and players are led by a coach.

21. **D**

A variation is a difference or a slightly modified or changed version. Though variations can be used for the purpose of comparison, *comparison* doesn't define as closely what a variation is. Remember, you're looking for the word that is closest in meaning to the word in the question. *Classification* is a distracter meant to trick you by including the *-tion* from *variation*.

22. **B**

The first two statements indicate that Frank is the most outgoing. Therefore, the third statement is false.

23. **D**

Postponed means moved to a later time, so a postponed appointment is delayed.

24. **C**

There is no way to know for certain if C is longer than D.

25. **C**

A unanimous vote is one that is completely agreed upon, or undisputed.

26. **C**

A practical person is sensible.

27. **D**

A director is one individual; the other choices are groups.

28. **C**

To abandon means to leave.

29. **A**

A dynamic speaker is full of life, or energetic.

30. **B**

A penniless person is without a penny, or poor.

31. **A**

A folder holds papers and a drawer holds clothes.

32. **D**

Sense is the general classification. The other choices are examples of senses.

33. **C**

All *googles* are *moogles*, but not all *moogles* must be *googles*, so some *moogles* might wear glasses.

34. **D**

Money is the general classification. The other choices are types of money.

35. **A**

To reduce means to lessen or decrease; the opposite is enlarge.

36. **C**

A ladle is used for soup, a shovel is used for sand.

37. **A**

To disperse means to scatter; the opposite is gather.

38. **A**

Because the first two statements are true and hiking trail L is longer than K and K is longer than J, L is longer than J as well.

39. **D**

To hamper means hinder or interfere with; the opposite is assist.

40. **A**

Aptitude is ability; the opposite is inability.

41. **C**

An agenda creates a plan for a meeting, and a program creates a plan for a play.

42. D

Car is the general classification. The other choices are parts of a car.

43. A

Sturdy means strong; the opposite is flimsy.

44. C

Gullible means naïve or easily deceived; the opposite is incredulous.

45. D

Rotund means round; the other choices are synonyms for thin.

46. D

A rag is not a type of container.

47. A

Genuine means real.

48. A

Content means satisfied or happy; the opposite is restless.

49. B

Because the first two statements are true and magazines are longer than catalogues, magazines cannot be the shortest of the types of writing.

50. D

All the other choices are types of boats, a submarine is different from a boat.

51. D

To replenish means to provide more; the opposite is deplete.

52. C

While the first two statements are true, they do not provide any information about Jaylene. Therefore, we cannot be certain whether she blocks more goals than Ellen or not.

53. B

To enlist means to join; the opposite is resign.

54. D

Robust is strong or sturdy; all the other choices are synonyms for breakable.

55. B

Because the first two statements are true and the small pizza is not as big as the jumbo, the third statement must be false.

56. C

A saucer is a plate; all the other choices are types of drink containers.

57. B

To renovate means to renew.

58. D

Gem is the general classification; all the other choices are types of gems.

59. A

Pacific means calm; the other words are all synonyms for energetic.

60. B

Because the first two statements are true and Mr. Thomas has more grandchildren than Mr. Blake, the third statement must be false.

Quantitative Skills

61. B

Begin by finding 10% of 100: $.10 \times 100 = 10$. Then, add 7: $10 + 7 = 17$.

62. C

The pattern in this series is made by adding 6 to each number; $33 + 6 = 39$.

63. D

The pattern in this series is made by subtracting 5 from each number; $36 - 5 = 31$.

64. D

Determine the amount of money for (a), (b), and (c). Then, calculate each answer choice to see which is correct. (a) is 10 cents, (b) is 50 cents, and (c) is 12 cents.

(A) (10 cents) plus (12 cents) is greater than (50 cents) is incorrect

(B) (50 cents) is equal to (10 cents) is incorrect

(C) (10 cents) is more than (12 cents) is incorrect

(D) (50 cents) minus (10 cents) is greater than (12 cents) is correct

65. D

5 divided by 8 (b) equals .625; .26 × 3.4 (c) equals .884. Clearly .884 (C) is greater than either (a) or (b), so answer (D) is correct. And (c) is less than (a) plus (b), which is why answer (A) is incorrect.

66. D

The cube of 4 is 64; 64 ÷ 8 = 8.

67. A

The sum of 12 + 8 + 15 + 6 + 29 = 70; 70 ÷ 5 = 14; $\frac{1}{2}$ of 14 = 7.

68. A

Count the number of small triangles shaded within each larger triangle and compare each choice. (a) only has two sections shaded and (b) only has one.

69. B

The pattern in this series is to subtract 3 from each term. 85 − 3 = 82.

70. C

Determine the amounts for (a), (b), and (c) and test each alternative to see which is correct. (a) 20% of 60 is 12, (b) 60% of 20 is 12, (c) 60% of 20% is .12.

(A) 12 is greater than 12 or .12 is not correct.

(B) 12, 12 and .12 are equal is not correct.

(C) 12 is greater than .12 is correct.

(D) 12 is equal to .12 and smaller than 12 is not correct.

71. C

The pattern in this series is to take $\frac{1}{2}$ of the previous term to get the next. One-half of 30 is 15.

72. A

The pattern in this series is +6, −2, +1 and so on.

73. D

Start this problem from the end and work backward.

First find $\frac{3}{5}$ of 75:

$$\frac{3}{5} \times \frac{75}{1} = 45$$

But remember, we need 3 more than 45, or 45 + 3 = 48.

So what number subtracted from 62 equals 48? The quickest way to find out: Subtract 48 from 62, and see what you get. 62 − 48 = 14.

Or, plug in each answer choice to see which one is correct.

Does 62 − 48 = 48? NO

Does 62 − 41 = 48? NO

Does 62 − 45 = 48? NO

Does 62 − 14 = 48? YES

74. D

Begin with $\frac{3}{4}$ of 24: $\frac{3}{4} \times \frac{24}{1} = 18$. Then, 8 + 18 = 26

75. C

First, determine the amounts of (a), (b), and (c). Then, test each alternative to see which is true. Remember to do the operations within the parenthesis first. (a) is 10, (b) is 31, (c) is 21.

(A) 21 is greater than 31 is incorrect.

(B) 31 is less than 10 and 21 is incorrect.

(C) 10 plus 21 is equal to 31 is correct.

(D) 10 is greater than 21 and less than 31 is incorrect.

76. A

The pattern in the series is made by adding 8 to each number; 252 + 8 = 260.

77. D

Count the squares in (a), (b), and (c). Then, test each alternative to see which is true. (a) and (c) each have 5 squares and (b) has 10.

78. D

Determine how much of each figure is shaded. Then, test each alternative to see which is true. Each circle has two equally-sized sections shaded, so they are shaded equally.

79. A

The pattern in this series is −5, −4, −3, −2 and so on. Therefore, 96 − 1 = 95.

80. B

Determine $\frac{1}{5}$ of 80: $\frac{1}{5} \times \frac{80}{1} = 16$. Multiply this result by 6 to find the answer. $16 \times 6 = 96$.

81. B

The pattern in this series is +4, with the result alternately expressed as an Arabic, then a Roman numeral; $14 + 4 = 18$.

82. C

Determine the amounts for (a), (b), and (c). Test each alternative to find the one that is true. (a) is 3, (b) is 8, (c) is 6.

(A) 8 and 6 are equal is incorrect.

(B) 3 and 8 are each greater than 6 is incorrect.

(C) 6 is greater than 3 is correct.

(D) 3, 8, and 6 are equal is incorrect.

83. C

First, find $5 \times 4 = 20$; 20 is one-half of what number? Double the result to find the answer: $20 \times 2 = 40$.

84. C

Each box has 2 sections shaded out of six, which is equal to $\frac{1}{3}$. Therefore, only (C) can be true.

85. D

First, determine the product of 5 and 3: $5 \times 3 = 15$

$2 \times 15 = 30$

Now, you need to find out which number plus 7 equals 30.

$30 = x + 7$

$30 - 7 = 23$

86. A

The pattern in this series is −4, +3, −4, +3 and so on. Therefore, the next term is $12 + 3 = 15$.

87. B

You can change (a), (b), and (c) so that they are all in the same form—either all fractions, decimals, or percents. However, knowing common decimal, fraction, and percent equivalents will help you do questions like these with greater ease. (a), (b), and (c) are all equal.

(A) 25% is greater than $\frac{1}{4}$ which is greater than .25 is incorrect.

(B) 25%, $\frac{1}{4}$, and .25 are equal is correct.

(C) .25 is greater than $\frac{1}{4}$ but less than 25% is incorrect.

(D) 25% and $\frac{1}{4}$ are each more than .25 is incorrect.

88. D

You can figure out this problem with algebra. First, translate the sentence into an equation.

$\frac{2}{5} \times x = 2 \times 20$

$\frac{2}{5} \times x = 40$

$x = \frac{40}{1} \times \frac{5}{2}$

$x = 100$

Another method is to plug in the answer choices to see which one works.

$\frac{2}{5} = \frac{40}{x}$

$\frac{2}{5} = \frac{40}{100}$

89. B

The pattern in this series is ×5, −2, ×5, −2, and so on. Therefore, the next term is $3 \times 5 = 15$.

90. **C**

The pattern in this series is +5, +1, +1, +5, +1, +1, and so on. Therefore, the next term is 20 + 5 = 25.

91. **B**

The line drawn from point A to point D divides this square into two right triangles. One of which is triangle ABC. In this triangle, AB and AC are legs and AD is the hypotenuse of this right triangle. The length of the hypotenuse will always be the longest side of a right triangle, so the length of AD is greater than both AB and AC.

92. **B**

Begin by subtracting 2 from 20. This number divided by 6 will provide the answer.

$20 - 2 = 18$

$18 \div 6 = 3$

93. **A**

The pattern in this series is ×2, +1, ×2, +1 and so on. Therefore, the next term is 50 + 1 = 51.

94. **A**

Determine the amounts for (a), (b), and (c) then choose the best alternative. Be sure to do the operations in parentheses first. (a) is 10, (b) is 6, and (c) is 10. Therefore, (a) and (c) are equal.

95. **C**

The pattern in this series is +2, −3, +2, −3 and so on. Therefore, the next two terms will be 73 + 2 = 75 and 75 − 3 = 72.

96. **C**

Because the figure is a cube, all edges and sides are equal. When a diagonal line is drawn across one side like AG, it forms a hypotenuse of a right triangle whose length is longer than the length of either of its sides. Because the sides of the cube are all equal, AG must also be longer than DE.

97. **A**

This can be done with algebra. If Z is the number you're looking for:

$Z \div 6 = 3 + 9$

$Z \div 6 = 12$

$Z = 12 \times 6$

$Z = 72$

98. **C**

Perform multiplication as indicated to arrive at these values:

(a) $6a + 6b$

(b) $6a + 6b$

(c) $6a + 6b + b = 6a + 7b$

It can now be seen that (a) and (b) are equal and that (c) is greater than both of them. Therefore, (C) is the best answer if a and b are greater than zero.

99. **A**

The pattern in this series is +3, ×2, +3, ×2 and so on. Therefore, the next term is 26 + 3 = 29.

100. **A**

To begin, find $\frac{1}{5}$ of 40. This is the same as 40 divided by 5, which equals 8. If a is the number you are looking for:

$12 - a = 8$

$a = 4$

101. **D**

The pattern for the letters in this series is made by using sequential letters in the alphabet, alternately uppercase or lowercase. The pattern for the numbers is made by using +2, +2, and so on. Therefore, the next term is E10.

102. **B**

Determine the values for each section of the chart. A = 2, B = 4, C = 6, and D = 8. Then, choose the correct alternative. Since 6 − 2 = 4 is true, the answer is choice (B).

103. **A**

This can be set up as an algebraic equation. If b is the number you are looking for:

$b = \frac{2}{3}(15) - 7$

$b = \frac{30}{3} - 7$

$b = 10 - 7$

$b = 3$

104. **A**

The pattern in this series is: ×4, −8, ×4, −8 and so on. Therefore, the next term is 8 × 4 = 32.

105. **D**

Determine the amounts for (a), (b), and (c). Then, decide which alternative is true.

(a) 2 × 2 = 4
(b) 3 × 3 × 3 = 27
(c) 4 × 4 × 4 = 64

Therefore, (c) > (b) > (a).

106. **C**

The pattern is made by subtracting $1\frac{1}{4}$ from each number. Therefore, the next term is $5\frac{1}{4} - 1\frac{1}{4} = 4$.

107. **C**

First, figure out $\frac{1}{4}$ of 60. This number multiplied by 6 will provide the answer.

$$\frac{1}{4} \times 60 = \frac{60}{4} = 15$$
$$15 \times 6 = 90$$

108. **D**

The pattern in this series is +1, +3, −2, +1, +3, −2, and so on. Therefore, the next three terms are 19 + 1 = 20, 20 + 3 = 23, and 23 − 2 = 21.

109. **D**

This can be set up as an algebraic equation. If y is the number you are looking for:

$$6 + \frac{1}{8}y = 2 \times 7$$
$$6 + \frac{1}{8}y = 14$$
$$\frac{1}{8}y = 14 - 6$$
$$\frac{1}{8}y = 8$$
$$y = 8 \times 8$$
$$y = 64$$

110. **C**

Test each alternative to find the correct one. To find the perimeter add the length of all four sides. Since the figure is a square, each of the sides measure 3 inches; 3 + 3 + 3 + 3 = 12 inches.

111. **B**

This can be set up as an algebraic equation. If z is the number you are looking for:

$$z = 8 + \frac{4}{5} \times 10$$
$$z = 8 + \frac{40}{5}$$
$$z = 8 + 8$$
$$z = 16$$

112. **B**

First, find the cube of 3 and then subtract four from the result.

$$3 \times 3 \times 3 = 27 - 4 = 23$$

READING

Comprehension

113. **D**

Paragraph 2 begins with the sentence, *Lepidoptera is one of the largest and most diverse insect orders.* Therefore, the answer is (D).

114. **B**

You might have missed this detail from the first sentence that states that *insects can be classified into fourteen different groupings.* Therefore, choice (B) is the answer.

115. **B**

Skim the passage for any mention of butterflies and moths to answer this question. The second sentence states, *butterflies and moths belong to the Lepidoptera order.*

116. **A**

Because of the nature of the information, this passage would most likely be found in a scientific journal.

117. **C**

This is a detail question. Find and reread the sentence in the passage with the keywords *butterfly species*, and *worldwide*. It states that there are 28,000 species.

118. **D**

Diverse most nearly means varied. Read the context or sentences in and around where the word is found. They discuss difference, which is an important clue in decoding the word's meaning. *Flying* and *winged* are trick answers because although they have to do with butterflies, they do not define diverse. Multiple means many and does not really imply difference.

119. **B**

This is an inferential question. Though not specifically stated, the answer can be assumed based on the words *so far* in sentence 7.

120. **C**

The word *comparing* is a clue that you are looking for a difference. The end of the passage discusses the *important differences*. One of these differences is that butterflies have *brightly colored wings*.

121. **A**

In this passage, distinguished means recognizable. If you don't know the answer, try using each of the answer choices in the sentence: are butterflies recognizable by their wings? Are they respectable by their wings? Are they similar by their wings? Are they organized by their wings? The best choice is (A).

122. **B**

Although each species may be beautiful, in this passage, unique most nearly means different.

123. **A**

The question directs you to the first two paragraphs of the passage. If you skim them, you will notice words such as *glimpse*, *aroma*, and *crackling*. These words describe sights and sounds of the battle. This answer can be verified by eliminating choices (B), (C), and (D). The commanders, weapons, and soldiers are not described in detail.

124. **B**

If you don't know what *skirmish* means, read the sentence in which it is used to understand the context. The sentence states that it is not *a skirmish, but rather…a battle.* The word *battle* is used to replace *skirmish*, so choice (B) is the answer.

125. **B**

Think about who might be writing this passage. Because there aren't many historical facts, you can eliminate choice (A). Choices (C) and (D) are not likely authors based on the information written in the passage, nor by the tone of the passage. Therefore, choice (B) is the best answer.

126. **A**

This question is asking you to make an inference, or guess, about the passage. In other words, the answer isn't stated directly in the passage. If you read the first paragraph again, it mentions that the British *far outnumber the man's own regiment*. Therefore, the battle was probably won by the British.

127. **B**

Reread the part of the passage that mentions lowering a musket. This information is found at the end of the first paragraph, and states: *A general gives the command, and the man lowers his musket to aim.* Therefore, choice (B) is the correct answer.

128. **B**

The man was most likely afraid when he saw the number of opposing troops.

129. **C**

Always read the context in which a word is used so that you don't choose the most obvious answer. In this case, you may think smart means intelligent. It does, but that is not its meaning in this passage. The sentence says, *the man's eyes smart and his vision dims.* Now you may be tempted to choose fog, because the man's vision is dimmed. However, the correct choice is (C); to smart also means to hurt.

130. **B**

The end of the passage talks about the re-enactors, so you should read this part again. The last sentence says that *reenactors feel that demonstrating what the War for Independence was really like* [is] *a way to bring history alive*. Therefore, choice (B) is the best answer.

131. **A**

Though the author mentions these other elements, the general topic is making history come alive through reenacting battles.

132. **D**

According to the last paragraph, reenactors enjoy what they do.

133. **D**

Skim the passage for any mention of methane gas. The second paragraph states that *wastes in the dump…create methane gas when they decompose*. Therefore, decomposition is the best answer.

134. **A**

If you are not sure of the answer, skim over the passage and think of the overall tone the author uses in this passage. Nothing in the passage conveys her affection for the dump, and the passage is matter of fact, not sarcastic. Although you might be tempted to choose *disgust*, because of the subject matter, that is not the author's tone. The author appreciates the usefulness of garbage dumps.

135. **C**

There is nothing in the passage that suggests that garbage dumps are clean or that they power automobiles, so eliminate choices (A) and (D). Choice (B) is a distracter, the passage says that *methane gas* (not garbage dumps) is *used to power electric generators*, so the answer is (C).

136. **A**

Since this is a detail question, you should look for the part of the passage that discusses the five-megawatt generator. The passage states: *A five-megawatt generator could produce 42 million kilowatt-hours per year* [which is] *enough electricity to supply about 3,200 homes with power*.

137. **A**

Significant most nearly means sizeable. You can test the meaning of the word by replacing the word significant with the answer choices. Only (A) makes sense in the context of the passage.

138. **B**

You may think you know the answer without referring to the passage. However, you should check your answer in the passage. The end of paragraph 2 says that *methane is the same gas sold by natural gas utility companies.* This supports answer choice (B).

139. **C**

This answer is supported by the last sentence of the passage. It says, *there's treasure in the trash.*

140. **A**

The last paragraph says: *Methane that is released directly into the atmosphere can contribute to global warming.* Therefore, an added benefit of recovering methane gas from garbage dumps is that it prevents the contribution to global warming.

141. **B**

Careful, choice (A) is a distracter. Although something that is decomposing might smell, decompose most nearly means rot.

142. **D**

The main topic of the passage is that garbage dumps produce methane. Therefore, the best answer is (D).

143. **B**

Because this passage does not contain any instructions or excessive medical detail, you can eliminate choices (A) and (D). It is also unlikely that this is a letter to a friend, so you can eliminate choice (C). Therefore, the answer is choice (B).

144. **C**

You should refer back to the passage if you don't know the answer. The first sentence says that bloodletting is *misguided by modern standards* and the end of the passage states: *as modern doctors know,* [bloodletting] *does not have restorative powers.* The best answer is (C).

145. C

There is nothing in the passage to support choices (A), (B), and (D), so you can eliminate them. The passage does support choice (C), so it is the correct answer.

146. D

This is a detail question, the only group mentioned in the passage are barbers. Reread the end of the second paragraph which mentions that *medieval doctors and barbers believed they were helping their patients by causing them to bleed.*

147. A

The question is testing your vocabulary. Misguided means using poor judgment, therefore wearing small shoes to keep your feet from growing is also using poor judgment.

148. D

This is an inference question. It is never stated in the passage that modern doctors think that bloodletting is unsafe, however the passage does say that doctors know that *draining a person's blood does not have restorative powers.*

149. D

The middle of the passage focuses on reverberation, which the author describes as the *most important factor in acoustic design* at the end of the passage.

150. A

Choice (A) is the correct answer because the author says that *few of us realize the complex process that goes into designing the acoustics of concert and lecture halls.*

151. C

According to the passage, *too little reverberation can make sound thin and weak.*

152. B

The final sentence of the passage says that *the most important factor in acoustic design is the reverberation time,* which makes (B) correct.

Vocabulary

153. C

To predict means to tell in advance, or foretell.

154. C

Mutual means exchanged, given and received, or common.

155. A

A gap is a hole, opening, or break.

156. A

Frank means clear, plain, or honest.

157. C

To allege means to assert without proof, or to imply.

158. B

A consequence is an outcome, a result, or an effect.

159. A

To confine means to imprison, to shut in, or to restrict.

160. B

To delete means to remove, to cancel, or to erase.

161. D

Glossy means slick, smooth, or shiny.

162. A

Outrageous means beyond reason, extravagant, extraordinary.

163. B

Sophisticated means worldly, refined, or cosmopolitan. Learned means educated which is not the same thing. Although we may think that sophisticated women are fashionable, this does not define sophisticated. The word *wealthy* is often associated with the word *sophisticated,* but it does not define the word.

164. **C**

A proposal is an idea, a plan, or a suggestion.

165. **A**

Radical means extreme, revolutionary, or subversive.

166. **C**

To interrogate means to examine, to ask, or to question.

167. **D**

Plausible means acceptable, credible, or valid.

168. **C**

Access means acceptance, admission, or entrance.

169. **A**

To compose means to create, to author, or to write.

170. **B**

Ostentatious means showy or conspicuous.

171. **A**

Essential means vital, required, or necessary.

172. **C**

An obstacle is a block, a barrier, or a difficulty.

173. **C**

Precise means accurate.

174. **D**

Gracious means warm as in friendly, not warm as in temperature.

MATHEMATICS
Concepts

175. **D**

A *rhomboid* is a type of quadrilateral; it has four sides, not three as in a triangle.

176. **A**

The symbol in the question stands for intersection. The intersection of two or more sets is the set of elements they share in common. In this case, the common elements are 1 and 6.

177. **B**

This problem requires you to round off the given number to the place one digit to the right of the decimal point, the tenth's column. Since the number in the hundredth's place is 9, round up to 75.9.

178. **B**

Start with the operations in the parentheses first:

$(-3)^2 = -3 \times -3 = 9$

Then, continue with the operations outside the parentheses:

$3 \times 9 = 27$

179. **B**

The digit farthest to the right is in the hundredth's place. This means $.12 = \frac{12}{100}$.

180. **C**

A straight line represents a straight angle of 180 degrees. An angle of 135 is given, so the measure of the interior angle must be 45 to complete the line. $180 - 135 = 45$. Knowing that all the angles in a triangle added together equal 180 degrees:

$$m\angle x + 45 + 35 = 180$$
$$m\angle x = 180 - 80 = 100.$$

181. **B**

When multiplying a number by 10, 100, 1,000, etc., move the decimal point one place to the right for each zero in the multiplier. In this example, 1,000 has three zeros, so the decimal point would be moved three places to the right.

182. **A**

Consecutive numbers are numbers that follow one after another, in order.

183. **B**

The formula for finding the diameter of a circle is 2 times the radius; $2 \times 2 = 4$ m.

184. **A**

100 centimeters = 1 meter. Each centimeter is $\frac{1}{100}$ of a meter.

185. **D**

State $\frac{25}{3}$ as a decimal number.

$\frac{25}{3} \approx 8.3$.

An integer is a whole number. Between 8.3 and 12.8 there are 4 whole numbers {9, 10, 11, and 12}.

186. **C**

To figure out whether your product is positive or negative, count the number of negatives you had to start. If you had an odd number of negatives, the product is negative.

187. **A**

$11^2 = 121$; $12^2 = 144$. Therefore, the square root of 122 is between 11 and 12.

188. **A**

When working with scientific notation, the exponent represents the number of places to move the decimal point in the multiplier. If the base of the exponent is 10, the decimal point moves to the right. If it is $\frac{1}{10}$, the decimal point moves to the left.

189. **A**

Since the ratio is 3:1, let $3x$ = the larger number and $1x$ the smaller number.

$3x + 1x = 52$

$\qquad 4x = 52$

$\qquad\ x = \frac{52}{4}$

$x = 13$, which is the smaller number.

So, $3(13) = 39$, which is the larger number.

190. **D**

To make the comparison more readily, we convert the fractions to decimals

$\frac{1}{5} = .20, \frac{4}{9} = .44$

Since $\frac{1}{3}$ has a value of .33, $\frac{1}{3}$ has a value between $\frac{1}{5}$ and $\frac{4}{9}$.

191. **A**

The sector *AOB* (which is shaded) is 60 degrees out of a total of 360 degrees, $\frac{60}{360}$ or $\frac{1}{6}$ of the circle.

192. **C**

$42 + 28 + 20 = 90\%$ voted.

$100 - 90 = 10$, so $\frac{10}{100}$ or $\frac{1}{10}$ did not vote.

193. **D**

$40\% = .4$; $0.4\ (5) = \$2$

194. **D**

Pythagorean refers to a formula used in geometry to find the unknown length of a right triangle's side.

195. **A**

Since triangles *ABC* and *ADE* are similar, their corresponding sides are in proportion.

If we separate the two triangles, we can see the proportion readily:

$\frac{AD}{AB} = \frac{DE}{BC}$

196. **A**

Prime factorization is factoring a number to the point where all factors are prime. $30 = 10 \times 3 = 5 \times 2 \times 3$. Seven is not a prime factor.

197. **A**

The least common multiple is the smallest number divisible by both given numbers.

198. **C**

The associative property of addition means that you may group the numbers to be added in different ways and still achieve the same result.

Problem Solving

199. **B**

$$12 + 3x = x + 40$$
$$2x = 40 - 12$$
$$2x = 28$$
$$x = 14$$

200. **D**

tubes of paint $11.25 \ (5 \times \$2.25)$
paint brushes $12.90 \ (3 \times \$4.30)$
total $24.15

201. **D**

$$2\tfrac{1}{3} = \tfrac{7}{3}, \ 1\tfrac{1}{4} = \tfrac{5}{4}$$
$$\tfrac{7}{3} - \tfrac{5}{4} = \tfrac{7(4)}{12} - \tfrac{5(3)}{12}$$
$$\tfrac{28}{12} - \tfrac{15}{12} = \tfrac{13}{12} = 1\tfrac{1}{12}$$

202. **A**

$\dfrac{\$850}{12} \approx 70.8333 \approx \$70.80.$

203. **B**

$$1\tfrac{1}{2} = \tfrac{3}{2}, \ 2\tfrac{1}{4} = \tfrac{9}{4}$$
$$\tfrac{3}{2} \times \tfrac{9}{4} \times \tfrac{2}{3} = \tfrac{9}{4} = 2\tfrac{1}{4}$$

204. **D**

$$(-5) + (-4) + (-8) = -17$$
$$+6 + (-17) = -11$$

205. **B**

First, multiply $102 by 2 to get $204. Then, subtract 3 from 204 to get $201.

206. **C**

Replace the C in the equation with 5 and solve:
$$F = \frac{9}{5(5)} + 32 = 9 + 32 = 41.$$

207. **B**

First, add all the positive numbers, then, add the negative numbers. Then, combine the results.
$$9 + 4 = 13, \ (-3) + (-5) = -8$$
$$13 + (-8) = 5$$

208. **D**

If the sum of the two numbers is a and one of the numbers is 4, then the other number is $a - 4$. Two times the other number is $2(a - 4)$.

209. **A**

This problem is done by ratios:
$$\frac{3}{1} = \frac{x}{12}$$
$$x = 12 \times 3$$
$$x = 36$$
$$36 = x$$

210. **C**

First, multiply 2 by 36 to get 72. Then, subtract 4 from 72 to get an answer of $68.

211. **B**

1 pound 2 ounces $= 1\tfrac{2}{16}$, or $\tfrac{18}{16}$
$$\tfrac{18}{16} \times \$2.00 = \$2.25$$

212. C

We may write the given equation, $a + 4 = b + 6$, as $a - b = 6 - 4$, or $a - b = 2$. This tells us that a is 2 more than b or $a > b$.

213. A

$3a - 2 > 10$
$\quad 3a > 12$
$\quad\quad a > 4$

If $a > 4$, then $a^2 > 16$

214. D

This can be set up as an algebraic equation. If x is the amount Mrs. Daly borrowed

$5\%(x) = \$35.50$

$\quad x = \dfrac{35.50}{.05} = \$710$

215. C

$3^3 + 3\left(\dfrac{1}{2}\right) + 2 = 27 + 1\dfrac{1}{2} + 2 = 30\dfrac{1}{2}$

216. D

Volume = length × width × height
Volume = $10 × 4 × 3 = 120 \text{ m}^3$

217. B

First, find the area of the room. Multiply the area by $4.00 to arrive at the cost.

Area = $12 × 15 = 180$ square feet

$180 × \$4 = \$720.$

218. B

This can be set up as an algebraic equation. If y equals the price of the roller blades is z, 6% of z equals $4.50 or

$.06z = 4.50$

$\quad z = \dfrac{4.50}{.06} = \$75$

219. A

Replace the letters in the problem with the numbers given.
$2XYZ = 2(2)(3)(4) = 48.$

220. D

$5.31\overline{)2.7633}$

First, move the decimal points

$$
\begin{array}{r}
.52 \\
531\overline{)276.33} \\
265.5 \\
\hline
10.83 \\
10.62 \\
\hline
\end{array}
$$

221. D

Remember that the number of decimal places to the right of the decimal point in the answer should equal the total number of places to the right of the decimal points in the two factors being multiplied; in this case 5.

$$
\begin{array}{r}
42.13 \\
\times\,.082 \\
\hline
8426 \\
337040 \\
\hline
3.45466 \\
\end{array}
$$

222. B

$2x - 7 > 9$
$\quad 2x > 9 + 7$
$\quad 2x > 16$
$\quad\ x > 8$

If $x > 8$, then $x^2 > 8^2$, and $x^2 > 64$.

223. C

When adding decimal numbers, line up the decimal points.

$$
\begin{array}{r}
.354 \\
7.9 \\
2.03 \\
\hline
10.284 \\
\end{array}
$$

224. A

$8x + 2 = 3x + 5$
$\quad 5x = 3$
$\quad\ x = \dfrac{3}{5}$

225. **C**

Let x = the number of goals in 15 games. We set up the proportion:

$$\frac{4}{10} = \frac{x}{15}$$
$$4(15) = x(10)$$
$$60 = 10x$$
$$\frac{60}{10} = 6$$

226. **A**

The only even integer less than −1, but greater than −4 is −2.

227. **C**

Plug in 18 for b in the equation:

$$3a - 6 = 18$$

Isolate a on one side of the equation:

$$3a = 18 + 6$$
$$3a = 24$$

Divide both sides by 3 to find the value of a: $a = 8$.

228. **C**

$22.75 \div 7 = 3.25$; $3.25 \times 4 = 13.00$

229. **B**

$30 \times .20 = 6 per week. Multiply that \$6 by 4 (since there are 4 weeks in a month) for a total of \$24 per month.

230. **A**

$$\begin{array}{r} 534 \\ \times\ 32 \\ \hline 1068 \\ 16020 \\ \hline 17088 \end{array}$$

231. **C**

If we square both sides of the equation, we have

$$a + 6 = 12^2$$
$$a + 6 = 144$$
$$a = 138$$

232. **A**

The area of the square is length × width or $4 \times 4 = 16$ m². The area of the semicircles on each side $= \frac{1}{2}(\text{radius})^2 \times \pi$, or $\frac{1}{2}(2)^2 \times \pi = 2\pi$. However, since there are four semicircles, the area of all of them put together $= 2\pi + 2\pi + 2\pi + 2\pi = 8\pi$ m². Therefore, the area of the whole figure = 1 6 + 16π.

233. **B**

$\frac{3}{4}x = 30$. Multiply both sides of the equation by the reciprocal to obtain:

$$x = 30 \times \frac{4}{3} = \frac{120}{3} = 40.$$

The value of $\frac{5}{8}x = \frac{5}{8}(40) = 25$.

234. **D**

Let x = the coworker's hourly wage.

And $x + 25$ = the supervisor's wage.

$$8x + 8(x + 25) = 600$$
$$16x + 200 = 600$$
$$16x = 600 - 200 = 400$$

$\frac{400}{16} = 25$. The coworker earns \$25, and the supervisor earns \$25 + \$25 = \$50 per hour.

235. **D**

$$\frac{2}{3} : \frac{3}{8} = \frac{2}{3} \div \frac{3}{8} = \frac{2}{3} \times \frac{8}{3} = \frac{16}{9}.$$

236. A

Let x = the amount of money Mark's younger brother has.

$$3x - 10 = x + 10$$
$$2x = 20$$
$$x = 10$$

Mark has three times much as his brother; therefore Mark has 3(5) = $15.

237. B

Since in the given inequality $6 > y > 3$, y must be an odd number integer, it must be 5, since that is the only odd number integer greater than 3 but less than 6.

238. D

Begin solving this equation by squaring both sides:

$$a + 12 = 7^2$$
$$a + 12 = 7(7) = 49$$
$$a = 49 - 12$$
$$a = 37$$

LANGUAGE

Usage

239. C

There should be a comma after *Tuesday*.

240. B

Day should be capitalized.

241. A

History should be capitalized.

242. C

There should be quotations before *where* and after the question mark.

243. D

There are no mistakes.

244. C

Me should be *I* since it is a subject in this sentence.

245. C

It is not standard English to use *may* to ask the question, *May you pass the salt?* The word *may* asks permission, so it should not be used in this question.

246. D

There are no mistakes.

247. D

There are no mistakes.

248. C

There should be quotation marks in this sentence to show that what Nancy said is a direct quote.

249. B

The word *their* is incorrect in this context. The word should be *they're* (they are).

250. D

There are no mistakes.

251. D

There are no mistakes.

252. A

The word *lay* is incorrect in this context. The word should be *lie*.

253. C

The word *who's* (*who is*) is incorrect in this context. The word should be *whose*.

254. B

The object of he preposition *to* is Frank and *me*.

255. B

The word *she* should be capitalized.

256. C

This is a question, so it should end with a question mark, not a period.

257. **C**

The past tense of the verb *to lie* is *lay*.

258. **A**

The word *we* is incorrect in this sentence. The word *us* should be used.

259. **C**

The tense is incorrect. The last part of the sentence should read *he'd ever gone*.

260. **D**

There are no mistakes.

261. **B**

Everyone is singular. The pronoun must be singular as well. Either *his* or *her* would be correct.

262. **D**

There are no mistakes.

263. **A**

There is a shift in verb tense in this sentence. It shifts from the past tense (*the show was over*) to the present tense (*everyone leaves*). Both verbs should be in the same tense.

264. **B**

The word *of* is incorrect in this context. The word should be *have*.

265. **B**

The apostrophe in *womens* should be placed before the *s* since *women* is a plural word.

266. **B**

The word *learning* is incorrect in this sentence. The word should be *teaching*.

267. **A**

California should be capitalized.

268. **B**

The preposition *to* is incorrect in this context. The word should be *too*, meaning too much.

269. **D**

There are no mistakes.

270. **C**

The object *me* is incorrect in this context. The correct pronoun is *I* since it is a subject.

271. **C**

Quick should be *quickly* since it is an adverb, describing how Shawn ran.

272. **C**

Using double negatives is incorrect. The sentence should be: *I can do nothing.* OR *I can't do anything.*

273. **D**

There are no mistakes.

274. **B**

Because there are three athletes mentioned, the superlative *fastest* (not the comparative *faster*) is required.

275. **C**

Money is a singular noun and can't be counted, so the word *less* should replace *fewer* to make the sentence grammatically correct.

276. **A**

The subject and verb of the sentence are *she has*.

277. **A**

Grand, Central, and *Station* should be capitalized.

278. **B**

There should be a comma after *said*, not a semicolon.

Spelling

279. A

The correct spelling is *cafeteria*.

280. B

The correct spelling is *composition*.

281. D

There are no mistakes.

282. C

The correct spelling is *prejudiced*.

283. B

The correct spelling is *immediately*.

284. B

The correct spelling is *specific*.

285. A

The correct spelling is *temperature*.

286. D

There are no mistakes.

287. A

The correct spelling is *surface*.

288. A

The correct spelling is *interrupt*.

Composition

289. A

The word *however* indicates the contrasting relationship of the two clauses.

290. D

The phrase *display of antique armor* should come immediately after the verb *is* in order to make the sentence as clear as possible. The phrase *dating back from the 12th century* describes the armor and should come after it.

291. B

The subject *we* must follow the introductory phrase.

292. A

Caring for your bicycle fits under the topic of bicycle maintenance.

293. D

The two clauses contradict one another, so *although* is the best answer choice.

294. A

The first sentence is the most clear and correct way of expressing the idea.

295. D

The second clause stands independently. No linking words are necessary.

296. D

Sentences 1, 2, and 3 are about Tom's enjoyment of the early morning. Sentence 4 talks about what he likes to cook and therefore, does not belong in the paragraph.

297. B

This topic is simple enough to be dealt with in a brief theme.

298. D

The given sentence should be after sentence 3 because it ties together the idea that a combination of events led to the extinction of the dinosaurs.

HSPT Practice Test 2
Answer Sheet

Remove (or photocopy) this answer sheet and use it to complete the practice test.

Verbal Skills

1. Ⓐ Ⓑ Ⓒ Ⓓ   13. Ⓐ Ⓑ Ⓒ Ⓓ   25. Ⓐ Ⓑ Ⓒ Ⓓ   37. Ⓐ Ⓑ Ⓒ Ⓓ   49. Ⓐ Ⓑ Ⓒ Ⓓ
2. Ⓐ Ⓑ Ⓒ Ⓓ   14. Ⓐ Ⓑ Ⓒ Ⓓ   26. Ⓐ Ⓑ Ⓒ Ⓓ   38. Ⓐ Ⓑ Ⓒ Ⓓ   50. Ⓐ Ⓑ Ⓒ Ⓓ
3. Ⓐ Ⓑ Ⓒ Ⓓ   15. Ⓐ Ⓑ Ⓒ Ⓓ   27. Ⓐ Ⓑ Ⓒ Ⓓ   39. Ⓐ Ⓑ Ⓒ Ⓓ   51. Ⓐ Ⓑ Ⓒ Ⓓ
4. Ⓐ Ⓑ Ⓒ Ⓓ   16. Ⓐ Ⓑ Ⓒ Ⓓ   28. Ⓐ Ⓑ Ⓒ Ⓓ   40. Ⓐ Ⓑ Ⓒ Ⓓ   52. Ⓐ Ⓑ Ⓒ Ⓓ
5. Ⓐ Ⓑ Ⓒ Ⓓ   17. Ⓐ Ⓑ Ⓒ Ⓓ   29. Ⓐ Ⓑ Ⓒ Ⓓ   41. Ⓐ Ⓑ Ⓒ Ⓓ   53. Ⓐ Ⓑ Ⓒ Ⓓ
6. Ⓐ Ⓑ Ⓒ Ⓓ   18. Ⓐ Ⓑ Ⓒ Ⓓ   30. Ⓐ Ⓑ Ⓒ Ⓓ   42. Ⓐ Ⓑ Ⓒ Ⓓ   54. Ⓐ Ⓑ Ⓒ Ⓓ
7. Ⓐ Ⓑ Ⓒ Ⓓ   19. Ⓐ Ⓑ Ⓒ Ⓓ   31. Ⓐ Ⓑ Ⓒ Ⓓ   43. Ⓐ Ⓑ Ⓒ Ⓓ   55. Ⓐ Ⓑ Ⓒ Ⓓ
8. Ⓐ Ⓑ Ⓒ Ⓓ   20. Ⓐ Ⓑ Ⓒ Ⓓ   32. Ⓐ Ⓑ Ⓒ Ⓓ   44. Ⓐ Ⓑ Ⓒ Ⓓ   56. Ⓐ Ⓑ Ⓒ Ⓓ
9. Ⓐ Ⓑ Ⓒ Ⓓ   21. Ⓐ Ⓑ Ⓒ Ⓓ   33. Ⓐ Ⓑ Ⓒ Ⓓ   45. Ⓐ Ⓑ Ⓒ Ⓓ   57. Ⓐ Ⓑ Ⓒ Ⓓ
10. Ⓐ Ⓑ Ⓒ Ⓓ   22. Ⓐ Ⓑ Ⓒ Ⓓ   34. Ⓐ Ⓑ Ⓒ Ⓓ   46. Ⓐ Ⓑ Ⓒ Ⓓ   58. Ⓐ Ⓑ Ⓒ Ⓓ
11. Ⓐ Ⓑ Ⓒ Ⓓ   23. Ⓐ Ⓑ Ⓒ Ⓓ   35. Ⓐ Ⓑ Ⓒ Ⓓ   47. Ⓐ Ⓑ Ⓒ Ⓓ   59. Ⓐ Ⓑ Ⓒ Ⓓ
12. Ⓐ Ⓑ Ⓒ Ⓓ   24. Ⓐ Ⓑ Ⓒ Ⓓ   36. Ⓐ Ⓑ Ⓒ Ⓓ   48. Ⓐ Ⓑ Ⓒ Ⓓ   60. Ⓐ Ⓑ Ⓒ Ⓓ

Quantitative Skills

61. Ⓐ Ⓑ Ⓒ Ⓓ   72. Ⓐ Ⓑ Ⓒ Ⓓ   83. Ⓐ Ⓑ Ⓒ Ⓓ   93. Ⓐ Ⓑ Ⓒ Ⓓ   103. Ⓐ Ⓑ Ⓒ Ⓓ
62. Ⓐ Ⓑ Ⓒ Ⓓ   73. Ⓐ Ⓑ Ⓒ Ⓓ   84. Ⓐ Ⓑ Ⓒ Ⓓ   94. Ⓐ Ⓑ Ⓒ Ⓓ   104. Ⓐ Ⓑ Ⓒ Ⓓ
63. Ⓐ Ⓑ Ⓒ Ⓓ   74. Ⓐ Ⓑ Ⓒ Ⓓ   85. Ⓐ Ⓑ Ⓒ Ⓓ   95. Ⓐ Ⓑ Ⓒ Ⓓ   105. Ⓐ Ⓑ Ⓒ Ⓓ
64. Ⓐ Ⓑ Ⓒ Ⓓ   75. Ⓐ Ⓑ Ⓒ Ⓓ   86. Ⓐ Ⓑ Ⓒ Ⓓ   96. Ⓐ Ⓑ Ⓒ Ⓓ   106. Ⓐ Ⓑ Ⓒ Ⓓ
65. Ⓐ Ⓑ Ⓒ Ⓓ   76. Ⓐ Ⓑ Ⓒ Ⓓ   87. Ⓐ Ⓑ Ⓒ Ⓓ   97. Ⓐ Ⓑ Ⓒ Ⓓ   107. Ⓐ Ⓑ Ⓒ Ⓓ
66. Ⓐ Ⓑ Ⓒ Ⓓ   77. Ⓐ Ⓑ Ⓒ Ⓓ   88. Ⓐ Ⓑ Ⓒ Ⓓ   98. Ⓐ Ⓑ Ⓒ Ⓓ   108. Ⓐ Ⓑ Ⓒ Ⓓ
67. Ⓐ Ⓑ Ⓒ Ⓓ   78. Ⓐ Ⓑ Ⓒ Ⓓ   89. Ⓐ Ⓑ Ⓒ Ⓓ   99. Ⓐ Ⓑ Ⓒ Ⓓ   109. Ⓐ Ⓑ Ⓒ Ⓓ
68. Ⓐ Ⓑ Ⓒ Ⓓ   79. Ⓐ Ⓑ Ⓒ Ⓓ   90. Ⓐ Ⓑ Ⓒ Ⓓ   100. Ⓐ Ⓑ Ⓒ Ⓓ   110. Ⓐ Ⓑ Ⓒ Ⓓ
69. Ⓐ Ⓑ Ⓒ Ⓓ   80. Ⓐ Ⓑ Ⓒ Ⓓ   91. Ⓐ Ⓑ Ⓒ Ⓓ   101. Ⓐ Ⓑ Ⓒ Ⓓ   111. Ⓐ Ⓑ Ⓒ Ⓓ
70. Ⓐ Ⓑ Ⓒ Ⓓ   81. Ⓐ Ⓑ Ⓒ Ⓓ   92. Ⓐ Ⓑ Ⓒ Ⓓ   102. Ⓐ Ⓑ Ⓒ Ⓓ   112. Ⓐ Ⓑ Ⓒ Ⓓ
71. Ⓐ Ⓑ Ⓒ Ⓓ   82. Ⓐ Ⓑ Ⓒ Ⓓ

Reading

113. Ⓐ Ⓑ Ⓒ Ⓓ	126. Ⓐ Ⓑ Ⓒ Ⓓ	139. Ⓐ Ⓑ Ⓒ Ⓓ	152. Ⓐ Ⓑ Ⓒ Ⓓ	165. Ⓐ Ⓑ Ⓒ Ⓓ
114. Ⓐ Ⓑ Ⓒ Ⓓ	127. Ⓐ Ⓑ Ⓒ Ⓓ	140. Ⓐ Ⓑ Ⓒ Ⓓ	153. Ⓐ Ⓑ Ⓒ Ⓓ	166. Ⓐ Ⓑ Ⓒ Ⓓ
115. Ⓐ Ⓑ Ⓒ Ⓓ	128. Ⓐ Ⓑ Ⓒ Ⓓ	141. Ⓐ Ⓑ Ⓒ Ⓓ	154. Ⓐ Ⓑ Ⓒ Ⓓ	167. Ⓐ Ⓑ Ⓒ Ⓓ
116. Ⓐ Ⓑ Ⓒ Ⓓ	129. Ⓐ Ⓑ Ⓒ Ⓓ	142. Ⓐ Ⓑ Ⓒ Ⓓ	155. Ⓐ Ⓑ Ⓒ Ⓓ	168. Ⓐ Ⓑ Ⓒ Ⓓ
117. Ⓐ Ⓑ Ⓒ Ⓓ	130. Ⓐ Ⓑ Ⓒ Ⓓ	143. Ⓐ Ⓑ Ⓒ Ⓓ	156. Ⓐ Ⓑ Ⓒ Ⓓ	169. Ⓐ Ⓑ Ⓒ Ⓓ
118. Ⓐ Ⓑ Ⓒ Ⓓ	131. Ⓐ Ⓑ Ⓒ Ⓓ	144. Ⓐ Ⓑ Ⓒ Ⓓ	157. Ⓐ Ⓑ Ⓒ Ⓓ	170. Ⓐ Ⓑ Ⓒ Ⓓ
119. Ⓐ Ⓑ Ⓒ Ⓓ	132. Ⓐ Ⓑ Ⓒ Ⓓ	145. Ⓐ Ⓑ Ⓒ Ⓓ	158. Ⓐ Ⓑ Ⓒ Ⓓ	171. Ⓐ Ⓑ Ⓒ Ⓓ
120. Ⓐ Ⓑ Ⓒ Ⓓ	133. Ⓐ Ⓑ Ⓒ Ⓓ	146. Ⓐ Ⓑ Ⓒ Ⓓ	159. Ⓐ Ⓑ Ⓒ Ⓓ	172. Ⓐ Ⓑ Ⓒ Ⓓ
121. Ⓐ Ⓑ Ⓒ Ⓓ	134. Ⓐ Ⓑ Ⓒ Ⓓ	147. Ⓐ Ⓑ Ⓒ Ⓓ	160. Ⓐ Ⓑ Ⓒ Ⓓ	173. Ⓐ Ⓑ Ⓒ Ⓓ
122. Ⓐ Ⓑ Ⓒ Ⓓ	135. Ⓐ Ⓑ Ⓒ Ⓓ	148. Ⓐ Ⓑ Ⓒ Ⓓ	161. Ⓐ Ⓑ Ⓒ Ⓓ	174. Ⓐ Ⓑ Ⓒ Ⓓ
123. Ⓐ Ⓑ Ⓒ Ⓓ	136. Ⓐ Ⓑ Ⓒ Ⓓ	149. Ⓐ Ⓑ Ⓒ Ⓓ	162. Ⓐ Ⓑ Ⓒ Ⓓ	
124. Ⓐ Ⓑ Ⓒ Ⓓ	137. Ⓐ Ⓑ Ⓒ Ⓓ	150. Ⓐ Ⓑ Ⓒ Ⓓ	163. Ⓐ Ⓑ Ⓒ Ⓓ	
125. Ⓐ Ⓑ Ⓒ Ⓓ	138. Ⓐ Ⓑ Ⓒ Ⓓ	151. Ⓐ Ⓑ Ⓒ Ⓓ	164. Ⓐ Ⓑ Ⓒ Ⓓ	

Mathematics

175. Ⓐ Ⓑ Ⓒ Ⓓ	188. Ⓐ Ⓑ Ⓒ Ⓓ	201. Ⓐ Ⓑ Ⓒ Ⓓ	214. Ⓐ Ⓑ Ⓒ Ⓓ	227. Ⓐ Ⓑ Ⓒ Ⓓ
176. Ⓐ Ⓑ Ⓒ Ⓓ	189. Ⓐ Ⓑ Ⓒ Ⓓ	202. Ⓐ Ⓑ Ⓒ Ⓓ	215. Ⓐ Ⓑ Ⓒ Ⓓ	228. Ⓐ Ⓑ Ⓒ Ⓓ
177. Ⓐ Ⓑ Ⓒ Ⓓ	190. Ⓐ Ⓑ Ⓒ Ⓓ	203. Ⓐ Ⓑ Ⓒ Ⓓ	216. Ⓐ Ⓑ Ⓒ Ⓓ	229. Ⓐ Ⓑ Ⓒ Ⓓ
178. Ⓐ Ⓑ Ⓒ Ⓓ	191. Ⓐ Ⓑ Ⓒ Ⓓ	204. Ⓐ Ⓑ Ⓒ Ⓓ	217. Ⓐ Ⓑ Ⓒ Ⓓ	230. Ⓐ Ⓑ Ⓒ Ⓓ
179. Ⓐ Ⓑ Ⓒ Ⓓ	192. Ⓐ Ⓑ Ⓒ Ⓓ	205. Ⓐ Ⓑ Ⓒ Ⓓ	218. Ⓐ Ⓑ Ⓒ Ⓓ	231. Ⓐ Ⓑ Ⓒ Ⓓ
180. Ⓐ Ⓑ Ⓒ Ⓓ	193. Ⓐ Ⓑ Ⓒ Ⓓ	206. Ⓐ Ⓑ Ⓒ Ⓓ	219. Ⓐ Ⓑ Ⓒ Ⓓ	232. Ⓐ Ⓑ Ⓒ Ⓓ
181. Ⓐ Ⓑ Ⓒ Ⓓ	194. Ⓐ Ⓑ Ⓒ Ⓓ	207. Ⓐ Ⓑ Ⓒ Ⓓ	220. Ⓐ Ⓑ Ⓒ Ⓓ	233. Ⓐ Ⓑ Ⓒ Ⓓ
182. Ⓐ Ⓑ Ⓒ Ⓓ	195. Ⓐ Ⓑ Ⓒ Ⓓ	208. Ⓐ Ⓑ Ⓒ Ⓓ	221. Ⓐ Ⓑ Ⓒ Ⓓ	234. Ⓐ Ⓑ Ⓒ Ⓓ
183. Ⓐ Ⓑ Ⓒ Ⓓ	196. Ⓐ Ⓑ Ⓒ Ⓓ	209. Ⓐ Ⓑ Ⓒ Ⓓ	222. Ⓐ Ⓑ Ⓒ Ⓓ	235. Ⓐ Ⓑ Ⓒ Ⓓ
184. Ⓐ Ⓑ Ⓒ Ⓓ	197. Ⓐ Ⓑ Ⓒ Ⓓ	210. Ⓐ Ⓑ Ⓒ Ⓓ	223. Ⓐ Ⓑ Ⓒ Ⓓ	236. Ⓐ Ⓑ Ⓒ Ⓓ
185. Ⓐ Ⓑ Ⓒ Ⓓ	198. Ⓐ Ⓑ Ⓒ Ⓓ	211. Ⓐ Ⓑ Ⓒ Ⓓ	224. Ⓐ Ⓑ Ⓒ Ⓓ	237. Ⓐ Ⓑ Ⓒ Ⓓ
186. Ⓐ Ⓑ Ⓒ Ⓓ	199. Ⓐ Ⓑ Ⓒ Ⓓ	212. Ⓐ Ⓑ Ⓒ Ⓓ	225. Ⓐ Ⓑ Ⓒ Ⓓ	238. Ⓐ Ⓑ Ⓒ Ⓓ
187. Ⓐ Ⓑ Ⓒ Ⓓ	200. Ⓐ Ⓑ Ⓒ Ⓓ	213. Ⓐ Ⓑ Ⓒ Ⓓ	226. Ⓐ Ⓑ Ⓒ Ⓓ	

Language

239. Ⓐ Ⓑ Ⓒ Ⓓ 251. Ⓐ Ⓑ Ⓒ Ⓓ 263. Ⓐ Ⓑ Ⓒ Ⓓ 275. Ⓐ Ⓑ Ⓒ Ⓓ 287. Ⓐ Ⓑ Ⓒ Ⓓ

240. Ⓐ Ⓑ Ⓒ Ⓓ 252. Ⓐ Ⓑ Ⓒ Ⓓ 264. Ⓐ Ⓑ Ⓒ Ⓓ 276. Ⓐ Ⓑ Ⓒ Ⓓ 288. Ⓐ Ⓑ Ⓒ Ⓓ

241. Ⓐ Ⓑ Ⓒ Ⓓ 253. Ⓐ Ⓑ Ⓒ Ⓓ 265. Ⓐ Ⓑ Ⓒ Ⓓ 277. Ⓐ Ⓑ Ⓒ Ⓓ 289. Ⓐ Ⓑ Ⓒ Ⓓ

242. Ⓐ Ⓑ Ⓒ Ⓓ 254. Ⓐ Ⓑ Ⓒ Ⓓ 266. Ⓐ Ⓑ Ⓒ Ⓓ 278. Ⓐ Ⓑ Ⓒ Ⓓ 290. Ⓐ Ⓑ Ⓒ Ⓓ

243. Ⓐ Ⓑ Ⓒ Ⓓ 255. Ⓐ Ⓑ Ⓒ Ⓓ 267. Ⓐ Ⓑ Ⓒ Ⓓ 279. Ⓐ Ⓑ Ⓒ Ⓓ 291. Ⓐ Ⓑ Ⓒ Ⓓ

244. Ⓐ Ⓑ Ⓒ Ⓓ 256. Ⓐ Ⓑ Ⓒ Ⓓ 268. Ⓐ Ⓑ Ⓒ Ⓓ 280. Ⓐ Ⓑ Ⓒ Ⓓ 292. Ⓐ Ⓑ Ⓒ Ⓓ

245. Ⓐ Ⓑ Ⓒ Ⓓ 257. Ⓐ Ⓑ Ⓒ Ⓓ 269. Ⓐ Ⓑ Ⓒ Ⓓ 281. Ⓐ Ⓑ Ⓒ Ⓓ 293. Ⓐ Ⓑ Ⓒ Ⓓ

246. Ⓐ Ⓑ Ⓒ Ⓓ 258. Ⓐ Ⓑ Ⓒ Ⓓ 270. Ⓐ Ⓑ Ⓒ Ⓓ 282. Ⓐ Ⓑ Ⓒ Ⓓ 294. Ⓐ Ⓑ Ⓒ Ⓓ

247. Ⓐ Ⓑ Ⓒ Ⓓ 259. Ⓐ Ⓑ Ⓒ Ⓓ 271. Ⓐ Ⓑ Ⓒ Ⓓ 283. Ⓐ Ⓑ Ⓒ Ⓓ 295. Ⓐ Ⓑ Ⓒ Ⓓ

248. Ⓐ Ⓑ Ⓒ Ⓓ 260. Ⓐ Ⓑ Ⓒ Ⓓ 272. Ⓐ Ⓑ Ⓒ Ⓓ 284. Ⓐ Ⓑ Ⓒ Ⓓ 296. Ⓐ Ⓑ Ⓒ Ⓓ

249. Ⓐ Ⓑ Ⓒ Ⓓ 261. Ⓐ Ⓑ Ⓒ Ⓓ 273. Ⓐ Ⓑ Ⓒ Ⓓ 285. Ⓐ Ⓑ Ⓒ Ⓓ 297. Ⓐ Ⓑ Ⓒ Ⓓ

250. Ⓐ Ⓑ Ⓒ Ⓓ 262. Ⓐ Ⓑ Ⓒ Ⓓ 274. Ⓐ Ⓑ Ⓒ Ⓓ 286. Ⓐ Ⓑ Ⓒ Ⓓ 298. Ⓐ Ⓑ Ⓒ Ⓓ

HSPT Practice Test 2

TEST 1: VERBAL SKILLS

Questions 1–60
16 Minutes

Directions: For questions 1–60, choose the best answer.

1. Which word does *not* belong with the others?

   (A) lenient
   (B) light
   (C) mild
   (D) severe

2. Christine runs faster than Joanne. Joanne runs faster than Katie. Christine runs faster than Katie. If the first two statements are true, the third is

   (A) true
   (B) false
   (C) uncertain

3. Abundant is the *opposite* of

   (A) scarce
   (B) lush
   (C) collect
   (D) loyal

4. Shell is to egg as peel is to

   (A) rind
   (B) orange
   (C) omelet
   (D) helmet

5. If Mr. Johnson is not at work, he is at home. If Mr. Smith is not at home, he is at the golf club. If Mr. Johnson is not at the golf club, he must be at home. If the first two statements are true, the third is

   (A) true

   (B) false

   (C) uncertain

6. Endorse most nearly means

   (A) approve

   (B) check

   (C) wear

   (D) beg

7. Which word does *not* belong with the others?

   (A) expand

   (B) reduce

   (C) summarize

   (D) abbreviate

8. Hank has hit more home runs that Peter. Peter has hit more home runs than Joe. Hank has hit fewer home runs than Joe. If the first two statements are true, the third is

   (A) true

   (B) false

   (C) uncertain

9. Claw is to eagle as paw is to

   (A) bird

   (B) nest

   (C) hunt

   (D) lion

10. Fiction means the *opposite* of

   (A) imaginary

   (B) science

   (C) fact

   (D) invention

11. Territory most nearly means

    (A) land
    (B) border
    (C) capital
    (D) home

12. Impose means most nearly

    (A) question
    (B) interrupt
    (C) imply
    (D) force

13. Which word does *not* belong with the others?

    (A) diplomat
    (B) ambassador
    (C) representative
    (D) spy

14. Paddle is to canoe as pedal is to

    (A) road
    (B) bicycle
    (C) gear
    (D) engine

15. Infinite most nearly means

    (A) unending
    (B) miniscule
    (C) complex
    (D) undiscovered

16. Which word does *not* belong with the others?

    (A) kitchen
    (B) basement
    (C) attic
    (D) lot

17. Steak is more expensive than hamburger but less expensive than lobster. Chicken is more expensive than hamburger but less expensive than swordfish. Of all the foods mentioned, hamburger is the least expensive. If the first two statements are true, the third is

    (A) true
    (B) false
    (C) uncertain

18. Average is the *opposite* of

    (A) outstanding
    (B) individual
    (C) medium
    (D) general

19. Saw is to cut as handle is to

    (A) door
    (B) jar
    (C) open
    (D) tool

20. Mandate most nearly means

    (A) speak
    (B) command
    (C) vote
    (D) council

21. Embellish most nearly means

    (A) wipe out
    (B) embroider
    (C) polish
    (D) adorn

22. Wary means the *opposite* of

    (A) forgetful
    (B) wise
    (C) hopeful
    (D) careless

23. Serene most nearly means

    (A) mermaid
    (B) serious
    (C) peaceful
    (D) dangerous

24. Which word does *not* belong with the others?

    (A) solemn
    (B) elated
    (C) serious
    (D) grave

25. Small is to minute as large is to

    (A) toy
    (B) miniature
    (C) big
    (D) colossal

26. Acquainted most nearly means

    (A) familiar
    (B) distant
    (C) friendly
    (D) unknown

27. Which word does *not* belong with the others?

    (A) remote
    (B) distant
    (C) beside
    (D) far

28. Colleague means most nearly

    (A) coworker
    (B) manager
    (C) friend
    (D) university

29. Wolf Lake is larger than Rosebud Lake. Rosebud Lake is smaller than Beaver Lake. Wolf Lake is larger than Beaver Lake. If the first two statements are true, the third is

    (A) true
    (B) false
    (C) uncertain

30. The radioactive half-life of element A is longer than the radioactive half-life of element B. The half-life of element C is longer than the half-life of element D. The half-life of element A is longer than the half-life of element D. If the first two statements are true, the third is

    (A) true
    (B) false
    (C) uncertain

31. Underhanded most nearly means

    (A) easier
    (B) sneaky
    (C) graceful
    (D) lucky

32. Which word does *not* belong with the others?

    (A) choose
    (B) punish
    (C) sentence
    (D) condemn

33. Which word does *not* belong with the others?

    (A) condone
    (B) excuse
    (C) condemn
    (D) pardon

34. Praise is to admiration as insult is to

    (A) injury
    (B) contempt
    (C) annoy
    (D) barb

35. All mammals give birth to live young. All kangaroos are mammals. All kangaroos do not give birth to live young. If the first two statements are true, the third is

   (A) true
   (B) false
   (C) uncertain

36. Fortuitous most nearly means

   (A) hazardous
   (B) circular
   (C) lucky
   (D) safe

37. Ambivalent most nearly means

   (A) emotional
   (B) fair
   (C) ambidextrous
   (D) uncertain

38. Which word does *not* belong with the others?

   (A) letter
   (B) magazine
   (C) newspaper
   (D) tabloid

39. All X is Y. No Z is X. No Z is Y. If the first two statements are true, the third is

   (A) true
   (B) false
   (C) uncertain

40. Forge is to signature as counterfeit is to

   (A) create
   (B) fake
   (C) money
   (D) paper

41. Which word does *not* belong with the others?

   (A) detain
   (B) enlist
   (C) enroll
   (D) register

42. Renowned most nearly means

   (A) worldly
   (B) secretive
   (C) novel
   (D) famed

43. Implicit most nearly means

   (A) fake
   (B) inferred
   (C) stated
   (D) granted

44. Fool is to wisdom as pauper is to

   (A) humor
   (B) knowledge
   (C) grace
   (D) riches

45. Ingenious most nearly means

   (A) dull
   (B) clever
   (C) silly
   (D) unworthy

46. Which word does *not* belong with the others?

   (A) fool
   (B) mimic
   (C) jester
   (D) clown

47. Bombastic most nearly means

   (A) explosion
   (B) sturdy
   (C) overblown
   (D) refined

48. All myops are nearsighted. Lester is a myop. Lester is nearsighted. If the first two statements are true, the third is

    (A) true
    (B) false
    (C) uncertain

49. Which word does *not* belong with the others?

    (A) school
    (B) herd
    (C) pack
    (D) cub

50. Warrant is to search as visa is to

    (A) right
    (B) license
    (C) travel
    (D) charge

51. Sedentary means the *opposite* of

    (A) optimistic
    (B) calm
    (C) active
    (D) loyal

52. Which word does *not* belong with the others?

    (A) suit
    (B) shoe
    (C) hat
    (D) wardrobe

53. Rudimentary is the *opposite* of

    (A) advanced
    (B) polite
    (C) regulated
    (D) essential

54. Which word does *not* belong with the others?

    (A) fasten
    (B) tie
    (C) secure
    (D) unleash

55. Which word does *not* belong with the others?

   (A) battle
   (B) victory
   (C) win
   (D) triumph

56. Malevolent means most nearly

   (A) evil
   (B) smelly
   (C) bossy
   (D) kind

57. Which word does *not* belong with the others?

   (A) stage
   (B) actors
   (C) play
   (D) ticket

58. Chapter is to book as section is to

   (A) title
   (B) newspaper
   (C) heading
   (D) contents

59. City A is south of City B. City C is north of City D, but south of City A. City B is south of City D. If the first two statements are true the third is

   (A) true
   (B) false
   (C) uncertain

60. Transient means most nearly

   (A) transparent
   (B) fixed
   (C) temporary
   (D) electric

QUANTITATIVE SKILLS

Questions 61–112

30 Minutes

Directions: For questions 61–112, choose the best answer.

61. If three times a number is $34\frac{1}{2}$ then half the number is

    (A) $5\frac{1}{4}$
    (B) 11
    (C) $11\frac{1}{2}$
    (D) $5\frac{3}{4}$

62. What is the next number in the following series: 2, 5, 8, 11, ...

    (A) 14
    (B) 13
    (C) 12
    (D) 15

63. In the figure below, if A > B > C, which of the following is correct?

    (A) A < C
    (B) A > C
    (C) A = B + C
    (D) B > A

64. What is the next number in the following series: 54, 49, 44, 39, ...

    (A) 40
    (B) 35
    (C) 34
    (D) 36

65. When a number is subtracted from 36, the result is 4 more than the product of 5 and 6. What is the number?

    (A) 2
    (B) 4
    (C) 3
    (D) 5

66. In the diagram below, *A*, *B*, and *C* represent the angles of an equilateral triangle. Which of the following must be true?

   (A) $A < B$

   (B) $A = B + C$

   (C) $A - B = C$

   (D) $A + B > C$

67. Examine (a), (b), (c), and (d), and select the correct answer.

   (a) .33

   (b) $\frac{2}{3}$

   (c) 33%

   (d) 0.3

   (A) (d) is equal to (b)

   (B) (c) is greater than (a)

   (C) (b) is greater than (a)

   (D) of the numbers given, (d) is greatest

68. What is the missing number in the following series: 61, 57, 53, ___, 45

   (A) 50

   (B) 49

   (C) 48

   (D) 51

69. On a menu, each item from column A costs $2.25, each item from column B costs $4.50, and each item from column C costs $5.25.

   Terry ordered 4 items from column A and 1 from column C.

   John ordered 2 items from column A and 2 from column C.

   Maria ordered 1 item from column A, 1 from column B, and 1 from column C.

   Which of the following is correct?

   (A) Maria's meal cost more than Terry's but less than John's.

   (B) Terry's, John's, and Maria's meals all cost the same.

   (C) Terry's meal cost more than John's meal and also cost more than Maria's meal.

   (D) John's meal cost more than Terry's meal.

70. Examine (a), (b), and (c) and select the correct answer.

    (a) 11 − (6 + 3)
    (b) (8 − 2) − 3
    (c) 12 − (5 − 4)

    (A) (a) + (b) = (c)

    (B) (c) − (b) < (a)

    (C) (b) > (c)

    (D) (c) > (a) + (b)

71. In the figure below, lines *A* and *B* intersect in the center of circle *O*.

    Which of the following must be correct?

    (A) measure of angle *D* > measure of angle *E*

    (B) measure of angle *D* = measure of angle *E*

    (C) measure of angle *D* > measure of angle *F*

    (D) measure of angle *D* + measure of angle *E* = measure of angle *F* + measure of angle
    G

72. Examine (a), (b), and (c) and select the correct answer.

    (a) 50% of 20
    (b) 30% of 90
    (c) 25% of 80

    (A) 2(a) = (b)

    (B) (b) − (a) = (c)

    (C) (a) + (c) = (b)

    (D) 2(a) = (c)

73. What is the next number in the following series: 15, 12, 17, 14, 19, ...

    (A) 14

    (B) 13

    (C) 16

    (D) 15

74. If $\frac{3}{5}$ of a number is 6 less than 15, the number is

(A) 15

(B) 45

(C) 30

(D) 50

75. What percentage of the figure below is shaded?

(A) 33%

(B) 30%

(C) 25%

(D) 20%

76. If $\frac{1}{3}$ of a number is 2 more than $\frac{1}{4}$ of the same number, what is the number?

(A) 20

(B) 24

(C) 12

(D) 48

77. The number of fourths in $\frac{7}{8}$ is

(A) $3\frac{1}{2}$

(B) 8

(C) 28

(D) 14

78. A grocer purchased 3 super-sized cartons of eggs. A super-sized carton has 4 rows with 12 spaces for eggs in each row. He wants to repackage these in regular cartons that have 2 rows with 6 spaces for eggs in each row. How many regular cartons will he need?

(A) 4

(B) 3

(C) 6

(D) 12

79. What number represents the cube of 4 divided by 4?

(A) 16

(B) 64

(C) 12

(D) 32

80. What is the next number in the following series: 48, 24, 12, 6, ...

(A) 1

(B) 2

(C) 3

(D) 4

81. Triangle *ABC* is a right triangle. The measure of angle *BAL* is

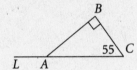

(A) 145°

(B) 45°

(C) 90°

(D) 75°

82. What fraction divided by $\frac{1}{5}$ is equal to $\frac{7}{8}$?

(A) $\frac{1}{6}$

(B) $\frac{7}{40}$

(C) $\frac{7}{45}$

(D) $\frac{35}{8}$

83. What is the next number in the following series: 1, 2, 4, 7, ...

(A) 14

(B) 9

(C) 10

(D) 11

84. What is the circumference of the circle below?

(A) 3π m

(B) 4π m

(C) 6π m

(D) 9π m

85. The circle below is divided into 8 equal sectors. What portion of the circle is shaded?

(A) $\frac{1}{3}$

(B) $\frac{1}{2}$

(C) $\frac{1}{4}$

(D) $\frac{2}{4}$

86. Which of the following is correct?

(A) $\frac{1}{5} > \frac{1}{3} > \frac{2}{3}$

(B) $\frac{1}{5} > \frac{2}{3} > \frac{1}{3}$

(C) $\frac{2}{3} > \frac{1}{3} > \frac{1}{5}$

(D) $\frac{2}{3} = \frac{1}{5} + \frac{1}{3}$

87. By how much does the average of 15, 24, 32, and 13 exceed 9?

(A) 12

(B) 9

(C) 16

(D) 8

88. What is the next number in the following series: 1, 4, 5, 8, 9, 12, ...

    (A) 15
    (B) 11
    (C) 14
    (D) 13

89. If $a = 3^2$, $b = 2 \times 2^2$ and $c = 3 \times 2^3$, which of the following is true?

    (A) $a < b$
    (B) $c > a + b$
    (C) $a + b > c$
    (D) $a + b + c > 100$

90. When a number is increased by 50% of itself, the result is 30. What is that number?

    (A) 15
    (B) 20
    (C) 40
    (D) 30

91. What is the missing number in the following series: 3, 2, 4, 3, 6, ___, 10, 9

    (A) 5
    (B) 12
    (C) 3
    (D) 8

92. What number is 12 more than 4^3 divided by 4?

    (A) 26
    (B) 28
    (C) 16
    (D) 30

93. The number of eighths in 10 is

    (A) 80
    (B) 8
    (C) 16
    (D) 12

94. What is the next number in the following series: 1, 4, 2, 8, 3, 12, 4, ...

    (A) 10

    (B) 5

    (C) 16

    (D) 18

95. Examine (a), (b), and (c) and select the correct answer.

    (a) $31 - 2 \times 7$
    (b) $5 \times 4 - 8$
    (c) $7 + 6 - 2$

    (A) (c) − (b) = (a)

    (B) (b) + (c) = (a)

    (C) (a) > (b) + (c)

    (D) (a) > (b)

96. Line *BD* bisects right angle *B* and right angle *D* in square *ABCD* below. *E* is the midpoint of line *BD*. What portion of the square is shaded?

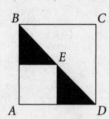

    (A) $\frac{1}{2}$

    (B) $\frac{1}{4}$

    (C) $\frac{1}{8}$

    (D) $\frac{1}{6}$

97. What is the next number in the following series: XI, 9, VII, 5, ...

    (A) 3

    (B) III

    (C) V

    (D) X

98. When a number is divided by 4, the quotient is 3 and the remainder is 1. What is the number?

    (A) 11
    (B) 12
    (C) 13
    (D) 14

99. Examine (a), (b), and (c) and select the correct answer.
    (a) $(5 + 1)^2$
    (b) $3^2 + 2^2$
    (c) $25 - 2 \times 3$

    (A) $(a) + (b) > (c)$
    (B) $(c) > (a) + (b)$
    (C) $(c) = (a) + (b)$
    (D) $(b) > (a) + (c)$

100. 15% of a school's student body rides a bicycle to school. If every student who rides chained his or her bicycle outside the school, and the number of bicycles chained outside the school is 12, what is the total number of students in the school?

    (A) 120
    (B) 800
    (C) 80
    (D) 1200

101. The sum of $\frac{3}{4}$ and $\frac{5}{6}$ is greater than $\frac{1}{2}$ by

    (A) $\frac{13}{12}$
    (B) $\frac{6}{14}$
    (C) $\frac{7}{8}$
    (D) $\frac{7}{14}$

102. $33\frac{1}{3}$ percent of a number is 15. What is the reciprocal of the number?
    (A) $\frac{1}{5}$
    (B) 5
    (C) 45
    (D) $\frac{1}{45}$

103. What is the next number in the following series:
      5, 10, 8, 7, 12, 10, 9, …

      (A) 7
      (B) 8
      (C) 11
      (D) 14

104. Examine the graph and select the correct answer.

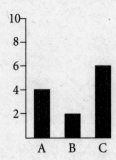

      (A) A + C = B
      (B) B + A = C
      (C) B + C = A
      (D) C > A + B

105. Examine the triangle and select the correct answer.

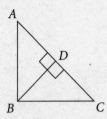

      (A) *AB* is greater than *AD*
      (B) *AD* and *DB* are greater than *AB* and *BC*
      (C) *AB* is equal to *AC*
      (D) *DC* is equal to *BC*

106. Examine (a), (b), and (c).

    (a) $3\frac{1}{2}\%$

    (b) $3\frac{1}{2}$

    (c) .33

    Which of the following is correct?

    (A) (b) > (a) + (c)
    (B) (a) > (b)
    (C) (a) = (b)
    (D) (a) = (c)

107. $\frac{2}{3}$ of what number added to 8 is 4 times 10?

    (A) 45
    (B) 96
    (C) 48
    (D) 32

108. What is the next number in the following series: $8, 6\frac{1}{2}, 5, 3\frac{1}{2}, \ldots$

    (A) 1
    (B) $1\frac{1}{2}$
    (C) 2
    (D) $2\frac{1}{4}$

109. What is the next number in the following series: 2, 4, 3, 6, 5, 10, …

    (A) 7
    (B) 8
    (C) 9
    (D) 5

110. What is the next term in the following series: Z1, Y2, X3, W4, …

    (A) V3
    (B) X3
    (C) X5
    (D) V5

111. What number is 8 less than 3 cubed?

(A) 18

(B) 27

(C) 19

(D) 20

112. Examine the parallelogram and select the correct answer.

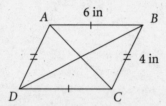

(A) The perimeter of the parallelogram is 10 inches.

(B) The area of triangle *ABD* is greater than the area of triangle *ACD*.

(C) The perimeter of triangle *BDA* is equal to the perimeter of parallelogram *ABCD*.

(D) The perimeter of parallelogram *ABCD* is 20 inches.

READING

Questions 113–174

25 Minutes

Comprehension

Directions: Read the passages and answer questions 113–152.

Read the following passage and answer questions 113–120.

In April 1861, when the Sixth Massachusetts Regiment arrived in Washington, D.C. without their baggage, one energetic woman set to work, supplying their needs. Clara Barton responded by supplying old sheets for towels and handkerchiefs, and cooking for the troops. Thus began an incredible career as a patriot and humanitarian.

After the battle of Bull Run, Barton was deeply affected by tales of shortages of supplies in the field. So, she advertised for <u>provisions</u> in a local newspaper. The public responded by sending huge amounts, and Barton established an agency to distribute them.

In 1862, the government granted Barton permission to <u>accompany</u> sick and wounded soldiers from the battlefield. Barton gave her sympathetic aid to many. After the war, she supervised a federal search for missing soldiers, eventually heading the Missing Soldiers Office. Barton was the first woman to run a government bureau. In her role, she tracked down information on nearly 22,000 soldiers before the office was closed in 1868.

From 1869 and 1873, Barton lived in Europe, where she worked with the International Red Cross distributing supplies in France and Germany during the Franco-Prussian War. She returned home in 1873 with Germany's Iron Cross for outstanding military service. She also returned with the goal of creating the Red Cross in the United States. She <u>campaigned</u> tirelessly for its establishment, educating the public through brochures and lobbying cabinet heads and Congress. Her efforts paid off, and in 1881, the National Society of the Red Cross was organized with a grant from John D. Rockefeller. The Red Cross' national headquarters were established in Washington, D.C., one block from the White House.

113. Barton began her career as a nurse in

(A) Washington, D.C.

(B) France

(C) Germany

(D) Massachusetts

114. As used in the passage, the word <u>accompany</u> most nearly means

(A) care for

(B) go with

(C) befriend

(D) cure

115. The best title for this selection would be

(A) Women of the Red Cross

(B) Battles of the Civil War

(C) Nursing Wounded Soldiers

(D) A Career of Caring

116. Clara volunteered to help soldiers because

(A) she was well-paid

(B) she was a school teacher

(C) she wanted to lessen their suffering

(D) she wanted to stop the war

117. As used in the passage, the word <u>provisions</u> most nearly means

(A) nurses

(B) soldiers

(C) supplies

(D) towels

118.   Clara won a medal for

(A) being a good soldier

(B) aiding soldiers during the Franco-Prussian War

(C) helping to locate missing soldiers

(D) establishing the Red Cross

119.   As used in the passage, the word <u>campaigned</u> most nearly means

(A) volunteered to help

(B) argued with politicians

(C) fought for recognition

(D) ran for office

120.   The author implies that it is patriotic to

(A) help one's fellow countrymen

(B) become a nurse

(C) join to the Red Cross

(D) travel in Europe

Read the following passage and answer questions 121–125.

   Since the invention of Henry Ford's first Model T, the automobile has had an enormous <u>impact</u> on life in the United States. What was once a novel form of transportation has become the source of two of the most powerful global industries: petroleum
and automobiles. Highways criss-cross our landscape, and automobile ownership
is at an astounding high. On average, we find three passenger vehicles for every four
Americans. But the American love affair with the automobile carries a high price.
   Almost all automobiles in the United States are powered by the combustion of petroleum. While these vehicles help make our lives easier, the combustion of fossil fuels is
an environmental hazard. Car emissions are a leading cause of global warming—the
gradual increase of our Earth's temperature. Yet, people seem to accept the sacrifices
that owning a car requires. We continue to buy more cars and bigger cars. The United
States leads the world in car ownership, at about 0.8 cars per capita. Meanwhile,
American motor vehicles consume more than 150 billion gallons of petroleum per
year. The manufacture and use of gasoline for consumer vehicles cause more environmental damage than any other single consumer spending category. Environmental
hazards could be considered a speed bump on the road of modern convenience.

121.   The main idea of this passage is that

(A) Henry Ford changed the face of America

(B) every step forward comes with a price

(C) the automobile causes global warming

(D) highways have taken the place of parks

122. As used in the passage, the word <u>impact</u> most nearly means

   (A) effect
   (B) damage
   (C) strike
   (D) benefit

123. The author of this passage

   (A) uses foreshadowing
   (B) discusses historical facts
   (C) includes statistics
   (D) uses quotations

124. Why did the author choose to begin by mentioning the Model T?

   (A) She wanted the reader to think about how cars have changed our lives.
   (B) She wanted the reader to realize how much cars have changed the environment.
   (C) She wanted the passage to be humorous in tone.
   (D) The Model T was the first car to be mass-produced.

125. In the last sentence of paragraph 1, what is the author really trying to say about
   the American love affair with the automobile carr[ying] a high price?

   (A) that cars are expensive in the United States
   (B) that the large number of cars in the United States will have a negative effect on the
   environment
   (C) that everyone in the United States can afford to buy a car
   (D) that Americans love to pay a lot of money for things

Read the following passage and answer questions 126–132.

   The first amendment to the Bill of Rights states, "Congress shall make no law …
abridging the freedom of speech…." This amendment was passed to protect our right
to express our opinions without fear. Yet, we must stop using the first amendment as a
justification to say whatever we want, whenever we want. No speech is "free" when it
has detrimental effects on the well-being of others, the protection of our privacy, the
safety of our borders, or the quality of our thinking.

   While censorship is not the way of this land, we must take into account the effect of
musical lyrics that influence young listeners. How often do we find ourselves singing a
tune, or repeating a phrase from a song instinctively, without stopping to ponder the
meaning of the words? When those words are <u>demeaning</u> to any group of people, or
when they incite violence, we are unknowingly repeating phrases of hate. How long
does it take until those phrases become worn into our patterns of thought and we find
ourselves believing the words we mindlessly hummed?

126. The best title for this selection would be

    (A) The Bill of Rights

    (B) Think About What You Say

    (C) The First Amendment

    (D) Ban Bad Music

127. As used in the passage, the word <u>demeaning</u> most nearly means

    (A) distasteful

    (B) complimentary

    (C) insulting

    (D) delightful

128. The author implies that the most important aim of the right to free speech is

    (A) the ability to disagree with Congress

    (B) the ability to say whatever you want whenever you want

    (C) the right to express our opinions freely

    (D) the right to listen to violent music

129. The author attempts to persuade the reader with

    (A) statistics

    (B) impassioned generalizations

    (C) historical quotations

    (D) anecdotes and examples

130. Phrases become *worn into our patterns of thought* when

    (A) we repeat them again and again

    (B) we listen to music

    (C) we agree with them

    (D) we think about them

131. According to the author, speech is not free when it

    (A) must be purchased

    (B) is ugly

    (C) is censored

    (D) harms others

132. This passage is most likely from a(n)

    (A) speech given to a radio station

    (B) textbook on the Constitution

    (C) magazine article on American music

    (D) editorial in a school newspaper

Read the following passage and answer questions 133–140.

Throughout the history of humankind, people have wondered why children take after one parent or another. Yet, it was research into plant biology that ultimately helped answer questions about human genetics. In the 1860s a little known Central European monk, named Gregor Mendel discovered the secrets of <u>heredity</u> through his observations growing pea plants. By selectively growing common pea plants over many generations, Mendel discovered that particular characteristics showed up in the off-spring pea plants again and again. For example, Mendel found that pea flowers are either purple or white; they are never a blend of these colors. In all, Mendel found seven traits could be <u>readily</u> observed in only one of two forms. These traits included flower color, flower position, stem length, seed shape, seed color, pod shape, and pod color. This observation was in direct contrast to the theorists of day, who believed that that traits blended from generation to generation. In cross pollinating plants, or breeding plants with different traits, Mendel found that the first generation always exhibited only one trait. For example, a short plant and a tall plant would only yield tall plants. However, the second generation would yield 3 tall and 1 short plants—a 3 to 1 ratio.

Observing many pea plants over many generations, Mendel concluded three important things. First, that traits were passed on to offspring unchanged. Second, that an individual inherits traits from each parent. And third, that even though a trait may not show up in one individual, it could still be passed on to the next generation. These three observations were enormously important in helping understand human heredity.

133. Which of the following definitions of <u>heredity</u> best fits its use in this selection?

    (A) genetics

    (B) inherited wealth

    (C) inherited personality

    (D) plant biology

134. The title that best fits the this selection is

    (A) Nature not Nurture

    (B) Peas in a Pod

    (C) Observing Life

    (D) It's All in the Genes

135. The number of traits Mendel observed in pea plants is

(A) three
(B) seven
(C) four
(D) innumerable

136. Which of the following is most likely true of Gregor Mendel?

(A) He was impatient.
(B) He was lonely.
(C) He was systematic.
(D) He was friendly with Charles Darwin.

137. Which of the following is true of traits?

(A) They blend from one generation to the next.
(B) They appear unchanged from one generation to the next.
(C) If they appear in one generation, they are never seen again.
(D) They are cross-pollinated.

138. Mendel's system of research was based on

(A) Central European education
(B) writings of his fellow monks
(C) existing theories
(D) careful observation

139. Within any offspring

(A) traits can be inherited from either parent
(B) traits can be inherited from the father only
(C) traits can be inherited from the mother only
(D) traits appear the same way in each generation

140. As used in the passage, the word readily most nearly means

(A) scientifically
(B) understandably
(C) easily
(D) surprisingly

Read the following passage and answer questions 141–146.

The dictionary tells us that the root of the word *communicate* comes from the Latin verb *comunicare*: to make common, to make known, to be connected, to have an interchange of thoughts, ideas, and feelings. <u>Genuine</u> communication is more than an exchange of words; it is the process of sharing meaning. This act of sharing <u>naturally</u> involves two individuals—the one sending the message, and the one receiving it. The ability to share your ideas effectively requires not only that you present an idea, but also that you also make sure your intended message is interpreted correctly by the receiver. In order to minimize any misunderstanding, you must pay careful attention to the words you choose, your body language, and your tone of voice. Research shows that people pay more attention to tone of voice and body language than they do to the actual words used in a message. In other words, if your behaviors transmit one message and your words transmit another, the listener will pay more attention to the behaviors.

141. The best title for this selection would be

    (A) How to Be a Good Listener

    (B) Sending Messages

    (C) Effective Communication

    (D) Body Language

142. As used in the passage, the word <u>genuine</u> most nearly means

    (A) real

    (B) intelligent

    (C) extraordinary

    (D) spontaneous

143. Communication takes place when

    (A) two people understand one another

    (B) one person talks, and one person listens

    (C) two people talk with one another

    (D) two people speak the same language

144. Which of the following is stressed in this passage as an advantage of choosing your words carefully?

    (A) influence others

    (B) communicate more often

    (C) make people pay attention

    (D) eliminate any misunderstanding

145. This passage most likely was printed in a

   (A) manual on how to run effective meetings

   (B) treatise on effective management

   (C) textbook on linguistics

   (D) social studies textbook

146. As used in the passage, the word <u>naturally</u> most nearly means

   (A) accidentally

   (B) purely

   (C) organically

   (D) obviously

Read the following passage and answer questions 147–152.

   Throughout the first few decades of American diplomacy, the first and foremost principle of American foreign <u>policy</u> was isolationism. As laid out by George Washington in his speech of 1796, isolationism meant that the United States should form no permanent alliance and should forge "as little political connection as possible" with foreign powers. However, this policy applied only to diplomatic relations, since trade with other nations was an essential element of the American economy.

   In the early 1800s, the United States expanded its isolationist policies to the entire western hemisphere. President Monroe, in his now famous address to Congress, stated that the United States would stay out of European affairs, and that in turn, Europe should not intervene in <u>affairs</u> of the Americas. This policy, known as the Monroe Doctrine, was designed to signal a clear break between the New World and the Old. However, it also was used to assert American influence in Latin America.

147. The best title for this selection would be

   (A) President Monroe

   (B) American Diplomacy Past and Present

   (C) Evolution of the Monroe Doctrine

   (D) American Neutrality

148. As used in the passage, the word <u>policy</u> most nearly means

   (A) guiding principles

   (B) strict regulations

   (C) exact measurements

   (D) political arguments

149. In the 1800s, isolationism came to mean

    (A) the United States' refusal to trade with other nations
    (B) the United States' influence over the western hemisphere
    (C) interference in European affairs
    (D) a break between the United States and Latin America

150. Isolationism does *not* mean

    (A) reluctance to form permanent alliances
    (B) minimizing political affiliations
    (C) American refusal to side with any one European nation
    (D) banning of all trade

151. Comparing the two paragraphs, we can say that

    (A) the first paragraph contains more statistics than the second
    (B) the second provides examples of ideas discussed in the first
    (C) the second shows a shift in the definition of isolationism
    (D) the second paragraph completely disagrees with the first

152. As used in the passage, the word affairs most nearly means

    (A) festivities
    (B) wars
    (C) meetings
    (D) business

Vocabulary

Directions: For questions 153–174, choose the word that is closest in meaning to the underlined word.

153. to <u>apprehend</u> a criminal

    (A) catch

    (B) understand

    (C) view

    (D) approach

154. to <u>secure</u> an agreement

    (A) break

    (B) protect

    (C) end

    (D) obtain

155. <u>blatant</u> disrespect

    (A) angry

    (B) unfair

    (C) youthful

    (D) obvious

156. <u>excessive</u> spending

    (A) exact

    (B) enormous

    (C) successful

    (D) necessary

157. an <u>unassailable</u> fortress

    (A) impenetrable

    (B) unprotected

    (C) undefeated

    (D) ancient

158. an added <u>incentive</u>

    (A) profit

    (B) rebate

    (C) motivation

    (D) demand

159. a <u>scowling</u> face

    (A) pale

    (B) ruddy

    (C) beautiful

    (D) frowning

160. an <u>ulterior</u> motive

    (A) concealed

    (B) alternate

    (C) unwise

    (D) ultimate

161. to <u>aggravate</u> one's mother

    (A) bother

    (B) embrace

    (C) boss

    (D) discuss

162. an <u>executive</u> decision

    (A) governing

    (B) friendly

    (C) stern

    (D) serious

163. to <u>contemplate</u> an idea

    (A) judge

    (B) consider

    (C) punish

    (D) decide

164. an <u>efficient</u> worker

    (A) expensive

    (B) shoddy

    (C) outgoing

    (D) capable

165. an <u>unprecedented</u> ruling

(A) strict
(B) extraordinary
(C) unanimous
(D) orderly

166. a <u>verbatim</u> quote

(A) brief
(B) historical
(C) wordy
(D) exact

167. to <u>resolve</u> an argument

(A) settle
(B) break
(C) win
(D) avoid

168. <u>subordinate</u> rank

(A) high
(B) military
(C) inferior
(D) organized

169. a <u>perilous</u> journey

(A) lengthy
(B) hazardous
(C) solitary
(D) adventurous

170. to <u>refrain</u> from eating

(A) cease
(B) return
(C) sing
(D) resolve

171. a <u>dilapidated</u> building

(A) luxurious
(B) overrated
(C) decayed
(D) renovated

172. a <u>prevailing</u> theory

(A) proven
(B) dominant
(C) technical
(D) antiquated

173. to <u>found</u> a business

(A) lead
(B) tax
(C) discover
(D) begin

174. a <u>credible</u> witness

(A) trustworthy
(B) legal
(C) unbelievable
(D) experienced

MATHEMATICS

Questions 175–238

45 Minutes

Directions: For questions 175–238, choose the best answer.

Concepts

175. Which of the following is *not* a type of angle?

    (A) obtuse
    (B) acute
    (C) positive
    (D) right

176. $\{4, 5, 7, 9, 11\} \cap \{5, 7, 10, 11\} =$

    (A) $\{4, 5, 7, 9\}$
    (B) $\{3, 6, 9, 12\}$
    (C) $\{5, 7, 11\}$
    (D) $\{5, 6, 7, 11\}$

177. What is 83.456 rounded to the nearest tenth?

    (A) 83
    (B) 83.45
    (C) 83.5
    (D) 83.46

178. Simplify: $2(-3)^3 =$

    (A) −52
    (B) −54
    (C) −27
    (D) −44

179. As a fraction, .45 equals

    (A) $\frac{45}{1000}$
    (B) $\frac{100}{45}$
    (C) $\frac{9}{20}$
    (D) $\frac{1}{2}$

180. The measure of angle *A* is

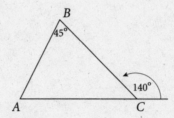

(A) 95°

(B) 90°

(C) 85°

(D) 80°

181. To divide a number by 100, move the decimal point

(A) two places to the right

(B) three places to the right

(C) two places to the left

(D) four places to the right

182. Which of the following is a pair of reciprocals?

(A) $(4 \times 2), (2 \times 4)$

(B) $2\frac{1}{2}, \frac{2}{5}$

(C) $2^4, 4^2$

(D) $.25, \frac{1}{4}$

183. The area of this circle is

(A) $3\pi \, m^2$

(B) $9\pi \, m^2$

(C) $6\pi \, m^2$

(D) $12\pi \, m^2$

184. The ratio of 36 inches to 2 yards is equivalent to

(A) 1 to 2

(B) 2 to 1

(C) 3 to 2

(D) 1 to 3

185. How many integers are between $\frac{17}{2}$ and 9.5?

(A) 1

(B) 2

(C) 12

(D) 0

186. Which of the following is true?

(A) $\frac{a+b+a}{b} = a(b+a)$

(B) $a(b+c) = ab + ac$

(C) $a + b + b^2 = a \, b(b)$

(D) $2a + 2b + 2c = 2(abc)$

187. Which of the following numbers is an example of a perfect square?

(A) 12

(B) 24

(C) 32

(D) 81

188. Which of these is correctly written in scientific notation?

    (A) $345 \times \left(\frac{1}{10}\right)^3 = 345,000$

    (B) $3.45 \times 10^2 = 345$

    (C) $.345 \times 10^4 = 345$

    (D) $.0345 \times 10^4 = 345$

189. Two integers are in the ratio 5:7. The sum of the two integers is 36. What is the larger integer?

    (A) 36

    (B) 15

    (C) 21

    (D) 7

190. The exact number of hundreds in 8,675 is

    (A) 875

    (B) 8675

    (C) 86.75

    (D) .8675

191. A luncheonette serves lemonade in 8-ounce glasses. How many servings can be obtained from 2 gallons of lemonade?

    (A) 32

    (B) 128

    (C) 256

    (D) 64

192. At a school bake sale, the marching band sold two more brownies than cupcakes. In total, the marching band sold 30 items. How many cupcakes did they sell?

    (A) 14

    (B) 28

    (C) 15

    (D) 10

193. What is the measure in degrees of each acute angle in an isosceles right triangle?

    (A) 50

    (B) 90

    (C) 36

    (D) 45

194. The formula for the area of rectangle is

(A) $A = (\text{length})(\text{width})$

(B) $A = \frac{1}{2}(\text{base})(\text{height})$

(C) $A = (\text{diameter})(\pi)$

(D) $A = (\text{width})(\text{base})(\text{height})$

195. If triangle DCE is similar to triangle ABC, the length of AB is

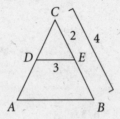

(A) 6 units

(B) 12 units

(C) 5 units

(D) 4 units

196. The prime factorization of 16 is

(A) 4^3

(B) 4×4

(C) 2×4

(D) $2 \times 2 \times 2 \times 2$

197. The lowest common denominator of $\frac{1}{3}$ and $\frac{2}{9}$ is

(A) 15

(B) 9

(C) 2

(D) 3

198. Which of the following is *not* equivalent to $75\frac{1}{2}\%$?

(A) $\frac{151}{200}$

(B) 75.5

(C) $\frac{75.5}{100}$

(D) .755

Problem Solving

199. Find the difference between $3\frac{1}{4}$ and $1\frac{1}{5}$.

    (A) $2\frac{1}{20}$

    (B) $2\frac{1}{4}$

    (C) $2\frac{1}{6}$

    (D) $1\frac{1}{2}$

200. Solve: $-2 + 6 + (-4) + (-1) =$

    (A) -3

    (B) -4

    (C) -7

    (D) -1

201. A family went to the amusement park and bought 10 ride tickets for the Ferris wheel at $3.25 each and 4 tickets for the roller coaster at $2.75 each. How much did they spend?

    (A) $31.50

    (B) $31.25

    (C) $43.50

    (D) $43.25

202. Find the product: $1\frac{1}{5} \times 2\frac{1}{4} \times 1\frac{1}{3} =$

    (A) $3\frac{3}{5}$

    (B) 3

    (C) $3\frac{4}{5}$

    (D) 4

203. If a building has a shadow 12 feet long when a 3-foot tall child has a shadow 1 foot long, what is the height of the building?

    (A) 36 feet

    (B) 12 feet

    (C) 34 feet

    (D) 4 feet

204. Solve for x in the following equation:

    $10 + 2x = x + 14$

    (A) 4
    (B) 14
    (C) 10
    (D) 8

205. Mrs. Young drove 1,250 miles last week. Approximately how much, on average, did she drive each day for the 7 days?

    (A) 205
    (B) 105
    (C) 125
    (D) 179

206. If the 8% tax on a new car was $1,600, how much was the car, not including tax?

    (A) $30,000
    (B) $2,000
    (C) $20,000
    (D) $25,000

207. Martin has 4 dollars less than 2 times the amount his sister has. If his sister has $36, how much does Martin have?

    (A) $36
    (B) $72
    (C) $68
    (D) $34

208. If $2a + 3 > 9$, then a^2 must be

    (A) equal to 6
    (B) less than 9
    (C) greater than 9
    (D) equal to 9

209. A salesman earns 5% commission on every piece of furniture he sells. If he sells 4 sofas at $1,200 each, what is his commission?

    (A) $280
    (B) $2,400
    (C) $120
    (D) $240

210. If 20 is added to an integer and the result is $\frac{3}{2}$ of the integer, what is the integer?

    (A) 30

    (B) 15

    (C) 20

    (D) 40

211. Solve: $1\frac{1}{2} + 2\frac{1}{3} + 2\frac{1}{4} =$

    (A) $6\frac{1}{12}$

    (B) $5\frac{1}{12}$

    (C) $6\frac{1}{2}$

    (D) $7\frac{7}{12}$

212. If the sum of two numbers is x and one of the numbers is 5, then three times the other number is

    (A) $3(x-5)$

    (B) $3(x+5)$

    (C) $3x+5$

    (D) $3x(5)$

213. The fancy chocolate shop charges $2 per ounce of chocolate. What is the cost of a gift box with 1 pound, 4 ounces of chocolate?

    (A) $40.00

    (B) $4.00

    (C) $8.00

    (D) $6.00

214. If $x + 5 = y + 10$, then

    (A) $x > y$

    (B) $x = y$

    (C) $x < y$

    (D) $x = y - 5$

215. Find the value of $3x^2 + 2y - 1$ if $x = \frac{1}{3}$ and $y = 2$.

  (A) $3\frac{1}{9}$

  (B) $3\frac{1}{3}$

  (C) $5\frac{1}{6}$

  (D) 30

216. The Smiths paid $ 420 interest on a loan that had a 6% simple interest rate. How much did they borrow?

  (A) $7,000

  (B) $8,000

  (C) $700

  (D) $800

217. What is the volume of this cube solid?

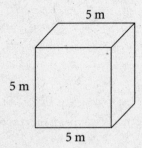

  5 m

  5 m

  5 m

  (A) $125\,m^3$

  (B) $250\,m^3$

  (C) $500\,m^3$

  (D) $150\,m^3$

218. How many strips of paper $1\frac{1}{3}$ inches long can be cut from a sheet of paper $4\frac{1}{4}$ inches long?

  (A) $5\frac{2}{3}$

  (B) $5\frac{1}{3}$

  (C) 4

  (D) $3\frac{3}{16}$

219. Solve: $3.22\overline{)1.5232}$ =

    (A) .57

    (B) .47

    (C) 47

    (D) 57

220. If P% of 60 is 12, then P =

    (A) 20

    (B) 200

    (C) 66

    (D) 60

221. Solve: $233.5 \times .051$ =

    (A) 1.19085

    (B) 11.9085

    (C) .119085

    (D) 119.085

222. Solve: $.784 + 8.2 + .31$ =

    (A) 9.294

    (B) 16.35

    (C) 11.914

    (D) 12.084

223. If the tax rate is $3.72 per $100, how much are the taxes on a home valued at 500,000?

    (A) $1,750

    (B) $1,860

    (C) $18,600

    (D) $17,500

224. If $5x - 8 > 2$, then

    (A) $x^3 > 8$

    (B) $x^3 > 16$

    (C) $x^3 > 9$

    (D) $x^3 > 7$

225. Mr. Battle earns $36,000 annually. He puts 5% of his salary in a savings account toward his retirement. How much does Mr. Battle save for retirement each month?

    (A) $150
    (B) $180
    (C) $1,800
    (D) $1,500

226. Given the series: 23.01, 23.04, 23.07, 24.0... What number should come next?

    (A) 24.02
    (B) 24.03
    (C) 25.01
    (D) 24.01

227. Solve: $726 \times 19 =$

    (A) 13,794
    (B) 12,794
    (C) 14,794
    (D) 13,804

228. What is the area of the figure shown in the diagram?

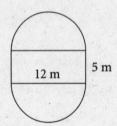

12 m   5 m

    (A) $(60 + \frac{3}{2}\pi)$ m^2
    (B) $(60 + 9\pi)$ m^2
    (C) $(60 + 3\pi)$ m^2
    (D) $(60 + 36\pi)$ m^2

229. Solve for x: $\left(\frac{2}{3} + \frac{2}{5}\right) - \left(\frac{1}{3} + \frac{1}{10}\right) = x$

    (A) $\frac{1}{6}$
    (B) $\frac{6}{5}$
    (C) $\frac{5}{6}$
    (D) $\frac{19}{30}$

230. The product of 8 and 9 is 12 more than x. What is x?

    (A) 50

    (B) 69

    (C) 68

    (D) 60

231. $ABCD$ is a rectangle in which $AD = 9$ inches and $DC = 15$ inches. What is the area, in square inches, of the rectangle?

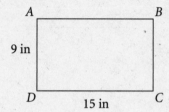

    (A) 135

    (B) 144

    (C) 120

    (D) 108

232. The ratio of $\frac{1}{3}$ to $\frac{5}{9}$ is equivalent to

    (A) $\frac{5}{3}$

    (B) $\frac{3}{5}$

    (C) $\frac{5}{27}$

    (D) $\frac{5}{18}$

233. If the square root of $y - 3$ is equal to 2, then $y =$

    (A) 7

    (B) 4

    (C) 9

    (D) 8

234. A ladder is extended to a length of 10 feet and is leaning against the side of a house. If the base of the ladder is 6 feet from the house, how high up the house does the ladder reach?

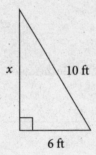

x 10 ft

6 ft

(A) 12 ft

(B) 10 ft

(C) 6 ft

(D) 8 ft

235. Which number is a multiple of 60?

(A) 213

(B) 350

(C) 540

(D) 1,060

236. On a cross-country tour, Rosemarie drove 60 miles in one day—40% of her planned mileage for that day. How many more miles did Rosemarie plan to drive that day?

(A) 70

(B) 90

(C) 60

(D) 150

237. The measure of two acute angels of a right triangle is in a ratio of 2:1. The measure of the larger acute angle is

(A) 35

(B) 50

(C) 60

(D) 30

238. Solve for x: $.8x + 5.5 = 9.7$

(A) 5

(B) 5.25

(C) 5.50

(D) .52

LANGUAGE

Questions 239–298

25 Minutes

Usage

Directions: For questions 239–278 choose the sentence that contains an error in punctuation, capitalization, or usage. If there is no error, select choice (D).

239. (A) It's been a very cold winter.
    (B) The Tigers won a victory over the falcons.
    (C) Why don't you bring your sister to the party?
    (D) No mistake.

240. (A) I had never been on a roller coaster before.
    (B) The students took off they're coats.
    (C) Marjorie asked, "Who is the fastest runner on the team?"
    (D) No mistake.

241. (A) Safety is our primary concern.
    (B) We should of voted in the election.
    (C) How often have you been to Los Angeles?
    (D) No mistake.

242. (A) Aunt Edith bought a new tractor.
    (B) They won't allow dogs in the store.
    (C) The Hudson River is a great place to sail.
    (D) No mistake.

243. (A) Neither Alice and John liked the book.
    (B) I prefer chocolate ice cream.
    (C) Maria, please sit down.
    (D) No mistake.

244. (A) She is a Professor at the college.
    (B) Veronica promised to visit this afternoon.
    (C) If you're ready, please let me know.
    (D) No mistake.

245. (A) There aren't any peaches left.
    (B) A swan lives by the community pond.
    (C) I looked, but I couldn't find the book nowhere.
    (D) No mistake.

246. (A) We still haven't agreed on a solution.
     (B) The situation will affect everyone.
     (C) If you finish quick, we will have time to go to the store.
     (D) No mistake.

247. (A) I wish you could have seen her reaction.
     (B) She lended her book to Thomas.
     (C) Doesn't she want to join us?
     (D) No mistake.

248. (A) He hung the clothes on the clothesline.
     (B) The faucet has been leaking for days.
     (C) I've been studying Spanish for five years.
     (D) No mistake.

249. (A) I believe you are the first to arrive.
     (B) That there boy lost his eyeglasses.
     (C) Which jacket belongs to Sally?
     (D) No mistake.

250. (A) If she had known there would be cake, Rachel would of come.
     (B) It's a long way from Boston to New York City.
     (C) Joseph and I are renting a canoe.
     (D) No mistake.

251. (A) Would you like a piece of pie?
     (B) My favorite season is summer.
     (C) The lion got a thorn in it's paw.
     (D) No mistake.

252. (A) The book was wrote by Jim.
     (B) The office will be closed on Memorial Day.
     (C) I saw the movie that you recommended.
     (D) No mistake.

253. (A) Who's coat is this?
     (B) Give the pen and paper to us.
     (C) We can take care of the mistake ourselves.
     (D) No mistake.

254. (A) Don't forget to wear your helmet.
     (B) The plants have grown since you watered them.
     (C) I hope you return back the library books on time.
     (D) No mistake.

255. (A) We go to school every day accept Saturday and Sunday.
     (B) Don't forget to study your lesson.
     (C) Carlos is teaching his brother how to spell.
     (D) No mistake.

256. (A) If you feel tired, why don't you lie down?
     (B) Actually, I'd rather not go.
     (C) Lisa asked, "Did you keep your receipt?"
     (D) No mistake.

257. (A) The policeman is controlling traffic.
     (B) We had never went bowling before.
     (C) That's a great kick!
     (D) No mistake.

258. (A) Each of the books is interesting.
     (B) We eat turkey on Thanksgiving.
     (C) Barb and me are going to play tennis.
     (D) No mistake.

259. (A) What is the capital of Illinois?
     (B) Which house is Mary's?
     (C) We telephoned her and Carol.
     (D) No mistake.

260. (A) Can you lift that heavy chair?
     (B) Aunt Charlene brought us each a present.
     (C) John plays the saxophone as well as Christopher does.
     (D) No mistake.

261. (A) Can I watch television tonight?
     (B) Please help me clean up.
     (C) George asked us all to come to his game.
     (D) No mistake.

262. (A) Donald told us to turn right from the corner.
     (B) "Hey," said Karen, "do you want to ride bicycles?"
     (C) It's a lovely day, isn't it?
     (D) No mistake.

263. (A) Have you seen Anthonys golf clubs?
     (B) I'd like to practice two or three hours a day.
     (C) The coach asked the team to take their uniforms home.
     (D) No mistake.

264. (A) We don't owe them nothing.
     (B) I would rather go to the beach than to the movies.
     (C) John enjoys reading novels.
     (D) No mistake.

265. (A) It is important to exercise daily.
     (B) She wouldn't of come if she knew he would be there.
     (C) Is it time to leave yet?
     (D) No mistake.

266. (A) Mary is taller then Pete.
     (B) Most people have some artistic talent.
     (C) How many apples are in the carton?
     (D) No mistake.

267. (A) How often does Jack bake?
     (B) Daniel and his friend John have made the Dean's List.
     (C) Its too late to begin the project now.
     (D) No mistake.

268. (A) I just called to say hello.
     (B) Patricia's mother will drive.
     (C) Why you don't come with us?
     (D) No mistake.

269. (A) Let's go to the store after lunch.
     (B) Why do you think she cancelled the meeting?
     (C) You and me are best friends.
     (D) No mistake.

270. (A) Us students must organize a petition.

(B) I'll let you know what time the game begins.

(C) Our whole band played well yesterday.

(D) No mistake.

271. (A) Drive slow in the center of town.

(B) Harry apologized for his mistake.

(C) This kind of behavior is unacceptable.

(D) No mistake.

272. (A) The men's room is down the hall to the left.

(B) My sisters and I all share a room.

(C) I've bought a new folder for my homework.

(D) No mistake.

273. (A) Clarence graduated at the head of his class.

(B) You should have spoken to your mother.

(C) The Great Lakes are in the northern United States.

(D) No mistake.

274. (A) The commander issued an order.

(B) Would you please pass the salt?

(C) Jim please set the table.

(D) No mistake.

275. (A) Can you describe what happened?

(B) Marie Curie was a brilliant scientist.

(C) I didn't see nothing.

(D) No mistake.

276. (A) I'm relieved that no one was hurt.

(B) If you have a question, raise your hand.

(C) Frank throws as well as her does.

(D) No mistake.

277. (A) We have more cousins than you.

(B) Sit down immediately!

(C) Dad's going to cook dinner tonight.

(D) No mistake.

278. (A) When she was finished the crowd applauded.
     (B) The baby is sleeping soundly.
     (C) Will you be joining us this evening?
     (D) No mistake.

Spelling

Directions: For questions 279–288, choose the sentence that contains a spelling error. If there is no error, select choice (D).

279. (A) Emily telephoned recently.
     (B) Did you recieve instructions?
     (C) Everyone except Claire will come.
     (D) No mistake.

280. (A) Please disregard my previous message.
     (B) Dad apologized for blaming Tim.
     (C) The principle patrolled the corridors of the school.
     (D) No mistake.

281. (A) The substitute teacher is very nice.
     (B) That was a terrific show.
     (C) I am going to cancel my subscription.
     (D) No mistake.

282. (A) What time will the room be availible?
     (B) Smoking is not allowed in public places.
     (C) We used various fruits in the salad.
     (D) No mistake.

283. (A) She gave me many encouraging words.
     (B) It is important to coopurate with the rest of the team.
     (C) Kate is concerned about her younger cousin.
     (D) No mistake.

284. (A) Martin pretended not to recognize me at the party.
     (B) We were disappointed that the show was mediocer.
     (C) I'm sure you are capable of completing the task.
     (D) No mistake.

285. (A) The doctor prescribed cough medicine.
     (B) Please complete the questionaire.
     (C) No one can predict the future.
     (D) No mistake.

286. (A) The hole is not noticeable.
     (B) We will conduct a formal inquiry.
     (C) Dana is an excelent athlete.
     (D) No mistake.

287. (A) We refered her to the proper authorities.
     (B) Everyone sympathized with the main character.
     (C) Forgive me, I bumped into you by accident.
     (D) No mistake.

288. (A) The audiance was amazed.
     (B) Whether or not you agree, I like this book very much.
     (C) Everyone except Mary attended the lecture.
     (D) No mistake.

Composition

Directions: For questions 289–298, follow the directions for each question.

289. Choose the word that is a clear connective to complete the sentence.

     The blizzard raged outside; _____ we remained cautiously at home, sitting rapt by the fire.

     (A) in addition,
     (B) for example,
     (C) therefore,
     (D) none of these

290. Choose the group of words that best completes the sentence.

     Before planting the seeds, _____.

     (A) watering the ground well was what Bob did
     (B) Bob first watered the ground
     (C) the ground was well watered, Bob made sure
     (D) water the ground was first for Bob

291. Choose the group of words that best completes the sentence.
      Most athletes find that it is essential _____ .

      (A) daily practicing
      (B) for practicing daily
      (C) to practice daily
      (D) daily to practice

292. Which choice most clearly expresses the intended meaning?

      (A) The violin was played by the musician beautifully.
      (B) The musician played her violin beautifully.
      (C) The violin played by the musician was beautiful.
      (D) The musician's violin, when played, played beautifully.

293. Which choice most clearly expresses the intended meaning?

      (A) After playing all afternoon, the hammock looked inviting.
      (B) The hammock looked inviting after playing all afternoon.
      (C) Playing all afternoon, the hammock looked inviting.
      (D) After we played all afternoon, the hammock looked inviting.

294. Which of the following pairs of sentences fits best under this topic sentence?
      John Wayne is best known for his cowboy roles in films of the wild west.

      (A) His portrayal of tough but fair cowboys won him a place in America's heart. He
           has become a symbol of our national spirit.
      (B) His incredible career spanned 50 years. He acted in more than 200 films.
      (C) There are not many cowboys around anymore. Nonetheless, kids still enjoy
           wearing cowboy costumes for Halloween.
      (D) His heroism was notable not only on screen, but in his life as well. He was a model
           of character for a generation.

295. Which of the following expresses the idea most clearly?

      (A) The 7 A.M. bus she took in order to arrive at work on time.
      (B) She took the 7 A.M. bus in order to arrive at work on time.
      (C) In order to arrive at work on time, the 7 A.M. bus she took.
      (D) The 7 A.M. bus she took, and she arrived at work on time.

296. Which of these best fits under the topic "Protecting Our Natural Resources"?

    (A) The National Parks system was created by Theodore Roosevelt to ensure that Americans could enjoy nature for generations to come.

    (B) It is important to regulate the high cost of petroleum.

    (C) Many zoos feature exhibits that allow the animals space to roam.

    (D) Uranium is an important source of energy.

297. Choose the best word or words to join the thoughts together.

In the North, textile mills and other industrial plants fueled the economy; _____ agriculture was the staple of the economy in the South.

    (A) therefore,

    (B) in contrast,

    (C) moreover,

    (D) none of these

298. Which of the following sentences best creates an element of foreshadowing?

    (A) The foghorn's deep and spine-tingling sound cut through the night as the ship approached Thunder Bay.

    (B) In the end, detectives determined that the watch had been stolen by the butler.

    (C) Mosquitoes are the most misunderstood members of the insect world.

    (D) The people of this enchanted isle lived isolated from the woes of modern society.

ANSWER KEY

Verbal Skills

1.	D	36.	C	70.	D
2.	A	37.	D	71.	B
3.	A	38.	A	72.	D
4.	B	39.	C	73.	C
5.	C	40.	C	74.	A
6.	A	41.	A	75.	C
7.	A	42.	D	76.	B
8.	B	43.	B	77.	A
9.	D	44.	D	78.	D
10.	C	45.	B	79.	A
11.	A	46.	B	80.	C
12.	D	47.	C	81.	A
13.	D	48.	A	82.	B
14.	B	49.	D	83.	D
15.	A	50.	C	84.	C
16.	D	51.	C	85.	C
17.	A	52.	D	86.	C
18.	A	53.	A	87.	A
19.	C	54.	D	88.	D
20.	B	55.	A	89.	B
21.	D	56.	A	90.	B
22.	D	57.	D	91.	A
23.	C	58.	B	92.	B
24.	B	59.	B	93.	A
25.	D	60.	C	94.	C
26.	A			95.	D

Quantitative Skills

27.	C	61.	D	96.	B
28.	A	62.	A	97.	B
29.	C	63.	B	98.	C
30.	C	64.	C	99.	A
31.	B	65.	A	100.	C
32.	A	66.	D	101.	A
33.	C	67.	C	102.	D
34.	B	68.	B	103.	D
35.	B	69.	D	104.	B
				105.	A

106. A	140. C	**MATHEMATICS**
107. C	141. C	**Concepts**
108. C	142. A	175. C
109. C	143. A	176. C
110. D	144. D	177. C
111. C	145. A	178. B
112. D	146. D	179. C
	147. C	180. A
READING	148. A	181. C
Comprehension	149. B	182. B
113. A	150. D	183. B
114. B	151. C	184. A
115. D	152. D	185. A
116. C		186. B
117. C	**Vocabulary**	187. D
118. B	153. A	188. B
119. C	154. D	189. C
120. A	155. D	190. C
121. B	156. B	191. A
122. A	157. A	192. A
123. C	158. C	193. D
124. A	159. D	194. A
125. B	160. A	195. A
126. B	161. A	196. D
127. C	162. A	197. B
128. C	163. B	198. B
129. B	164. D	
130. A	165. B	**Problem Solving**
131. D	166. D	199. A
132. A	167. A	200. D
133. A	168. C	201. C
134. D	169. B	202. A
135. B	170. A	203. A
136. C	171. C	204. A
137. B	172. B	205. D
138. D	173. D	206. C
139. A	174. A	207. C

208. C
209. D
210. D
211. A
212. A
213. A
214. A
215. B
216. A
217. A
218. D
219. B
220. A
221. B
222. A
223. C
224. A
225. A
226. B
227. A
228. D
229. D
230. D
231. A
232. B
233. A
234. D
235. C
236. B
237. C
238. B

LANGUAGE

Usage

240. B
241. B
242. D
243. A

244. A
245. C
246. C
247. B
248. D
249. B
250. A
251. C
252. A
253. A
254. C
255. A
256. D
257. B
258. C
259. D
260. D
261. A
262. A
263. A
264. A
265. B
266. A
267. C
268. C
269. C
270. A
271. A
272. D
273. D
274. C
275. C
276. C
277. D
278. A

Spelling

279. B
280. C
281. D
282. A
283. B
284. B
285. B
286. C
287. A
288. A

Composition

289. C
290. B
291. C
292. B
293. D
294. A
295. B
296. A
297. B
298. A

ANSWERS AND EXPLANATIONS

Verbal Skills

1. D

Severe means the opposite of the other choices, which are all synonyms for easygoing.

2. A

In terms of speed, the order is Christine, Joanne, Katie, so (A) is true.

3. A

Abundant means plenty, so the opposite is *scarce*.

4. B

A shell surrounds and protects an egg; a peel surrounds and protects an orange.

5. C

We are not told where Mr. Johnson would be if he were not at the golf club.

6. A

To endorse most nearly means approve.

7. A

To expand means to grow.

8. B

The order from most homeruns to least according to the first two statements is: Hank, Peter, Joe. Therefore, Hank has hit the most home runs.

9. D

A claw is the foot of an eagle, while a paw is the foot of a lion.

10. C

Fiction means made up, so the opposite is fact.

11. A

Territory most nearly means land.

12. D

To force most nearly means to impose.

13. D

A spy seeks out hidden information; the other choices are all examples of people who represent a country or region.

14. B

A paddle makes a canoe move and a pedal makes a bicycle move.

15. A

Unending fits the definition of infinite. While something that's infinite may also be complex and undiscovered, those are not actual synonyms of infinite.

16. D

A lot is an empty space; the other choices are spaces found in a house.

17. A

Hamburger is named as the least expensive food in both statements.

18. A

Average means typical or medium; outstanding is atypical or superb.

19. C

A saw is used to cut and a handle is used to open.

20. B

Mandate means command or decree. It may be used as a noun or as a verb. For example: *Before the city council voted to mandate 'no parking' rules, many citizens spoke out against the mandate.*

21. D

To embellish most nearly means to adorn. To embroider would be one way to embellish something, but embroider is too specific to be a close synonym for embellish.

22. **D**

Wary means careful; the opposite is careless.

23. **C**

Serene means peaceful.

24. **B**

Elated means happy; solemn, serious, and grave are synonyms that mean the opposite of happy.

25. **D**

This is a degree relationship. Minute means extremely small and colossal means extremely large.

26. **A**

Only the word *familiar* fits the definition of the word *acquainted*.

27. **C**

Beside means close to. All the other choices are synonyms of far.

28. **A**

A colleague is a coworker.

29. **C**

We have no information regarding the size relationship between Wolf Lake and Beaver Lake.

30. **C**

There is no information comparing the half-lives of elements A and D.

31. **B**

Underhanded means sneaky.

32. **A**

The word *choose* is unlike the other choices which are all synonyms for punish.

33. **C**

To condemn means to judge. The other answer choices all mean to overlook or to excuse.

34. **B**

Praise is an expression of admiration, while insult is an expression of contempt.

35. **B**

Since the first two statements are true, and kangaroos are mammals, kangaroos must give birth to live young.

36. **C**

Fortuitous means lucky or fortunate.

37. **D**

Ambivalent means having mixed feelings or being uncertain.

38. **A**

The word *letter* does not belong with the other choices, which are examples of published writing.

39. **C**

The key word is *all*. All *X* is *Y* doesn't mean all *Y* is *X*, so some *Z* could be *Y*.

40. **C**

One forges a signature and one counterfeits money.

41. **A**

To detain means to keep back, while all the other choices mean to enter.

42. **D**

Renowned means well-known or famed.

43. **B**

Implicit means implied or inferred.

44. **D**

A fool lacks wisdom and a pauper lacks riches.

45. **B**

Ingenious means clever.

46. B

A mimic imitates. The other choices are synonyms for clown.

47. C

Bombastic means loud, exaggerated, or overblown.

48. A

The key word is *all*. Since Lester is a myop and all myops are nearsighted, Lester must be nearsighted.

49. D

A cub is a young animal. All the other choices are names of groups of animals.

50. C

A warrant grants permission to search while a visa grants permission to travel.

51. C

Sedentary means seated or inactive; the opposite is active.

52. D

Wardrobe is the general classification; all the other choices are types of clothing.

53. A

Rudimentary means basic; the opposite is advanced.

54. D

The word *unleash* is the opposite of the other choices.

55. A

Although a battle may result in success, the other words are synonyms for success.

56. A

Malevolent means evil.

57. D

Although a ticket may be needed to watch a play, the other words are all elements of a theatrical performance.

58. B

A chapter is a piece of a book, a section is a piece of a newspaper.

59. B

According to the first two statements, the order of cities from north to south is B, A, C, D. Therefore, the third statement is false.

60. C

Transient means passing or temporary.

Quantitative Skills

61. D

Let x = the number

$$3x = 34\frac{1}{2} = \frac{69}{2}$$

$$x = \frac{69}{2} \div 3 = 11\frac{1}{2}$$

Half the number $= \frac{1}{2} \times 11\frac{1}{2} = \frac{1}{2} \times \frac{23}{2} = \frac{23}{4} = 5\frac{3}{4}$.

62. A

The pattern in the series is +3. Therefore, the next term is $11 + 3 = 14$.

63. B

If $A > B > C$; A must also be greater than C.

64. C

The pattern in the series is −5; $39 − 5 = 34$.

65. A

The product of 5 and 6 is $5 \times 6 = 30$.

The product plus $4 = 30 + 4 = 34$.

$$36 − x = 34$$
$$x = 36 − 34 = 2$$

66. D

Since all three angles in an equilateral triangle are equal (each angle is 60 degrees), $A + B$ must be greater than C.

67. C

Calculate the value of each number as a decimal to readily compare them.

(A) = .33, (B) = .66, (C) = .33, (D) = 0.30. We see therefore that (B) has the greatest value.

68. B

The pattern is −4; 53 − 4 = 49.

69. D

Terry's meal cost 4(2.25) + 5.25 = $14.25

John's meal cost 2(2.25) + 2(5.25) = $15

Maria's meal cost 2.25 + 4.50 + 5.25 = $12

70. D

Calculate the value of each answer choice, performing the operation within the parentheses first.

(a) 11 − (6 + 3) = 11 − 9 = 2
(b) (8−2) − 3 = 6 − 3 = 3
(c) 12 − (5 − 4) = 12 − 1 = 11

Then, plug in the numbers to the equation in each answer choice to arrive at the correct equation; 11 > 2 + 3.

71. B

Since the vertical angles formed by two intersecting lines are equal, and a circle totals 360 degrees: angles D and E each equal 80 degrees, and angles F and G each equal 100 degrees. Therefore, the only correct answer is (B).

72. D

(a) = .50 × 20 = 10
(b) = .30 × 90 = 27
(c) = .25 × 80 = 20

The correct choice is (D) because 2(a) = 20 = (c).

73. C

The pattern in the series is −3, +5, −3, +5, −3 and so on. Therefore, the next number is 19 − 3 = 16.

74. A

6 less than 15 = 15 − 6 = 9

Let x = the number

$$\frac{3}{5}x = 9$$

$$3x = 9 \times 5 = 45$$

$$x = \frac{45}{3} = 15$$

75. C

Count the shaded boxes, 3 of 12 are shaded.

$$\frac{3}{12} = \frac{x}{100}$$

$$12x = 300$$

$$x = 25$$

Expressed as a percent, $\frac{25}{100}$ = .25, or 25%.

76. B

Let x = the number

$$\frac{1}{3}x = 2 + \frac{1}{4}x$$

$$\frac{x}{3} = 2 + \frac{x}{4}$$

If we multiply both sides of the equation by 12, we have

$$4x = 24 + 3x$$

$$4x − 3x = 24$$

$$x = 24$$

77. A

$\frac{7}{8} \div \frac{1}{4} = \frac{7}{8} \times \frac{4}{1} = \frac{28}{8} = 3\frac{4}{8}$ or reduced, $3\frac{1}{2}$.

Another way to approach this problem is with cross-multiplication:

$$\frac{7}{8} = \frac{x}{4}$$

$$\frac{8x}{8} = \frac{28}{8}$$

$$x = \frac{7}{2} = 3\frac{1}{2}$$

78. D

The grocer will need 12 cartons.

He has: 3 super-sized cartons.

Each holds 4 rows × 12 spaces = 48 eggs

A regular carton holds = 2 rows × 6 spaces = 12 eggs

$\frac{48}{12}$ = 4 cartons × 3 super-sized cartons = 12 cartons total

79. **A**

Let x = the number

$$x = \frac{4^3}{4} = \frac{4 \times 4 \times 4}{4} = \frac{16 \times 4}{4} = 16$$

80. **C**

Each successive number in the series is obtained by dividing the preceding number by 2. In this case, $6 \div 2 = 3$.

81. **A**

The angles of a triangle total 180 degrees. Two angles are given: 90 and 55.

$180 = 90 + 55 + A$
$180 = 145 + A$
$180 - 145 = A$
$A = 35$

Furthermore, a straight line represents a straight angle of 180 degrees. Since the measure of angle $A = 35$ degrees, angle BAL must measure 145 degrees, since $35 + 145 = 180$.

82. **B**

Let x = the unknown fraction

$$x \div \frac{1}{5} = \frac{7}{8}$$
$$x \times 5 = \frac{7}{8}$$
$$5x = \frac{7}{8}$$
$$x = \frac{7}{8} \div 5 = \frac{7}{8} \times \frac{1}{5} = \frac{7}{40}$$

83. **D**

The pattern is +1, +2, +3 and so on. The subsequent number in the series should be $7 + 4 = 11$.

84. **C**

The equation for circumference = diameter $\times \pi$.

Since the radius of the circle is 3 m, the diameter = 6 m; therefore the circumference is 6π m.

85. **C**

Of 8 sectors, 2 are shaded: $\frac{2}{8} = \frac{1}{4}$.

86. **C**

By writing each fraction as a decimal, we can readily compare.

$$\frac{1}{5} = .20, \frac{1}{3} = .33, \frac{2}{3} = .66$$

Since $.66 > .33 > .20$, (C) is the correct answer.

87. **A**

The average of 15, 24, 32, and 13 = and the sum of these numbers, divided by 4.

$84 \div 4 = 21$
$21 - 9 = 12$

88. **D**

Note that odd and even terms alternate. Each odd term is followed by that term +3. Each even term is followed by that term +1. Thus, $12 + 1 = 13$.

89. **B**

$a = 3^2 = 3 \times 3 = 9$
$b = 2 \times 2^2 = 2 \times (2 \times 2) = 2(4) = 8$
$c = 3 \times 2^3 = 3 \times 2 \times 2 \times 2 = 3 \times 8 = 24$

(B) is the correct answer since $24 > 8 + 9$

90. **B**

Let x = the number

$30 = x + x(.50)$
$30 = 1.5x$
$30 \div 1.5 = 300 \div 15 = 20$

91. **A**

The pattern is to subtract 1 from the preceding number, and then double the result; $6 - 1 = 5$

92. **B**

$$\frac{4^3}{4} = 4^2 = 16$$
$16 + 12 = 28$

93. **A**

$$10 \div \frac{1}{8} = 10 \times \frac{8}{1} = 80$$

94. C

In moving from left to right in the series, we note that the odd-numbered terms follow the counting numbers: 1, 2, 3 Each even-numbered term is 4 more than the preceding number: 4, 8, 12. In this case, the even-numbered term following 12 is $12 + 4 = 16$.

95. D

Find the values of each answer choice and compare. Remember in order of operations, multiplication comes before addition or subtraction.

(a) $31 - 2 \times 7 = 31 - 14 = 17$
(b) $5 \times 4 - 8 = 20 - 8 = 12$
(c) $7 + 6 - 2 = 13 - 2 = 15$

We can therefore see that (a) is greater than (b).

96. B

Since the square is bisected into two equal triangles, and E is the midpoint of line BD, $\frac{1}{2}$ of 1 triangle is shaded, or $\frac{1}{4}$ of the square is shaded.

97. B

The pattern alternates Roman numerals and Arabic numerals. Each subsequent number is two less than the preceding number. $5 - 2 = 3$. This should be expressed as a Roman numeral.

98. C

Let $x =$ the number

$\frac{x}{4} = 3\frac{1}{4}$

$x = 3 \times 4 + 1 = 13$

99. A

Calculate the value of each answer choice.

(a) $(5 + 1)^2 = 6^2 = 6 \times 6 = 36$
(b) $3^2 + 2^2 = 3 \times 3 = 9 + 2 \times 2 = 9 + 4 = 13$
(c) $25 - 2 \times 3 = 25 - 6 = 19$

100. C

Let $x =$ the number of students

$.15x = 12$

$x = \frac{12}{.15} = \frac{1200}{15} = 80$

101. A

$\frac{3}{4} + \frac{5}{6} = \frac{3 \times 6}{24} + \frac{5 \times 4}{24} = \frac{18}{24} + \frac{20}{24} = \frac{38}{24} = 1\frac{14}{24}$

Compare $\frac{38}{24}$ to $\frac{1}{2}$. $\left(\frac{1}{2} = \frac{12}{24}\right)$

$\frac{38}{24} - \frac{12}{24} = \frac{26}{24}$. Reducing: $\frac{26}{24} = \frac{13}{12}$.

102. D

Let $x =$ the number. Recall that $33\frac{1}{3}\%$ of a number is equal to $\frac{1}{3}$ of the number.

$\frac{1}{3}x = 15$

$x = 15 \times 3 = 45$.

The reciprocal of 45 is $\frac{1}{45}$.

103. D

The pattern is $+5, -2, -1, +5, -2, -1$ and so on. Therefore, add 5 to get the next value in the pattern: $9 + 5 = 14$.

104. B

Determine the values for each bar in the graph using the number scale to the left. Then, choose the correct alternative. $B + A = 2 + 4 = 6 = C$.

105. A

AB must be greater than AD since it is the hypotenuse of a right triangle whose length must be greater than the base.

106. A

Write each number as a decimal to readily compare.

(a) $3\frac{1}{2}\% = .035$

(b) $3\frac{1}{2} = 3.50$

(c) $.33 = .33$

Therefore we see that (b) > (a) + (c)

Or $3.5 > .035 + .33$

$\quad 3.5 > .365$

107. C

Let $x =$ the number

$\frac{2}{3}x + 8 = 40$

$\quad \frac{2}{3}x = 40 - 8 = 32$

$\quad\quad x = 32 \times \frac{3}{2} = \frac{96}{2} = 48$

108. C

The pattern is $-1\frac{1}{2}$ from each term in the series.

Therefore, $3\frac{1}{2} - 1\frac{1}{2} = 2$.

109. C

The pattern is ×2, −1 and so on. Therefore, 10 − 1 = 9.

110. D

The pattern works backward from end to beginning in the alphabet. Each letter is paired with a subsequent integer, working forward from 1. The letter before W is V; the next number after 4 is 5.

111. C

Let $x =$ the number

$x = 3^3 - 8$

$x = 3 \times 3 \times 3 - 8$

$x = 9 \times 3 - 8$

$x = 27 - 8 = 19$

112. D

Test each of the alternatives to find the true one. To find the perimeter, add the length of all sides; 6 + 4 + 6 + 4 = 20 inches.

READING

Comprehension

113. A

Although you might be tempted to choose (D) because it is mentioned first in the passage, you need to read carefully. The first sentence says that Clara Barton started her work in Washington, D.C.

114. B

In this passage, the word *accompany* means go with.

115. D

Choices (A), (B), and (C) are not correct because they are too general. The passage only discusses the career of Clara Barton, so (D) is the best choice.

116. C

There is nothing in the passage to support choice (A), (B), or (D). We can infer that Clara volunteered to help because she felt compassion for the soldiers.

117. C

The second paragraph tells how there were *shortages of supplies* and Clara *advertised for provisions*. Therefore, supplies is a synonym for provisions.

118. B

Although it is not clearly written that the Iron Cross is a medal, you can infer that from the context in the fourth paragraph. Locate the sentence about the Iron Cross. It says *she returned home…with Germany's Iron Cross for outstanding military service*. Although it doesn't directly say that it was for aiding soldiers during the war, the other choices are not supported by the passage.

119. C

Read the sentence in which the word *campaigned* is used. The sentence mentions that she worked at *educating the public…and lobbying cabinet heads*. Although you may be tempted to choose (B) and (D), they are not closest in meaning to how the word is used in the passage.

120. **A**

This is an inference question. If you read the last sentence in paragraph 1, the word *patriot* is used to describe Clara Barton after discussing how she helped other people. Therefore, (A) is the best choice.

121. **B**

Choices (A), (C), and (D) are supporting the main idea that our love affair with automobiles, a step forward, comes with a price.

122. **A**

Even if you know the meaning of the word, you should refer its context to confirm your choice. In this passage, impact means effect.

123. **C**

Choices (A) and (D) are incorrect because there is no use of foreshadowing or quotations. Choice (B) is incorrect because the historical fact is only an introduction to the topic.

124. **A**

By mentioning the Model T, the author shows that automobiles were not always part of our lives; they are an invention that changed our lives.

125. **B**

You need to understand the context of this statement in the passage. The author is not talking about the financial cost of automobiles, but rather about the environmental cost. Therefore, the best answer is (B).

126. **B**

The author is arguing for more careful use of the right to free speech, therefore, (B) is the best choice.

127. **C**

Even if you know the meaning of the word, you should check its context in the passage. In this passage, demeaning means insulting.

128. **C**

This is an inference question. Although the author never explicitly states the most important aim, the second sentence of the passage gives us a clue. The author says freedom of speech *protect*[s] *our right to express opinions without fear.*

129. **B**

There are no statistics, quotations, or anecdotes (stories) offered. The argument is based on the author's impassioned opinions.

130. **A**

You need to understand the context of this quote. If you reread the second paragraph, the authors asks, *How often do we find ourselves…repeating a phrase…without stopping to ponder the meaning of the words?* Choice (A) is the best answer.

131. **D**

The word *free* is used in quotations in the first paragraph to show that speech is not free if it is harmful to any group.

132. **A**

Because the passage discusses musical lyrics, this selection was most likely intended as a speech to a radio station.

133. **A**

This selection discusses inherited traits, or genetics.

134. **D**

This selection discusses Gregor Mendel's study of how traits are inherited. It concludes that traits are passed on through genes. Therefore, choice (D) is the best title for the passage.

135. **B**

This is a detail question. Look for the part of the passage that discusses traits. The first paragraph includes the sentence that gives the answer: *In all, Mendel found seven traits that could be readily observed in only one of two forms.*

136. C

Mendel must have been systematic in his approach, to achieve the results that he did over time.

137. B

This is another detail question. Paragraph 2 gives the answer: *Traits* [are] *passed on to offspring unchanged.*

138. D

The selection explains that Mendel did his research by breeding and observing pea plants over many generations.

139. A

The second paragraph says *that an individual inherits traits from each parent.* Therefore, choice (A) is the best answer.

140. C

Readily means easily. Mendel could *easily* see these traits and study them.

141. C

There is nothing in the passage that supports choices (A), (B), and (D). The passage is mostly about effective communication.

142. A

Even if you know the meaning of the word, you should refer to its context in the passage. In this example, genuine means real.

143. A

According to the passage, two people must understand one another for communication to have taken place.

144. D

The passage discusses effective communication. The sentence that mentions minimizing misunderstanding supports choice (D).

145. A

Since this passage discusses communication, it would be helpful information in a manual on effective meetings.

146. D

The word *naturally* here is used to mean obviously; it *obviously* takes two people to share something—in this case, a message.

147. C

This passage discusses how interpretation of the Monroe Doctrine has evolved or changed.

148. A

Based on the context of the word, policy means guiding principles.

149. B

This is a detail question. You see that the 1800s are mentioned in paragraph 2. The first sentence in that paragraph states: *In the early 1800s, the United States expanded its isolationist policies to the entire western hemisphere.* This supports answer choice (B).

150. D

The answer to this question might not be obvious. If you skim the passage again for information about isolationism, you will notice that the last sentence in paragraph 1 states that isolationism *applied only to diplomatic relations, since trade with other nations was an essential element of the American economy.*

151. C

The second paragraph expands on the idea of the Monroe Doctrine and explains how it has shifted in meaning.

152. D

You need to understand how the word is used in context. In this passage, *affairs* most nearly means business.

Vocabulary

153. A

To apprehend means to nab, to grab, or to catch.

154. D

To secure means to obtain or to acquire.

155. **D**

Blatant means apparent, showy, or obvious.

156. **B**

Excessive means exaggerated, needless, or enormous.

157. **A**

Unassailable means safe, secure, or impenetrable.

158. **C**

Incentive means stimulus, encouragement, or motivation.

159. **D**

Scowling means unhappy or frowning.

160. **A**

Ulterior means covert or concealed.

161. **A**

To aggravate means to annoy, to irritate, or to bother.

162. **A**

Executive means controlling or governing.

163. **B**

To contemplate means to think, to speculate, or to consider.

164. **D**

Efficient means effective, competent, or capable.

165. **B**

Unprecedented means unheard of, exceptional, or extraordinary.

166. **D**

Verbatim means word for word or exact.

167. **A**

To resolve means to solve, to decide, or to settle.

168. **C**

Subordinate means lowly or inferior.

169. **B**

Perilous means dangerous, difficult, or hazardous.

170. **A**

To refrain means to abstain, to avoid, or to cease.

171. **C**

Dilapidated means crumbling, damaged, or decayed.

172. **B**

Prevailing means dominant, popular, or current.

173. **D**

To found means to create, to initiate, or to begin.

174. **A**

Credible means reliable, believable, or trustworthy.

MATHEMATICS
Concepts

175. **C**

There is no such thing as a positive angle.

176. **C**

The symbol stands for intersection. The intersection of two or more sets is the set of elements they share in common. In this case, the common elements are 5, 7, and 11.

177. **C**

This problem requires you to round off the given number to the place one digit to the right of the decimal point, the tenth's column. Since the number in the hundredth's place is 5, round to 83.5.

178. **B**

Start with the operations in the parentheses first:
$(-3)^3 = -3 \times -3 \times -3 = -27$
Then, continue with the operations outside the parentheses:
$2 \times (-27) = -54$

179. **C**

$.45 = \frac{45}{100}$; $\frac{45}{100}$ can then be reduced to $\frac{9}{20}$.

180. **A**

A straight line represents a straight angle of 180 degrees. An angle of 140 degrees is given, so the measure of angle C must be 40 degrees to complete the line. Knowing that all the angles in a triangle added together equal 180 degrees:

$m\angle A + m\angle B + m\angle C = 180$

$m\angle A + 45 + 40 = 180$

$m\angle A = 180 - 85$; $m\angle A = 95$ degrees

181. **C**

When dividing a number by 10, 100, 1000, etc., move the decimal point one place to the left for each zero in the divisor. In this example, 100 has two zeros, so the decimal point would be moved two places to the left.

182. **B**

The reciprocal of a fraction is the fraction reversed. In other words, the numerator and denominator are switched. Change $2\frac{1}{2}$ to an improper fraction; $\frac{5}{2}$ is the reciprocal of $\frac{2}{5}$.

183. **B**

The formula for finding the area of a circle is $\pi \times$ the radius squared. The radius is 3, so $3^2 = 9$; the area is 9π.

184. **A**

The components of this problem must be stated in the same units. Therefore 36 inches = 1 yard. So, the ratio is 36:72 or 1:2 simplified.

185. **A**

State $\frac{17}{2}$ as a decimal number.

$\frac{17}{2} = 8.5$.

Between 8.5 and 9.5 there is only 1 integer; the number 9.

186. **B**

This is an example of the distributive property of multiplication over addition.

187. **D**

A perfect square is a number whose factors multiplied by itself equal the number. In this case the perfect square is 81 since $9 \times 9 = 81$.

188. **B**

When working with scientific notation, the exponent represents the number of places to move the decimal point in the multiplier. If the base of the exponent is 10, the decimal point moves to the right. If it is $\frac{1}{10}$, the decimal point moves to the left.

189. **C**

The easiest way to approach this problem is to add multiples of 5 and 7 until you find a pair of multiples that equals 36.

$5 + 7 \neq 36$.   Try again.

$10 + 14 \neq 36$.   Try again.

$15 + 21 = 36$.   And what is the larger of these two multiples? 21

190. **C**

To find the exact number of hundreds in 8,675 we must divide by 100.

$8,675 \div 100 = 86.75$

191. **A**

1 quart = 32 fluid ounces

1 gallon = 4 quarts

$4 \times 32 = 128$ fluid ounces

$2 \times 128 = 256$ ounces

$256 \div 8 = 32$

192. **A**

Let x = number of cupcakes sold and $x + 2$ = the number of brownies.

$x + x + 2 = 30$

$2x + 2 = 30$

$2x = 28$

$x = 14$

193. **D**

Together, all the angles in a triangle add up to 180. A right angle is 90 degrees, so the sum of the remaining angles must also be 90 degrees. Since the triangle is isosceles, the two acute angles must be equal to one another. $\frac{90}{2} = 45$ degrees.

194. **A**

The area of a rectangle is determined by multiplying its length times its width.

195. **A**

The two triangles are similar. Therefore we can solve this problem by ratios. Let x = the base AB

$3:2 = x:4$

$$\frac{3}{2} = \frac{x}{4}$$

$12 = 2x$

6 units $= x$

196. **D**

Prime factorization is factoring a number to the point where all factors are prime numbers.

$16 = 4 \times 4$

$16 = 2 \times 2 \times 2 \times 2$

197. **B**

The lowest common denominator is the least number that is a product of both denominators. In this case 9 is the lowest number both denominators can factor into.

198. **B**

For (B) to be equal, it would need the percent symbol after it.

Problem Solving

199. **A**

$$\frac{13}{4} - \frac{6}{5} = \frac{65}{20} - \frac{24}{20} = \frac{41}{20} = 2\frac{1}{20}.$$

200. **D**

$(-2) + (-4) + (-1) = -7$

$\qquad\quad +6 + (-7) = -1$

201. **C**

tickets for the Ferris wheel	$32.50 (10 × $3.25)
tickets for the roller coaster	$11.00 (4 × $2.75)
total	$43.50

202. **A**

$1\frac{1}{5} = \frac{6}{5}$, $2\frac{1}{4} = \frac{9}{4}$, $1\frac{1}{3} = \frac{4}{3}$

$$\frac{6}{5} \times \frac{9}{4} \times \frac{4}{3} = \frac{54}{15} = 3\frac{9}{15} = 3\frac{3}{5}.$$

203. **A**

This problem is done by ratios:

$$\frac{x}{3} = \frac{12}{1}$$

36 ft $= x$

204. **A**

$10 + 2x = x + 14$

$\qquad\quad x = 14 - 10$

$\qquad\quad x = 4$

205. **D**

$$\frac{1250}{7} \approx 178.57 \approx 179 \text{ miles}$$

206. **C**

This can be set up as an algebraic equation. If y equals the price of the car, 8% of y equals 1,600 or $.08y = 1,600$

$$y = \frac{1600}{.08} = 20,000$$

207. **C**

First, multiply $36 × 2 = $72. Then subtract 4 from $72 to get $68.

208. **C**

$2a + 3 > 9$
$2a > 6$
$a > 3$
If $a > 3$, then $a^2 > 9$

209. **D**

$.05(\$1,200 \times 4) = .05(4,800) = \$240.$

210. **D**

Solve this as an algebraic equation with x as the unknown integer.

$x + 20 = x\left(\dfrac{3}{2}\right)$
$20 = \dfrac{3}{2}x - x$
$20 = \dfrac{3}{2}x - \dfrac{2}{2}x = \dfrac{1}{2}x$
$20 \times 2 = x$
$40 = x$

211. **A**

Convert the mixed numbers into improper fractions. Then, find the common denominator and add:

$\dfrac{3}{2} + \dfrac{7}{3} + \dfrac{9}{4} = \dfrac{18}{12} + \dfrac{28}{12} + \dfrac{27}{12} = \dfrac{73}{12} = 6\dfrac{1}{12}.$

212. **A**

If the sum of the two numbers is x and one of the numbers is 5, then the other number is $x - 5$. Three times the other number is $3(x - 5)$.

213. **A**

1 pound = 16 ounces; 1 pound 4 ounces = 20 ounces.
$20 \times \$2 = \$40$

214. **A**

We may write the given equation, $x + 5 = y + 10$ as
$x - y = 10 - 5$ or $x - y = 5$. Therefore, $x > y$.

215. **B**

$3\left(\dfrac{1}{3}\right)^2 + 2(2) - 1$ if $x = \dfrac{1}{3}$ and $y = 2$

$3\left(\dfrac{1}{9}\right) + 4 - 1$

$\dfrac{3}{9} + 3 = 3\dfrac{1}{3}$

216. **A**

This can be set up as an algebraic equation. If x is the amount the Smiths borrowed, then

$6\%(x) = 420$
$x = \dfrac{420}{.06} = \$7,000.$

217. **A**

Volume = length $\times$ width $\times$ height
Volume = $5 \times 5 \times 5 = 125$ m^3.

218. **D**

Convert the mixed numbers into improper fractions. Then divide the total length of the paper by the length into which it must be cut.

$\dfrac{17}{4} \div \dfrac{4}{3} = \dfrac{17}{4} \times \dfrac{3}{4} = \dfrac{51}{16} = 3\dfrac{3}{16}.$

219. **B**

First, move the decimal points in order to divide by a whole number. Then, carry out the division.

$$
\begin{array}{r}
.47 \\
322\overline{)152.32} \\
128\ 8 \\
\hline
23\ 52
\end{array}
$$

220. **A**

P% of 60 is 12
$P\% = \dfrac{12}{60} = \dfrac{1}{5}$
$P\% = .20$
$P = 20$

221. **B**

Remember that the number of decimal places to the right of the decimal point in the answer should equal the total number of places to the right of the decimal points in the two factors being multiplied; in this case 4.

$$\begin{array}{r} 233.5 \\ \times\ .051 \\ \hline 2335 \\ 116750 \\ \hline 11.9085 \end{array}$$

222. **A**

When adding decimal numbers, line up the decimal points.

$$\begin{array}{r} .784 \\ 8.2 \\ +\ .31 \\ \hline 9.294 \end{array}$$

223. **C**

First, determine how many times $500,000 can be divided by 100; $500,000 \div 100 = 5,000$. Then multiply by 3.72 since that is the amount due per hundred; $5,000 \times 3.72 = \$18,600$

224. **A**

$5x - 8 > 2$
$\quad 5x > 10$
$\quad\ x > 2$

If $x > 2$, $x^3 > 2^3$; thus $x^3 > 8$.

225. **A**

.05 of 36,000 = 1,800 saved per year. Divide 1,800 by 12 to arrive at how much Mr. Battle saves each month; $\frac{1,800}{12} = 150$

226. **B**

The pattern is made by adding .03 to each number.

227. **A**

$$\begin{array}{r} 726 \\ \times\ 19 \\ \hline 6534 \\ 7260 \\ \hline 13794 \end{array}$$

228. **D**

The area of the rectangle is length × width or $5 \times 12 = 60$ m².

The area of the semicircles on each side $= \frac{1}{2}(\text{radius})^2 \times \pi$, or $\frac{1}{2}(6)^2 \times \pi = 18\pi$ m². However, since there are two semicircles, the area of both of them put together $= 36\pi$ m². Therefore, the area of the whole figure $= (60 + 36\pi)$ m²

229. **D**

Rename the fractions with a common denominator, then do the operations in parenthesis first.

$$\left(\frac{2}{3} + \frac{2}{5}\right) - \left(\frac{1}{3} + \frac{1}{10}\right)$$
$$\left(\frac{20}{30} + \frac{12}{30}\right) - \left(\frac{10}{30} + \frac{3}{30}\right)$$
$$\frac{32}{30} - \frac{13}{30} = \frac{19}{30}$$

230. **D**

First, translate into an equation and then solve.

$8 \times 9 = x + 12$
$\quad 72 = x + 12$
$\quad 60 = x$

231. **A**

The formula for area is length × width; $9 \times 15 = 135$ square inches.

232. **B**

$$\frac{1}{3} : \frac{5}{9}$$
$$\frac{1}{3} \div \frac{5}{9} = \frac{1}{3} \times \frac{9}{5} = \frac{9}{15} = \frac{3}{5}$$

233. **A**

If we square both sides of the equation, we have

$y - 3 = 2^2$
$y - 3 = 4$
$\quad y = 7$

234. D

Since this is a right triangle, you can use the Pythagorean theorem to solve this problem.

$$x^2 + 6^2 = 10^2$$
$$x^2 + 6^2 = 100$$
$$x^2 = 100 - 36 = 64$$
$$x = 8$$

235. C

A number that is a multiple of 60 must be both a multiple of 10 and a multiple of 6. A number that is a multiple of 10 ends in a 0, so you can eliminate (A). A multiple of 6 meets the requirements for multiples of 2 and 3. Choices (B), (C), and (D) are all divisible by 2. The one that is divisible by 3 is the correct answer.

236. B

Let x = the total number of miles planned for that day.

$$.40x = 60$$
$$x = \frac{60}{.4} = 150$$

Of that 150 planned miles, Rosemarie has already driven 60. Therefore, the number of miles she has left to drive to reach her total planned miles = 150 − 60 = 90 miles.

237. C

All the angles in a triangle = 180. We know that 1 angle of this triangle is right, or 90 degrees. The remaining angles must therefore = 90 degrees. (For a total of 180 degrees) Since the ratio is 2:1, set up the equation:

$$2x + 1x = 90$$
$$3x = 90$$
$$x = 30$$

Therefore, the larger angle is 2(30) = 60 degrees, and the smaller is 30 degrees.

238. B

Multiply both sides of the equation by 10 to make it more manageable.

$$8x + 55 = 97$$
$$8x = 97 - 55$$
$$8x = 42$$
$$x = \frac{42}{8} = 5.25.$$

LANGUAGE

Usage

239. B

The name of the team, the *Falcons,* should be capitalized. While you might have been on the lookout for incorrect contractions, *It's* in choice (A) is the correct contraction for *it has,* and *don't* in choice (B) is used correctly as well.

240. B

They're is the subject/verb *they are. Their* is the possessive.

241. B

The correct verb is *should have,* not *should of.*

242. D

There are no mistakes.

243. A

The correct phrase is *neither…nor.*

244. A

Professor does not need to be capitalized, since it is a general job classification, not a title.

245. C

The double negative is incorrect. The correct usage would be *couldn't find the book anywhere.*

246. C

Quick should be *quickly* as it is an adverb, describing the verb *finish.*

247. **B**

The past tense of *to lend* is *lent.*

248. **D**

There are no mistakes.

249. **B**

That means the one there; the word *there* is not needed.

250. **A**

The correct verbal phrase is *would have come.*

251. **C**

It's is the contraction for *it is. Its* is the possessive which should be used here.

252. **A**

Was wrote is incorrect. The correct passive verb is *was written.*

253. **A**

Who's is incorrect; it is the contraction *who is.* The correct word here should be *whose.*

254. **C**

Return back is incorrect; it is repetitive to *return back.*

255. **A**

Accept means *welcome* or *receive*; in this case, the word should be *except.*

256. **D**

There are no mistakes.

257. **B**

The correct verbal phrase is *had never gone.*

258. **C**

Barb and me should be Barb and *I* since the pronoun is a subject. If you thought that choice (A) should use the plural verb *are* instead of the singular verb *is*, look again at the sentence and see that the verb is correctly paired with the singular noun *each.*

259. **D**

There are no mistakes.

260. **D**

There are no mistakes.

261. **A**

Can refers to ability. The correct word here should be *may.*

262. **A**

The correct prepositional phrase is *to turn right at the corner.*

263. **A**

There should be an apostrophe in *Anthonys* to show possession.

264. **A**

The double negative, *don't...nothing*, is incorrect. The correct wording should be *don't owe anything*, or *we owe nothing.*

265. **B**

The word *of* is incorrect. The correct word should be *have.*

266. **A**

Then is incorrect. The correct word should be *than.*

267. **C**

Its is incorrect. The contraction *it's (it is)* should be used here.

268. **C**

The word order *you don't* is incorrect. When asking a question, the correct word order is *don't you.*

269. **C**

Me is incorrect; the subject pronoun is *I.*

270. **A**

If we omit the word *students* we see that *we*, the subject form of the pronoun, is required: *We students must...*

271. **A**

The adverb *slowly* is required.

272. **D**

There are no mistakes.

273. **D**

There are no mistakes.

274. **C**

A noun in a direct address should be followed by a comma: Jim, please set the table.

275. **C**

The double negative is incorrect. The sentence should read: *I didn't see anything.*

276. **C**

Her is incorrect. The sentence should read: *Frank throws as well as she does.*

277. **D**

There are no mistakes.

278. **A**

A comma is needed between the clauses: *When she was finished, the crowd applauded.*

Spelling

279. **B**

The correct spelling is *receive*. The spelling rule is *i* before *e*, except after *c*.

280. **C**

Principle is incorrect. Remember, the princi*pal* is your *pal*.

281. **D**

There are no mistakes.

282. **A**

The correct spelling is *available*.

283. **B**

The correct spelling is *cooperate*.

284. **B**

The correct spelling is *mediocre*.

285. **B**

The correct spelling is *questionnaire*.

286. **C**

The correct spelling is *excellent*.

287. **A**

The correct spelling is *referred*.

288. **A**

The correct spelling is *audience*.

Composition

289. **C**

The connective must convey the idea of the blizzard being the reason we remained inside.

290. **B**

The subject *Bob* must follow the introductory phrase.

291. **C**

The infinitive *to practice* should not be split.

292. **B**

The sentence needs to imply that the musician is playing the violin. Therefore, choice (B) is correct.

293. **D**

Choices (A), (B), and (C) are incorrect because they imply that the hammock had been playing. (D) is the only choice that makes it clear that *we* were the ones who were playing, not the hammock.

294. A

Tough cowboys are roles in wild west films. These are part of the American spirit.

295. B

The second clause offers the reason why she took the 7 A.M. bus.

296. A

The creation of the National Park system fits under the topic of protecting natural resources.

297. B

The second clause provides a contrasting statement.

298. A

The foreshadowing is based on the sense of doom that the sound of the foghorn invokes.

NOTES

NOTES

How Did We Do? Grade Us.

Thank you for choosing a Kaplan book. Your comments and suggestions are very useful to us. Please answer the following questions to assist us in our continued development of high-quality resources to meet your needs. Or go online and complete our interactive survey form at **kaplansurveys.com/books**.

The title of the Kaplan book I read was: _____

My name is: _____

My address is: _____

_____

My e-mail address is: _____

What overall grade would you give this book?   (A)   (B)   (C)   (D)   (F)

How relevant was the information to your goals?   (A)   (B)   (C)   (D)   (F)

How comprehensive was the information in this book?   (A)   (B)   (C)   (D)   (F)

How accurate was the information in this book?   (A)   (B)   (C)   (D)   (F)

How easy was the book to use?   (A)   (B)   (C)   (D)   (F)

How appealing was the book's design?   (A)   (B)   (C)   (D)   (F)

What were the book's strong points? _____

How could this book be improved? _____

Is there anything that we left out that you wanted to know more about?

Would you recommend this book to others?   ☐ YES   ☐ NO

Other comments: _____

_____

_____

Do we have permission to quote you?   ☐ YES   ☐ NO

Thank you for your help.
Please tear out this page and mail it to:

　　Managing Editor
　　Kaplan, Inc.
　　1440 Broadway, 8th floor
　　New York, NY 10018

Thanks!

Test Prep and Admissions

Need help preparing for the SAT?

We've got some recommended reading.

Guides for students taking the SAT on or before January 22, 2005

Guides for students taking the SAT beginning in March 2005

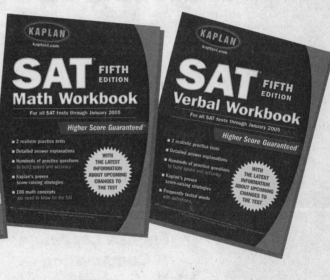

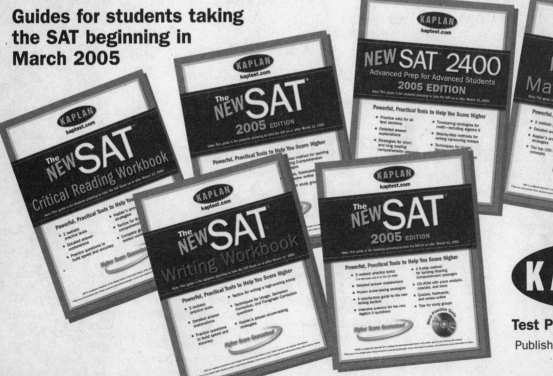

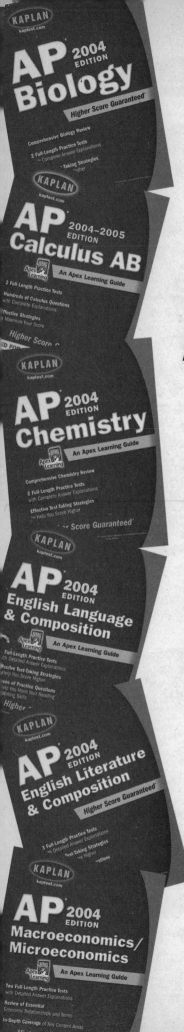

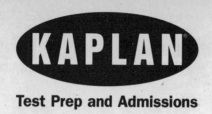